SKEWED

SKEWED

A CRITICAL THINKER'S GUIDE TO MEDIA BIAS

Larry Atkins

Prometheus Books

59 John Glenn Drive
Amherst, New York 14228

Published 2016 by Prometheus Books

Cover design by Jacqueline Nasso Cooke
Cover design © Prometheus Books

Inquiries should be addressed to
Prometheus Books
59 John Glenn Drive
Amherst, New York 14228
VOICE: 716–691–0133
FAX: 716–691–0137
WWW.PROMETHEUSBOOKS.COM

20 19 18 17 16   5 4 3 2 1

Library of Congress Cataloging-in-Publication Data

Names: Atkins, Larry, 1961- author.
Title: Skewed : a critical thinker's guide to media bias / by Larry Atkins.
Description: Amherst, New York : Prometheus Books, 2016. | Includes bibliographical references and
    index.
Identifiers: LCCN 2016014340 (print) | LCCN 2016024553 (ebook) |
    ISBN 9781633881655 (hardback) | ISBN 9781633881662 (ebook)
Subjects: LCSH: Journalism—Objectivity—United States. | Mass media—Objectivity—United
    States. | Journalism—Political aspects—United States. | BISAC: SOCIAL SCIENCE / Media
    Studies.
Classification: LCC PN4888.O25 A875 2016 (print) | LCC PN4888.O25 (ebook) |
    DDC 302.230973—dc23
LC record available at https://lccn.loc.gov/2016014340

Printed in the United States of America

CONTENTS

ACKNOWLEDGMENTS

Special thanks to my mother, Phyllis Zebin; my deceased father, Robert Atkins; and deceased grandmother, Edith Dubin; my stepfather, Jack Zebin; various friends and family; my professional colleagues at Temple University, Arcadia University, Montgomery County Community College, and the Philadelphia Writers Conference; my photographer, Jack Kapenstein; my agent, Maryann Karinch of The Rudy Agency; and the staff at Prometheus Books, especially Steven L. Mitchell and Sheila Stewart, my editors on the project.

INTRODUCTION

Over the past fifteen years, as newspaper circulation has declined, more and more people are turning to advocacy journalism via websites, talk radio, cable TV, and blogs to get their news. These outlets are often entertaining, provocative, and thought provoking. The problem is that many of these news sources, especially those run by just one person or a handful of people, are biased, have an agenda, don't have the resources or time to do much fact-checking, aren't heavily or carefully edited, and aren't held accountable when they get their facts wrong. Cable TV networks like MSNBC and Fox News and websites like *CounterPunch* and TheBlaze have a clearly biased agenda. Often, many of these outlets are primarily sources of opinion. Yet many people rely on advocacy journalism as their main source of news.

Perhaps most importantly, advocacy journalism has a polarizing effect on society, and I hope that this book deepens readers' understanding of this polarization. The book will also explore aspects of media literacy and ways to navigate the echo chamber of modern media. (By echo chamber, I am referring to the tendency for people to get news and opinions from sources that "echo," or reinforce, their own or similar viewpoints.)

Advocacy journalism continues to be a popular media format. It is a type of reporting in which the reporter gives an opinion or point of view and uses stories to advance an agenda. On May 28, 2014, Fox News marked its 149th consecutive month as the most-watched cable news network, beating MSNBC and CNN combined in total viewers and ranking sixth among all ad-supported cable networks in both total daytime and primetime audience size. The network had the top fourteen shows in total viewers and the top eight shows in the demo (meaning the key demographics—the specific type of viewers the shows are trying to reach) in all of cable news. Some of Fox News's shows are relatively straight news presentations, meaning that they are not projecting a specific point of view, but many others do embody advocacy journalism.

Don't be fooled by the title of this book. This will not be a diatribe against the so-called liberal media. When people think of media bias, they seem to instantly associate it with the Republican conservative mantra and complaints about what these folks broadly describe as the "liberal media." The point of this book is to examine media bias on both ends of the political spectrum, whether liberal or conservative.

In an effort to be completely transparent, I should note that I am a staunch liberal. I am a frequent guest blogger for the *Huffington Post*, and I've written articles for liberal outlets like *OpEdNews*, *CounterPunch*, and *Z Magazine*. I published a book that is a collection of my various liberal-leaning op-eds. As I've joked in past op-eds, I tended to root for the apes against Charlton Heston's character in *Planet of the Apes* (Heston was a staunch conservative and a past president of the National Rifle Association). In this book, however, I am attempting to give a balanced, objective, and centrist presentation; even though I am liberal, I can recognize that news organizations such as MSNBC and various websites have a staunchly liberal agenda. I acknowledge that my attempt at balance may not be perfect, but I will try my very best to both acknowledge and critique conservative and liberal advocates. During my writing career, I have written both straightforward—or what used to be considered objective—types of articles as well as works of advocacy journalism, so I think I have pretty good insight into both approaches.

If I am to be successful in my task, I feel that it's important for me to continue to watch Fox News, read conservative websites, and listen to conservative talk radio to get that particular perspective. It doesn't occur often, but there are times when they convince me to rethink my position on an issue.

I also wish to admit here and now that I am a fan of advocacy journalism, yet I know that it has its flaws, especially with respect to bias. There are also different types and levels of advocacy journalism. Whenever there is a mass shooting in the United States, liberal media outlets like the *New York Times* editorial page, MSNBC hosts such as Rachel Maddow and Lawrence O'Donnell, and liberal websites like *Salon* will push the discussion to advocate for more gun control. In contrast, conservative media pundits like Fox News hosts Sean Hannity and Tucker Carlson, and talk radio hosts like Rush Limbaugh and Mark Levin will staunchly defend the Second Amendment right to bear arms and vehemently oppose any type of regulation. Very rarely would liberal or conservative outlets recognize some validity in the other side's point of view on the gun issue.

People can make a distinction between hard-hitting investigative reporting with a point of view versus clearly opinion-based advocacy journalism. I am a strong advocate of the view that the mainstream media needs to continue to strive toward the goals of objectivity, balance, impartiality, and fairness, even though perfect objectivity is impossible given that all reporters have preconceived worldviews, philosophies, perspectives, and biases.

There is a debate among journalists as to how best describe traditional media's approach when covering news events. Among the debated labels, one will find such descriptions and goals as objectivity, fairness, accuracy, balance, straightforwardness, impartiality, lack of bias, neutrality, and transparency. The ideal of objectivity certainly sounds good, but many journalism and media-literacy professionals are now shying away from using the term. They assert that there is no such thing as true objectivity; they point out that the code of the Society of Professional Journalists (SPJ) no longer lists objectivity as a core goal. According to Brent Cunningham of *Columbia Journalism Review*, SPJ dropped the term "objectivity" from the code due to the dilemma that the term tends to mean different things to different people. As Cunningham observes, "Ask ten journalists what objectivity means and you'll get ten different answers."[1] Some urge reporters to strive for balance, yet others complain that not all issues lend themselves to a balanced approach—such as global warming or the events that led to the 2003 invasion of Iraq and the downfall of Saddam Hussein. Efforts at transparency (as, for example, when a reporter admits his or her personal bias), are good things to point out, since the reader or viewer will then be aware of it, but this effort might prove insufficient since the information presented will have likely been skewed by the admitted bias of the reporter and may therefore be difficult for the audience to interpret accurately. As for impartiality, Margaret Sullivan, public editor of the *New York Times*, says that impartiality does not mean an even split between opposing beliefs: "Getting at the truth can require setting aside personal views to evaluate evidence fairly. If that's impartiality, it remains not only worthwhile but crucially necessary."[2] Terms like impartiality, objectivity, fairness, and so on do not have some agreed-upon meaning that reporters and journalists universally accept. Therefore, for the purposes of this book, I will use many of these labels interchangeably.

Some of the critical questions this book will address include:

1. What is the history of advocacy journalism?
2. What are its goals?
3. How did today's media landscape become so polarizing and confusing?
4. What are the positive and negative aspects of advocacy journalism?
5. Does the mainstream media have a liberal bias?
6. To what extent does the mainstream media strive to provide balanced and objective reporting?
7. Is advocacy journalism polarizing our country?
8. How can readers separate facts from opinions?
9. How can viewers, listeners, and readers understand the difference between balanced reporting and advocacy journalism?
10. How can all of us become more savvy news and media consumers?

The first chapter will provide insight on advocacy journalism and how it has led to the echo chamber that dominates a large part of American media.

CHAPTER 1

GOING INSIDE THE ECHO CHAMBER

Advocacy journalism outlets are notorious for taking readers and viewers way off track when trying to advance their agenda.[1] Both conservative and liberal media have elements within their ranks that engage in demeaning the other side and promoting their own viewpoints, and sometimes their zealous nature results in mistakes that confuse the consumer.

In November 2009, Fox News's Sean Hannity used misleading video when reporting on an anti-healthcare rally held by Republican Rep. Michele Bachmann in order to bolster the crowd estimate. Hannity aired video from the Tea Party's September 12 march on Washington while discussing Bachmann's much smaller healthcare protest. Hannity alleged that over 20,000 people had attended Bachmann's protest. The September rally reportedly drew over 70,000 people, while the crowd for Bachmann's anti-healthcare event was estimated to be only around 4,000. Hannity later apologized for using the wrong video.[2]

Fox News is hardly alone in making such errors. MSNBC's political pundit Ed Schultz misrepresented Republican Texas governor Rick Perry's alleged maligning of President Obama during a segment in August 2011. Schultz showed a clip of Perry at a campaign event telling the crowd that America's trillion-dollar debt was a "big black cloud" hanging over America. Schultz then stated, "That black cloud that Perry is talking about is President Barack Obama." It turned out that Perry was referring to this country's debt, causing Schultz to later apologize on air for not showing the full context of Perry's statements.[3]

The political landscape of the United States has been highly polarized for a number of years now. It is harder than ever to get members of Congress to break with their party on a key vote in the hope of reaching compromise on even the smallest of legislative items. Many in the general public blame the polarized media landscape for contributing to this political gridlock. Generally, the public mistrusts the media almost as much as they do trial lawyers, used car salesmen, and politicians.

As reported by Rebecca Riffkin, a September 2015 Gallup Poll revealed that only 40 percent of Americans trusted the media. This result tied the all-time lows from 2012 and 2014, continuing a ten-year trend. Before 2004, from 1977 on, a slight majority of people indicated in polls that they trusted the media. The 2015 poll indicated that people under age fifty and those who were acknowledged Republicans had a greater mistrust of the media: only 36 percent of those under fifty trusted the media, while only 32 percent of Republicans trusted the media.[4]

Perhaps most importantly, advocacy journalism is seen by many to be polarizing our country. A new Pew Research Center poll indicates that Americans are more politically polarized than ever. The Pew study states, "Republicans and Democrats are more divided along ideological lines— and partisan antipathy is deeper and more extensive—than at any point in the last two decades. These trends manifest themselves in myriad ways, both in politics and in everyday life. And a new survey of 10,000 adults nationwide finds that these divisions are greatest among those who are the most engaged and active in the political process."[5]

As reported by Andrew Beaujon of Poynter, the website for the prestigious and influential Poynter Institute for Media Studies, on June 10, 2014, a newly released survey by the Public Religion Research Institute and the Brookings Institute on religion, values, and immigration reform revealed that "People's media choices have a strong effect on their beliefs."[6] For example, with regard to the volatile topic of immigration, the study stated that "Only 42% of Republicans who most trust Fox News to provide accurate information about politics and current events support a path to citizenship, compared to 60% of Republicans who most trust other news sources."[7]

Advocacy journalists do not just set out to inform; they attempt to advance an agenda, whether it be conservative or liberal. Fox News and conservative talk radio show hosts like Rush Limbaugh and Sean Hannity are examples, along with Rev. Al Sharpton and Rachel Maddow, among others, on the liberal side. They are all giving their opinion and reporting news with a goal of swaying their audience via a biased agenda. This results in echo chambers and parallel universes of Red State (tradition-ally Republican) and Blue State (traditionally Democratic) viewpoints. The red state/blue state distinction became fairly standardized during the 2000 election, as the media used this color scheme on maps to describe Republican and Democratic states, and has since become commonplace and widely understood.[8]

Advocacy journalism is not a new phenomenon. In fact, it has a long and, depending on how one looks at it, distinguished or checkered past. During the late 1700s to the early 1800s in the United States, as our nation was emerging and developing its roots, each political party had its own newspapers to advance its unique agenda—the only real source of news with the exception of word-of-mouth, pamphleteering, and private letters. (This will be discussed in the next chapter.) The late 1800s and the 1900s saw the rise of large-scale corporate media with syndicates of many news-papers owned by one person or company, reflecting early attempts at providing the public with objective journalism, although there were still muckraking or yellow journalists who reveled in publishing scandalous and sensational stories, and numerous newspapers started publishing op-ed pages featuring the opinions of noted persons or groups on issues of the day. The emergence of talk radio in the late 1980s and 1990s, spearheaded by Rush Limbaugh, G. Gordon Liddy, Oliver North, Bob Grant, and Dr. Laura Schlessinger, among others, started the reemergence of clearly biased, agenda-driven media. There had been earlier examples of such opinion-based programs, such as Father Coughlin on radio and Edward R. Murrow on television, but they were in the minority. In the late 1990s, biased blogs and websites, such as *Salon*, *Slate*, and the *Drudge Report*, started to sprout and become immensely popular. Then came Fox News and MSNBC.

In summarizing these journalism phases and contemplating the future, former *New York Times* executive editor Howell Raines wrote, in 2008, "In little more than a century, journalism has been conducted under a variety of short-lived labels. Yellow journalism begat objective journalism, which begat investigative journalism, which begat advocacy journalism. To some of us, the New Journalism looked like a destination, but that was before the passage through gossip journalism to our next stop: fact-free journalism."[9]

Advocacy journalism can be a powerful tool, and sometimes it can be misused. In general, I am wary of some journalists advocating for a cause and using biased reporting to advance their agenda. An example of this was the ACORN incident a few years ago, where two conservative activists, James O'Keefe and Hannah Giles, went undercover with a hidden camera into ACORN offices nationwide, pretending to be a prostitute and either a pimp or her boyfriend and making up a specific scenario about seeking alleged tax advice on how to conceal the source of illegal income while managing underage Salvadoran prostitutes who were in the United States illegally.

ACORN was a community organizing and voter registration organization that drew the ire of conservatives due to its alleged past voter registration irregularities. In light of these undercover videos, Congress shut down ACORN's funding and the group's contributions diminished significantly. O'Keefe and Giles released their heavily edited videos through conservative web entrepreneur Andrew Breitbart. Their reporting was clearly agenda-driven—to expose and embarrass ACORN. While they were celebrated as heroes among conservatives, others viewed their actions as an unethical prank. Richard W. Rahn, in a *Washington Times* op-ed, called Giles and O'Keefe "true American patriots."[10] In contrast, according to *AdWeek*, *Baltimore Sun* TV critic David Zurawik wrote in his blog, "Only on the cube-sided Bizarro Planet are [James] O'Keefe and Giles champions of the First Amendment"[11]

Another concern advocacy journalism poses is when the host of a news program gets too involved with the story. Rev. Al Sharpton seems to do this often when he reports on incidents in which he is involved as an activist, such as the Ferguson, Missouri, protests over the death of Michael Brown at the hands of a police officer, or the George Zimmerman case in Florida, in which Mr. Zimmerman was tried for killing Trayvon Martin.

Sharpton's close connection with the people involved in these news stories gives him a definite advantage with respect to gaining access to the victim's relatives and their legal representatives, but due to his support for the victims and their families, many people would conclude that he is unable to report fairly and objectively.[12]

Many critics of journalist Glenn Greenwald believe that he was too close to National Security Agency whistleblower Edward Snowden, who leaked agency communications regarding surveillance of various individuals, and that he was not impartial regarding Snowden's motives for such damaging disclosures. Glenn Greenwald, a journalist, lawyer, activist, columnist, and author, broke the news in his *Guardian* column on June 6, 2013, that the National Security Agency was collecting the phone records of millions of Americans. His source was Edward Snowden, a former computer security specialist for a defense contractor, who leaked classified documents to Greenwald, along with *Washington Post* reporter Barton Gellman and documentarian Laura Poitras. As Malcolm Forbes wrote regarding Greenwald in *Columbia Journalism Review*, "Attempts are made to discredit him by certain media figures. For some, he was not engaged in 'journalism' but embroiled in 'activism.'"[13] Some people, including Congressman Peter King, claimed that Greenwald should be criminally charged for aiding and abetting Snowden's effort to avoid criminal extradition and criminal prosecution, while *Meet the Press* host David Gregory asked Greenwald this very question. Greenwald responded that the assumption that he had aided and abetted Snowden was completely without evidence. House Intelligence Committee chairman Mike Rogers (R-Mich.) told reporters, "For personal gain, he's now selling his access to information, that's how they're terming it. . . . A thief selling stolen materials is a thief."[14] While some people felt that Greenwald was too close to his source (Snowden) and was acting as an enabler, others praised him as a crusading journalist who broke an important story that the public needed to know. In fact, Greenwald, Gellman, Poitras, and Ewen MacAskill received the prestigious George Polk Award for National Security Reporting for their coverage on the Snowden documents.[15] In 2014, the *Guardian* and the *Washington Post* won Pulitzer Prizes for Public Service for their reporting on the NSA's secret surveillance.

Rolling Stone magazine's flawed reporting of the allegation by a female University of Virginia student that she was raped by members of a university-sanctioned fraternity resulted from a reporter wanting to satisfy her particular narrative regarding sexual assault on America's campuses. As reported by T. Rees Shapiro of the *Washington Post* on January 8, 2016, the student, Jackie, was the main figure in *Rolling Stone*'s nine-thousand-word article that reported a brutal gang rape in a UVA campus fraternity house. After discrepancies and inconsistencies in Jackie's story were reported by the *Washington Post*, and Charlottesville, Virginia, police determined that no gang rape had occurred, *Rolling Stone* retracted the story. A Columbia University Graduate School of Journalism report commissioned by *Rolling Stone* concluded that magazine's investigation was a journalistic failure that could have been avoided.[16]

As Shapiro reported on May 12, 2015, the complaint of a civil lawsuit against *Rolling Stone*, its parent company, and Sabrina Rubin Erdely, the writer of the article, by UVA associate dean of students Nicole Eramo, alleged, "Rolling Stone and Erdely's highly defamatory and false statements about Dean Eramo were not the result of an innocent mistake," according to the lawsuit, which was filed in Charlottesville Circuit Court. "They were the result of a wanton journalist who was more concerned with writing an article that fulfilled her preconceived narrative about the victimization of women on American college campuses, and a malicious publisher who was more concerned about selling magazines to boost the economic bottom line for its faltering magazine, than they were about discovering the truth or actual facts."[17]

Edward Wasserman, dean of University of California at Berkeley's journalism school, told Paul Farhi of the *Washington Post* that although journalists can have a social commitment, people should be skeptical of reporters who are also advocates. Wasserman asked, "Do we know if he's pulling his punches or has his fingers on the scale because some information that he should be reporting doesn't fit [with his cause]? If that's the case, he should be castigated."[18]

Advocacy journalism can also lead to overemphasis and overexaggeration of certain stories. This overemphasis through constant and continuous coverage can reflect a bias, especially when most of the coverage is negative. MSNBC succumbed to this with respect to New Jersey governor Chris Christie and the "Bridgegate" matter, and Fox News was equally excessive with its coverage of the Benghazi, Libya, attack that killed the US ambassador to that country while Hillary Clinton was serving as secretary of state. The Bridgegate scandal involved the intentional closing of the George Washington Bridge from Fort Lee, New Jersey, to New York City. While Christie was cleared of wrongdoing, federal authorities eventually conducted criminal investigations and charges were filed against three of Christie's former political allies for plotting together to create lane closures and traffic jams on the bridge, allegedly to punish Democratic Fort Lee mayor Mark Sokolich for not endorsing Christie's reelection bid.

Regarding Clinton and Benghazi, Jim Tankersley of the *Washington Post*, citing Internet archive data compiled by the GDELT Project, stated that there were 1,500 individual shows mentioning Benghazi on Fox News in 2015, compared to about 650 on CNN. Tankersley noted that it was "likely that the extra airtime Clinton is receiving on Fox has often been spent discussing scandals related to her."[19] According to the *Washington Examiner*, MSNBC's constant and obsessive focus on the Bridgegate scandal was mocked and criticized by many people, including MSNBC's own Joe Scarborough, HBO's Bill Maher, CNN's Don Lemon, the *Daily Kos*, and David Axelrod.[20] As noted by PolitiFact, the night that the Bridgegate story broke, MSNBC spent 211 minutes, nearly all of its evening programming on the scandal, while CNN dedicated 53 minutes to it.[21] As *Daily Kos* liberal blogger James Fidlerten (who posts with the byline "fidlerten") noted, "Unfortunately, of late I have had to either turn to CNN or just give up on the news entirely to watch sitcoms. The reason is that it seems to be wall-to-wall coverage on my favorite news channel (MSNBC) of New Jersey Governor Chris Christie's travails concerning the George Washington bridge lane closures. . . . MSNBC has of late become obsessed with Chris Christie as much as Fox News obsesses over Obama."[22]

After seeing each network spend days, weeks, and months on the

Bridgegate and Benghazi incidents, it made many viewers want to say, "Enough already. Let it go." I know that these were my feelings. It got to the point that if the show's host indicated that the next segment would be about either of these two issues, I switched channels. I pretty much knew what the hosts and guests would be saying and arguing. It was too predictable.

Sometimes advocacy journalism is used to promote a narrative even if the facts don't fit. The host's bias can be shown through tone, choice of stories, opinions, and the way he or she interviews guests. Rachel Maddow from MSNBC often comes across as sarcastic and snarky to her detractors, while Bill O'Reilly of the Fox News channel comes across as pompous and arrogant. Most of the time, it's a lovefest, where the host and his or her guests all agree on a certain position. Other times, if a guest has a different opinion than the host, the latter will frequently interrupt the guest and not let the person get a word in edgewise. With the host in control, it's a bigger mismatch than the Harlem Globetrotters going against the Washington Generals. Viewers of the show are fans of the host and will more often agree with the host. Frequently, such adversarial confrontations reach a point at which all parties to the discussion talk at the same time and try to be heard over each other in such a cacophonous fashion that it reaches a crescendo and the viewer can't understand what either side is saying.

There is also a tendency to demonize the other side. If you watch Fox News long enough, you will believe that President Barack Obama is an incompetent elitist and a socialist. And if you watch MSNBC long enough, you would believe that President George W. Bush was never smarter than a fifth grader.

Contrary to what some might think, though, there actually are positive features of advocacy journalism. Sometimes it can be used to highlight important stories that are ignored by the mainstream media, such as stories involving third-world countries—for example, the 2015 Nepal earthquake, trafficking and smuggling worldwide, lack of cellphones and electricity in African countries, overworked healthcare professionals misapplying malaria treatments in the Congo, fatal pre-election violence in Nigeria, the hesitation of Argentinian emergency medics to respond to Buenos Aires slums due to safety fears, or the 2006 landslide in Java, Indonesia, that killed over one hundred people.[23]

When it's at its best, advocacy journalism can be used positively, as a watchdog on government to keep an eye on those in power. It can also be entertaining through the hosts' use of humor, sarcasm, and conflict with guests. It can validate the viewpoints of the viewer, listener, or reader and give them useful talking points when arguing with friends and family about some major social issue or world event. Some people love to see the passion when opposing sides get into verbal brawls over an issue. The hosts are passionate about the causes they believe in and will fight for what they think is right. On the MSNBC side, Al Sharpton fights for civil rights for African-Americans, Rachel Maddow fights for gay and lesbian rights, and José Diaz-Balart fights for the rights of Mexican immigrants. On the conservative side, Sean Hannity crusades against Islamic extremism, Bill O'Reilly rails against "The War on Christmas," and Glenn Beck advocates traditional American values. The hosts' views and passions can stir people to action and influence public opinion. It's a stark contrast to the network news, in which the anchorperson has a calm demeanor and doesn't argue with his or her guests.

Another positive aspect of advocacy journalism is that there are times when a host can discredit a guest through vigorous questioning. I like to show my students videos of two of these incidents. One case in 2008 involved MSNBC program host Chris Matthews and his aggressive questioning of conservative radio host Kevin James, who was defending President George W. Bush's comparison of then-senator Barack Obama to Nazi appeasers because of Obama's willingness to talk with enemies of the United States, such as Iran. James claimed that Obama was appeasing terrorists much like British prime minister Neville Chamberlain had appeased Adolf Hitler. For over three minutes, Matthews tried nearly twenty times to get James to explain what Chamberlain had done and how he had appeased Hitler. "What did he do?" Matthews repeated over and over and over. Finally, the exchange culminated with this:

MATTHEWS: You don't know what you're talking about, Kevin. You don't know what you're talking about. Tell me what Chamberlain did wrong.

JAMES: Neville Chamberlain was an appeaser, Chris. Neville Chamberlain was an appeaser, all right? [. . .]

MATTHEWS: I've been sitting here five minutes asking you to say what the president was referring to in 1938 at Munich.

JAMES: I don't know.

MATTHEWS: You don't know, thank you.[24]

While Matthews's detractors would find his interrogation and frequent interruptions to be obnoxious, his supporters would claim that his interviewing technique exposed a guest as a buffoon for not knowing what he was talking about. Personally, I enjoyed it.

Similarly, in an August 2014 interview, Sean Hannity smacked down controversial Muslim imam Anjem Choudary, who threatened the West and claimed that ultraconservative sharia law would become the law in the United Kingdom and the United States. Hannity badgered him for several minutes about his views, questioning Choudary's support of ISIS, his views on punishing women who do not cover themselves, as well as punishment of women who commit adultery, punishment of gay people, whether sharia law would be implemented worldwide, and whether he wanted a worldwide Islamic caliphate. One of the exchanges went like this:

HANNITY: You support Hamas, Hezbollah, ISIS, ISIL. You support al Qaeda. You once said about 9/11—you were very clear that you were on team bin Laden, not team Obama. So you supported what happened on 9/11 and you said it was a good thing. So I know where you're coming from. I just want America to . . .

(CROSSTALK)

HANNITY: . . . see you for who you are! . . .

HANNITY: You support evil and death and demise of innocent people! . . .

(CROSSTALK)

HANNITY: That makes you an enemy of freedom!

CHOUDARY: We can talk over each other . . .

HANNITY: And I don't want your sharia law, and neither does anybody in Great Britain that has a brain!

CHOUDARY: You will have no choice, in fact, Sean. It's coming to a place near you. It's coming to a place near you.

HANNITY: Coming—so you're threatening to come and get me, is that what you're saying?

CHOUDARY: I'm saying that the sharia will be implemented in the whole world . . .

HANNITY: Thank you. You've answered my question. You want a worldwide Islamic caliphate.

CHOUDARY: Of course we do . . .

CHOUDARY: You will be liberated from the shackles of (INAUDIBLE). Let me tell you something . . .

HANNITY: I don't need to be liberated by Islam. I'm a Christian! (CROSSTALK)

HANNITY: I don't want your religion. I don't want sharia.

(CROSSTALK)

HANNITY: I believe in women's rights. I believe in freedom[25]

For Hannity's supporters and to many Americans, this was interesting and informative because it gave some perspective on how people like Choudary really think.

There is a clear distinction between advocacy journalism and the reporting done by the mainstream media, such as (theoretically, anyway) the network news and major newspapers. Even if one accepts the conservative dogma that the mainstream media has a liberal bias (more on that in a later chapter), it is much more subtle than what can be found on MSNBC or on liberal websites.

Every semester, I give my journalism students an exercise in which they have to watch and analyze three different news shows. One is a Fox News program, hosted by someone such as Sean Hannity, Bill O'Reilly, or Megyn Kelly; another is an MSNBC program, with someone like Al Sharpton, Rachel Maddow, or Chris Matthews; the third is one of the national network news programs on ABC, NBC, or CBS. The point of the assignment is to show the students how bias can affect news coverage. For instance, Fox News's coverage of a Tea Party rally will attempt to portray happy, flag-waving, patriotic people speaking out against their government and proudly exercising their First Amendment rights; the MSNBC coverage will focus on ostensibly racist signs and comments from the crowd such as "Obama, go back to Kenya"; meanwhile, the national network coverage of ABC, NBC, and CBS tends to be more objective and balanced and show elements of both. To my surprise and satisfaction, most of my students prefer the straightforward, objective, balanced journalism, and many are repulsed by advocacy journalism. After seeing YouTube clips of five minutes of cable news hosts and guests screaming and yelling and talking over each other, some students have complained that it was giving them a headache. They laugh when I play them the clips of Chris Matthews and Sean Hannity berating their guests, but they generally say that they wouldn't watch their shows as a news source.

Despite claims that the mainstream media is liberally biased, it does seem to do a much better job of being fair and impartial than Fox News or MSNBC. You'll never hear ABC's David Muir call President Bush a moron or President Obama a socialist. The hosts have a calm, professional, straightforward demeanor and do not badger or abruptly interrupt their guests during interviews. They also try to give both sides' positions on the issue. For instance, after a State of the Union address, the network news will get reaction from both Republicans and Democrats. At most, any bias from the network news tends to be subtle or demonstrated by the selection of which stories to cover. Granted, there is no such thing as true objectivity, since reporters have their own views and beliefs. However, they do strive, it seems, to be balanced and objective. The hosts just read the news from the teleprompter and cut away to live reporters or taped stories. Some people find this approach to be outdated and boring, but many still like to rely on this style of delivery as their main news source.

As Judy Woodruff of PBS told aspiring journalists in a Facebook chat,

> I draw a bright line between news reporting of the type we do regularly on the *NewsHour* and advocacy journalism, where the writer or commentator is clearly taking sides and giving his or her opinion. We

don't do that here, except on Fridays when I interview Mark Shields and David Brooks for their analysis of the week's news. Even then, they don't express their opinions without explaining the background. I don't engage in advocacy journalism—it's just not what I do. As a reporter, I was trained to understand the public doesn't care what I think, or what my opinion is. My job is to report, and sometimes offer analysis when it's clearly labeled as such, and to stop there.[26]

Despite its flaws and the many complaints it attracts, advocacy journalism isn't going to go away. It continues to remain immensely popular. In addition to cable television shows, websites and blogs are prominent outlets for advocacy journalism. Liberal websites include the *Daily Kos*, *Counter-Punch*, *OpEdNews*, *Salon*, Media Matters, *AlterNet*, *ThinkProgress*, *Democratic Underground*, and *Huffington Post*. Conservative websites include the *Drudge Report*, Breitbart, Townhall.com, Free Republic, *WorldNet-Daily*, *RedState*, GOPUSA, and TheBlaze. Like their television counterparts, these websites report news but have a clear bias and agenda and provide opinions and commentary. They are also immensely popular and influential. According to eBizMBA, a website that tracks Internet usage and traffic, in February 2016, the *Huffington Post* had over 110 million monthly visitors, while TheBlaze had 25 million monthly visitors.[27]

Talk radio shows continue to be a thriving source of advocacy journalism, as well. As noted in Hannah Karp's *Wall Street Journal* article of February 3, 2015, "More than 50 million people in the U.S. tune in each week to news-talk radio stations that carry advertising, making it radio's second-most popular format, behind country music, according to Nielsen."[28]

In light of the explosion of media outlets ranging from cable news, talk radio, blogs, and websites, we need to be more savvy news consumers. As I tell my journalism students, it's important to consider the source of the information before we make our judgments. We need to stop elevating advocacy journalists as our main news sources. In some cases, advocacy journalists might be giving their audience accurate facts; however, in many cases, they will slant those facts and present them in a manner that advances their argument or agenda. A Fox News host like Tucker Carlson will cherry-pick facts and statistics that support his position that

Obamacare is and will be a disaster. Likewise, MSNBC's Chris Hayes will choose facts and statistics that show the Affordable Care Act in a positive light. There's nothing wrong with either side doing this. Their shows are like video editorial/op-eds. Such programs have value in rallying their base audience, presenting information and arguments in an entertaining manner, and giving viewers and listeners talking points for their own discussions and arguments.

However, if our country is ever to get out of its current polarized rut, our media habits need to change. People need to get their news from a wide range of sources and go beyond their own self-reinforcing echo chambers to get various perspectives on the news. They need news that they can rely on. Yes, watch your favorite advocacy journalism programs, but also watch programs with opposing viewpoints, as well as the national network nightly news and public television. Media literacy is an emerging field of study that is attempting to help consumers navigate this polarized and confusing environment. Many people are unaware of a news outlet's bias, and literacy as it relates to sources for news and information is very important in today's adversarial media landscape. Fortunately, there are organizations and universities that are focused on teaching people the needed skills to become more discriminating when choosing media sources and in evaluating the information they receive as consumers (something I will discuss later in the book).

How do readers, listeners, and viewers determine what news is? How can they understand the difference between balanced, fair, objective, impartial, unbiased journalism and advocacy journalism? It's important to be able to sort facts from opinion. One of the most important roles of journalism is to educate and inform people, but advocacy journalism only provides a partial education. More people need to be aware of this and learn how to distinguish what is balanced from what is skewed. So what is the goal and purpose of advocacy journalism? How does it work? That will be addressed in the next chapter.

CHAPTER 2

WHAT'S THE GOAL AND PURPOSE OF ADVOCACY JOURNALISM?

A dvocacy journalism has a long tradition and has served many purposes. Its goal is to inform people and give them information in a manner that attempts to convince the receiver of a certain viewpoint. It can validate people's views and give them information and talking points; it can shed light on issues that are not getting much attention and can educate the public to the fact that the issue needs to be addressed. The journalist takes a side on an issue, has a specific point of view, and then argues as persuasively as possible to justify it. Reporters, bloggers, and others who engage in advocacy journalism use journalistic techniques and their specific medium—be it writing, radio, or audiovisual—as a method of advancing their cause or belief. These journalists often start with a certain premise or objective and then use their reporting skills to support that premise. Unlike outright and blatant propaganda, which often trades in false, hyperbolic, or extremely exaggerated claims, advocacy journalism uses carefully chosen facts to support a certain viewpoint or bias. This approach is often used as a tool to expose the hypocrisy or corruption of governments, organizations, or individuals. Some claim to use advocacy journalism as a watchdog, as the eyes and ears of the public. Others believe that they are using it as a voice for the oppressed, the voiceless, and the marginalized segments of society. Some advocacy journalists seek to pinpoint and expose social ills and atrocities and engage in a campaign designed to cause social change for the better, urging people to take action.

What makes it so difficult to assess the accuracy of advocacy journalism reportage is that what is stated is not outright propaganda filled with lies and mistruths. In many cases, there are kernels or even chunks of truth in its reports. The problem is that the journalist or host is interpreting the facts with spin, or a skewed perspective, which makes it doubly difficult to distinguish what is actual fact from what is a more weighted interpretation.

Advocacy journalism is practiced by newspaper op-eds and editorials pages, magazine editorials and columns, radio commentary and talk show programs, television and cable news outlets, websites, blogs, books, social media, and television and movie documentaries. Nowadays, a lot of advocacy journalism is loud, passionate, entertaining, and humorous. It is a tool used by both sides of the political spectrum to act as a counterbalance to what the advocates consider the opposition's point of view. Each side claims that the other side should not be allowed to control the public narrative when it comes to important issues that shape our society. They insist that the "other side" should be questioned, challenged, and rebutted, if not completely refuted.

Use of advocacy journalism can also be a wise business decision. Many people, especially younger persons, see the mainstream media as bland and uninteresting. They like to see news presented in a passionate and humorous way. This is often reflected in the strong ratings for talk radio shows, cable news talk shows, and comedic analysis of news via programs such as *Real Time with Bill Maher* on HBO, *The Michael Medved Show* on syndicated radio, and the hugely popular *Daily Show*, most recently hosted by comedian Jon Stewart and now anchored by Trevor Noah, as well as *The Colbert Report* (Stephen Colbert's late-night show, which went off the air at the end of 2014). This is good business, because these shows achieve high ratings, which leads to more advertising revenue, which leads to even more similar shows, due to the large number of people who watch these programs. As noted by a Comedy Central press release from April 2013, "'The Daily Show with Jon Stewart' and 'The Colbert Report' Top the Competition During 1Q 2013 as the Most-Watched Late Night Talk Shows among Adults 18–49, Adults 18–34, Adults 18–24, Adults 25–34, Men 18–49, Men 18–34 and Men 18–24."[1]

How does advocacy journalism operate? It seeks to give viewers, listeners, and readers news in an argumentative, biased manner. Its goal is to pick and choose facts that support a certain viewpoint, whether it is a political or social issue. It primarily reports news or provides information with a clear agenda or bias. It doesn't strive to be objective, balanced, straightforward, non-opinionated, or neutral. New journalism, also sometimes referred to as gonzo journalism, immersion journalism, participatory journalism, or embedded journalism is a form of journalism where the reporter's point of view is encouraged. Tom Wolfe and Hunter Thompson were among the pioneers in this field, which emerged in the 1960s and 70s. They used a first-person style of writing, with the writer immersing himself in the story, becoming an essential character and using literary techniques to tell feature stories. Gonzo journalism focuses on the writer's life, rather than just the experience. Thompson wrote for *Rolling Stone* magazine, and he also wrote several books, including *Fear and Loathing in Las Vegas* and *Fear and Loathing: On the Campaign Trail '72*. Wolfe wrote for *Esquire* and *Rolling Stone*, among other magazines, and he too wrote several books, including *The Right Stuff*, *The Bonfire of the Vanities*, and *The Electric Kool-Aid Acid Test*. There is also public or civic journalism, which seeks to both inform readers and engage them in public debate as to how to solve problems or take action.

According to *Media Ethics* magazine, "Public journalism and, for the most part, citizen journalism can be viewed as examples of *advocacy* journalism, a form of journalism that endeavors to be fact-based, but does not separate editorial opinion from news coverage and often approaches the news from a specific viewpoint."[2]

In his defense of advocacy journalism and his criticism of objective journalism, Robert Niles, former editor of USC's *Online Journalism Review*, wrote that advocacy journalism was necessary to restore credibility to the journalism profession. He noted that his journalism students were motivated by idealism and advocating for worthy causes, not by a big payday, and that people want reporters to make their communities better: "The problem some journalists have with 'advocacy' is not the concept itself, but those who put advocacy ahead of the truth, instead of behind it, where it belongs. Objectivity is a means to an end—that end being truthful reporting. And if truthful reporting leads to an obvious conclusion, a reporter and publication cheat their readers if they pull back and don't follow their reporting to that conclusion, and fail to advocate for their community reading it."[3]

Thus, while advocacy should not get in the way of truth due to the reporter wanting to use his reporting to support his viewpoint, he shouldn't hesitate to provide his own conclusions if the reporting supports it.

In defending Univision's Jorge Ramos as an advocacy journalist who confronted Republican presidential candidate Donald Trump during a press conference in 2015 regarding Trump's stance on immigration, *Detroit News* columnist Bankole Thompson compared him to notable and admirable advocacy journalists of the past, such as Ida B. Wells, who crusaded against lynching and fought for women's rights: "There is also precedent of journalists holding politicians accountable over controversial issues. During the Vietnam War, CBS's venerable Walter Cronkite was openly against the war. *Washington Post* reporters Bob Woodward and Carl Bernstein helped bring down former President Richard M. Nixon for abuse of power in the Watergate scandal."[4]

Walter Cronkite discussed his on-air objections to the Vietnam War in his book *A Reporter's Life*. He explained that this was a rare situation and that he didn't make his decision lightly. He wrote:

> So I flew home and did a special report on the Tet offensive. It was as factual as we at CBS News could make it. But I ended it with a clearly labeled editorial. This was a radical departure from our normal practice. I had only once or twice stepped out of my role as an impartial newscaster, and on both those occasions I was defending freedom of the press on the theory that if we members of the press did not speak up for this democratic essential, no one else would. As we discussed the broadcast, [CBS News president Richard] Salant warned that I was placing my reputation, as well as CBS's, on the line and that we were putting ourselves in jeopardy; that given the delicate state of the bitterly divided American public opinion, we might well lose a substantial part of our audience. I had no problem making my decision. . . . In the broadcast, I made it clear that my subsequent words represented my opinion and that this was an extraordinary affair.[5]

I don't think that Cronkite's objections to the war negatively impacted his ability to accurately report the nightly news. As he explained, his commentary was a rare situation.

There was also a time in the 1960s and 70s when news anchors like Eric Sevareid, David Brinkley, Howard K. Smith, and John Chancellor would give commentaries during nightly network newscasts, but this custom fell out of fashion.

There are different levels of advocacy journalism. Some are blatantly biased and opinionated, such as when foreign governments have state-run media that spews propaganda with little regard for the facts. Then there are editorials, op-eds, talk radio, and blogs that have strong opinions but are often fact based (although the facts are frequently cherry-picked in a skewed manner). Some feel that the most credible types of advocacy journalism would be investigative reporting and solutions journalism, in which reporters often have a point of view and an agenda, but the research is extensive and designed to uncover some wrongdoing or conflict of interest. The last fifty years or so have seen the rise of interpretative journalism, explanatory journalism, solutions journalism, investigative journalism, and literary journalism. Reporters use interpretive journalism and investigative journalism to give context to stories and explain complex issues. They use solutions journalism to try to solve problems and focus on successful stories, such as which approaches have worked in reducing the dropout rates in schools and why they were successful. Another example would be a *New York Times Magazine* article that focused on how Xavier University in New Orleans, a historically black college, was successful in sending its students to medical school.[6]

Mark Bowden, a former reporter for the *Philadelphia Inquirer* for twenty years, and an award-winning author of many bestselling books, including *Black Hawk Down: A Story of Modern War*, noted in an e-mail interview that there are different types of advocacy journalism:

> There is good advocacy and poor advocacy. Good advocacy is honest, well-reported, and persuasive; poor advocacy is just cheap salesmanship, readily dismissed. Good journalism reports new information, or

offers some new way of understanding things. It can advocate a point of view, or try to present information in such a way that allows the reader to decide how she feels. In either case, the trustworthiness of the journalist and the quality of the work determines its import, and in the case of advocacy, its effectiveness.[7]

According to Dan Gillmor of the online publication *Slate*, many organizations are engaging in advocacy journalism. "Yes, *BuzzFeed*, *Vox*, and ESPN's new *FiveThirtyEight*, and a host of other large and small new media operations are extending the news ecosystem," he writes. "But so are Human Rights Watch, the American Civil Liberties Union, the Cato Institute, and a host of other organizations that do serious reporting about some of the key issues of our time. The latter are doing advocacy journalism—coverage with a clearly stated worldview—and often leading the way for traditional journalists."[8] Gillmor writes that groups like these are going deeper into issues that the public needs to understand or that traditional media has ignored or treated shallowly, and that they are doing it through twenty-first-century technology.

With great power comes great responsibility, however. While advocacy journalism can be used as an effective tool to illuminate and combat social ills, it can also be misused by those who are so agenda driven that they mislead or ignore certain facts in their zealous efforts to make their case. Their passion for a cause may well impede their judgment as to what is accurate and what is not. As described in detail in the next chapter, advocacy journalism is not a new phenomenon. It has existed in various forms since America's colonial days.

CHAPTER 3

THE EARLY HISTORY OF ADVOCACY JOURNALISM: THE LATE 1700S AND THE 1800S

A case can be made that many of the writers during America's colonial period were advocacy journalists and muckrakers. Thomas Paine's 1776 pamphlet *Common Sense* challenged the authority of royal English rule and helped convince people in the colonies that independence from England was essential. Benjamin Franklin was an advocacy journalist whose *Pennsylvania Gazette* contained many columns critical of British rule and even featured a 1754 cartoon showing a severed snake with the phrase "Join or Die," which helped inspire the call for American independence.[1] Boston printer Benjamin Harris's *Publick Occurrences, Both Foreign and Domestick*, was the first American newspaper, but it was banned after only one issue because it expressed negative views of English rule and reported that the king of France had an affair with his daughter-in-law.[2] The publisher of the *New York Weekly Journal*, John Peter Zenger, was arrested in 1735 and tried for libel after accusing New York's colonial governor of corruption. He was acquitted based on the argument that truth was a defense.[3] The *Federalist Papers*, a series of newspaper articles designed to support ratification of the US Constitution, featured eighty-five persuasive essays by lead editors Alexander Hamilton, James Madison, and John Jay.[4]

As these examples clearly demonstrate, advocacy journalism is not a new phenomenon. During the late 1700s and early 1800s, various political parties put out their own newspapers. As President George Washington's secretary of state, Thomas Jefferson founded the *National Gazette*, a newspaper that was created to attack Secretary of the Treasury Alexander Hamilton and the Federalists, who wanted a strong central government that would have certain powers over the various state governments. John Adams and the Federalist Party had the *New York Commercial Advertiser* and the *Connecticut Courant*, which skewered Jefferson during the presidential election campaign of 1800 against incumbent president John Adams.[5]

This was an extremely partisan era and many of the publications were scathingly critical of the other side, including vicious personal attacks. According to the University of Virginia's Miller Center, the presidential election of 1800, between Federalist incumbent John Adams and Democratic-Republican Thomas Jefferson, featured an especially high level of animosity:

> The Federalists attacked the fifty-seven-year-old Jefferson as a godless Jacobin who would unleash the forces of bloody terror upon the land. With Jefferson as President, so warned one newspaper, "Murder, robbery, rape, adultery, and incest will be openly taught and practiced, the air will be rent with the cries of the distressed, the soil will be soaked with blood, and the nation black with crimes." Others attacked Jefferson's deist beliefs as the views of an infidel who "writes aghast the truths of God's words; who makes not even a profession of Christianity; who is without Sabbaths; without the sanctuary, and without so much as a decent external respect for the faith and worship of Christians."[6]

To some extent, this early presidential election in our nation's history was a precursor to today's polarized media environment. As Joanna Weiss of the *Boston Globe* states, "For those of you despairing about the nasty tenor of elections today, the ugly partisanship of politics, the polarity of the press: Be happy you weren't around in the nineteenth century."[7] As Leonard Downie Jr. and Michael Schudson of *Columbia Journalism Review* point out in a 2009 article, the American media of the late 1700s and early 1800s were mostly opinion based and stridently partisan because the newspapers owed their livelihoods and loyalties to political parties: "Not until the 1820s and 1830s did they begin to hire reporters to gather news actively rather than wait for it to come to them."[8] And according to *The Atlantic*, there was a synergy between the political parties and their newspapers:

> Political parties at this time were only loose coalitions of leaders; they had no ongoing organization except their newspapers, and in practice, the parties

and their newspapers were almost indistinguishable. Local editors were key party organizers, and local party leaders often met in the newspaper office. According to some historians, this partisan press belonged to the "dark ages" of American journalism. But it played a central role in mobilizing political participation and creating a vibrant democracy. And at no time was that more the case than in 1828, when [Andrew] Jackson's supporters built a network of Democratic papers across the country [against National Republican John Quincy Adams], and voting turnout increased sharply.[9]

Carolyn Kitch, professor and chair of the Department of Journalism at Temple University and associate editor of *Journalism and Mass Communication Quarterly*, offered these observations in an e-mail interview:

The "Party Press" era is an interesting period for several reasons. Most commonly, historians point to this era as an early example of what we think of as a present-day phenomenon, today's increasingly polarized news climate, in which political parties align themselves with particular news outlets and their audiences consume the news coverage with which they already agree. But to me the more interesting parallel is that the Party Press era is an early example of how bureaucracy and economics determine the structure and nature of journalism. Prior to the Penny Press era, newspapers depended heavily on revenue from backers and subscribers; there weren't many options for newsstand sales, and although the papers were full of notice-style ads, advertising wasn't yet an organized industry and so wasn't yet a predictable revenue source. So targeting a particular audience was a more viable strategy for economic survival. Also, after the American revolution, several major newspaper publishers gained government printing contracts—because there were many new laws and policies to print—and this revenue stream aligned them with federal and local governments in a structural way.[10]

Why did this early polarized political era end? Dr. Kitch contends that "Many newspapers continued to have political agendas throughout the nineteenth century, but the arrival of the Penny Press newspapers in major cities in the early 1830s signaled an important change in the nature of American journalism." And, she continues,

Although some historians locate the origins of journalistic "objectivity" to the Penny Press papers, they occurred mainly because of—again—economics. These papers were made possible because of the emergence of the Industrial Revolution in America. New technologies made production faster and cheaper, at the same time that a significant advertising industry emerged to market mass-manufactured goods. Both of these developments enabled publishers to greatly lower the price of a newspaper (to a penny, although that price rose to two or three cents pretty quickly in the case of most major "Penny Press" papers), which meant that more people could buy them, which meant that the publishers could raise advertising prices because of bigger audiences. Concurrently, waves of immigrants were arriving in American cities, swelling the numbers of potential readers and creating population concentrations that favored newspaper sales made on the street.[11]

The Penny Press of the 1830s and 1840s reflected a transition away from the partisan press and featured a philosophy of producing newspapers for the common people that cost only a penny or so. Being less partisan, they focused extensively on coverage of crime, local news, and human interest stories. This era featured strong publishers like Benjamin Day, James Gordon Bennett, and Horace Greeley. Greeley and other publishers used their newspapers to advocate their own personal or corporate positions on social issues, through strongly worded and passionate editorials. Famed poet Walt Whitman was a columnist and editor for the *Brooklyn Eagle* and wrote editorials in support of the US war with Mexico in 1846–47.

In lamenting the current state of advocacy journalism in today's media environment, *Newsweek* compared it to the early days of the American press: "The United States is now in danger of drifting toward a more European or nineteenth-century American 'partisan' press. This kind of journalism can be more satisfying and exciting, but it's less reliable and authoritative."[12] In the mid to late 1800s, another form of journalism emerged: corporate, objective journalism, with the inverted-pyramid, straightforward, informational style of writing. This was a turn from opinionated reporting.

CHAPTER 4

THE RISE OF CORPORATE, OBJECTIVE JOURNALISM, AND THE INVERTED PYRAMID

During the late 1800s and early 1900s, the concept of corporate, objective journalism was established. Most newspaper outlets embraced the view that reporters should be unbiased, neutral, objective observers, and storytellers. This is still the predominant model for much of the mainstream media today, whether they adhere to it or not. This era gave rise to the concept of the inverted pyramid formula for producing news stories, which features the "Who, What, When, Where, Why, and How" model.[1] The philosophy is that most readers are busy and want their information quickly. They will often scan stories and just read the first paragraph or two to get the essential information right away. The inverted pyramid is a straightforward approach that strives to give the reader the essential information quickly in a nonbiased, "just the facts" manner. Therefore, it is inverted because most of the essential information is given up front, followed by less-important descriptive material that the reader can skip if need be. The reporter's job is simply to present the news, not to give opinions or commentary about it. Generally, the reporter stays in the third person and does not insert himself into the article. As I tell my journalism students, don't say "I went to the pumpkin festival," or "John Smith, the pumpkin festival coordinator told me," or "This was the greatest pumpkin festival I've ever seen." The reporter lets the people involved in the story give their opinions and perspectives. The inverted pyramid formula tends to be used in describing events. The beginning of the article, through the summary lead (also spelled lede), or hard lead, should answer the essential questions that the reader is expecting to have addressed. It's especially useful for breaking news stories, for which readers want to get right to the point. The inverted pyramid also makes it easier for editors to cut the article's content from the bottom up and for headline writers to come up with headlines by reading the first paragraph.

Samuel Morse's invention of the telegraph in 1845 helped to spur the invention of this inverted pyramid approach to journalism. Due to the expense of using the telegraph, newspapers abandoned their practice of using long-winded storytelling and instead moved to shorter, more concise reporting. The advent of wire services and the Associated Press, a national news-gathering organization, expanded and flourished during this time period, providing news content to a variety of newspapers throughout the country in an objective, unbiased manner.[2] In 1999, Jonathan Alter of the *Washington Monthly* wrote about the origins of the inverted pyramid, noting that, according to journalism historian David T. Z. Mindich's book *Just the Facts: How Objectivity Came to Define American Journalism*, the formula was first used nationally to cover the assassination of President Abraham Lincoln.[3] While many newspapers buried the lead and didn't mention that Lincoln had been fatally assassinated until much later in the article, those using the inverted pyramid gave the essential information right away. Eventually, the chronological, storytelling approach started to fade away. "Lincoln's Secretary of War, Edwin Stanton, the greatest press censor in American history, also originated the inverted pyramid. While war correspondents still filed flowery narratives, Stanton, who had total control of all new information, telegraphed the first terse bulletins from the War Department. Stanton was also the first to use the convention of 'objectivity' to bolster authority. By the 1880s, it was standard for newspapers. The telegraph, which placed a premium on speed and economy of style, became an important technological tool of 'objectivity.'"[4]

One of the main reasons for this type of straightforward and balanced reporting was clearly economic. In order to appeal to more readers and increase circulation and profit, media companies determined that they should be as even-handed as possible and not alienate a substantial number of readers through biased and partisan content. When people want information as opposed to opinion, they need somewhere reliable to turn.

Why did the straightforward, objective model of journalism arise and gain considerable popularity and success in the mid to late 1860s? Dr. Carolyn Kitch offers this explanation:

> Because of the new business model of the Penny Press papers, newspaper publishers became less economically reliant on political backers and therefore less obligated to run articles with a particular political slant. At the same time, the large new audiences wanted a wider variety of news content covering the subjects of ordinary life such as crime and sports. And so what we recognize as the modern newspaper came into being during the mid-nineteenth century. Mid-nineteenth-century news wasn't necessarily "objective" in our twenty-first-century definition of that word, but it was a more general mix of local news necessitating a routine process of newsgathering. Certainly reporting during the Civil War wasn't objective—war coverage differed in content as well as tone in the North and the South—but one journalism historian, David Mindich, attributes the first appearance of the inverted-pyramid story format to the Civil War era, when reporters feared that telegraph lines could be cut at any time and therefore put the important news first.[5]

In 1896, Albert Ochs, the new owner of the *New York Times*, decided to transform the *Times* from the sensationalist style and approach used by competitors—such as newspaper moguls William Randolph Hearst and Joseph Pulitzer—to instead incorporate an objective journalistic style emphasizing a neutral and impartial voice. He phrased it as "clean, dignified, trustworthy and impartial." The paper also adopted the motto "All the news that's fit to print."[6] The practice of interviewing and quoting sources also emerged as a common journalism technique in the early 1900s. In addition, the political parties were less polarized and fractured than they are today. The media's movement toward more objective reporting was geared toward selling papers to the average person rather than as a vehicle for wealthy media owners to curry favor with high-powered politicians.

Some critics of this type of middle-of-the-road journalism, which focuses on facts and tries not to have a strong point of view, claim that at its core this reporting is boring, uninspired, and doesn't adequately serve the public. Stephen A. Smith, a journalism professor at Idaho University and former editor of the *Spokesman-Review* in Spokane, Washington, suggested on his blog *Journalism Still Matters* that today's newspapers should have "More voice and attitude on the news pages, a stronger editorial voice complemented by a wide-open, interactive op-ed strategy, more emotion in the writing, more nuance in the reporting and more respect for the intelligence of readers."[7]

However, it can be pointed out that the mainstream media acts much more like an honest broker or the adult in the room compared to the shouting and hyperbole that takes place in advocacy journalism media outlets. When people want to confirm breaking news and get accurate information, many will still turn to the mainstream media.

Despite the lament over the death of newspapers following the introduction of radio, television, and the Internet, many people still read them. According to the Alliance for Audited Media, in March 2014 the *Wall Street Journal*'s total average circulation of print and digital formats combined was 2,294,093 readers, the *New York Times*'s was 2,149,012, and *USA Today*'s was 3,255,157.[8]

In discussing the rise of market-driven objectivity in the mid-1900s, Albert Oetgen of Poynter stated that the marketplace "had created the environment for those stalwarts of fair and balanced coverage to develop into icons of American journalism. The mid-century journalism community . . . superimposed the idea that fairness and balance were ideals that journalists should strive for."[9] John Timpane, media editor for the *Philadelphia Inquirer* and former op-ed page editor for that paper, wrote in an e-mail interview, "Objectivity was a creation of the new newspapers of the 1910s and 1920s that sought to separate themselves from the partisan, obviously skewed papers of the era. It was a marketing tool. What we want, what we live and work for, is honesty apart from our personal preferences."[10] He also criticizes the concept of fairness in reporting: "The entire notion of 'fairness' has been rendered perilously close to meaningless in the current struggle between the two private clubs named left and right. My head aches when I think of all the ruses employed to leverage 'fairness' to make sure 'my position' wins in the public space. Creationism is the best example. I am a religious person, but that whole thing makes me ill. There has been a repeated push to allow biblical creation stories 'equal time' or 'fair time' alongside scientific accounts of the emergence of the physical universe. And those attempts have met with repeated slapdowns in the courts. But the push is still very much on, and the claim is of 'fairness.'"[11]

The straightforward, inverted pyramid approach is still common today, especially for wire services such as the Associated Press and Reuters, and it is also still used in many newspaper articles. It's a common style for covering a sporting event, for example, especially for games involving out-of-town teams. Many press releases also use this approach, along with reporting on crimes and trials. Inverted-pyramid–style reporting might seem dull and uninspiring to many, but it is a viable approach to presenting news, and it is still taught and emphasized in university journalism schools and departments.

However, subsequent models and approaches to journalism took a biased and opinionated turn toward the end of the nineteenth and twentieth century. The op-ed page, editorial page, columnists, editorial cartoons, yellow journalism, muckraking journalism, and investigative reporting will be discussed in the next chapter.

CHAPTER 5

THE OP-ED PAGE, EDITORIAL PAGE, COLUMNISTS, EDITORIAL CARTOONS, YELLOW JOURNALISM, MUCKRAKING JOURNALISM, AND INVESTIGATIVE REPORTING

There is a long tradition of having opinion articles in newspapers—op-eds, editorials, columns, and reviews of movies, music, and restaurants. According to Kenneth Rystrom's *The Why, Who, and How of the Editorial Page*, editorials moved from being highly personalized, strong, and opinionated in the mid-1800s, to being anonymous, bland, and boring in the late 1800s and early 1900s.[1]

The editorial page is the voice of the editorial board. It was invented in the 1850s by noted publisher Horace Greeley, who was the founder and editor of the influential newspaper the *New York Tribune*, which was nicknamed "The Great Moral Organ." Greeley wrote extensively for the paper, espousing his views in opposition to slavery, criticizing corporate monopolies, advocating economic improvement for workers, arguing for educational reform and women's rights, and opposing capital punishment.[2]

The editorial page has long been considered prestigious and influential. Most newspapers have staff columnists who write on a weekly or biweekly basis. The staff columnists are often former reporters, or experts on a certain topic. "Op-ed," on the other hand, stands for opposite the editorial page and debuted in the *New York Times* in September 1970. While the staff-written editorials tend to be more academic and stuffy, the op-ed page has more humor, voice, and personal connection. Writers for the op-ed page include regular columnists, syndicated columnists, freelance writers, noted experts, government officials, or people with standing affected by an issue. Op-eds and editorials usually appear in the last few pages of the front section of the paper, but there are rare occasions when the paper will put an editorial on the front page for special emphasis. In 2015, for the first time since 1920, the *New York Times* put an editorial on the front page, fiercely arguing for gun control measures to be enacted.[3]

THE MUCKRAKERS

In the late 1800s and early 1900s, something known as muckraking journalism became popular, as noted reporters began exposing important societal ills that needed to be remedied. Their writing, in fact, led to significant social change. In 1890, for example, Jacob Riis published a book titled *How the Other Half Lives*, exposing the poverty-stricken conditions of slums in New York City's Lower East Side through photographs and essays. Riis, an immigrant from Denmark who had at first struggled financially in America, had become a police reporter for the *New York Tribune*, which exposed him to poor, crime-ridden areas. Riis's writings and photos of overcrowded tenement slums provoked social reform, and led to important policy changes.[4]

Lincoln Steffens, in his 1904 book *The Shame of the Cities*, published a collection of articles he had written for *McClure's* magazine, which exposed political corruption by government officials and local businessmen in several American cities, including New York, Chicago, Minneapolis, Pittsburgh, Philadelphia, and St. Louis.[5] *McClure's* also published works by journalist Ida Tarbell. Tarbell, in her nineteen-part series "The History of the Standard Oil Company," wrote about the abusive practices of John D. Rockefeller's oil monopoly, which sought to suppress industry competition through gaining control in various industries. Her series was printed in a 1904 book and it helped lead to the breakup of Standard Oil and other large trust companies through the congressional passage of the federal Sherman Anti-Trust Act in 1911.[6]

Novelist Upton Sinclair's 1906 book, *The Jungle*, exposed contaminated beef and horrible working conditions in Chicago stockyards, which led to federal regulation of the food industry in the form of the Pure Food and Drug Act (1906) and the Meat Inspection Act (1906).[7] Ida B. Wells, an African American journalist and suffragist, wrote an extensive report on the lynching of black people in America for the *New York Age*, an African-American newspaper, in 1893. She also wrote a book titled *The Red Record*, which described lynchings in America during the previous three years.[8] Congress never passed an anti-lynching law, but Wells is viewed as a civil rights pioneer.

Dr. Carolyn Kitch, department chair of Temple University's Journalism Department, commented on this muckraking journalism era:

> Although in its own time the term was meant as an insult to reporters, "muckraking," or investigative journalism, emerged in response to a litany of urban problems (including lack of sanitation and education, rising crime and poverty, few quality or price standards in manufacturing and business, and much more) and alongside the emergence of Progressive-era [ca. 1880s to the 1920s] reform and new fields such as social work. This era's muckraking journalism was "long-form"—not only in-depth, but extremely long and often serialized reports that took months or years to investigate and that therefore often appeared not in newspapers but in magazines such as *McClure's* (which published the work of some of the most famous muckrakers, Ida Tarbell and Lincoln Steffens), or in book form. The most famous muckraking book, Upton Sinclair's *The Jungle*, was actually a novel. Economics and technology were factors in the emergence of this kind of investigative journalism, too: muckraking exposés drew big audiences (they, too, were sensational), and newspapers' and magazines' ability to print photographs expanded the audience for the investigative projects of social reformers such as Jacob Riis.[9]

This era also saw the beginning of undercover reporting. Elizabeth Cochrane, a.k.a. Nellie Bly, faked mental illness in order to be committed to the insane asylum at New York's Blackwell Island. After seeing the poor living conditions and abuse and torture of the inmates during her ten-day stay—which included ice-cold baths, undrinkable water, crawling rats, and beatings by nurses—lawyers from the *New York World* secured her release.

Her serialized report on the asylum was later published in book form as *Ten Days in a Mad-House*, which led to reforms of the conditions at New York's mental asylums.[10]

Not everyone was pleased with muckraking journalists, especially government officials and employees. As Amanda Foreman of the *Wall Street Journal* wrote, "Many U.S. presidents have shared Nixon's exasperation with the press. Theodore Roosevelt coined the term 'muckraker' during a speech in 1906. He compared investigative reporters to the narrow-minded figure in John Bunyan's seventeenth-century religious fable, *The Pilgrim's Progress*: the man that could look no way but downwards, with a muck-rake in his hand."[11]

Nonetheless, many admire the work that the muckraking journalists did in those early days and the social change that they inspired. Their efforts also encourage many modern-day journalists who want to write important stories that have an impact.

YELLOW JOURNALISM

The yellow journalism era of the late 1800s led to the Spanish–American War. A feud between major newspaper owners William Randolph Hearst and Joseph Pulitzer resulted in a series of sensationalized stories and headlines that stoked the flames of public support for United States military intervention against Spain in Cuba and the Philippines. According to the US Department of State's Office of the Historian's website, the term "yellow journalism" arose from a popular *New York World* cartoon strip called "Hogan's Alley" and its well-known character, the Yellow Kid. Hearst hired the Yellow Kid cartoonist Richard F. Outcault away from Pulitzer's *New York World* in a fierce bidding war, but Pulitzer hired another cartoonist to continue the Yellow Kid strip.

The competition between Hearst and Pulitzer led to a sensationalized style of covering world events, particularly focusing on Cuba's struggle for independence from Spain and fanning anti-Spanish sentiment in America. Both papers ran sensationalized stories about executions, rebels fighting, and starving women and children, with bold headlines and creative drawings of events, many of which turned out to be false. After an explosion sank the US battleship the *Maine* in Havana harbor, Hearst and Pulitzer published rumors of Spanish plots to sink the vessel, and shouts of "Remember the *Maine*" filled the news. The dramatic stories helped to fuel American support for the Spanish–American War in 1898. Hearst's supposed quote, "You furnish the pictures, I'll provide the war!" came from this period.[12]

In describing the era, Dr. Carolyn Kitch observes that yellow journalism was a continuation of the impact of technology and economics on journalism that had been going on throughout the nineteenth century. Immigration from southern and eastern Europe helped create this second period of enormous circulation growth, as did advances in printing speed and the ability to print illustrations (even in color) and then photographs: "These developments made it more affordable to print a visually appealing publication that could be sold cheaply to bigger and bigger audiences, which brought in more and more advertising revenue. And sensational content sold newspapers! There are some cultural historians who also point out that, at the turn of the twentieth century, modern life, especially in American cities, was pretty sensational itself . . . and thus they argue that in this era journalists were following, rather than creating, public fascination with sensational topics."[13] Kitch also noted that while Pulitzer and Hearst owned the biggest-circulation newspapers, the *New York World* and the *New York Journal*, it was Pulitzer, an immigrant, who was committed to serving working-class readers and addressing urban problems through undercover reporting, like Nellie Bly's famous infiltration of the insane asylum.

OP-EDs

Op-eds consist of opinion articles not written by the newspaper staff. The predecessor to the modern op-ed page was created by the *New York World* in the 1920s, which, unlike the *New York Times* in the 1970s, only published in-house op-ed columnists and did not publish outside contributors. The typical newspaper op-ed page consists of articles from regular staff columnists, nationally syndicated columnists, national and local freelance writers, and local and national experts on topics. It's a highly competitive process to get op-eds published, since many op-ed page editors will receive over a thousand submissions per week and they can only choose around ten to publish in their newspaper. From a personal standpoint, I can attest to how competitive the process can be. I've published hundreds of op-eds in major newspapers over the last twenty-five years, but there are times when my articles get rejected due to space restrictions. If I want to write an op-ed on breaking news, I know that I need to submit it within hours after the event was initially reported in order to have a chance of being published, since dozens of other freelance writers and experts know this as well. There were also times when I had submitted an op-ed on a topic to a newspaper only to be told that one of their staff columnists was already covering that topic. Some papers have started publishing additional op-eds solely on their website. Unlike the editorials written by members of the editorial board, representing the viewpoint of the newspaper, op-eds often tend to be more personal and passionate, with a stronger voice. Op-eds and columns will often relate the personal experience of the writer, which doesn't happen in the unsigned editorials. From a personal standpoint, op-eds are my favorite type of writing, because I can express opinions on controversial and important issues that I feel passionate about. I don't have to be balanced or objective, and I can freely emphasize the points that I want to make with a skewed, biased perspective. Sometimes, I like to give a contrarian position that goes against what most people think. As a reader, I enjoy op-eds and columns that take a strong stand and demonstrate passion, as opposed to a "captain obvious" point of view. Some editorial pages are staunchly liberal, while others are staunchly conservative, and still other such pages try to be more centrist and have varied political and social viewpoints. In some cases, the op-eds tend to mostly reflect the political philosophy of the paper, while others like to feature opposing viewpoints. Some editorial boards and op-ed pages are heavily controlled by the publisher or owner, while others, if not most, are allowed to make independent decisions, including candidate endorsements. In some cases, the publisher or owner might get a vote or one voice in the editorial board's positions on an issue. Most of the editorial board members of newspapers are former reporters.

The editorial board and the group that manages the editorial page are separate entities at most newspapers. They generally meet in separate parts of the newsroom and generally do not collaborate. Most readers don't make that distinction and therefore believe that the rest of the newspaper adheres to the philosophy expressed by the editorial board. If the paper has a liberally slanted editorial page, many readers believe that the rest of the paper's reporters are liberal as well and that their news reporting will also have a liberal bias. My own impression is that newspapers do not make a big enough effort to publicize this distinction for readers, and they make a big mistake with respect to the public's perception of their newspaper by not doing so.

Unlike the rest of the newspaper, the editorial and op-ed pages take a strong stand on the issues. The writers of these articles don't lie or misrepresent facts; however, these definitely aren't objective, balanced articles either. As with any opinion piece, the editorial writer will cherry-pick facts, data, statistics, and expert quotes that support the position being offered.

CANDIDATE ENDORSEMENTS

One of the most important features and traditions of the editorial page and editorial board is the process of evaluating and endorsing political candidates. It's an endeavor that they take very seriously, since they do extensive research on the candidates and their positions, and they will often interview the candidates in the editorial board meeting rooms so that they can assess their demeanor and competence. However, not everyone is happy with that tradition and process. There is a debate currently underway as to whether newspapers should ever endorse political candidates. It's a longstanding tradition, but is it outdated? I offered my views on the subject in an op-ed piece I wrote for *Philadelphia* magazine and the *Huffington Post* in 2012. What follows contains substantial portions of that article.[14]

In the weeks prior to elections, newspapers around the country endorse political candidates. Most papers still do it, but some decide not to. Even foreign newspapers get involved in candidate endorsements: for example, the *Economist*, based in London, has endorsed US presidential candidates since 1980. In general, the influence of newspapers and newspaper endorsements has been decreasing. Many papers see their political endorsements as a journalistic obligation to their readers.

In January 2012, the *Chicago Tribune* defended its tradition of endorsing candidates, stating that endorsements are consistent with the editorial board's general function of expressing opinions on vital public issues ranging from government pension costs, educational shortcomings, and political dysfunction: "We want to inform our readers and encourage them to push an agenda for a more vital community. The most direct way they do that is in choosing who will lead their government. . . . To arrive at our choices, we send out questionnaires, scrutinize voting records and public statements, and interview hundreds of candidates. We make our evaluation of which ones will best serve the interests of the public."[15]

There still is some prestige that emerges from receiving a newspaper endorsement, especially during the presidential primaries. In 2004, John Kerry's floundering campaign got a boost from endorsements by several Iowa papers, while John McCain's 2008 comeback was helped by newspaper endorsements in New Hampshire. New Jersey governor Chris Christie received a temporary bump from an endorsement from New Hampshire's *Union Leader* in November 2015, and it helped raise his poll numbers and bump him up from the children's table preliminary debate back to the main stage in the next debate. Some candidates mention newspaper endorsements in their TV ads, and an endorsement can be even more powerful, influential, or newsworthy if it comes as a surprise or goes against the grain. For instance, if a newspaper that typically endorses Democratic candidates for president were to endorse a Republican candidate for a change (or vice versa), that could be influential.

However, as everyone knows, newspaper circulation has been in steep decline over the last decade. In addition, these days people can get plenty of political opinions from the Internet, cable and network TV, and talk radio. Celebrities get into the act as well, with Madonna and Oprah endorsing Obama, and Chuck Norris endorsing Mike Huckabee in 2008. In 2012, Leonardo DiCaprio, George Clooney, Aretha Franklin, and Neil Patrick Harris endorsed President Obama. Musician Gene Simmons and actor Scott Baio from *Happy Days* endorsed Mitt Romney, while Clint Eastwood "sort of" endorsed Romney when he interviewed an empty chair signifying President Obama during the Republican National Convention.[16]

A 2007 Pew Research Center for People and the Press survey found that 69 percent of respondents said that newspaper endorsements had no impact on their vote and that they were slightly more likely to be swayed by an endorsement from Oprah Winfrey or their minister, priest, or rabbi.[17] In her 2000 book, *Everything You Think You Know About Politics . . . and Why You're Wrong*, University of Pennsylvania communications professor Kathleen Hall Jamieson found that only 1 percent of people said that newspaper endorsements greatly impacted their vote, while 10 percent said they somewhat impacted their vote.[18]

In many cases, the presidential endorsements are predictable. Most liberal-oriented papers endorse the Democrat, while most conservative papers endorse the Republican. According to *Editor & Publisher* magazine, in 2004, John Kerry received 213 newspaper endorsements, while President George W. Bush received 205. In 2008, Barack Obama received 273 newspaper endorsements, while John McCain received 172. In 2008, some newspapers, including the *Philadelphia Inquirer*, endorsed Obama but also ran an endorsement of McCain by dissenting editorial board members.[19]

Most American newspapers still endorse presidential candidates. However, some major newspapers choose not to, including *USA Today* and the *Wall Street Journal*—which stopped the practice after its 1928 endorsement of Herbert Hoover. In January 2012, the *Chicago Sun-Times* announced that it would halt endorsements (although it went back to endorsing in 2014), and the *Atlanta Journal Constitution* stopped endorsing in 2009. Other major US papers that no longer endorse presidential candidates include the St. Paul (Minnesota) *Pioneer Press*, the Milwaukee *Journal-Sentinel*, the *Virginian Pilot*, the *Dayton Daily News*, Salt Lake City's *Deseret News*, Knoxville's *News Sentinel*, and Sarasota, Florida's *Herald-Tribune*.[20]

One reason why newspapers should halt national endorsements is that they lead people to believe the papers' coverage will be biased. In reality, since the editorial board meets separately from the rest of the newsroom, the paper's endorsement has no effect on the paper's coverage. If a paper's editorial board endorsed Barack Obama, the rest of the paper wouldn't hesitate to give extensive coverage of a scandal involving Obama, if one arose. The public, likely not being aware of the separation between the editorial board and the rest of the paper, might easily assume that the paper's coverage of anything to do with Obama would be skewed in his favor.

In response to extensive reader criticism that the *Los Angeles Times*'s presidential endorsement of Barack Obama in October 2012 indicated a bias favorable toward him in news coverage, Deirdre Edgar of the *Times* wrote that readers were confusing the editorial board with the newsroom. The editorial board gives the views and judgments of the paper, while the newsroom reports the news in an unbiased manner: "The two are separate, and the editorial board's views do not influence news articles." Editorial page editor Nicholas Goldberg told Edgar, "When the *Los Angeles Times* covers the news, it tries to do so in as objective and unbiased a manner as possible. Reporters are expected to present both sides of every argument but to withhold judgments about which side is right and which side is wrong. Readers are to be presented with the facts but should be left to draw their own conclusions. But the editorial page is different. . . . Not only is opinion allowed—it's expected."[21]

Newspapers are very wary about reporters' conflicts of interest due to their concern that the reporting will be deemed biased by their readers. Most media outlets prevent their reporters from expressing their own political views, and they are not permitted to wear campaign buttons, volunteer or donate to political campaigns, put up political signs on their front lawns, or attend campaign rallies. This would include editorial writers and members of the editorial board. Yet that concern doesn't seem to translate to endorsements by the editorial board in the name of the newspaper and the editorial board. Part of the editorial board's rationale is that their endorsements are not reporting. They are intended to explain why, in the board's opinion, person x is a better candidate for some position than person *y*. Nonetheless, some people and readers find this inconsistent, confusing, and a blurring of the lines.

The best solution would be for newspapers like the *Philadelphia Inquirer*, *Chicago Tribune*, *Dallas Morning News*, *Houston Chronicle*, and other major regional papers across the country to just stick to giving endorsements for local races—state representatives, local judges, mayors, governors, members of the US Senate and House, state auditors, township commissioners, and ballot initiatives. Those types of endorsements tend to have more sway with the voters.

Local newspapers have a distinct advantage when it comes to local races. For most of the major local races in the Philadelphia area, the *Inquirer* and *Daily News* editorial boards will interview each candidate and get a sense of their demeanor and where they stand on positions important to local voters. A great many local candidates can't afford significant TV ad time, so most people don't know much about them. Many people don't even know the names of their local congressman or state representatives. In Pennsylvania and some other states, judges are elected. Pretty much no one knows anything about the people running for positions on the state supreme court. The local paper's informed endorsement can help voters make up their minds.

Another possible approach is for editorial boards to just set forth the candidates' positions on the issues, without giving their opinion on whom to vote for. This is the approach taken by many newspapers' voters' guides for local races. That way, the newspapers could give the readers detailed and accurate information about the presidential candidates' positions, without taking sides. Voters can get a sense of where the major candidates stand on important issues like national security, immigration, healthcare, gun rights and gun control, raising or lowering taxes, and whether to raise the minimum wage. Alternatively, newspapers could also decide to run competing endorsements written by different members of the editorial board, setting forth reasons to vote for either candidate.

At any rate, as print newspapers continue to fade away, so should their tradition of endorsing presidential candidates on the national level.

In contrast to this view, John Timpane of the *Philadelphia Inquirer* defends the endorsement practice. In an e-mail interview, he says that endorsements are part of giving an editorial perspective to the news:

> In the editorial pages, it's very OK. The editorial pages exist to provide a very important service, one you can get nowhere, and I mean nowhere, else.
>
> They model an adult decision-making process. You may agree with where an editorial comes down, or you may not, but at least you have seen an adult mulling over the issues and giving reasons for a decision. Where else is that ever done?
>
> This is why, this is supremely why, newspapers should continue to endorse candidates. I realize there is a push—again, on the factitious basis of "fairness"—to eradicate endorsements. One or another "side" claims, in essence, that "our candidates don't get endorsed as often as theirs do." If these advocates can get to owners and editors and persuade them that, on that basis, the paper should stop endorsing candidates, that will be a terrible day. I have no problem with a main endorsement and then an opposing view.
>
> That's fun. That can be instructive. But to junk one of the most important things an editorial board can provide, that's nigh to insane.
>
> The *Inquirer* endorsements, since about 1970, if you take all federal, state, and local races into account, are quite nearly 50–50. One place we haven't endorsed many Republicans, however, is the presidential endorsement, where I think the last one might have been Eisenhower.
>
> But nobody should be forced to "count up" endorsements and look to "make a different choice" on the basis of past choices. Why? Clearly, obviously, because each such endorsement is made on different bases, local to that election. We chose Eisenhower in 1956 for this, this, and this reasons, and none of those reasons need guide us for the [19]92 or 2016 elections. Any argument that says, "Oh, no, you should stay aware of what you've done in the past, and make sure that that awareness operates in all your choices NOW" is simply a bid to tie the hands of powerful media that could affect your side's fortunes. No: all hands should remain untied, and they should be allowed to address the crazily complicated political sphere case by case, election by election.[22]

POLITICAL CARTOONS

Political cartoons are a staple of editorial pages and another form of advocacy journalism with a long tradition. They are a prime example of a picture painting a thousand words. English cartoonist James Gilray was known for his biting caricatures of Napoleon. According to *U.S. News & World Report*, American political cartoonists lampooned President Andrew Jackson as a ruthless strongman. Editorial cartoons mocked Democratic presidential nominee Grover Cleveland for fathering an illegitimate child. Cartoonists portrayed William Jennings Bryan as a backward Bible thumper during the 1896 presidential race. Thomas Nast, often dubbed as the father of American cartoonists, was an influential cartoonist in the 1800s, who lampooned New York's Boss Tweed and created the modern image of Santa Claus, as well as the Democrat Donkey and Republican Elephant.[23]

Newspaper cartoons continue to be controversial in the modern era. The *New York Post* was criticized for publishing a cartoon that featured two white police officers shooting a monkey, with the tagline, "They'll have to find someone else to write the next stimulus bill."[24] There was a great deal of criticism of the cartoon, with many calling it racist because the monkey allegedly depicted President Obama. The creator of the cartoon was not fired or suspended, despite the outcry.

Some newspapers have their own staff cartoonist, while others use syndicated cartoonists. There are liberal cartoonists as well as conservative ones. The visual depictions, as well as the statements made in the cartoons, can reflect a strong bias and point of view. They often use sarcasm, humor, and irony to express their opinions. They make us laugh and make us think. Cartoons are often provocative and can stir debates and controversy. The Danish newspaper *Jyllands-Posten* printed several offensive cartoons depicting the Prophet Muhammad, including one with a bomb in his turban. Worldwide protests ensued, and death threats were made against the cartoonists. In 2015, the world was stunned by the murder of several employees of the satirical French publication *Charlie Hebdo* by radical Islamists. There arose a worldwide debate as to whether media outlets should reprint the controversial cartoons, which satirized Islam and its prophet. Defenders of media outlets that reprinted the cartoon alleged that it is essential to show the cartoons to adequately explain the issue, to show solidarity with the slain cartoonists, and to show terrorists that the press will not be intimidated. Those who believed that the cartoons should not have been reprinted cited multicultural sensitivity and a concern for safety and retribution.[25]

As I noted in WHYY's NewsWorks in 2015, although the pen is mightier than the sword, there are times when the pen should be kept in the pocket.[26] There was justifiable outrage worldwide over the Islamist terrorist massacre of twelve journalists at *Charlie Hebdo*. While there was appropriate emphasis on the need for free speech and satire, many people lost sight of the fact that free speech needs to be balanced against multicultural sensitivity. Many media outlets had to weigh this balance in deciding whether to reprint the offending cartoons. It could be deemed appropriate to reprint the cartoons to describe the controversy and explain the issue. However, in general, media outlets should use restraint and self-censorship regarding content that is blatantly offensive to religious or racial groups. At the time, I felt and wrote that most mainstream media outlets showed appropriate restraint in declining to reprint the controversial cartoons.

Just as most US newspapers and mainstream media outlets chose not to show the controversial Danish cartoons in 2006, US papers and media outlets like the *New York Times*, ABC News, NBC, Fox News, and the Associated Press declined to show the controversial *Charlie Hebdo* cartoons after the shootings in France. On the other hand, some outlets, like the *New York Daily News* and London *Telegraph*, ran the magazine's controversial covers but blurred the offending images. Explaining their reasons for not publishing the cartoons, the *New York Times* told *BuzzFeed*, "Under *Times* standards, we do not normally publish images or other material deliberately intended to offend religious sensibilities. After careful consideration, *Times* editors decided that describing the cartoons in question would give readers sufficient information to understand today's story."[27] Santiago Lyon, a vice president of the Associated Press and its director of photography, offered this explanation for not running the cartoons: "We've taken the view that we don't want to publish hate speech or spectacles that offend, provoke or intimidate, or anything that desecrates religious symbols or angers people along religious or ethnic lines. We don't feel that's useful."[28] There were some exceptions, of course, with outlets like the *Washington Post* op-ed page, *Huffington Post*, *Slate*, *Vox*, *Daily Beast*, and *BuzzFeed* publishing the cartoons.

Every semester, I discuss the delicate balance between free speech and multicultural sensitivity with my journalism students. I give them a series of articles to read, starting with one defending the right to free speech and to express controversial and provocative ideas. But then I give them others that show that this right is not absolute.

Many media personalities have been penalized for exercising their right to free speech. Radio talk show host Don Imus was fired for his "nappy-headed hos" comment about the Rutgers University women's basketball team;[29] Dr. Laura Schlessinger resigned from her radio program after public outcry over her repeated use of the full "N-word," allegedly as part of a philosophical discussion;[30] an ESPN headline writer was fired for the headline "Chink in the Armor" after a loss by the New York Knicks and its Asian-American star, Jeremy Lin;[31] Jimmy "the Greek" Snyder was taken off the air by CBS after his controversial explanation of why blacks were better athletes than whites;[32] the editor of *Golfweek* magazine was fired after he put a noose on its cover in response to a controversy when, during a discussion as to whether Tiger Woods's challengers might want to gang up on him, a television commentator quipped that possible challengers to Woods might want to "lynch him in a back alley."[33] Sometimes, these sanctions are the result of threats made to boycott the programs' sponsors.

There is a great tradition of editorial cartoons pushing people's buttons, criticizing public officials, and mocking groups and institutions to make a point. It's part of the Fourth Estate, the media, which keeps the government in check and exposes corruption. Free speech does include the right to offend, and that right has been upheld in the US Supreme Court time and again.

The government cannot and should not stifle or censor controversial viewpoints. The right to publish controversial ideas should be absolute in theory, but in practice it's not that simple. Generally, while the media should not hesitate to criticize religious and racial groups, they should consider self-censorship for outrageous or deliberately offensive content that simply serves to insult those groups.

There are times when media outlets go too far. For example, as a hypothetical situation, what if during the Israel-Hamas war in 2014, an American newspaper published a cartoon showing Palestinian victims, with the tagline "Hitler was right"? In that hypothetical case, the cartoonist would likely be fired, editors would be forced to resign, and the newspaper would face justifiable outrage and boycotts. Yes, we have a right to express outrageous and controversial ideas, but sometimes it's best to show restraint and have respect for certain segments of the readership. This is especially the case for mainstream media outlets that serve a widely diverse audience.

Many free-speech advocates consider self-censorship to be cowardly. In the *Charlie Hebdo* case, they alleged that media outlets that declined to show the controversial cartoons were allowing the terrorists to win. Free speech is a valuable right, but it's not absolute. Restraint should not be mandated, but sometimes it's appropriate.

By the way, not many people were tweeting #jesuischarlie after *Charlie Hebdo* ran a controversial cartoon in January 2016 suggesting that the three-year-old Syrian boy whose drowning death raised awareness of the migrant crisis would have grown up to be a sexual molester, which was an implied reference to a wave of sexual attacks of women in Germany by men of Arab appearance.[34]

INVESTIGATIVE JOURNALISM

The twentieth century also saw the rise of interpretative journalism, explanatory journalism, service journalism, watchdog journalism, solutions journalism, investigative journalism, and literary journalism. Reporters use interpretive journalism to give context to stories and explain complex issues, making judgments and conclusions about them. An example would include Bob Woodward and Carl Bernstein's coverage of the Watergate scandal for the *Washington Post*.[35] Don Barlett and James B. Steele's

Philadelphia Inquirer series, "America: What Went Wrong," giving a narrative portrayal and explanation of the loss of American manufacturing jobs as a result of mergers, acquisitions, and plant closures, is another example.[36] Barlett and Steele are one of the most acclaimed and influential investigative teams in American journalism history and won two Pulitzer Prizes, among other journalism awards, while writing for the *Philadelphia Inquirer* from 1971 to 1997.

In explaining the difference between investigative journalism and advocacy journalism, Steele offered me this explanation in a phone interview:

> In advocacy journalism, the reporter starts with a specific intent to make a point. In investigative journalism, the reporter examines the issue or problem to find out what's going on and explain it. For example, in one of my early *Inquirer* projects with Don Barlett, we looked into charges by politicians that Philadelphia judges were too soft on crime. We researched the data and showed how the judges meted out justice. We didn't set out to prove either side. That's a big difference from advocacy journalism, where they would set out to prove that certain judges were a pox on the judicial system and then find facts that fit that narrative. That's different from investigative journalism, where you do the research and see where the facts fall.[37]

Investigative journalism started in the 1960s as part of a society that was looking for political and social change. Aside from Woodward and Bernstein's 1972 *Washington Post* stories about the Watergate break in, examples of investigative journalism include the 2013 articles by the *Washington Post* and the *Guardian* giving details about the National Security Agency's surveillance; Seymour Hersh's article about the My Lai massacre during the Vietnam war and the subsequent government cover up; Sydney Schanberg's reporting in Cambodia in the 1970s, which inspired the movie *The Killing Fields*; the *Chicago Tribune*'s exposure of faulty government regulation of toys, car seats, and cribs; Clifford Levy's *New York Times*'s series "Broken Homes," which exposed abuse of mentally ill adults in state-regulated homes; and reporting on the Three Mile Island nuclear disaster and the British Petroleum oil spill in the Gulf of Mexico.

Unfortunately, due to budget restrictions, there is much less investigative journalism conducted by newspapers today. Many are struggling financially to survive and are constantly laying off or firing staff. Investigative stories are expensive; it often takes weeks, months, or even years to research and develop a story. Many news outlets now see these stories as a luxury that they can't afford.

In response, nonprofit news sites, such as *ProPublica* and the Center for Investigative Reporting are trying to fill that investigative journalism void. *ProPublica*, based in Manhattan, started publishing in 2008. It is a nonprofit, nonpartisan, independent organization that uses investigative journalism to spur reform through exposure of wrongdoing. Employing around forty-five journalists, it won a Pulitzer Prize in 2010 for Investigative Reporting and a Pulitzer in 2011 for National Reporting. It is funded by many individuals, institutions, and foundations, including the Carnegie Corporation of New York, the Sandler Foundation, the Ford Foundation, the MacArthur Foundation, and the John S. and James L. Knight Foundation. Some people might be concerned that such foundation support would skew *ProPublica*'s research or reportage, especially, say, if the publication was investigating charitable foundations or major corporations connected to them. However, *ProPublica* emphasizes its independence, writing, "Our donors support the independence of our work, and do not influence our editorial processes."[38] These donors also allow *ProPublica* to carry out lengthy research that many news outlets cannot afford: *The Atlantic* reported that *ProPublica*'s major investigative series on the dangers of acetaminophen took two years and cost over $750,000.[39]

Thus far, our focus has mainly been on print publications. However, radio, television, and the Internet have featured many forms of advocacy journalism. The next chapter will focus on the rise of talk radio and its influence.

CHAPTER 6

THE START OF THE BIG CHANGE: THE RISE OF TALK RADIO IN THE LATE 1980S

"**D**id you listen to Rush yesterday?" That's the question that Rush Limbaugh's devoted conservative "Ditto Heads" have asked each other for over twenty-five years. They love Limbaugh's brash style, strong opinions, condemnation of liberalism, and biting sense of humor. Whether he's calling John Kerry "Lurch" (i.e., the *Addams Family* TV butler), featuring parody songs such as "Barack the Magic Negro," railing against political correctness, or berating the mainstream "drive-by media," Limbaugh gives his conservative audience what they want—an ongoing, entertaining, and blistering attack on liberalism and an unwavering defense of unapologetic conservatism. After nearly three decades on the air, he still remains hugely popular and influential. His avid defense of Donald Trump's comments about illegal immigrants from Mexico, when Trump announced his candidacy for the Republican nomination, was one of the main reasons conservatives rallied behind Trump. Limbaugh's blessing made it acceptable for conservatives to support Trump.

The repeal of the Federal Communications Commission's Fairness Doctrine in 1987 cleared the way for the rise of talk radio. On-air shows no longer had to present both sides of an issue, as the Fairness Doctrine had required, if they were to provide programming "in the public interest." Rush Limbaugh quickly emerged as the most influential, controversial, and prominent radio host. Talk radio became very popular with conservatives. Brian Rosenwald of *Politico*, writing in 2014 about Limbaugh's rise, wrote, that Limbaugh "tapped into the widespread feeling among conservatives that the 'mainstream media' neglected their needs—and looked down upon them. By contrast, Limbaugh expressed their views in a fun and entertaining manner. . . . His success—by 1993, his audience had reached seventeen million—begot the development of entirely conservative and political talk stations, and as those stations succeeded, an increasing number of stations adopted the format."[1]

Conservative talk radio and shock jocks have become very influential since the late 1980s. Their shows draw large audiences, and they are able to influence public opinion. They helped oppose healthcare reform in the 1990s and immigration reform in the 2010s. They helped spur the Republican revolution of 1994 and the second Iraq War. Talk radio has been criticized, especially by liberals, as being too inflammatory, factually incorrect, and controversial.[2]

Six days after the Oklahoma City bombing in 1995, President Bill Clinton criticized the tone of talk radio for helping to create the climate of hate that led to the incident: "We hear so many loud and angry voices in America today whose sole goal seems to be to try to keep some people as paranoid as possible and the rest of us all torn up and upset with each other. They spread hate. They leave the impression that, by their very words, that violence is acceptable. You ought to see—I'm sure you are now seeing the reports of some things that are regularly said over the airwaves in America today."[3]

Yet, as far as their conservative base and following is concerned, the more incendiary the rhetoric, the better. Dan Shelley, a former news director for a conservative talk radio station, wrote in the *Milwaukee* magazine in 2009 that framing Democrats, government bureaucracy, and the mainstream media as the enemy is a successful approach for conservative talk radio: "To succeed, a talk show host must perpetuate the notion that his or her listeners are victims, and the host is the vehicle by which they can become empowered. The host frames virtually every issue in us-versus-them terms. There has to be a bad guy against whom the host will emphatically defend those loyal listeners."[4]

Rush Limbaugh's influence is undeniable. Republican politicians have learned to be careful not to cross or disparage him. He can be a kingmaker, but he can also ruin reputations of politicians and government officials with whom he disagrees. According to Simon Maloy of Media Matters, a liberal media watchdog organization, when a high-profile Republican criticizes Limbaugh, they will almost immediately give a follow-up statement clarifying that they did not really intend to insult him. For example, Maloy described one incident involving Limbaugh and Michael Steele: "On the March 1, 2009, edition of CNN's *D. L. Hughley Breaks the News*, then-Republican National Committee chairman Michael Steele attacked Limbaugh's rhetoric, saying: 'Rush Limbaugh is an entertainer. Rush Limbaugh, his whole thing is entertainment. Yes it's incendiary. Yes, it's ugly.' The next day, Limbaugh unloaded on Steele: 'Why are you running the Republican Party? Why do you claim you are leading the Republican Party when you are obsessed with seeing to it that President Obama succeeds?'" Maloy continued, "Later that same day, Steele apologized to Limbaugh, telling *Politico*: 'My intent was not to go after Rush—I have enormous respect for Rush Limbaugh,' Steele said in a telephone interview. 'I was maybe a little bit inarticulate. . . . There was no attempt on my part to diminish his voice or his leadership.'"[5] Maloy also cited incidents in 2009 involving Republican congressmen Phil Gingrey and Todd Tiahrt, in which they criticized Limbaugh and later clarified or apologized for their remarks.[6]

In 2012, Limbaugh received extensive criticism and scrutiny for his statements criticizing Georgetown law student Sandra Fluke for her advocacy of women's access to birth control, asserting that she wanted the government to subsidize her sex life by providing healthcare coverage for contraception. Fluke had testified at an unofficial congressional hearing hosted by Congresswoman Nancy Pelosi, arguing that birth control should be covered by health insurance at religious institutions such as Georgetown. Limbaugh quipped, "What does that make her? It makes her a slut, right? It makes her a prostitute. She wants to be paid to have sex. She's having so much sex she can't afford contraception. She wants you and me and the taxpayers to pay her to have sex." He later added, "If we are going to pay for your contraceptives, thus pay for you to have sex, we want something for it, and I'll tell you what it is: We want you to post the videos online so we can all watch."[7]

Media outlets reported that dozens of advertisers pulled their ads from Limbaugh's show in the weeks following his comments, and Limbaugh apologized. His show stayed on the air despite the controversy because he subsequently picked up new advertisers and continued to thrive. Surprisingly, one of Limbaugh's defenders during the incident was liberal-leaning television host Bill Maher, who tweeted, "Hate to defend #Rush Limbaugh but he apologized, liberals looking bad not accepting. Also hate intimidation by sponsor pullout."[8]

Naturally, Limbaugh has many detractors. Liberals tend to view him as a bombastic blowhard. Former *Saturday Night Live* comedian Al Franken wrote a bestselling book titled *Rush Limbaugh Is a Big, Fat, Idiot* in 1996, which helped to propel him to a position as a liberal talk show host on Air America and eventually helped to win him a US Senate seat from the state of Minnesota.[9]

Limbaugh's brash style didn't translate well when he was briefly hired to be a commentator on *Monday Night Football*'s pregame show on ESPN. He resigned in the wake of sharp rebuke after he criticized Philadelphia Eagles quarterback Donovan McNabb, alleging that he was not as good as the media made him out to be. "I think what we've had here is a little social concern in the NFL. The media has been very desirous that a black quarterback do well," Limbaugh said. "There is a little hope invested in McNabb, and he got a lot of credit for the performance of this team that he didn't deserve. The defense carried this team."[10] This incident showed the importance that the audience can have. Limbaugh's criticism of McNabb would have been fine with his regular conservative radio audience, but it didn't translate well to a broader audience with more diverse political and social views.

Nonetheless, in the 1980s, Limbaugh was a breath of fresh air to conservatives who were tired of what they perceived as the constant liberal slant of the mainstream media. As Kathleen McKinley wrote in 2009, the media became more liberal in the 1980s, and it became painful for conservatives and libertarians to watch the news: "This, quite simply, is why Rush began his incredible rise to the top of talk radio. Finally someone was speaking to the conservative values that we embraced. It's almost like when someone lives in a foreign country and you miss America terribly. Then you find a radio station that is American based. You turn it on every day to hear your native language and hear the news from where you grew up. You didn't feel so alone."[11]

Being edgy, provocative, and controversial is part of the job for a talk radio host. A dull, boring host will get fired for low ratings. But sometimes it's determined that these radio talking heads go too far. In 2007, popular radio host Don Imus lost his show due to backlash over his offhand remark about Rutgers University's female basketball team. *Time* magazine had at one point named him one of the twenty-five most influential Americans, and he was a member of the National Broadcaster Hall of Fame. According to MSNBC's *Imus in the Morning*, this was part of the offensive portion of the transcript of his show that day:

> IMUS: So, I watched the basketball game last night between—a little bit of Rutgers and Tennessee, the women's final.
> ROSENBERG: Yeah, Tennessee won last night—seventh championship for [Tennessee coach] Pat Summitt, I-Man. They beat Rutgers by 13 points.
> IMUS: That's some rough girls from Rutgers. Man, they got tattoos and—
> McGUIRK: **Some hard-core hos.**
> IMUS: **That's some nappy-headed hos there.** I'm gonna tell you that now, man, that's some—woo. And the girls from Tennessee, they all look cute, you know, so, like—kinda like—I don't know. . .[12]

Imus argued, among other things, that he was just using language that many rappers use in their songs. Despite his attempts at damage control and repeated apologies, CBS fired him from his show due to the threats of boycotts and advocacy by many people, including Rev. Al Sharpton and Jesse Jackson.[13] Imus was subsequently brought back by WABC radio in New York to host his radio show, which is syndicated nationally through Cumulus Media.

In another well-publicized incident, Dr. Laura Schlessinger, a popular conservative talk radio host, came under fire for using the full N-word multiple times during one of her broadcasts. She claimed that she was using the word in order to have a philosophical discussion as to whether it was okay to use the word, but she eventually decided not to renew her contract, saying that she grew tired of the criticism. "I want my First Amendment rights back, which I can't have on radio without the threat of attack on my advertisers and stations," Schlessinger told Larry King on his television show.[14]

In 2015, Washington, DC, radio station WMAL fired conservative host Michael Graham after his repeated comments describing Islam as a terrorist organization resulted in protests against the station and its advertisers led by the Council on American-Islamic Relations (CAIR). As reported by the *Washington Post*, Graham issued a statement saying, "As a fan of talk radio, I find it absolutely outrageous that pressure from a special interest group like CAIR can result in the abandonment of free speech and open discourse on a talk radio show."[15]

In 1996, Bob Grant, a popular New York radio host for over twenty-five years, was fired from his WABC show after a series of racially tinged comments, including calling African American mayor David Dinkins a "washroom attendant," and an insensitive remark regarding the death of Commerce Secretary Ron Brown in an airplane crash. He later returned to the station in 2007.[16]

To this day, most radio talk show hosts are conservative. The *Conservative Talk Directory* lists 110 shows, including Rush Limbaugh, Sean Hannity, Laura Ingraham, Dennis Prager, Hugh Hewitt, Michael Medved, Michael Savage, Glenn Beck, and Bill Bennett. They usually reflect how the conservative base feels about polarizing issues. For instance, in December 2015, radio talk show host Erick Erickson shot bullet holes into the *New York Times* front page editorial that urged gun control measures.[17]

Kathleen Hall Jamieson told *NOW on PBS* producer William Brangham, "What political talk radio hosts do is pick the facts that advantage their case and then make those facts the most salient facts for their audience. They fall within the range of omission that characterizes contemporary politics. When you look at political debates, for example, Republicans [and] Democrats both do it. The biggest sin is a sin of omission. They don't tell you what would hurt their case. Well, that's what political talk radio does. It selectively moves to feature the facts that best make the case for the ideology that advances the candidate in the moment that supports the agenda of the conservative talk radio host. So, the notion that talk radio hosts are just up there polluting the political process by egregiously lying is simply not true."[18]

Liberals attempted to counter the dominance of conservative talk radio with Air America, but the radio network went bankrupt a few years later due to poor ratings. Air America announced in 2003 that it would be launched in January 2004, financed primarily by Chicago venture capitalists and Democratic campaign contributors Sheldon and Anita Drobny. I wrote an op-ed for the *Philadelphia Inquirer* in October 2003 in support of the concept.[19] I noted that after years of being abused and ignored, liberals deserved a way to fight back, a forum in which to vent about President Bush without being called dopes, morons, traitors, feminazis, evildoers, and communists. They needed a place where the host felt their pain. Even assuming that most reporters are liberal, many of those who spin the news in this country—columnists, pundits, and opinion makers—are conservative. For every Maureen Dowd, there is an Ann Coulter, a Linda Chavez, a Jonah Goldberg, and a Cal Thomas. And network news anchors at the time usually wouldn't launch into partisan diatribes against the Bush administration. I noted that, in the past, liberal radio hosts haven't done as well (in terms of market share) as conservative hosts. The problem is that liberal hosts weren't angry or entertaining enough, like their conservative counterparts were. They couldn't survive if they served up tofu and snow peas. They needed to deliver red meat to the base—they needed to expose the failures and arrogance of the Bush administration. They needed to tap the untapped anger of their liberal audience. There was no shortage of potential hosts with the gumption to take on the radical right in an aggressive and entertaining way: Michael Moore, Al Franken, Janeane Garofalo, Paul Begala, and James Carville among them.

In the run-up to the invasion of Iraq, most major media outlets served as cheerleaders for the Bush administration. The media did not cover the protest movement until it was too late, raising few questions about what turned out to be lousy intelligence regarding weapons of mass destruction and Saddam's ties to al-Qaeda.

Conservative talk radio is fundamentally unfair and unbalanced. It spent eight years lampooning and ridiculing President Clinton through vicious personal attacks. Many felt it played a role in cementing a dedicated minority voting bloc that helped Republicans gain majorities in the House and Senate and helped George Bush succeed in his controversial defeat of Al Gore in the 2000 election. Liberal callers would never get a fair hearing on the Rush Limbaugh show regarding the unconscionable tax cuts for the wealthiest Americans and the incompetence of the Bush administration in planning for the postwar situation in Iraq. A successful liberal radio network could have given voice to the discontent with President Bush.

Air America had limited success, in that it launched the career of Rachel Maddow and helped give Al Franken a political forum that helped him eventually get elected to the United States Senate in November 2008. Unfortunately for liberals, Air America only lasted a few years before it went bankrupt and went off the air in January 2010.

People had varied opinions as to why the network failed, but most analysts felt that the programming and hosts weren't interesting or entertaining enough—unlike many conservative talk show hosts. Richard Corliss, of *Time* magazine, in discussing why political talk radio was dominated by Rush Limbaugh, wrote that Limbaugh was extremely entertaining, even if you disagreed with his viewpoints: "He and his clones may dominate as a radio format and energize the conservative base and annoy liberal politicians, but their success is not a reflection of the mood of the country at large. And in the ratings, the whole contingent of the radio right is outpointed by NPR's *Morning Edition* and *All Things Considered*. That's where the liberal listeners so desired by Air America went for their news and (covert) commentary. At the same time, MSNBC was showing how liberals could make TV that was appealing and sometimes competitive with the Fox News behemoth. When Air America's stars went into the public—and cable-TV sectors, the radio network lost its strongest voices. And now it's lost its voice—forever."[20]

According to Mackenzie Weinger of *Politico*, the network didn't understand the economics of the talk radio business. She said that progressive radio hosts "would do well to remember that one of the reasons the liberal talk radio network Air America flopped was that they 'forgot they were in the radio business, not in the get my candidate elected business,' said Al Peterson, publisher and editor of talk radio trade *NTS MediaOnline Today*."[21] SiriusXM's Mark Thompson also told Weinger, "We have an opportunity and a responsibility to even challenge our progressive leadership and our progressive politicians."[22]

Political talk radio today continues to thrive, and it remains primarily conservative. During the Obama administration, it gave listeners a chance to vent about Obama's policies. James B. Steele pointed out that talk radio has changed considerably and has become more and more conservatively biased: "I don't necessarily see talk radio as journalism, but talk radio is a radical shift from what it was twenty years ago. Back then, there were many radio stations that had all different viewpoints, and many shows would listen to moderate and liberal ideas. Those stations and programs have shrunk drastically over the last ten years. That's why conservatives focus so much on NPR, which tries to balance multiple viewpoints. Talk radio is more powerful than the advocacy journalism practiced through newspapers or television. Talk radio has helped to polarize the United States. It often has bad information distributed by outlets for political purposes."[23]

Are talk radio hosts journalists? Are they just pundits and commentators spouting their strong opinions? Are they primarily entertainers? These are hard questions to answer because the answers depend on the programs and the hosts being considered. There are some talk radio programs, such as NPR's *Radio Times*, with Marty Moss-Coane, and *Fresh Air*, with Terry Gross, that do engage in traditional journalism techniques like interviewing guests. In many situations, these programs use a mix of formats, including an opening opinion statement, guest interviews, and interaction with callers. Many listeners rely on talk radio as one of their main news sources.

Interactivity is an essential element of talk radio. Hosts interact with guests and callers, and often it is the callers who provide the most interesting and provocative contributions. It's not a total free-for-all, because the producers screen calls. Sometimes it's a total lovefest, where the caller and host have an identical opinion. Other times, the hosts take on callers who disagree with them. Personally, I wish this would happen more often, since conflict can be interesting, educational, and entertaining.

Without the phasing out of the Fairness Doctrine, conservative talk radio would not have flourished. The doctrine was officially eliminated in 2011.[24] Since radio stations no longer had to present opposing points of view, hosts were free to present a biased and unbalanced viewpoint. Radio stations could feature a lineup consisting entirely of conservative talk show hosts and were not obligated to have a token liberal voice.[25]

While some criticize this concept and long for the day of equal time and balance, others claim that the free marketplace means that if liberals don't like what's currently available on the airwaves they are free to create their own radio networks, just like they tried with Air America. Personally, I would like to experience some voluntary balance on talk radio and the presence of more liberal hosts just to inject some variety, not only for my own sake but for the sake of exposing the public to various perspectives on major issues like healthcare and gun control. I think there is a market for liberal talk radio, but it needs to approach its role in a more entertaining and interesting manner than Air America did.

Robert F. Kennedy Jr. blamed the lack of enforcement of the Fairness Doctrine for many of the problems in the media of his day, telling PBS,

> [Radio stations] no longer have an obligation to serve the public interest. Their only obligation is to their shareholders. They serve that obligation not by informing us, telling us the things we need to understand to make rational decisions in a democracy, but rather by entertaining us. . . . We know we're the best entertained, the least informed, people on the face of the world.[25]

Sports talk radio has also emerged over the last twenty-five years. Like political talk radio, the hosts tend to be provocative and opinionated. Reporting tends to be woven with strong opinions, along with praise and criticism for players, coaches, general managers, owners, athletic directors, and universities. Like political talk radio, sports talk show hosts will usually be opinionated and entertaining. Naturally, the hosts, guests, and callers will have their own biases and opinions. Many tend to be polarizing. For some of them, part of their shtick is how they criticize, argue with, and put down their callers. Their opinions can influence whether a general manager or a coach gets fired or hired or a player gets traded. As a Philadelphia Eagles fan, I hate when my team loses on Sunday, but the loss does make the call-in shows more entertaining, with the hosts and callers ranting about how dumb the coach is or how bad the players are. Misery loves company.

Talk radio is a powerful force in American society. It continues to thrive, even though there is a huge proliferation of other news and entertainment options. It continues to be primarily conservative and heavily influential on conservatives, the Republican Party, and Republican elected officials. Unfortunately, some people listen to it as their main news source and aren't exposed to objective, balanced reporting or liberal viewpoints presenting an opposing point of view. These skewed viewpoints of the conservative hosts are fine, but ideally there should be some prominent liberal counterbalance on the radio.

In addition to talk radio, there is another media format that has exploded onto the scene during the last thirty years or so—namely, fake entertainment news and celebrity journalism. That type of media has been around for a long time, but it has increased in recent years.

CHAPTER 7

THE RISE OF FAKE ENTERTAINMENT NEWS AND CELEBRITY JOURNALISM

There is a long history of political satire, ranging from Geoffrey Chaucer, Jonathan Swift, Charles Dickens, Mark Twain, Will Rogers, George Orwell, Kurt Vonnegut, Johnny Carson, Lenny Bruce, the Smothers Brothers, George Carlin, Dave Barry, and Dennis Miller to *Boondocks*, *Doonesbury*, *South Park*, *Family Guy*, David Letterman, Jay Leno, and *Monty Python's Flying Circus*. While these satirical persons and programs make people laugh, they often harbor underlying messages and purposes. During the last few years, there has been a rise in fake entertainment news and celebrity journalism. Entertaining and funny hosts like Jon Stewart, Bill Maher, Stephen Colbert, and Trevor Noah have arisen, and what's more, many young people have actually come to rely on these programs as their main news source.

In an e-mail interview with me, Mark Bowden, journalist and author of many bestselling books (including *Black Hawk Down*), wrote, "Such shows are entertaining and are often quite effective as advocacy. A smart viewer/reader always considers the source."[1] In recent years, more and more of my journalism students tend to cite these satirical news shows as their primary news source. They assert that the regular nightly news is too boring and that they like to be entertained while getting their news. I hope that they can tell what is news and what is purely entertainment or a gag, but I'm not so sure. Most of the time, Jon Stewart acted like a satirist, but there were times, especially when he interviewed notable politicians, government officials, journalists, and celebrities that he acted more like a journalist. As noted by the Pew Research Center, his show combined elements of traditional news shows and late-night variety programs: "Stewart has always insisted that his show isn't journalism and given its comedic core, its blurring of truth and fiction, and its ignoring of many major events, that is true in a traditional sense. But it's also true that, at times, the *Daily Show* aims at more than comedy. In its choice of topics, its use of news footage to deconstruct the manipulations by public figures and its tendency toward pointed satire over playing just for laughs, the *Daily Show* performs a function that is close to journalistic in nature—getting people to think critically about the public square."[2]

Fake news and satirical commentary often function as forms of advocacy journalism. Arguably, one could also throw into this mix the fake news segments on *Saturday Night Live* and the monologues of late night talk show hosts such as Johnny Carson, Jay Leno, David Letterman, Conan O'Brien, Jimmy Fallon, Jimmy Kimmel, and Seth Meyers, who start their shows with a five-to-ten-minute comedic overview of the current news stories of the day. Other television shows and hosts such as Oprah Winfrey, Phil Donahue, Morton Downey Jr., and Ellen DeGeneres often tackle important and controversial social issues with a distinct slant, bias, and point of view. In addition, daytime programs like *The View* often take on current events, political news, and controversies with a primarily liberal viewpoint.

Conservative presidential candidate Carly Fiorina had a heated exchange with the hosts of *The View* in November of 2015 regarding their criticism of her looks. As noted by *USA Today*'s Kirsten Powers, after the second GOP Primary debate, cohost Michelle Collins told the other *View* panelists that Fiorina's smile during the debate made her look "demented," to which fellow panelist Joy Behar added, "I wish it was a Halloween mask, I'd love that." Collins then said, "A 'smiling Fiorina.' Can you imagine that? It'd give me nightmares."[3] According to Jesse Byrnes of *The Hill*, Behar later defended herself by saying that she was a comedian and had also made fun of Hillary Clinton's looks and choice of wardrobe.[4]

Bill Maher is another television pioneer who presents and analyzes news in an entertaining manner. From 1993 to 2002, Maher hosted *Politically Incorrect* on ABC, talking politics and social issues with a panel of guests and poking fun at politicians and leaders in an irreverent manner.

In 2003, he started *Real Time with Bill Maher* on HBO, in which he mixed humor, commentary, and interviews with well-known people in politics, media, and entertainment. The goals of his program are to entertain and provoke people by analyzing current events and news in an opinionated and sarcastic style. In 2015, Maher told Brian Steinberg of *Variety* that while he doesn't like network news, people shouldn't rely on his show primarily for their news: "And while Maher scoffs at traditional evening newscasts—'All of the network newscasts blow,' he remarked. . . . He realizes that *Real Time* functions as a sort of news outlet. In each broadcast, he said: 'I want to touch what I consider to be every important story that happened that week. I don't mean it's every story the media thought was important.' But he also wonders if people who rely on just his program for the news are on the right information diet: 'It's like saying I get all my nutrients from the Cheesecake Factory.'"[5]

Jon Stewart's *Daily Show* emerged in 1999 and Stewart grew to become perhaps the most popular and influential satirical news host. Thomas Kent, standards editor for the Associated Press, wrote that Stewart was important and brought in new audiences, but that traditional reporting was important as well: "News commentary, especially acid commentary, is on the rise. . . . Jon Stewart was its master. But alongside commentary, citizens—and comedians—need the fundamentals: solid sources of fast, aggressive and balanced reporting."[6] Supporters of such programs argue that they act as a check on politicians, government, and the media. For example, it was the *Daily Show* that exposed Sean Hannity's use of footage from an entirely different rally to make it look as though the crowd for an anti-Obamacare rally was substantially larger than it actually was.[7]

While it is definitely not a good idea to rely on entertainment programming as a primary source for news, due to its various biases, often overt agendas, and obvious selectivity when it comes to the types of news it chooses to focus on, it nevertheless appears that many millennials do in fact rely on these entertaining shows as their news source of choice. They see such programming as a more interesting way of being informed, as opposed to newspapers or standard network news, which they find boring and hard to relate to, as many of my students have indicated during class discussions.

Shows like Stewart's are and were entertaining, but they also provide clever insight and perspective on current events and controversies. As noted by Amber Phillips of the *Washington Post*, a Public Religion Research Institute poll found that more than 10 percent of young adults say they trusted *The Daily Show* or *The Colbert Report* the most for their news sources. Phillips wrote, "Young people like Jon Stewart. Young people trust Jon Stewart."[8]

According to Stephen Collinson of CNN Politics, Stewart's show was entertaining, but it also served to inform people. Collinson noted a 2012 Pew Research Center survey showing that "39% of the *Daily Show*'s regular viewers were between 18 and 29, but the group makes up just 23% of the public as a whole." He also noted a 2007 survey showing that "Americans who knew most about what was going on in the world also tended to be viewers of the *Daily Show* and its recently shuttered Comedy Central spin-off, the *Colbert Report*."[9] In light of these studies, Collinson observed that "Stewart frequently denied that his program was a news show and insisted that it was merely about entertainment, [but] his work appeared to serve much the same function as traditional network news shows. Both his dissection of social and political issues of the day and his forensic dismissal of political hypocrisy performed much the same roles as fact checkers in traditional media."[10] A May 2015 Reuters/Ipsos online poll found that Stewart was the most fearless and most admired commentator, and he topped the list of being the commentator that people agreed with the most on the issues.[11] TV journalist Howard Kurtz said that although Stewart was liberal and focused more on attacking Republicans, when he did criticize President Obama, it stung: "Stewart's great dodge . . . is the just-a-comic line. But that undercuts the importance of what he does. Sure, he selectively and sometimes misleadingly edits the clips, but he's trying to get at a core argument—one that you may agree or disagree with, but which breaks through the usual blather."[12]

Personally, as a news junkie, I don't watch these shows to get news. I watch them to be entertained and to get a humorous take on the news of the day. I like to see the hosts call out politicians and public figures on their hypocrisy and inconsistencies. However, most people aren't news junkies and are busy with their daily lives, so they don't have the time to watch an hour newscast or to read several newspapers every day. Therefore, watching Jon Stewart is a way for them to get news in an entertaining way that doesn't feel like they're taking cough medicine, prune juice, or cod liver oil.

As Howard Homonoff, a regular contributor to *Forbes* magazine and director of Homonoff Media Group, wrote, news satire shows are just another medium for people to get news: "I'm not advocating eliminating the line between news and entertainment. As I've written about very recently, there is still a vital place for serious, sober-minded news journalism on television, even as the public expands its own definition of 'news.' But the work of Stewart, Colbert, and Maher, websites like *BuzzFeed* and *Politico*, and even the now-iconic bloggers in pajamas . . . shows us how many different ways people today are getting news from unexpected places."[13]

In some cases, alleged breaking news is provided by Internet trolls and troublemakers who have an agenda or simply want to cause mischief or confusion. They post false or misleading information on social media or make assumptions that turn out to be false. Among the *Washington Post*'s list of the worst Internet hoaxes of 2014 were: the "three boob girl," a woman who falsely claimed that she had gotten a third breast implant in order to get a reality show; a miracle machine that allegedly could turn water into wine; death hoax claims that Betty White and Macaulay Culkin had died; and the false claim (fortunately) that a solar storm would block out the sun for six days.[14] It's important to be able to distinguish satire—whether well-meaning or malevolent—from real news. Sources of parody like the *Onion* have fooled people into believing made-up stories. Several publications were duped by the *Onion*'s article declaring North Korea's Kim Jong Un the world's sexiest man.[15] Other publicized incidents in which officials erroneously relied on *Onion* stories have also taken place: Jack Warner of the international governing organization for soccer, FIFA, cited an *Onion* article that jokingly announced that the United States would be hosting the World Cup in 2015.[16] And an Iranian news agency cited an *Onion* article that jokingly claimed that a new Gallup poll indicated that 77 percent of rural white Americans would rather go to a baseball game and drink beer with Iranian President Ahmadinejad than President Obama.[17]

Weekly World News was a mostly fictional (one hopes) tabloid that was published from 1979 till 2007. It was relaunched as an online publication in 2009. It has featured outlandish stories on a regular basis, with headlines like "Hillary Clinton Adopts Alien Baby"; "Dick Cheney Is a Robot"; "Bigfoot Diet (He can lose 150 lbs.—it can work for you too!)"; and "Obama Appoints Martian Ambassador," along with stories about Bat Boy, a half-bat, half-human. I loved their covers and miss not seeing the print version at the checkout counters of stores.[18]

I'm embarrassed to admit that I was guilty of failing to evaluate a source while teaching one of my classes. In my Mass Media Law and Ethics course, I was teaching the topic of censorship. I found an article for my students to read titled "12 Reasons to Boycott 'Game of Thrones' in 2012" by Stephenson Billings, for the website *Christwire*. *Game of Thrones* is one of my favorite television shows, but I knew that it had come under fire for its graphic violence, nudity, and rape scenes. Therefore, I erroneously assumed that the article was legitimate. It turned out that one of my students recognized the website as a parody site similar to the *Onion*. Its goals are to mock Christian conservatives in America and those who do not question what they hear on the news.[19] As noted in the TV show the *Odd Couple* and one of the *Bad News Bears* movie sequels, "Don't assume, because it makes an ass out of u and me."

The conservative magazine the *National Review*, described how a satirical Facebook page titled "Stop the World, the Teabaggers Want Off" has been sending fake tweets with fabricated and outrageous quotes allegedly provided by Republican presidential candidates. In one example, the page gave a quote they attributed to Marco Rubio, asking, "Why wouldn't I trust Josh Duggar to babysit my children? I'd rather leave my daughters alone with him than with Beyonce or Miley Cyrus or Taylor Swift."[20] The Facebook page does contain a disclaimer that it is for entertainment purposes only, is primarily satire, and is not to be taken seriously. However, as PolitiFact, a noted fact-checking journalism website affiliated with the *Tampa Bay Times*, noted, "This caveat would be far from obvious to anyone simply seeing the group's memes on their own news feeds or those of their friends."[21]

As we have seen, tabloid journalism dates back to the 1800s. It often focuses on sensationalized stories of crime and celebrity gossip. Notable examples include the *Globe*, the *National Enquirer*, and the *Star*. At the checkout counter of almost every store, tabloids like the *Globe*, the *National Enquirer*, and the *Star* can usually be found. Despite the questionable nature of the stories they print, these magazines remain hugely popular. According to the Alliance for Audited Media, The *National Enquirer* had the tenth highest single-copy sales rate of US consumer magazines in the first half of 2014, with a total of 360,612 readers.[22] The *American Journalism Review*, citing the Audit Bureau of Circulations, reported that the *National Enquirer* had a circulation of over three million readers in 1994.[23] To the surprise of many, it was a finalist for a Pulitzer Prize in 2010, both for national news reporting and investigative reporting, for breaking the story about presidential candidate John Edwards's affair and love child. According to Ashley Lutz of *Business Insider*, the *National Enquirer* was the first media outlet to report, among other stories, Tiger Woods's extramarital affairs in 2009, Jesse Jackson's affair and out-of-wedlock child in 2001, Rush Limbaugh's addiction to painkillers in 2003, and the divorces of Billy Joel in 2009 and Mel Gibson in 2008.[24] In 1985, Michael H. Randall wrote in *Serials Review* that polls showed that 75 percent of tabloid readers do not believe what they read in the tabloids.[25] According to a June 2004 Pew Research Center survey, only 5 percent of the polled group believed all or most of what the *National Enquirer* said, and that 77 percent believed almost nothing.[26] One could infer that reading tabloids is just a diversion, a guilty pleasure. People know that the information might not be true, but it's still interesting and fun to read. When I was in the checkout line at a supermarket, I always liked reading about Bigfoot, Obama's Martian ambassador, and Bat Boy.

Another component of today's media landscape is the rise of celebrity journalism. These days, celebrities are no longer just the focus of gossip and tabloid magazines. The TV celebrity gossip program *TMZ* has emerged as a go-to source for celebrity news. Mainstream media and cable outlets have determined that it is a good business decision to emphasize the lifestyles and activities of celebrities to boost ratings and circulation, since many people care about celebrities and want to know as much as they can about their lives. They will watch celebrity-focused stories, resulting in higher ratings and advertising rates for the shows. If one media outlet doesn't cover a particular story, many people will go to other media outlets looking for the celebrity story they want. Media outlets know this, and it can affect how they cover the news. One of the most famous recent incidents highlighting this trend was when MSNBC host Andrea Mitchell interrupted her interview with former California congresswoman Jane Harman, on the topic of national security and alleged eavesdropping by the National Security Agency, to cut to "breaking news" of a preliminary hearing involving the entertainer Justin Bieber for DUI and drag racing charges. Mitchell wasn't the only one to do this, and other cable networks cut to Bieber coverage as well.[27] This is a sad reflection of what the news media's definition of news is and their determination of which stories should take precedence. I'm sure that the interruption wasn't Mitchell's call; she must have been cringing inside when she had to cut off the former congresswoman. In the grand scheme of things, national security is much more important than a court proceeding involving a celebrity's criminal charges—but ratings matter. If your network doesn't cover celebrity news, people will click to another channel that is.

An additional drawback of celebrity journalism is that some celebrities (encouraged perhaps by their agents or managers) appear on talk shows in which they know they will not be confronted with tough, challenging, or difficult questions. They do these interviews to promote a new album, movie, play, book, or television show, and they want the focus to be on that, as opposed to on controversies that they might be involved in. Such interviews are often a public relations lovefest filled with softball questions, and news outlets will write puff pieces on celebrities, focusing only on the positive.

Relying on celebrity news outlets as primary news sources generally won't keep people well-informed, due to their emphasis on trivial matters. Yet many people crave these news outlets because they're entertaining and a welcome break from serious and depressing news. Obviously, there have been exceptions in which celebrities have been pointedly questioned, such as the Barbara Walters specials, Diane Sawyer's interview with Bruce Jenner as he was transitioning to become Caitlyn, Oprah Winfrey's interview with bicyclist Lance Armstrong about his admission that he had used performance-enhancing substances, and interviews conducted by Dick Cavett, David Frost, and Phil Donahue. Also, there are many viewers who just don't want to think very much about what goes on in their world. They just want to be entertained. Actually thinking about the news of the day or having an opinion about issues doesn't interest them. These entertainment stories are a diversion from their own lives. Others feel helpless about their potential role in creating problems or in finding solutions. There's also a "kick them when they're down" mentality. Some people just gain pleasure from learning about celebrities who suffer misfortune.

Celebrity journalism is like crack, as I wrote in the *Huffington Post* in 2010.[28] Many Americans are addicted to it. They need to hear the Mel Gibson tapes from 2010, released by *Radar Online*, which contained rants to his ex-girlfriend filled with curses, epithets, threats, and racist comments, or see Lindsay Lohan report to jail for violating the terms of her court order. So why do newspapers, magazines, and television programmers keep feeding this habit? As Janice Min, editor in chief of *Us Weekly* told the *Washington Post*'s Ariana Eunjung Cha, the public wants to be entertained constantly since they see grim news every day about war and natural disasters: "Celebrities have become a sort of national distraction. They are hired entertainers."[29] If the mainstream media doesn't cover celebrities, those who clamor for such information will get their "news" through outlets like *Radar Online*, *TMZ*, the *Drudge Report*, the *National Enquirer*, or Perez Hilton's popular blog, known for Hilton's snarky comments about celebrities. Of course, even these media avenues can serve the greater good, such as when Matt Drudge broke the Clinton-Lewinsky sex scandal that put him and his website on the map, or when the *National Enquirer* breaks the occasional legitimate news stories. But these rare occurrences don't change the fact that tabloid journalism is generally an extremely poor source for substantive news.

In 2010, hundreds of photographers and journalists camped out at the Beverly Hills courthouse to cover actress Lindsay Lohan's perp walk for her trial on charges that she had violated her probation, imposed in a prior drug case, by not attending alcohol education classes. In the lead-up to the spectacle, MSNBC cut away from its coverage every fifteen minutes or so to show the scene outside the courtroom. They even had the O. J. Simpson-like helicopter shots of the two SUVs that brought team Lohan to court. MSNBC wasn't alone; Fox News and others also ran the live helicopter shots. According to CNN's Nancy Leung, there were numerous satellite trucks and almost a hundred camera crews, including one from Australia, present to film Lohan's arrival at the courthouse. Many shots featured one man who held up a "Free Lindsay" sign and repeatedly screamed "Let her go." All of this led up to Lohan being whisked out of her car and briskly walking past the media, many of whom were shouting questions. It all lasted around ten seconds.[30] Lindsay Lohan's booking into jail just made you want to tweet "Eeeks! Don't these media folk have anything better to do?" There were many other national and world news stories that merited coverage on the day of the Lohan spectacle. Most significantly, British prime minister David Cameron made his first White House visit to meet with President Obama to discuss British Petroleum's alleged involvement in freeing Abdel Basset Ali al-Megrahi, convicted of planning the 1988 terrorist bombing of Pan Am Flight 103, and returning him to Libya.[31] The Afghanistan conflict with al Qaeda and the global economy, still reeling after the great recession of 2007, were also important stories that day. Secretary of State Hillary Clinton met with Hamid Karzai in Afghanistan.[32] The Senate voted on extending unemployment benefits in light of the recession and growing joblessness.[33] West Virginia governor Joe Manchin announced that he would run in the 2010 special election to fill the late Robert Byrd's Senate seat.[34] Yet, despite all of these newsworthy events, Lindsay Lohan's court appearance stole the show.

Journalists consider many things when deciding whether to cover a story. Journalism textbooks, such as *Writing and Reporting News: A Coaching Method* by Carole Rich, indicate that factors influencing what constitute news include timeliness, proximity, unusual stories, celebrities, human interest, conflict, impact, helpfulness, entertainment, community issues, and trends.[35] Regarding celebrities and entertainment, if a hypothetical Lindsay Smith in, say, Peoria, Illinois, violates her DWI probation, it won't get extensive news coverage—at most a short blurb in the local newspaper. But when Lindsay Lohan violates her probation, it becomes a national obsession. This hypothetical Lindsay Smith isn't a well-known person and isn't a celebrity, so she won't garner much media attention. The assumption is that people care more about prominent, well-known people. Granted, there are notable exceptions where celebrity coverage might be merited, such as the recent coverage of the allegations against Bill Cosby for sexually assaulting a number of women and his court appearance to enter a plea on some of those charges. This could be deemed newsworthy because Cosby has for years been viewed as a very moral and upstanding person whom many Americans saw as the epitome of fatherhood.

Economics also drives the decision about what constitutes news— meaning the selection of stories covered are chosen based on which will keep revenues flowing into the media's coffers. If American newspapers regularly focused on issues like copper mining in Argentina, the ups and downs of the value of the US dollar, or political feuding in eastern European countries, people would soon cancel their subscriptions. But when American teenager Natalee Holloway was reported missing in 2005 in Aruba, news hosts like Greta Van Susteren went to Aruba to air their shows. Doing so brought Van Susteren some of her highest-rated shows for that year. She wasn't alone in the obsessive coverage; true-crime show host Nancy Grace and legendary talk show host Larry King constantly focused on that case as well. It was a tragic and important story, but many people believe that it garnered too much coverage.

According to the Alliance for Audited Media, celebrity profile magazine *People* was fourth in consumer magazine circulation at the end of 2013, with a circulation of over 800,000 readers.[36] In an ideal world, media outlets would ignore the trivial banalities of celebrity meltdowns and focus primarily on the real-world issues that concern all of us. However, given that many newspapers are going out of business and that network and cable news programming has to compete against the Internet for audience share, media executives no doubt feel that they need to give "the people" what they appear to want if they are to survive in a twenty-four-hour news cycle.

Most reporters and editors don't want to keep acting as celebrity journalism crack dealers, but many view this type of reporting as a necessary part of the business. During a 2004 conference panel titled "Reporting on Celebrities: The Ethics of News Coverage," Dan Rosenheim, news director of KPIX-TV in San Francisco, said that a person's celebrity status should be a factor in determining news value: "One ignores viewers or reader interests at your own peril. We risk trivializing ourselves and marginalizing ourselves."[37] Thus, legitimate news sources can't ignore celebrity status when deciding which stories to cover or else they might lose a portion of their audience to competing media outlets. The prominence of the people involved in a news story is a traditionally recognized factor in deciding what news events get covered.

Unfortunately, celebrity journalism still thrives in 2016, and it doesn't appear as though it is ever going to go away. Such stories give the audience the gossipy, human interest—and even voyeuristic—content they seem to crave, and, while they also occasionally do shed a glimmer or two of light on important issues—exposing political intrigue, highlighting a charity fundraiser after a tragedy or natural disaster, or giving much-needed attention to serious health conditions that befall celebrities—these stories generally detract from serious news. However, if mainstream media outlets choose to ignore celebrity stories, especially when they involve controversy, they risk losing those viewers and readers to outlets like *TMZ*, who focus on those stories like a laser beam and provide thorough coverage. Another element blurring the lines of genuine reporting and journalism is the fairly new technique of major reputable news outlets using sponsored content, or native advertising, in which advertising content appears as news articles.

CHAPTER 8

THE RISE OF SPONSORED CONTENT

A recent trend in journalism is the concept of sponsored content, also referred to as native advertising, paid content, advertorials, or infomercials. This is content that definitely reflects a bias, since it is not intended to appear as fair and balanced news reporting. It is information presented in the form of a news article, which is paid for by a particular sponsor with the intent to sell a product, service, or idea. In effect, it is public relations or advertising. Companies pay media outlets to let them run editorial content that looks like real news but in fact is written by employees of the corporate sponsor. Even though the content is labeled as advertising or sponsored content, it still can be misperceived by the reader, listener, or viewer. Companies have also teamed up with magazines and local and national television networks to sponsor segments or portions of a publication or program. Internet podcasts are also used to feature native advertising.[1]

Even though I'm aware of the practice, there are still times when I don't notice it at first. Sometimes, I click on a story online and it takes me a little while to figure out that it sounds like an ad or a press release. Then I look at the top or click back and notice the small "advertising" disclaimer that I missed the first time. There are many well-known publications that use sponsored content. It's almost becoming an industry standard, as news outlets are looking for new ways to generate revenue in this competitive media environment. For example, *BuzzFeed* is a popular website known for its articles that use lists. The Native Advertising Institute, whose goal is to help marketers become successful with native advertising, listed several examples of native advertising used by *BuzzFeed*, including TV Land's "13 Things You'll Miss Most from Your Twenties," which ran in March 2015 to help promote the comedy-drama *Younger*; HBO's "10 Feelings All

NYC Girls Have at Least Once," which ran in January 2014 to promote its comedy-drama show *Girls*; and Spotify's "15 Bands that Probably Wouldn't Exist Without Led Zeppelin," which ran in December 2013 as a way to mention some of the musical acts that consumers can listen to through Spotify's music streaming service.[2] Lists like these are a clever and creative way to promote shows and products. As noted by Michael Sebastian of *Advertising Age*, some of the major media companies and outlets that use native advertising are *The Atlantic*, *Bon Appetit*, *BuzzFeed*, the *Chicago Tribune*, *Facebook*, *Forbes*, the *New York Times*, *Quartz*, *Slate*, *Twitter*, the *Wall Street Journal*, and the *Washington Post*.[3] In 2014, the *New York Times* created T Brand Studio and ran its first paid post in January 2014. An example of a T Brand Studio story was the native ad "The Surprising Cost of Not Taking a Vacation," which was sponsored by MasterCard. At the top of the ad article was the phrase "Paid Post" in small print, with a small MasterCard logo right below it. At the end of the post in small print was the disclaimer, "The news and editorial staffs of The New York Times had no role in this post's preparation."[4] When going onto AOL, some of the stories shown are advertised content, but the labeling is often in small type in the upper right hand corner. I admit that I've sometimes missed the advertising disclaimer, at least at first.

According a 2015 article in Poynter, by Benjamin Mullin, many newspapers, including most recently the *Boston Globe*, are now offering sponsored content as a way to make up for decreasing print revenue through normal advertising channels. They are able to charge high rates for sponsored content or native advertising. Mullin said, "Hearst Newspapers . . . has installed advertising agencies at the *San Francisco Chronicle* and the *Houston Chronicle* in an attempt to reach clients seeking (high tech) high-touch advertising and marketing services." Mullin cited the *Washington Post*, *New York Times*, Conde Nast, and Time Inc. as other media companies using similar techniques.[5] There is also an emerging form of sponsored content in which companies provide ready-made articles that appear as supplements in newspapers, magazines, and on websites. Native advertising has also appeared in television programs and video games. *Super Lawyers* magazine, owned by Thomson Reuters (which I used to write for), includes lists and profiles of selected attorneys, is distributed to attorneys, and also appears as special advertising sections in major American newspapers and magazines. Some of the articles are round-up articles in which selected "Super Lawyers" (chosen as a resource for attorneys and potential clients) are interviewed for quotes regarding certain issues. For instance, in one of my articles I wrote about what it was like for an attorney to argue before the United States Supreme Court and I interviewed and quoted four Illinois Super Lawyers to get their perspective and quotes. At the top of each page of the article and the entire supplement was a prominent statement that it was an advertising supplement that was published, at that time, in *Chicago Magazine*. In those cases, I felt as though the disclaimers were prominent and sufficient.[6]

Newspapers need advertisers and sponsors to make money and stay in business. Sponsored content is an effective way of doing this. It's a subtle way of promoting a product or service. It's a clever and creative way to reach people who don't want to read print ads, click on online ads, or look at television commercials. Sponsored content probably won't go away any time soon. But it is important for readers and news consumers to be aware that it exists and to realize that they should view this specific type of content as an ad as opposed to real news. Part of the rationale behind using native advertising is to avoid ad blocking by those who program their computers to ignore online ads. So how can people identify sponsored content? Some media outlets, like *Time* and *The Atlantic*, post their guidelines regarding sponsored content on separate sections of their websites. Michael Sebastian of *Advertising Age* wrote that even though companies assert that their native ads are clearly labeled so as to inform readers which content is produced by the publication's writers and which content is paid for and produced by advertisers, an analysis of two dozen news and lifestyle sites, social media platforms, and mobile apps showed that none of the native advertising is actually referred to as an advertisement. Instead, the companies often label native ads as "sponsored," "sponsored content," "brand publishing," "brand publisher," "promoted," "paid for and posted by," "sponsor generated content by," or "presented by." The media outlets also vary as to where the labeling is placed, with some placing it above the article, and others above the headline, in the byline with the advertiser's name, to the immediate left of the headline, or at the bottom of the article with the advertiser's name.[7]

If such sponsored information becomes too pervasive, people might just get quite used to it and accept it as part of the general media landscape, not unlike product advertising in television shows or movies where, for example, an actor or host drinks from a cup with a product logo on it, or like televised sporting events in which ads are superimposed behind home plate or along the perimeter of the baseball field, soccer field, or race car track. As a soccer fan, I actually appreciate this type of advertising, because it means that the network doesn't have to go to a commercial during the game action, which could result in missing a rare goal. However, I'm more wary of content that is portrayed in a journalistic manner, which can lead to confusion. According to Erin Griffith of *Fortune* magazine, a new study/survey conducted by Contently, an organization that connects brands with writers, who then create sponsored content, showed that "People feel deceived when they realize an article or video is sponsored by a brand, and believe it hurts the digital publisher's credibility." The article noted the recent debate in the publishing and advertising industry about sponsored content, "more recently called 'native advertising' and once known as 'advertorial'—the sort of advertising that looks very much like editorial content but is, in fact, directly paid for by an advertiser." Noting that websites like *BuzzFeed* and websites for magazines like *Forbes* and *The Atlantic* were using this technique, Griffith said, "Industry peers watched and discussed: Is it deceptive? Is it ethical? Does it even work?"[8]

One of the biggest concerns with sponsored content is that the content and articles are presented in a journalistic manner. David Weinberger of the *Harvard Business Review* expressed his concerns about paid content in 2013, writing, "My problems with paid content come from asking the obvious question: Does it make the place better or worse? The answer seems clear to me. It puts partisan work that looks like journalism literally next to actual journalism. Even when it is properly labeled as paid for by a company, the proximity of actual journalism can elevate the seriousness with which the paid content is taken. Readers may mistake it for actual journalism if the label is too small or unclear. The wall can be too thin."[9]

In response to this confusion, the FTC has given warnings and issued guidelines. In 2013, the *New York Times* reported that the Federal Trade Commission (FTC) was warning advertisers that it planned to enforce its rules against misleading advertisers in regard to sponsored content, quoting FTC chairwoman Edith Ramirez as saying that "it's equally important that advertising not mislead consumers. By presenting ads that resemble editorial content, an advertiser risks implying, deceptively, that the information comes from a nonbiased source."[10]

According to *PR Week* (an online and print publication for public relations professionals), the Edelman public relations firm published its new ethical framework in 2013, which it would use as a guideline for sponsored content: "The agency will also clearly disclose editorial-style sponsored content on major news sites. It also plans to work with publishers to ensure that the distinction between paid and earned content is clear."[11] Paid content is advertising, while earned content is word-of-mouth social media shares, reviews, and blog posts by other external sources, such as readers and consumers who voluntarily share their content and sources.

However, in response to continued confusion surrounding native advertising, the FTC took even further measures. According to Sydney Ember of the *New York Times* on December 22, 2015, "On Tuesday, the Federal Trade Commission issued a guide on native advertising intended to prevent customers from being deceived. The long-awaited guidelines function as a warning shot to the online ad industry and lay out for the first time how advertisers and publishers should deploy and label native ads."[12]

The FTC's eleven-page guideline states in part, "In assessing whether a native ad presented on the main page of a publisher site is recognizable as advertising to consumers, advertisers should consider the ad as a whole, and not just focus on individual phrases, statements, or visual elements. Factors to weigh include an ad's overall appearance; the similarity of its written, spoken, or visual style or subject matter to non-advertising content on the publisher site on which it appears; and the degree to which it is distinguishable from other content on the publisher site. The same assessment applies to any click- or tap-into page—the page on which the complete ad appears." The FTC guidelines set forth numerous examples and hypothetical situations of how companies should act. It also states, regarding disclosures, "In general, disclosures should be: in clear and unambiguous language; as close as possible to the native ads to which they relate; in a font and color that's easy to read; in a shade that stands out against the background; for video ads, on the screen long enough to be noticed, read, and understood; and for audio disclosures, read at a cadence that's easy for consumers to follow and in words consumers will understand."[13]

According to *Advertising Age*, the Interactive Advertising Bureau (which constitutes over 650 online, interactive advertising companies and is committed to professional development and advocating for its members) stated that while this new FTC guidance on native advertising was helpful, the bureau was concerned that some of the guidelines might stifle innovation and creativity and impinge on commercial speech protection.[14]

Given the amount and variety of sponsored content on the market today, it seems to be here to stay. However, readers and news consumers need to be aware of this growing trend and to consider the context when reading such articles or watching online videos. Media outlets should make the advertising disclaimers more prominent and bold in order to alert readers. I am hoping that the new FTC guidelines will help in this process. As someone who struggles with reading small print, I hope that these disclaimers will be in large bold print and bright colors and appear in multiple places, such as at the beginning and the end. As of February 2016, I hadn't noticed much of a change. For instance, on aol.com, the advertising disclaimers for sponsored content were there, but I found them easy to miss unless one was specifically looking for them. That's the problem: most people don't go through the conscious thought process of whether the online article they're reading is journalism or an ad created by a public relations or marketing team. They're just interested in reading about the topic.

While sponsored content has the overt goal of selling products and services, a different form of nontraditional news presentation emerged on television a few years ago. Rather than present news impartially, politically one-sided television stations have appeared. The Fox News channel was the first of these, and it has become the main television news source for conservatives.

CHAPTER 9

THE RISE OF FOX NEWS

Launched in 1996, Fox News, as part of the Fox network, was established as a response to what conservatives believed to be the overwhelmingly liberal media. Owner Rupert Murdoch hired former Republican consultant Roger Ailes to oversee the network.[1] Fox News quickly became a haven and the go-to network for conservatives who believed that the network news outlets were part of the mainstream media liberal bias that did not treat conservatives fairly. It became the platform for popular conservative hosts, guests, with regular pundits and contributors over the years including people like Bill O'Reilly, Sean Hannity, Megyn Kelly, Mike Huckabee, Greta Van Susteren, Glenn Beck, Tucker Carlson, Chris Wallace, Oliver North, Charles Krauthammer, Sarah Palin, Mark Levin, Ralph Peters, Jeanine Pirro, Stuart Varney, Karl Rove, Laura Ingraham, Neil Cavuto, and Greg Gutfeld. Fox News made them stars and influential thought leaders.

Approximately a decade later, in 2007, Fox expanded its brand by establishing the Fox Business Network, which provides financial news with a conservative slant. In 2015, the Fox Business Network had its highest ratings and was considered the fastest growing cable television network, according to Nielsen Media Research.[2]

Conservatives claim that they like Fox News because it heralds and supports traditional conservative values, which they see as running counter to the mainstream media and its alleged liberal agenda. Deborah Potter, formerly of CBS News and CNN news bureaus and now executive director of NewsLab, an online training center and resource for journalists, wrote in 2006, "What Ailes created was a channel with a clear identity and plenty of attitude, aimed directly at viewers fed up with what he calls the liberal slant of the mainstream media. While his competitors stuck to a broadcast model and tried to appeal to the widest possible audience, Fox found its niche by narrowcasting to viewers who wanted news from a particular perspective."[3]

Fox News tends to focus on stories that paint liberals in a negative light. It gives extensive coverage to Democratic scandals, such as Hillary Clinton's use of a private e-mail account and server while secretary of state and her involvement in the attack on the US compound in Benghazi, Libya, resulting in the death of our ambassador. This is especially the case with the Fox News primetime lineup, its morning show, and many of its weekend shows. These programs do offer a decent amount of hard news coverage during the day, but even then much of it is ideologically slanted toward a conservative bias. Most of the hosts also reflect a pro-conservative, anti-liberal bias through their tone and demeanor. Fox News continues to use the tagline "Fair and Balanced," even though its reporting and its hosts often prove otherwise. Nevertheless, the network is immensely popular and influential, and its ratings have remained strong over the years. Many conservatives see it as the only television news source that they can trust.

With Fox News's popularity has come criticism, frequently from liberally biased sources. As Chris Mooney of *Mother Jones* stated in a June 2014 article, partisan news outlets like Fox News have led to factual and political polarization: "Political polarization has increased in the decade since the invasion. The influence of Fox News has also increased, as the channel's viewership and revenues have grown since 2002. And disagreements about facts appear to have gotten worse. A 2010 PIPA [Program on International Policy Attitudes] study found that in the 2010 election, 'almost daily' Fox News viewers were 'significantly more likely' to believe 9 out of 11 false claims, including the assertions that scientists don't agree that climate change is happening, that 'most economists have estimated' that Obamacare will 'worsen the deficit,' and that 'most economists estimate' that the 2009 stimulus bill 'caused job losses.'"[4]

A study conducted by Bruce Bartlett, a former adviser and officer for Presidents Reagan and George H. W. Bush, found that Fox viewers were misguided and misinformed as to many important issues, including climate change and President Obama's citizenship. Bartlett said, "Republican voters get so much of their news from Fox, which cheerleads whatever their candidates are doing or saying, that they suffer from wishful thinking and fail to see that they may not be doing as well as they imagine, or that their ideas are not connecting outside the narrow party base."[5] Bartlett also argued that Fox and other conservative news outlets create a bubble that reinforces marginal or false views: "Conservatives engage in self-brainwashing, where certain ideas are repeated so often and with no contrary or alternative point of view that it fulfills the classic definition of brainwashing."[6]

Journalist and contributing editor Ben Adler wrote in the *Columbia Journalism Review* in 2011 that it would be valid for Fox to be a network of conservative opining as long as it openly proclaimed itself to be doing that: "But pretending to do straight reporting while choosing stories and dishonestly presenting nuggets of information in order to advance a political agenda perniciously undermines the work of the entire press and ill serves American democracy."[7] That's one of my main issues with Fox News, as well. It's clear to most viewers that the network is not engaged in fair and balanced journalism, but it tries to present itself as doing so. Fox's news reporting has a clear conservative slant and bias. It shouldn't be ashamed to admit that, especially in light of its huge ratings and influence among conservatives. Most of its conservative audience want the skewed presentation of the news that the Fox hosts deliver.

The Fox hosts have defended themselves and their approach. As journalists with a conservative perspective, many of them either felt unwelcome at liberal mainstream media outlets or else believed that they wouldn't fit in. Greg Gutfeld, host of the *Greg Gutfeld Show* and a cast member of *The Five*, wrote on the Fox News website that his network was a safe haven for conservative journalists who didn't feel welcome working for mainstream media outlets. He stated that the mainstream media dishonestly reported their favorite issues due to their advocacy: "Which leads me to FNC (Fox News Channel). Few of us are welcome in those other places, because we reject this deal. We chose this uncool world pushing an inconvenient fairness."[8]

Megyn Kelly, host of Fox News's analysis show the *Kelly File*, told *USA Today* that she is nonideological: "I'm not a partisan person. Our news division is truly fair and balanced. I've voted for Democrats and Republicans. I don't care about either of these parties. I care about America. I care about my audience."[9] And former ABC News journalist and current Fox political commentator Brit Hume told Paul Bedard of *U.S. News & World Report* that Fox aims to cover a side that the liberal mainstream media ignores and that he believed "there were two sides of the street and the mainstream were basically working one side. And that there was a journalistically legitimate set of opportunities on the other side of the street that if anybody ever worked would have a distinctive product, and that a lot of people would like it."[10] Fox News's critics have accused it of being unfair and unbalanced and an embarrassment to journalism, but the network has defied its critics over the years. It knows that it caters to a conservative audience that distrusts the mainstream media, and it gives its viewers a view of the country and the world that fits their perspective and ideology. Just from my own experience in talking to my conservative friends and relatives, I get the impression that most of them do trust what they see on Fox News, at least much more than they trust mainstream media television networks.

As Justin Peters of *Slate* has noted, "The chattering classes [a pejorative term referring to rich, well-educated people who comment publicly in the media on politics and current affairs] might view Fox News as an embarrassment, but it is a popular one, and that has been Ailes's consistent salvation. . . . It's downright obvious that Fox succeeds at least partially for the same reason that conservative talk radio succeeds where liberal alternatives fail: There is a bigger audience for conservative bloviation than for liberal bloviation."[11]

While some of Fox News's programming does focus on hard news during part of the day, its evening programming is highly skewed toward a conservative perspective. To some extent, its daytime programming also has a subtle conservative bias. Erik Wemple of the *Washington Post* wrote,

As the *New York Times*'s Brian Stelter reported, Fox News executives tout the weekday hours between 9 a.m. and 4 p.m. (as well as 6 p.m. to 8 p.m.) as "objective" coverage. In a memorable exchange last year with respected newsman Ted Koppel, Fox News's Bill O'Reilly cited this block as the difference-maker between Fox News and the competition: "We actually do hard news here from 9 in the morning until 5 in the afternoon," said O'Reilly, overstating the network's official position by an hour. "MSNBC doesn't do one hour of hard news. It's all, let's push the liberal Democratic agenda from sign-on to sign-off. So this is a news agency here." However, Wemple's viewing of Fox News led him to conclude, "*Fox News produces a fair amount of ideologically tilted coverage in the daytime hours*" (Wemple's emphasis). The Erik Wemple Blog counted 14 meaty, beefy segments totaling around 64 minutes in which a rightward tilt was somewhere between slight and overwhelming.[12]

Although I've never conducted my own similar detailed analysis, I always observe this conservative leaning, either through story choices, selection of biased guests, or reporters' tone. Much of Fox News's audience embraces this conservative slant. They want this perspective and bias, which they feel they can't get elsewhere. After the August 2015 Republican presidential primary debate, former CBS journalist Bernard Goldberg stated that many conservatives were upset with the hard-hitting questions because they were expecting the Fox News moderators to ask questions that were biased toward a conservative viewpoint and audience. Goldberg opined that many Fox News viewers didn't want fair and balanced news and opinion: "If they could get the weather from a conservative who would bash liberals while telling us it's going to rain today, that would be just dandy with them. . . . They want a news organization that caters to their own biases; that validates their own biases. . . . But they didn't get it during the GOP debate."[13]

There are times when Fox strays from the standard format, as, for example, when Bill O'Reilly occasionally defends a Democrat or when Chris Wallace or Megyn Kelly asks tough questions to a Republican candidate or government official. Fox News's debate moderators received praise for their tough questioning of Republican candidates during two of the many 2015 GOP primary debates. I have to give their moderators credit; I thought that, for the most part, they asked tough, relevant questions in a respectful manner. But generally Fox News and its hosts stick to the regular playbook of demonizing liberals, which continues to play to their primary audience. Despite its many critics, Fox News continues to be a ratings powerhouse and the media outlet of choice for conservatives. In light of its success, MSNBC was developed as an attempt to provide a liberal counterbalance to the conservative spin of Fox News.

CHAPTER 10

THE RESPONSE OF MSNBC

I n 1996, Microsoft teamed up with NBC to form MSNBC. In the 2000s, MSNBC started to put an emphasis on politics and opinion in prime-time. The network found its voice and an audience during the Bush administration and the Iraq War. It served as one of the few broadcast outlets where progressive liberals could get passionate, unapologetic, unfiltered, unsubtle liberal viewpoints on news and current events. The network arose as a counterbalance to the conservative spin of Fox News and talk radio.

To many staunch liberals, the mainstream media is not liberal because it is owned by conservative corporations. They believe that the mainstream media is timid and afraid to criticize conservatives because they will be accused of having a liberal bias. This was especially the case during the President George W. Bush administration.[1] MSNBC helped to fill that void. This especially became the case when Air America, the liberal talk radio network, went bankrupt.

After the devastation of Hurricane Katrina and the media's aggressive questioning of the Bush administration's mishandling of the aftermath, *Salon*'s Eric Bohlert wrote that it was about time the media woke up from its timid slumber: "Forgive some of us for not celebrating the press's coming-out party. The fact that this kind of aggressive questioning of people in power during times of crisis now passes as news itself only highlights just how timid the mainstream press corps has been during the Bush years."[2]

At its peak, MSNBC's strongest voice was Keith Olbermann, a former sports anchor at ESPN. Evoking the spirit of legendary CBS broadcast journalist Edward R. Murrow, Olbermann frequently delivered long, opinionated commentary rants, often criticizing the Bush administration and its conduct in the Iraq war. He also mixed in humor with features like "Oddball" and the "Worst Person in the World." Olbermann and MSNBC abruptly parted ways in 2011. According to CNN, on January 25, 2011, Olbermann had complained publicly about NBC's management and its suspension of him for two days in November 2010 for making financial political donations to three Democrats who were seeking congressional seats.[3]

Rachel Maddow also emerged as a popular MSNBC host, being named a "Breakout Star of 2008" by the *Washington Post*. Previously, she had been a successful host on Air America. Maddow, a lesbian, became the first openly gay anchor of a major primetime news show. Phil Griffin, MSNBC's president, told *New York* magazine in 2008, "[When] you come out of the gate as fast as she came out, it gives me incredible excitement. We are stronger than we've been in twelve years. We have more swagger today than we have ever had. It's because of Rachel. And trust me. The other guys see it. They are watching. And they are scared."[4] Maddow's interview of Senator Rand Paul regarding his views on civil rights caught viewers' attention when Paul hedged and sounded uncomfortable in answering her question as to whether private businesses had the right to deny service to black people.

Maddow's critics dismiss her as another predictable liberal who ridicules Republicans and Fox News. David Zurawik, a *Baltimore Sun* critic, once described her as acting like "a lockstep party member."[5] Jon Stewart once mocked and criticized her for politicizing the Haiti earthquake by saying how much better the Obama administration handled this than the Bush administration through use of the United States Agency for International Development (USAID)[6] Others are offended by her smug and snarky demeanor.[7] However, her fans love that demeanor and love it when she pokes fun at conservative Republicans.[8]

MSNBC focuses on issues and gives a voice to groups that are often marginalized in society, such as women, blacks, Latinos, the LGBTQ community, poor people, and immigrants. Many times, the mainstream media doesn't portray those stories. MSNBC's slogan of "Lean Forward" reflects its progressive viewpoint. It often focuses on people and stories that the mainstream news outlets tend to overlook. According to Leslie Kaufman of the *New York Times*, MSNBC entered into a collaboration agreement with Vocativ, a media and technology company that mines the deep web to discover stories and generate original content. Vocativ has produced documentaries and segments for MSNBC on stories such as an abandoned building in Venezuela that has become the world's tallest slum and Colorado marijuana dealers evading taxes on their drug sales.[9]

Over the years, MSNBC has displayed a clear liberal bias. According to Dylan Byers of *Politico*, a Pew Research Center's Project for Excellence in Journalism survey in 2012 found that 71 percent of MSNBC's coverage of Mitt Romney was negative, while Fox News's negative coverage of President Obama was 46 percent. Byers also wrote, "During the 2012 election, the ratio of unfavorable to favorable treatment in stories on Barack Obama and Mitt Romney on MSNBC 'was roughly 23-to-1; the negative-to-positive ratio on Fox News was 8-to-1.'"[10]

In 2015, due to declining ratings, MSNBC decided to cancel three of its afternoon programs: the *Ed Schultz Show*, *Now with Alex Wagner*, and *The Cycle*. Ed Schultz was a no-holds-barred liberal firebrand who pulled no punches when it came to criticizing conservatives and Republicans. My favorite part of his show was his slanted poll questions that had results of 96 percent to 4 percent in some cases. Some examples, cited by David Rutz of the *Washington Free Beacon* and Maxwell Strachan of *Salon*, included, "Will Republicans ever have the character to admit Obamacare saves lives? 98.1 percent are sure that will never happen"; "Will conservatives ever have the character to truly condemn racism in America? 95.1 percent said no way"; and "Do you think John Boehner cares more about playing golf or helping Americans? 89 percent golf; 11 percent helping Americans."[11] These polls, with their blatantly leading questions, played to his liberal-leaning audience and demonstrated just how liberal his audience was.

Alex Wagner's show provided perspective on news stories and featured her interviews of guests. *The Cycle* was a panel ensemble opinion show similar to *The View* on ABC, which featured regular panelists Ari Melber, Krystal Ball, Toure, and Abby Huntsman. MSNBC kept Al Sharpton's show, but moved it to the weekend. The network announced that it would be putting more emphasis on news coverage.[12] Why did MSNBC make the changes? According to Dylan Byers of *Politico*, a former NBCUniversal executive (MSNBC is a part of NBCUniversal's news group) told

Politico earlier that year that "MSNBC got boring. . . . You'll hear a lot of people talking about it being too far left, too political—all that matters is that it's entertaining." Byers also observed, "MSNBC's viewership hit historic lows this year: George W. Bush wasn't around to beat up on, and Barack Obama was no longer the candidate of hope, change and soaring rhetoric. The programming started to get stale."[13]

Joe Scarborough, conservative host of MSNBC's *Morning Joe*, praised NBC's Andy Lack for the programing shakeup.[14] Ironically, Scarborough's show is one of the most successful on the liberal network, mostly because it is entertaining and provides a wide variety of perspectives through its guests. Scarborough is usually also willing to criticize Republicans and praise Democrats.

Although Fox News has had a few token regular liberal guests and contributors, such as Juan Williams, Alan Colmes, Bob Beckel, Tamara Holder, Kirsten Powers, Susan Estrich, Doug Schoen, Pat Caddell, and, at times, Geraldo Rivera, it doesn't have any liberal hosts of its shows, although Sean Hannity's show was originally Hannity and Colmes, which Hannity usually dominated. Unfortunately, many of the Fox News democratic and liberal guests and commentators often come across as tepid or milquetoast, often agreeing with the conservative host. As noted by a headline in an article by Steve Rendall on the Fairness and Accuracy in Reporting (FAIR) website, "With Fox News Liberals, Who Needs Conservatives?"[15]

In 2015, I wrote an op-ed in the *Huffington Post* regarding MSNBC's decision to tweak its format.[16] I noted that MSNBC's announced rebranding was a welcome change in many ways, but that it needed to keep its liberal voice. In my view, the network needed to mend its voice, not end it. MSNBC canceled the three shows already mentioned. *Meet the Press* host Chuck Todd was given a daily show and former NBC nightly news anchor Brian Williams was given a prominent role dealing with breaking news. This was part of MSNBC's shift from opinionated advocacy journalism to more straightforward hard news. In 2016, the network added a show-sharing arrangement with Bloomberg TV because it would be replaying Bloomberg's centrist and moderate program *With All Due Respect*, hosted by John Heilemann and Mark Halperin, in the time slot once held by Al Sharpton.

The changes had come as a result of MSNBC's plummeting ratings. According to Rick Kissell of the show biz publication *Variety*, MSNBC's Nielsen ratings for the second quarter of 2015 dropped 5 percent in total viewers and 17 percent in the key adult demographic of 25 to 54. Its prime-time lineup's ratings dropped by 10 percent.[17] However, ratings announced just before the news release about the programming shuffle showed a significant increase in MSNBC's ratings, by 17 percent in the daytime and 12 percent in primetime.[18]

Despite that encouraging ratings news, I opined that many MSNBC programs had become boring and predictable over the last few years. Most of their hosts were either too wonkish or had become cartoonish caricatures. Chris Hayes, host of *All In with Chris Hayes*, is knowledgeable, likeable, and informative, but boring. Chris Matthews is a good down-to-earth Philly guy with spot-on opinions, but he is hard to watch—too rude, obnoxious, bombastic, in your face, and out of touch with twenty-first-century culture. He needs to get over the mispronunciation of Dick Cheney's last name (he frequently gets testy with guests when they pronounce the last name as CHAYNEY, like everyone else in the world commonly does, instead of CHEENEY, which Matthews always reminds people is the correct pronunciation) and stop living in the early 1960s, with never-ending references to the Kennedys and movies and TV shows from that era. Al Sharpton is too predictable, mistake-prone, and is a better activist than a journalist or commentator. They ended up moving him to Sunday.

The network tends to beat the same stories to death, most notably the Chris Christie Bridgegate scandal of 2014. The talking points get old and predicable after a while—e.g., Bush is a moron, Cheney is evil, Republicans are cold-hearted racists, and Obama is wonderful and flawless. Most of MSNBC's shows feature guests who share the same liberal view and don't have real debates with opposing viewpoints. The shows are basically four guests echoing each other's opinions. Even viewers who agree with the liberal positions of the MSNBC hosts and programs—like me and many of my friends and relatives—were getting tired of the repetition and lack of variety.

I noted that, like MSNBC, Fox News is clearly not fair and balanced.

It is just as predictable, with conservative opinions and talking points, beating to death topics like Obamacare, Benghazi, the alleged IRS scandals, Hillary Clinton scandals, and making Obama out to be an evil, anti-American, terrorist-loving anti-Christ. However, Fox News's hosts and shows generally are more entertaining; they deal with more interesting and varied controversies, and they have arguments with guests that they disagree with. They also have a more passionate and loyal conservative following, unlike MSNBC, which has to compete with CNN.

I argued that among the shows on MSNBC worth keeping are *Morning Joe* with Joe Scarborough and Mika Brzezinski, which is one of the few MSNBC programs that have real debates; thorough news veteran Andrea Mitchell's program; and the insightful and sarcastic Rachel Maddow, who led all MSNBC shows with over 700,000 viewers in the second quarter of 2015, topping CNN's Anderson Cooper.[19]

The network also needs to stop mailing it in on weekends and holidays. Enough of its ongoing documentaries, *Lockup* and *Caught on Camera*. News continues to break twenty-four hours a day, even on weekends and holidays. While the other major news networks continue to run news-related programs seven days a week, even on holidays, MSNBC will constantly run *Lockup* and *Caught on Camera* throughout the weekend and on holidays. For instance, during MSNBC's scheduled weekend programming for the weekend of January 8–10, 2016, starting at January 8 at 10 p.m., there were eighteen one-hour episodes of *Lockup* and twelve one-hour episodes of *Caught On Camera*.[20] As reported by *Mediaite*, MSNBC host Chris Hayes stated in a Facebook Q & A that the main reason they have so many *Lockup* reruns during the weekends is because these shows get good ratings.[21] But to many news junkies like me, this extensive schedule of ongoing documentaries is a turnoff. I want to turn to MSNBC to get news and analysis on a regular basis, not this other type of programming. While the network will break into regular programming if a major news story takes place, it's frustrating to see the scarcity of MSNBC's news programs and shows during the weekend. However, during the early part of 2016, as the presidential primaries started heating up, I noticed that MSNBC did start having a little more news coverage during the weekends.

I hope they will continue such coverage in the future, not just at the peak of election season.

Though I considered it unlikely, I felt MSNBC should try to think outside the box and attract more entertaining hosts with liberal views and star power for their prime-time lineup, people the likes of David Letterman, Jon Stewart, Bill Maher, Billy Crystal, Rosie O'Donnell, Katie Couric, or Whoopi Goldberg. It might have even been sensible to bring back Keith Olbermann, even though he is high maintenance and frequently clashed with his bosses at MSNBC and ESPN. As noted by Eric Kelsey of Reuters, after ESPN rehired Olbermann in 2013, "Olbermann . . . is as famous for his acrimonious departures from ESPN, MSNBC and Current TV as for his sharp tongue and wit."[22] I believed that MSNBC needed to convince a high-profile person to take on the noble goal of toppling Bill O'Reilly and Sean Hannity. It needed to give the viewers some ice cream with their vegetables. It needed to inform its viewers but keep them entertained and make them laugh.

While going to a straight news format during the day is a smart ratings move, I urged MSNBC to keep its liberal voice during primetime as a counterbalance to the bloviating Fox News prime-time lineup of Bill O'Reilly, Sean Hannity, and Megyn Kelly. Despite the Republican mantra complaining about the liberal media, there aren't enough strong liberal voices on television and talk radio to counterbalance the onslaught of conservative commentators on Fox News and talk radio, which has people such as Rush Limbaugh, Mark Levin, Michael Savage, Dennis Prager, and Laura Ingraham. As I mentioned earlier, Air America was an attempt at having a liberal voice on the radio, but the station went bankrupt in 2010, after only six years.

In light of the upcoming presidential campaign and the potential for a Republican to be elected president, there is a definite need for a consistent and strong liberal voice to even the playing field of advocacy journalism. During the next few years, MSNBC can serve to rebut the conservative spin and bias of Fox News and talk radio, which is highly influential. While MSNBC needs some programming changes, it shouldn't give up its liberal soul or its progressive values.

MSNBC, like the other cable news networks, tends to shift gears in response to a breaking news story when it deals with tragedy—earthquakes, floods, wildfires, plane crashes, terrorism incidents, snow storms, and military conflicts. As the news breaks, the focus tends to be more on straightforward informational reporting, as opposed to opinionated, biased reporting. This became especially evident when Brian Williams joined the network, and it was obvious during the terrorist shootings in Paris and San Bernardino in late 2015, as MSNBC suspended its regular programming to feature Williams anchoring the coverage of those incidents.

Like Fox News, MSNBC usually stacks its panels of guests to favor their own views, with most of the MSNBC guests having liberal opinions and viewpoints. Panels will frequently feature three liberals and one conservative or two liberals and one conservative, with the host asking questions from a liberal perspective and rebutting the token conservative. This was pointed out during one program by noted journalist Jeff Greenfield, who has worked for CBS, ABC, and CNN. According to Evan McMurry of *Mediaite*, a website that covers the intersection between media and politics, on October 23, 2013, during a panel discussion about the rollout of the Affordable Care Act/Obamacare on *Now with Alex Wagner* (on either October 16 or October 23) Yahoo News columnist and MSNBC contributor Jeff Greenfield got into a heated debate with the largely liberal panel when he said that he was not speaking as an "advocate" but as a "journalist," unlike the rest of the panelists:

> "I'll tell you the other thing," he continued. . . . "I realize sometimes networks can be—I want to just—I want to be a counter-arguer."
>
> "You're allowed to do whatever you want," Wagner said.
>
> "Because I represent myself as a humble country journalist, not an advocate."
>
> "I think many people at this table would consider themselves journalists, too," Wagner objected.
>
> "Who are also advocates," Greenfield countered. "Progressives and liberals."
>
> "Or not," Wagner said, more seriously, and then moved the segment along: "We can get into that discussion later."[23]

MSNBC's hosts do occasionally stray from the norm. Chris Matthews, for example, has frequently praised Ronald Reagan for his ability to work with then Speaker of the House Tip O'Neill to pass bipartisan legislation. In February 2016, Lawrence O'Donnell praised Republican presidential candidate Ted Cruz for having the courage to go against the ethanol industry in Iowa by saying that it shouldn't be receiving government subsidies.

MSNBC is clearly a liberally biased news outlet, but it is an important news and opinion source for liberals. It also serves as a check and balance to Fox News's conservative slant. The nighttime hosts are quick to point out mistakes or inaccuracies in stories reported by Fox News. While its recent programming changes make economic sense for the network, many liberals like me hope that it will keep its passionate and unapologetic liberal voice, which is absent in most of television and radio.

These last chapters have showcased the two main cable television networks primarily engaged in reporting and commentary with a clear bias. Another battleground and format for advocacy journalism has been the Internet, including blogs, biased websites, YouTube, social media, and citizen journalism. With the advent of this new form of communication came an explosion of people who were able to express their strong opinions to a large audience without the gatekeeper of the mainstream media.

CHAPTER 11

THE RISE OF BLOGGING, BIASED WEBSITES, YOUTUBE, SOCIAL MEDIA, AND CITIZEN JOURNALISM AND THEIR RELEVANCE TODAY

Blogging emerged as a turn-of-the-century phenomenon. According to *New York Magazine*, the first blog was created in 1994 by Justin Hall, a Swarthmore College student. Online diarist Jorn Barger created the term "Weblog" in 1997, and programmer Peter Merholz shortened it to blog in 1999. Subsequent milestones included the launch of *The Dish* on Andrew-Sullivan.com in 2000, which was a popular and influential blog on politics and social issues; the 2002 launch of *Gawker*, a website that covers media and pop culture; and the 2005 launch of the liberal-leaning digital news source the *Huffington Post*.[1]

One of the most influential political websites has been the conservative-slanted *Drudge Report*, founded as an e-mail newsletter by Matt Drudge in the mid-1990s. Drudge rose to fame when he broke the story of the affair between President Clinton and White House staffer Monica Lewinsky.[2]

Unlike twenty-five years ago, today there are endless media outlets for people to get a vast amount of information. Mainstream media (i.e., newspapers, magazines, radio, network news) are no longer the sole gatekeepers of what is made public. These sources no longer have a stranglehold on the flow of information. Any person with a cell phone, a blog, or Twitter account can be a provider of information or act like a reporter.

The creation of blogs and websites gave everyone in the world a soapbox or microphone. In many cases, blog and website creators are able to cultivate a worldwide audience. Most of these blogs and websites tend to be very opinionated and present a strong voice that reflects the positions of the website creators, unfiltered by the constraints of mainstream media gatekeepers who have to play it safe by covering a wide area of topics to satisfy the needs of the diverse audiences that they reach. The language used in these blogs tends to be more natural and conversational rather than scripted. They convey a personality and passion that often doesn't come across in many traditional media outlets. And in doing so they often build a loyal and engaged following.

In many cases, people who develop popular blogs and huge audiences are gobbled up by mainstream media, such as Ana Marie Cox (*Wonkette*), Bill Simmons (ESPN), and Nate Silver (first by FiveThirtyEight, then the *New York Times*, then ESPN). Cox founded the online magazine *Wonkette*, a liberal and snarky political blog and website, in 2004. Originally owned by Gawker Media, the website had a strong, colorful, and edgy voice and provided gossip, news, and commentary on the political scene. Cox, frequently referred to as Wonkette, left the website in 2006 to promote her new book *Dog Days*. She eventually became an editor for Time.com, a contributing editor for *Playboy*, a correspondent for Air America, a Washington correspondent for *GQ*, a political blogger for the *Guardian*, and a columnist for the *Daily Beast*.[3] In 1997, Bill Simmons created his website the Boston Sports Guy, in which he commented on Boston sports. By 2001, his website averaged 10,000 readers and 45,000 hits per day, according to the College of the Holy Cross website, his alma mater. His colorful writing style caught the attention of sports network ESPN, which hired him to write guest columns for its website. He eventually became its lead columnist and then served as editor in chief of ESPN's Grantland website, which covered sports and pop culture.[4] Nate Silver, a statistician and writer, founded the political website and blog FiveThirtyEight (which is the total number of Electoral College votes). He gained notoriety for accurately predicting 49 of 50 states correctly in the 2008 presidential election. In 2010, his website was licensed for publication by the *New York Times*. In 2013, Silver sold FiveThirtyEight to ESPN but remained its editor in chief.[5]

The social media website YouTube is fast emerging as a source for news. As of 2015, there were nearly one hundred news and politics channels listed on YouTube. Some are affiliated with traditional news organizations, such as CNN, *Time* magazine, the *New York Times, USA Today*, and BBC News, while others include the *Huffington Post*, TheBlaze, *The Young Turks, Secular Talk, Mashable*, On Demand News, *Vice News*, RT America, TheLip.tv, *The David Pakman Show*, the Daily Conversation, *The Thom Hartmann Program*, and *Jesse Ventura: Off the Grid*. These channels have become extremely popular. According to VidStatsX, a website that provides YouTube rankings and statistics, *Albernameg*, an Egyptian news satire program, and *The Young Turks* had over 2.4 million subscribers and *Vice News*, an international news channel, had over 1.7 million subscribers. Over fourteen YouTube news and politics channels had over one million subscribers each.[6] How does one find these channels? On its website at youtube.com/channels, YouTube lets people browse the various channel options and manage their subscriptions, in categories such as paid channels, music, comedy, film and entertainment, gaming, beauty and fashion, automotive, animation, sports, tech, science and education, cooking and health, and news and politics.

Anyone can use YouTube to find their voice and build an audience. You don't even have to be old enough to vote. Thirteen-year-old CJ Pearson of Georgia became well known as a conservative who was critical of President Obama. His YouTube channel had over five million viewers and he had over 100,000 Facebook "likes." In November 2015, he told CNN that he was renouncing his conservatism, that he would be unbound by party ideology, and that he was endorsing Bernie Sanders for president. Pearson told CNN, "I don't want to be the conservative wonder kid that people follow because I make them feel good and like young people are part of their movement. I want to be followed because I'm the voice of a generation that doesn't have a voice at the table."[7]

There are also thousands of Internet radio stations, many of which focus on news and politics. Anyone with a phone and computer can host a live Internet talk show on Blog Talk Radio, a podcasting platform that enables podcasters to broadcast, upload, record, and livestream their shows. Bloggers often use online radio shows as a way to increase their

Internet traffic.[8] According to the website "Web Hosting Secret Revealed," a site that gives advice and information to website hosting shoppers, bloggers, and web marketers, researchers for Harris Interactive, working on behalf of Radio Ad Effectiveness Lab, found "out of those who listened to Internet radio, a whopping 57 percent visited a website mentioned during the program. Even better, the site was visited almost immediately. Internet browsers are getting better and better at multi-tasking, which means a user might listen to the radio, open a new tab to visit a site mentioned and check e-mail all within a span of a few minutes."[9]

Blogs and websites have an increasing influence over their followers. Dismissed at first as the result of the pajamarati—disgruntled young people living in their parents' second bedroom and venting their personal and social frustrations online—today's websites are now the go-to place millennials rely on for news and information. Millennials often visit these sites because of their strong voice, passion, and opinions. Many feel that a person doesn't need to have a mainstream media platform to have valid and interesting opinions. Website operators can now get press passes to press conferences, political conventions, concerts, and sporting events. These venues don't just give these press passes to any Joe Schmo who has a U2 website with only a hundred Twitter followers and wants to get into a U2 concert for free, or to someone with a Philadelphia Eagles fan website that gets only a hundred online hits a day and wants free tickets to an Eagles game. They give those passes to those with websites that have earned credibility or have a large audience, and they make those determinations on a case-by-case basis.

Many politically oriented news websites, such as *Salon*, *Slate*, the *Daily Beast*, *Politico*, and the *Huffington Post*, have emerged as serious and well-respected news sites. Part of their credibility comes from the fact that they have hired away many prominent reporters from mainstream media outlets. Several news websites have been finalists or won Pulitzer Prizes and other prestigious journalism awards. David Wood of the *Huffington Post* won a Pulitzer Prize in 2012 for National Reporting; Jessie Eisinger and Jake Bernstein of *ProPublica* won a Pulitzer for National Reporting in 2011; Sheri Fink of *ProPublica*, in collaboration with the *New York Times*

Magazine, won a Pulitzer in 2010 for Investigative Reporting; Tobi Tobias of *ArtsJournal* was a finalist for a Pulitzer for criticism in 2012; and Matt Wuerker of *Politico* won a Pulitzer in 2012 for Editorial Cartooning and was nominated in 2009 and 2010. It's no longer a stigma to write for a website; in fact it's often seen as a primary destination for beginning and experienced reporters. It's likely that in the near future, more Pulitzers and prestigious journalism awards will be won by online media publications.[10] Among the most influential conservative blogs and websites are *Instapundit*, Newsmax, TheBlaze, the *Drudge Report*, *Town Hall*, *RedState*, *HotAir*, Free Republic, Breitbart, *WorldNetDaily*, the *Daily Caller*, and *NewsBusters*.[11] Among the most influential liberal blogs and websites are the *Huffington Post*, *CounterPunch*, the *Daily Kos*, *Salon*, *Eschaton*, the *Daily Beast*, *AlterNet*, *Common Dreams*, *ThinkProgress*, Media Matters, *OpEdNews*, and Truthout.[12]

As to how political websites have changed the media landscape over the last few years, Rob Kall, operator and creator of the popular and influential website *OpEdNews*, said in an e-mail interview, "They offer counter-narratives that did not exist before. And they offer on-line communities where like-minded people can share ideas."[13] According to the website, *OpEdNews* has 90,000 registered members, more than forty volunteer editors, over 185,000 content items (which store webpage-specific content), and an audience of between 200,000 and 800,000 unique visitors a month. It is consistently listed as one of the most popular and influential liberal, progressive websites.[14] Websites like Kall's make it much easier for like-minded people to communicate with each other. Before the Internet, such exchanges would have occurred by mail, phone, fax, or at in-person meetings.

Kall explains that the goal and purpose of his website and Internet radio program is to provide a content management, social networking website that supports bottom-up progressive visions, communications, and tools for activism and organizations. His site enables users to post articles and links to articles so activists and advocates can share information, and it hosts hundreds of volunteer writers and thousands of bloggers who write articles and blog diaries covering news from a different perspective and narrative—usually much more liberal—than that offered by the mainstream media. Kall goes on to say, "A strong press is essential to democracy. When big media becomes owned by and influenced by big corporations, smaller, bottom-up media becomes more essential to supporting truth, light, justice and democracy. The new technologies have enabled small media to do good journalism."[15]

Most major mainstream media outlets have blogs written by their reporters, and most reporters expand their reach and influence by using social media like Twitter and Facebook. They will promote newly posted or upcoming articles on Twitter and Facebook with a corresponding link. They will break stories on Twitter and then link to a more detailed article when it's ready. This is a good marketing tool, and it helps to promote their stories. It also gives readers insight into reporting that they couldn't have gotten years ago, such as the reporter's behind-the-scenes description of covering a story that just aired that night. Because of their pervasive use of social media in recent years, media outlets, like many other businesses and industries, have needed to establish ethical guidelines regarding the use of social media. For example, the *Washington Post* social media guidelines for its journalists require that reporters: maintain credibility, avoid real or apparent conflicts, be professional, be transparent, look before linking, think in real time (regarding breaking news), and mind the medium (engaging with followers).[16] *American Journalism Review*'s Katie Takacs reported in January 2015, "This fall, AJR contacted over a dozen news organizations, ranging from The Seattle Times to The Wall Street Journal, and found they pursue a range of strategies. Some provide specific guidelines on how reporters should use Twitter, typically with training sessions on how to implement them. Others give broad direction to their staffs and decline to specify what exactly should and should not be done on social media platforms."[17]

Part of the appeal of websites, blogs, and social media is that like-minded people can get together in these venues to share information and ideas. It's a concept similar to the niche-audience approach that made magazines successful. People who want sports information will go to a sports website, and not to a website that just plays cat videos. Topics are limitless and could include politics, sports, religion, pets, relationships, science, technology, media, art, psychology, and much more. Many websites use feed reader applications, which is software or web applications that aggregate content and display it in one location for easy viewing, and blogs serve in part as news aggregates because they show short summaries and provide links to articles and stories from many other news sites. This makes it easier for people to get news from one source, instead of clicking around from website to website. Google News, Yahoo News, Feedly, the *Drudge Report*, News360, Pulse, and the *Huffington Post* are just a few that provide this vital service. Google News determines placement through its automated algorithms, while sites like Yahoo News and the *Huffington Post* use human input.[18] User-generated and updated websites such as *Wikipedia* are immensely popular for quick information. According to *The Atlantic*, *Wikipedia* has tens of thousands of volunteer editors who update the site regularly.[19]

Social media has become a valuable news tool during tragedies. During the aftermath of the Boston Marathon bombings in 2013, someone live-tweeted the shootout between police and the Tsarnaev brothers. And when US Airways flight 1549 safely crash-landed in the Hudson River in 2009, social media captured the immediate aftermath of the landing.[20] During the terrorist attack in Paris on November 13, 2015, people used social media to let friends and family know they were safe. The hashtag #PorteOuverte (open door) let stranded people in the aftermath of the Paris attacks know that they could come to local houses for temporary shelter during the ordeal.[21] In the United States, the hashtag #strandedinUS let French citizens who had return flights to Paris canceled due to the terrorism know that they could stay temporarily with people in their American homes.[22]

Social media played a prominent role in the Arab Spring movement in 2011 as well. Tweets, videos, photos, and Facebook posts broadcasting the various revolutionary events went viral, which may well have emboldened other groups in surrounding areas to consider starting revolutionary movements in their own countries.

While these many social media venues offer the promise of instantaneous information flow and virtually immediate contact with others, one of the factors that can affect accuracy is the desire to scoop competing news outlets or websites and the pressure to be the first to break a hot news story. Social media makes this competition even more intense. There are pros and cons when using these vehicles for reporting news.

As Mark Bowden, journalist and bestselling author, said in an e-mail interview, "Social media has vastly muddied the believability of news. In most cases there is no way of knowing the source, much less knowing whether to trust it. It has the advantage of being able to spread information quickly, but it is often impossible to know how trustworthy that information is." He goes on to say, "A serious news organization ought to have rules governing its employees' use of social media, just as when I was hired years ago by the *Philadelphia Inquirer*, I was advised to not engage in political activism."[23]

In a *Huffington Post* op-ed in 2011, I noted that news consumers need to be careful about relying on Twitter and Facebook for breaking news.[24]That year, several incidents of rumors and false reporting on Twitter made national news. For a brief time, journalists on Twitter spread a false rumor that CNN's Piers Morgan had been suspended due to his alleged role in phone hacking when he was an editor for a British tabloid.[25] Earlier in the year, hackers took control of Fox News's Twitter account and posted several tweets erroneously reporting that President Obama had been assassinated in Iowa.[26] These incidents raised the issue of journalistic credibility, especially in light of the fact that reporters can use the lightning speed of social media to briefly report breaking news. The incidents served as another reminder that news consumers need to verify breaking news through multiple sources in this new world of instant communication.

Within the last decade, Twitter and other forms of social media have become effective tools for journalists, especially in augmenting foreign coverage, such as during the Arab Spring protests. It's also a valuable approach for covering breaking news and tragedies, like the Missouri tornado news coverage in May 2011 by Brian Stelter of the *New York Times*, who was on the scene as the tragedy took place.[27] Twitter allows the reader to follow the development of breaking news in real-time by a reporter on the scene. It also allows the readers to feel more of a personal connection with the reporter. In light of declining reader circulation, print media needs to continue to evolve its websites and use emerging technology to expand and improve its reporting capability.

However, as demonstrated by the Piers Morgan and Fox News Twitter-hacking incidents, among others, there are major concerns about the accuracy of instant reporting using Twitter and social media. Also in 2011, many news outlets erroneously reported through tweets and retweets that Congresswoman Gabrielle Giffords was one of the victims who died in the Tucson, Arizona, shooting incident.[28] For one thing, given Twitter's 140-character limit for single feeds at that time—as of early 2016, it was rumored to be in the process of removing this restriction—reporters couldn't give essential details or context to their stories, let alone provide explanations.

Despite the enormous changes in journalism over the last twenty years, there still exists a scoop mentality by media outlets, in which there is prestige in being the first one to report a major story. As I noted in my *Huffington Post* article, the number-one principle of journalism remains accuracy. Being right trumps being first. However, it is becoming more difficult to ensure accuracy due to the 24/7 news cycle in which breaking news is posted immediately on the media outlet's website or Twitter feed. In breaking news stories, journalists have little time to check facts and verify sources. Still, this needs to be done if the public's trust is to be maintained. While media outlets should use every avenue at their disposal to report newsworthy events, including use of Twitter and other such venues for breaking news, they need to be careful and judicious in how they use them. In some cases, they should state that information in a breaking story is preliminary and has not yet been fully confirmed. Digital journalist and blogger Mandy Jenkins published an accuracy and accountability checklist for journalists who use Twitter and Facebook. Among the questions that she believes journalists should ask before using Twitter are: "How do I know this information? Is this information independently confirmed? Does this tweet have/need attribution [a stated source] for reported facts?"[29] News outlets also need to be up front when they make mistakes on Twitter. As Mallary Jean Tenore pointed out in 2011 article on Poynter, "While sites such as Twitter and Facebook make it easy for misinformation to be spread rapidly, they also give journalists the opportunity to correct mistakes in real-time and be more open with their audiences about what's confirmed."[30]

The Piers Morgan and Fox News Twitter-hacking cases indicate the need for all of us to be savvy news consumers, especially when it comes to breaking news. In 2012, a Twitter hack of the Associated Press resulted in a false tweet reporting that the White House had been hit by two explosions and that President Obama had been injured.[31] In 2013, TMZ's Twitter feed incorrectly reported that rap star Lil Wayne was in a coma and being given last rites in a hospital.[32] That same year, the *New York Post*'s "Bag Man" cover incorrectly inferred that the two men on the cover of the paper were suspects in the Boston Marathon bombing. The two men sued the *Post* for defamation and the suit was settled.[33] In 2012, CNN and Fox News erroneously interpreted the US Supreme Court ruling on the Affordable Care Act, incorrectly reporting at first that the individual mandate had been struck down.[34] Unfortunately, the burden is shifting from the media being self-correcting to news consumers being careful about relying on and trusting breaking news reports. In March 2011, a Pew Research Report indicated that for the first time, more people said they got news from websites than from newspapers, and that the Internet now trails only television among American adults as their news destination, with this gap closing.[35]

As news consumers, we need to double check our sources before we retweet information or text our family and friends, erroneously telling them that the president was assassinated or that Justin Bieber died in a car accident. Living celebrities are frequently killed off on the Internet, such as Abe Vigoda (now actually dead), Betty White, Bill Cosby, and Morgan Freeman. We should treat instant news from tweets in the same way we handle reading *Wikipedia* or message board rumors, by thinking to ourselves, "Wow, that's interesting. I'd better double check to confirm." While news outlets have an obligation to be responsible on their end, we as readers need to be careful as well.

There is an expanding army of journalism entrepreneurs who are creating their own news outlets, websites, and blogs. Some of them are not familiar with or trained in the traditional news-gathering techniques of investigating and verifying facts and information. In some cases, they don't care about traditional news values; they see their purpose as setting forth strong opinions in an entertaining manner. Others take accuracy and reporting more seriously. Bill Reed of the *Philadelphia Inquirer* said in an e-mail interview, "Bloggers admit freely that they rely on the mainstream media for information and ideas on which to expound. Responsible bloggers credit the sources of their information, allowing their readers to decide whether the blogger's opinions stand up."[36] While there is no universal blogger code of ethics, there are attempts to ensure reliability and credibility. As reported by Jessica Blais on Poynter in 2010, the Ford Foundation gave the Poynter Institute a $750,000 grant to help Poynter fund its Sense-Making Project. Calvin Sims, Program Officer for News Media and Journalism for the Ford Foundation, told Blais, "With the advent of the Internet, consumers now have at their fingertips access to more sources of news and information than ever before, however, the integrity of these new media sources remains uncertain. Through our support for the research and training programs of the Poynter Institute, we seek to infuse standards and ethics in the new digital media space to help insure that the information the public consumes is both reliable and responsible."[37]

Reporters have been using social media both for sources and information gathering. That can be useful, but reporters need to be careful in relying on such sources and in attributing them. As noted by Amanda Hess in *Slate*, "Reporters interested in public opinion used to have to actually go outside, meet people—or at least call them on the phone—and identify themselves as journalists. Now, Twitter connects us to 230 million active users who publish a combined 500 million tweets every single day, giving us a direct line to random acts of advocacy and casual expressions of bigotry. The new, virtual man on the street doesn't even need to be aware of a reporter's existence in order to turn up on a highly trafficked news source with name, photo, and social media contact information embedded. It's the journalist's 'right' to reproduce these public statements, sure. But our rights are expanding radically, while our responsibilities to our sources are becoming more and more optional."[38]

Conservative and liberal websites will often slant news in a way that attacks the other party, often in a harsh, personal manner. One day, a conservative friend of mine gleefully asked me, "Did you hear about Obama and Rahm Emanuel having gay sex in a Chicago bath house?"

"No, I didn't hear that," I replied.

"Yeah, it's true," he said. "I read it on a conservative website."

I was skeptical about this, since I knew that conservative websites were consistently critical of President Obama. I found that many conservative websites were making the same claim, with many of the reader comments referring to Obama as "bath house Barry."[39]

However, Neil Gabler of *The Nation* rebutted this claim, stating, "Of course, there's nothing unusual about the wing-nuttery fabricating stories to rally their fellow nuts, and nothing unusual about the homophobes among them, especially on the religious right, attacking Obama as gay. But the persistent charges of his unmanliness—as if all gay men are unmanly and all women fainthearted—are part of a skein of Republican accusations and innuendoes against Democrats that goes back decades. . . . Gay becomes a proxy for effeminacy so that Republicans, in their antediluvian view of the world, can present themselves as tough he-men, Democrats as weak girls. . . . Indeed, 'feminized' is one of the dirtiest words in the Republican lexicon."[40]

Every once in a while, widely circulated conspiracy claims emerge on the Internet. I had a student in one of my classes who vehemently asserted that the Sandy Hook shooting was a false government conspiracy and that the children were not killed. Fortunately, another student in the class rebutted him by saying that he knew one of the parents of the deceased victims. I did some research and found that there was a viral Internet conspiracy rumor that either the Sandy Hook shootings didn't really happen and that the grieving parents were actually crisis actors, or that it did happen but that the government used the shooter Adam Lanza to do the shootings to advance the gun control movement. Many media outlets, such as Snopes, debunked the conspiracy rumor as false. I was really disappointed that many people seemed to have fallen for that rumor.[41]

Interactivity between those who produce the news and those who consume it is a major component of the modern media. Twenty years ago, letters to the editor or phone calls were the only way that readers could communicate with reporters. Today, readers can comment on message boards, post comments at the end of web articles, e-mail reporters, participate in online polls, communicate with and follow reporters via Twitter and Facebook, and engage in online live chats or delayed question and answer sessions. It's a way of connecting with readers, some of whom now correspond with reporters on a regular basis. This interactivity sometimes can influence which stories reporters cover. The readers might give the reporters tips or suggestions on stories that are underreported, or they might complain about stories, photos, or videos that should not have been published or broadcasted. However, there is a problem with the interactivity of modern media. Many of the producers, reporters, or commenters are anonymous people flexing their Internet muscles. They feel that they are free to say anything, no matter how outrageous. As we have seen, without being able adequately to source the information being reported, the credibility of what is offered can be seriously jeopardized.

Are online comments on articles a good thing? To those who support them, they are a way to fact-check the media outlets and point out mistakes. They can also lead to intelligent and vigorous debate by readers on an issue. Ideally, this can expand the audience and make readers feel connected to the media outlet. To detractors, the comments often deteriorate into verbal food fights, with ad hominem attacks on the other posters, the writer of the article, and the subject of the article. This can lead to readers' animosity toward comments sections due to the constant influx and bombardment of Internet trolls who just enjoy causing trouble. Some media outlets have either banned online comments or made the commenters register, often through Facebook, to avoid anonymity. As reported by Rob Lever of Agence France-Presse (AFP), media outlets such as Vice Media, Vox Media, Medium, the *Chicago Sun Times*, the *Daily Beast*, Mic, and *Popular Science* all had either turned off their comments section, hidden them, or edited them for the benefit of their readers.[42] "Newsrooms are really struggling with this," Jennifer Stromer-Galley, a professor of information studies at Syracuse University, told Lever. "They like the idea of the comments because it brings readers back, it creates a community of people who are dedicated and that's good for advertising. But the downside is that when people see lots of vitriol and attack, even if they are not using bad language, it turns people off. The worry is that instead of fostering communication, you lose readers."[43]

I often read the online comments to articles. Sometimes I get a chuckle out of how silly the comments can get, and it can be entertaining to read the arguments. Other times, the online commenters might correctly point out a reporter's mistake. This happened to me when I erroneously stated in a 2015 *Huffington Post* op-ed that when I saw the rock group Yes perform in the late 1970s it was the last time that those members of the band had played together. My article was meant to be a tribute to Chris Squire, a member of Yes who had just died, but only a few of the dozens of comments about the article were positive. Many of the other comments pointed out angrily that those members of Yes had reunited for a tour in the early 2000s.[44]

However, many times the online comments to articles are mean-spirited and they aren't vetted for accuracy. Posters can pretty much throw out false information and personal attacks without ramifications. Unfortunately, I think that some people might read these anonymous comments and give them just as much credibility, if not more, than the reporter's story.

Another aspect of blogging to be considered is the extent to which reporters for mainstream media outlets are doing it. Steve Outing, a columnist for *Editor & Publisher Online* since 1995, described in Poynter in 2004 the response to his most recent column for *Editor & Publisher*, in which he discussed how journalists must be careful in their personal blogs not to write anything too controversial or opinionated for fear of compromising their objectivity, even in their off-hours: "While some of the journalists I interviewed for the column were content to blog while walking on eggshells, others . . . are seething with anger over this issue."[45]

If a media outlet has its reporters blogging, is it necessary or important for it to have bloggers who have different political perspectives? If it's a mainstream media outlet that purportedly strives for objectivity and balance, it's probably a good idea to have bloggers with varied viewpoints, just like having opposing views on the op-ed page.

Does participating on social media like Twitter and Facebook affect the objectivity of journalists or the public's perception of their objectivity? It's possible that it might influence perception, since blogging gives reporters more of a personal voice, and their viewpoints and biases are likely to be more apparent than they would be in a regular news story. On social media, reporters are more likely to give their opinions, show emotion, and present their views in a stronger voice. Sometimes doing so can get them into trouble. CNN suspended global affairs correspondent Elise Labott for two weeks because she tweeted her disappointment after the House voted to deny Syrian refugees entry into the United States. Labott tweeted, "House passes bill that could limit Syrian refugees. Statue of Liberty bows head in anguish," along with a link to CNN's story on the piece, which Labott did not write.[46] According to *Fortune*, "Insiders say CNN head Jeff Zucker doesn't like social media and doesn't want his journalists being accused of bias because of a tweet or a Facebook post. And he's likely also concerned about appealing to advertisers."[47]

In November 2015, Mike Bell, an afternoon sports talk radio host in Atlanta, was suspended after making several derogatory Twitter comments about ESPN baseball commentator Jessica Mendoza, mocking her baseball knowledge since she had been a softball player. In one tweet, he joked that his wife was sending her resume to offer commentary on the Daytona 500 because she occasionally speeds.[48]

Reporters also have to be careful about what they choose to retweet or show that they like on Facebook, since these gestures can be interpreted to reflect a bias. In 2013, the Associated Press updated its guidelines on retweeting to state, "Retweets, like tweets, should not be written in a way that looks like you're expressing a personal opinion on the issues of the day. A retweet with no comment of your own can easily be seen as a sign of approval of what you're relaying. . . . However, we can judiciously retweet opinionated material if we make clear we're simply reporting it, much as we would quote it in a story. Introductory words help make the distinction. . . . These cautions apply even if you say on your Twitter profile that retweets do not constitute endorsements."[49]

The Internet era has seen a rise in citizen journalism, where average people use blogs, websites, and social media to comment on societal problems and to advocate change. As part of this, hashtag activism has risen. Citizen journalism and hashtag activism is especially important for stories around the world that tend to get ignored by the American media, which tends to focus on parts of the world where there are American interests. Generally, stories about Africa and South America are not covered. For example, Boko Haram killed more people than ISIS during 2014. According to the Global Terrorism Index report in 2015, deaths attributed to Boko Haram rose to 6,644, compared to 6,073 blamed on ISIS. However, articles and coverage about Boko Haram in the American media were few and far between, aside from the focus that took place after the "Bring Back Our Girls" Twitter campaign.[50] In my *Huffington Post* op-ed, titled "Hashtag Activism Is a Good Thing, Despite Its Conservative Critics," I noted, "Forget protest marches on Washington. The newest way for people to raise their voices is hashtag activism. Despite the criticism, it is a good thing."

This type of activism was pushed front and center in 2014 when First Lady Michelle Obama posted a tweet with the hashtag #BringBackOurGirls, in order to raise awareness of the kidnapping of 234 Nigerian school girls by the terrorist group Boko Haram. Many celebrities, such as Amy Poehler, Ellen DeGeneres, Malala Yousafzai, and Jesse Jackson also joined the campaign.[51]

Of course, not everyone approved of Michelle Obama's campaign, especially those in the conservative media. A Fox News panel that included George Will and Brit Hume ridiculed the movement, calling it "an exercise in self-esteem," presuming that people just wanted attention or wanted to feel as though they were being socially conscious.[52] Naturally, Rush Limbaugh expressed his outrage: "I just think this is pathetic. I'm just stunned. We got three hundred Nigerian girls kidnapped by an Al Qaeda group, and nobody cared or talked about it for a while; Hillary [Clinton] wouldn't call 'em a terror group. Now all of a sudden, for some reason, we're on a big push to get 'em back. . . . The sad thing here is that the low-information crowd that's puddling around out there on Twitter is gonna think we're actually doing something about it." Limbaugh indicated that this sent a message that the United States was powerless to do anything and that President Obama was to blame.[53] Jon Stewart proceeded to mock Limbaugh, calling him a "quivering rage heap who is apparently desperately trying to extinguish any remaining molecule of humanity that might still reside in the remains of a Chernobyl-esque super-fund cleanup site that was his soul."[54]

As I noted, hashtag activism might seem naive to some, but it actually serves a purpose. For the most part, the American media ignore global stories unless they directly involve US interests. Therefore, most coverage focuses on Europe, Asia, and the Middle East. Stories about South America and Africa are ignored, unless there is a natural disaster that results in mass casualties. A good example would be the Somali pirates who hijacked foreign ships for years. It wasn't until an American ship with Captain Phillips was captured that the story garnered media attention in this country.[55] Generally, stories of famine, war, disease, and starvation in Africa are ignored.

In the minds of today's young millennials (i.e., those born between the early 1980s and the early 2000s), Twitter is the equivalent of the town square or the National Mall in Washington, DC. Most millennials do not read physical newspapers or watch *Meet the Press*. Most of my college journalism students don't listen to news radio. It's not that they are stupid; it's that they receive news and information in a different way than their parents and grandparents did. People don't use written petitions anymore to express their grievances. Twitter and other social media are ways to get news instantaneously or to report news, and it has played a major role in news stories dealing with catastrophes, acts of terror, domestic mayhem, political uprisings in foreign lands, domestic struggles over police brutality in our nation's cities, and natural disasters such as earthquakes and tsunamis. President Obama's appearance on *Between Two Ferns*, a popular Emmy Award–winning Internet television series with Zach Galifianakis, was a major part of his successful effort to get young people to sign up for health insurance under the Affordable Care Act.[56]

This new trend of hashtag activism isn't likely to go away, as evidenced by the #YesAllWomen response to Elliot Rodger's shooting spree in which six people died and fourteen others were injured in May of 2014. According to the *Washington Post*, before his shooting spree, Rodger had posted a video on YouTube in which he gave misogynistic rants against women for rejecting him. He had also posted similar feelings on online forums. As noted by *Time*, the #YesAllWomen hashtag emerged in response to Rodger's video rant, as a forum for women to criticize how society teaches men to feel entitled to women at the expense of their health and safety.[57]

On Wednesday, April 30, two weeks after the kidnapping of the Nigerian schoolgirls, *Salon* ran an article with the headline "Why Is the Media Ignoring 200 Missing Girls?" (The actual number was 234.)] As *Salon*'s Mary Elizabeth Williams noted, the media was fixated on the missing Malaysian airline and the sports world's outrage over basketball team owner Donald Sterling's public remarks that many deemed racist.[58] There was also regular coverage of Benghazi, Chris Christie and Bridgegate, and a South Korean ferry tragedy during this time. Michelle Obama proceeded to tweet about the missing girls on May 6, which helped to raise awareness and media exposure. And as I have pointed out, tweeting about atrocities in Nigeria and elsewhere won't solve the problem, but it can raise awareness. It wasn't until the hashtag activism on this incident started that the media paid attention and the politicians started to care and get involved. That's a far cry from being pathetic. In fact, Nigeria announced in May 2015 that it had rescued over two hundred girls taken by Boko Haram since 2014, although it was unclear whether any of them were the missing girls abducted in April 2014.[59] Hashtag activism is, in a sense, a form of citizen journalism, in that regular people bring attention to news stories and social issues and comment on them.

Admittedly, in retrospect, the hashtag campaign didn't bring back all of the missing girls, and Boko Haram continues to thrive. However, the hashtag campaign was a noble one because it attempted to shed light on an important topic. It's still essential for people and governments to pressure the Nigerian government to do more to save all of the girls. Citizen journalism, through hashtag activism, can be that catalyst.

The media and news consumption habits of millennials significantly differ from that of their parents and grandparents. Young people get most of their news from Facebook, Twitter, YouTube, Instagram, and websites like *BuzzFeed*, Mic, Vocativ, *Ozy*, and *Vice*. They generally don't read newspapers or watch broadcast news. Their cell phones are virtually glued to their hands. They want information instantaneously. An article by Julia Greenberg on June 8, 2015, on *Wired* indicates that millennials like news stories that appeal to a diverse audience, and they like stylish design, colorful writing, humor, attention-grabbing headlines, and sexy flair.[60] Sonia Yamada of the *New York Times* pointed out in April 2015 that social media is a way to reach millennials and cultivate them as news consumers: "Emerging Millennials are comfortable with serious news and 'junkier' news appearing side-by-side in their social streams, but they also recognize [that some] news they get from social media is often silly. They are discerning and want reliable sources for serious news. News reporting organizations like the *New York Times* are often their next destination after they have found a topic on social media that they want to dive into."[61]

There is also a substantial likelihood that people using Twitter to get their news will be mostly exposed to viewpoints that bolster, agree with, and support their own. Conservatives are most likely to follow Conservative pundits and media outlets, and Liberals are more likely to follow Liberal pundits and media outlets.

According to the Pew Research Center's journalism website, a June 2015 Pew Research poll showed that 61 percent of Millennials get their news from Facebook and only 37 percent rely on local television news. In contrast, 60 percent of Baby Boomers get their news from local television and 39 percent rely on Facebook. The survey also showed that Millennials were less familiar with most news outlets than Baby Boomers or GenXers (i.e., those born from the early 1960s to the early 1980s), with the exception of *BuzzFeed* and Google News. The poll showed that Millennials were generally less interested in politics than their elders and that the most distrusted sources of news for all three age groups were the *Glenn Beck Program*, the *Rush Limbaugh Show*, the *Sean Hannity Show*, and *BuzzFeed*."[62]

Claire Cain Miller of the *New York Times* cautioned against the echo chamber of social media, citing a study of Twitter usage during the 2012 election by Brian Knight, an economist at Brown University, and Yosh

Halberstam, an economist at the University of Toronto: "Social media like Twitter and Facebook can create an echo chamber in which people are exposed only to opinions in line with their own. . . . Both conservatives and liberals were disproportionately exposed to like-minded information, and like-minded tweets reached them much more quickly than those from people who disagreed with them. This effect matters because people increasingly rely on social media as a main source of news."[63]

I would say that just like conservatives turn to Fox News and liberals turn to MSNBC as primary news sources, many people's social media feeds are similarly highly skewed toward providing information that is consistent with the person's values. Conservatives are more likely to follow conservative news outlets and commentators on Twitter, while liberals would be more likely to follow liberal news outlets and pundits. Also, their Facebook friends are likely to share links to stories that support their similar ideology. Thus, the skewed nature of people's social media news might have an effect on the reliability of the news and information they receive.

Knight told Miller that, based on who they are following on Twitter, people will be exposed to different content.[64]

How has the explosion of social media affected the reliability of the news? What are its benefits and drawbacks? Will Bunch, who won a Pulitzer Prize as a reporter for *Newsday* and is now a senior writer and blogger for the *Philadelphia Daily News*, maintains a blog called Attytood that focuses on, among other things, politics, world affairs, the media, and sports. He believes that reporters should be able to express opinions in their reporting. In a phone interview Bunch said, "On the whole, I think that social media has been a positive. Don't dwell on the times when false information is relayed. That's horrible, but it's corrected quickly. Twitter has been more effective than Facebook, and it's been a positive as a whole. It should be held to the same standards of accuracy, fairness, and transparency. It's just as important in social media as it is traditional media."[65]

John Timpane of the *Philadelphia Inquirer*, in an e-mail interview, reflected on how the explosion of social media had affected the reliability of news:

It has hurt. I love social media. But you have to be your own filter, and most of us just aren't equipped. As a professional media person and thoroughgoing skeptic of everything I read and see, I have a few advantages here (and I'm far from the best at this). For most folks, the effort (the necessity) to be your own filter is too long, difficult, and exhausting. Social media, however, can make you smart if you know how to surf them. But you have to know how to surf. One great disappointment in social media is the failure of any one site, or group of sites, to become authoritative filters. It'd be a tough assignment. I have evolved a grid of sieves and filters, and a series of methods for checking what I read. Mostly, the crud sites, garbage like Drudge, are easily caught, but I sure have been fooled from time to time.[66]

Like Timpane, there have been times when I've been fooled as well, as I noted in an earlier chapter. If people like us, who know to be on the lookout for less credible websites, get fooled on occasion, it's easy to see how average people and news consumers would be fooled as well.

Steven Beschloss is an award-winning writer, journalist, author, and filmmaker, who was nominated for a Pulitzer Prize and has been a featured guest on MSNBC, Fox Business, and NPR. He is a senior communications specialist for Arizona State University. In an e-mail interview, he offered the following observation:

I think much of social media—while offering a fantastically valuable way of communicating information and experience quickly and comprehensively (by the sheer volume of input from around the world)—has intensified hysterical reactions and responses that often lack awareness of facts. That can lead to bad decision-making when politicians feel compelled to swiftly enter the fray. What we lack these days is sufficient reflection and careful consideration of how to act; social media, as information-rich as it is, has magnified this problem.[67]

In light of the revolution in journalism that the Internet has sparked, it often becomes confusing as to who exactly is a journalist. That isn't just an interesting, academic discussion. That determination can have real-world ramifications. One example is whether bloggers can qualify as journalists in order to receive protection under shield laws, which give reporters protection from being forced to reveal their confidential sources. As of early 2016, most states had shield laws, but there was no federal shield law. I wrote an op-ed in the *Huffington Post* on this topic in 2014.[68] At the time, the United States Senate was considering the Free Flow of Information Act, a federal media shield law that would protect journalists and media organizations from revealing the identities of their confidential sources. It was the third time that Congress had considered such a federal shield law. Unfortunately, once again, the law failed to pass.

One of the main sticking points in getting the law passed remains trying to define who a journalist is. The proposed bill defined it as a person "with the primary intent to investigate events and procure material in order to disseminate to the public news or information concerning local, national or international events or other matters of public interest" who collects the information by conducting interviews and directly observing events, and has the intent of gathering news. The person also must intend to report on the news at the start of obtaining any protected information and must plan to publish that news.[69] I noted that one of the troublesome aspects of the bill was an amendment proposed by Sen. Dianne Feinstein (D-CA) and cosponsored by Sen. Richard Durbin (D-IL), which "defines a journalist as a salaried agent of a media entity," such as a newspaper, broadcast news station, news website, or another type of news service distributed digitally. There was also a "look back" option to protect legitimate reporters not tied to a specific news organization. Feinstein said, "This bill is described as a reporter shield law—I believe it should be applied to real reporters." She was also concerned that the bill "would grant a special privilege to people who aren't really reporters at all, who have no professional qualifications."[70]

Sen. Charles Schumer (D-NY), a cosponsor of the bill, objected to Feinstein's definition, stating that bloggers and others don't necessarily receive salaries: "The world has changed. We're very careful in this bill to distinguish journalists from those who shouldn't be protected, WikiLeaks and all those, and we've ensured that. But there are people who write and do real journalism, in different ways than we're used to. They should not be excluded from this bill."[71]

Under Feinstein's definition, an unpaid blogger for the *Huffington Post* might not be eligible for the shield-law privilege, even though the site is one of the top ten news sites in the country, with more than twenty million readers per month. Bloggers and website operators like Nate Silver, Ana Marie Cox, and Bill Simmons wouldn't have been protected when they were blogging on their own, but once they were hired and started blogging for the *New York Times*, the *Guardian*, and ESPN, respectively, they would be protected. In light of massive newspaper layoffs, how would former reporters who start reporting and interviewing sources on their own unpaid websites and blogs be handled? What about people who self-publish nonfiction books that contain interviews from sources? What about student newspapers at universities and high schools that want to engage in investigative journalism? There is also an increase of citizen journalism, where average people are muckraking and reporting news. It's common sense to believe that many bloggers are trying to become modern-day Thomas Paines.

Earlier in 2014, a New Jersey Superior Court judge ruled that a blogger, Tina Renna, was entitled to protection under the state's shield law because she had a connection to news media, her purpose was to gather or disseminate news, and she obtained her information through professional news-gathering activities. Renna was a self-declared citizen watchdog who wrote stinging, partisan, and snarky critiques of Union County government on her website, the County Watchers.[72] Courts in California and New Hampshire have extended shield-law protection to new media outlets, including bloggers. In the 1987 case of *von Bulow v. von Bulow*, involving eligibility for a reporter's privilege, the Second US Circuit Court emphasized the intent or purpose to disseminate information to the public during newsgathering as opposed to the medium used to do so.[73]

Many people still have the stereotypical notion of the blogger as the pajamarati, typing and ranting away in their parents' second bedroom. While there is a lot of ranting and raving in the blogosphere, many bloggers and website operators do engage in real reporting. While many bloggers rely on the mainstream media for information, just as many, if not more, mainstream media reporters often rely on and cite blogs and websites for their information to aid their own reporting. Many bloggers and website operators are now granted press passes to cover political conventions and sporting events, among other things. The determination of whether a blogger or website operator is a journalist should be made on a case-by-case basis.

The definition of who is a journalist or reporter should be interpreted broadly in light of the changing media landscape. The writer's intent and activities should be considered, not whether the writer is paid or affiliated with a news organization. Shield laws should not just extend to paid reporters from mainstream media outlets, but should extend to unpaid bloggers engaged in reporting as well. At the end of 2015, no federal shield law had yet been passed. This is a shame, because many issues arise with whistleblowers at the federal level. And as the Internet continues to grow as one of the most popular sources of news and information, many reporters and journalists who had been working in print formats will flock to Internet news outlets or create their own sites.

I don't mean to imply that everyone who blogs or has a website should be considered a journalist. Most probably wouldn't fall within that category because they don't interview anyone, don't engage in news-gathering or reporting, and are just ranting or venting. My point is that the designation of journalist or reporter should be given a case-by-case determination.

Many of the websites and blogs mentioned in this chapter have a clear bias and point of view. But what about the mainstream media? Conservatives have argued for many years that the mainstream media is liberally biased and can't be trusted. Is this a valid assertion, or have these concerns been overblown?

CHAPTER 12

IS THE MAINSTREAM MEDIA LIBERALLY BIASED? DOES THE MEDIA TRY TO BE OBJECTIVE AND BALANCED?

The mainstream media is biased. This is the claim frequently asserted by conservatives, who allege that most of the major national newspapers, magazines, and television networks have a strong liberal slant. Conservatives cite surveys indicating that a strong majority of journalists consider themselves liberal. Countering this view, liberals contend that the media corporations are owned mostly by conservatives, and so there can't be a liberal bias as conservatives insist. For instance, liberals were critical of the media for not being aggressive enough in challenging the Bush administration's effort to justify the invasion of Iraq. Conservatives, for their part, would point to the fawning media coverage of Barack Obama when he ran for president the first time in 2008.

Whether a liberal media bias actually exists depends a great deal on who you ask. Research on this issue has had mixed results, with some studies finding a liberal media bias and others rejecting the claim. As noted by journalist and University of Scranton professor Dr. Matthew H. Reavy in *Media Ethics* magazine, several books and studies show that there is an inherent liberal bias in the media, that journalists are more liberal than average Americans, and that they donate more to Democrats and vote for them as well. Among the books Reavy cites that assert a liberal media bias are *Weapons of Mass Distortion: The Coming Meltdown of the Liberal Media*, by Brent L. Bozell, and *Bias: A CBS Insider Exposes How the Media Distort the News*, by Bernard Goldberg. However, Reavy writes that many other books and studies show that there is no significant ideological liberal bias in the media, including *Guardians of Power: The Myth of The Liberal Media*, by David Edwards, David Cromwell, and John Pilger, and the article "The Liberal Myth Revisited: An Examination of Factors Influencing Perceptions of Media Bias," by Tien-Tsung Lee, published in the *Journal of Broadcasting & Electronic Media*.[1]

Allegations that the media demonstrated a liberal slant started to gain ground around the time of the Vietnam War (1964–1975) and the Watergate scandal (1972–1974). During President Richard M. Nixon's administration, Vice President Spiro Agnew complained about the liberal media and labeled them "nattering nabobs of negativism."[2] In his 2002 column, political commentator and two-time Republican presidential candidate Pat Buchanan referred to the *New York Times* as "a battering ram of the Left."[3]

Chris Matthews of *Fortune* magazine (not MSNBC's Chris Matthews) wrote in a November 2015 column that studies have consistently shown that the mainstream media is liberal. He observed that economists Tim Groseclose and Jeff Milyo had written that "an almost overwhelming fraction of journalists are liberal." Matthews opined, "The extent of this bias, of course, depends on what your definitions of liberal and conservative. And the media has other, arguably more important, biases: towards controversy and producing content that is profitable. But it is safe to say that median journalist in America is to the left of the median American voter, and that this affects how the news is presented."[4] Based upon such claims, many conservatives believe that they are not adequately represented in newsrooms. Timothy P. Carney, a visiting fellow at the American Enterprise Institute (a conservative think tank) and a *Washington Examiner* columnist, wrote in the *New York Times* that liberal media bias is real due in part to the sparse numbers of conservative reporters, which leads to liberally slanted coverage that conservatives rightfully distrust: "This breeds the perception that the mainstream media is out to get conservatives, and this perception has truly harmful consequences."[5]

Conservatives point to many purported examples of liberal media bias, including coverage of global warming and the environment; gun control; critical coverage of Republican vice-presidential candidate Sarah Palin (2008) and Republican vice president Dan Quayle (1989–1993); the police shooting of Michael Brown in Ferguson, Missouri; the Confederate flag debate; the Affordable Care Act of 2010 (Obamacare); anti-Israel coverage; anti-Tea Party coverage; the Dan Rather/60 Minutes Bush memos incident (2004); favorable coverage of Senator Edward Kennedy after his car accident on a Chappaquiddick River bridge that killed a female staff member (1969); coverage of the Vietnam war; coverage of normalized relations with Cuba; illegal immigration; the question of whether the Guantanamo Bay detainees should be relocated; President Obama's 2008 campaign; the Robert Bork (1987) and Clarence Thomas (1991) Supreme Court confirmation hearings; Operation Fast and Furious (a botched government effort to track gun sales); Secretary of State Hillary Clinton's e-mail scandal; the IRS scandal (that targeted Tea Party organizations); the Duke University lacrosse rape allegation case; the Occupy Wall Street movement (2011) and income inequality; abortion; anti-Christian bias; and critical coverage of corporations. In 2008, Republicans felt that the media had a bigger crush on Obama than the Obama Girl viral video (2007).

In contrast, many liberals refer to the media as the "corporate media" and view it as favoring business interests. Among the major media corporations are Disney, Viacom, Time Warner, Clear Channel, Comcast, CBS, Gannett, Media Newsgroup, and McClatchy. Examples liberals point to of conservative media bias include the media's obsessive criticism of the government's and Hillary Clinton's handling of the Benghazi incident; the IRS scandal; Planned Parenthood and its performing of abortions; the Association of Community Organizations for Reform Now (ACORN) and accusations of voter fraud; lax immigration policies; Obamacare; the Iran nuclear deal; as well as negative coverage of Bill and Hillary Clinton and President Obama; favorable coverage of Wall Street and corporations; coverage of the Clinton impeachment; stereotyping of minorities; the anti-Obama birthers, coverage of the Iraq war and the lead up to it; and opposition to raising the minimum wage.

In a phone interview, James B. Steele, Pulitzer Prize–winning journalist and author, disagreed with the view that the media is blatantly liberal, saying,

The mainstream media isn't as liberal as conservatives make it out to be. Sometimes they bend so far backwards to give both sides that the reader or viewer doesn't know what to believe. Sure, you can find some bias in almost every television network, magazine, or newspaper, where you can point to a liberal or conservative viewpoint. I think that most reporters try to do a reasonable job and to be fair and accurate. When they fail is where the facts are clear, and they try to balance the issue equally, but only one view is accurate. The best examples of the media not being as liberal as conservatives believe is the *New York Times*'s coverage of WMD [weapons of mass destruction] supposedly in Iraq, which was invented by a conservative Republican administration. The *Times* was also the principal investigator of the Whitewater [real estate] controversy in the Clinton administration, and we know how that all worked out. Now, most journalists who I know tend to be sympathetic to underdogs, the abused, those with no voice, and those with no power to express themselves and push back. In that sense, some might consider that to be liberal.[6]

A 2011 Media Matters study showed that 60 percent of America's daily newspapers printed more conservative syndicated columnists than liberal syndicated columnists, while only 20 percent of daily papers printed more liberal syndicated columnists. Nationally syndicated liberal columnists reached 125 million people in circulation, while conservative columnists reached 152 million.[7] In debunking Republican presidential candidates' claims that the media was liberally biased, Conor Lynch of *Salon* pointed to the companies that own the media:

Consider this: In 1983, 90 percent of American media was owned by 50 companies, and by 2011, that number had fallen to six companies: CBS, Time Warner, Viacom, News Corp, Disney and GE, which subsequently sold its media holding, NBC Universal, to cable giant Comcast (which would, in turn, later try to merge with Time Warner Cable, although that deal eventually fell apart). Thus, the media at large has one crucial goal: to make a profit. Not to serve the public, but to make money by selling advertisement spots to other corporations, whether they are selling new cars or tech products or pointless new drugs. All of this profit-making hardly sounds like the socialist media that Republicans would have everyone believe.[8]

In an e-mail interview, Rob Kall, founder and operator of *OpEdNews*, said, "All the people I know on the left believe the mainstream media is biased towards corporate interests."[9]

According to Ron Dzwonkowski of the *Detroit Free Press*, according to the 4th Estate project (an offshoot of news media analysis company Global News Intelligence) there was no liberal media bias during the 2012 presidential election. The 4th Estate project was an apolitical effort to test conventional wisdom about news coverage. The project monitored news reports from thirty-five publications, thirteen television broadcasts, and National Public Radio. Dzwonkowski said, "From May 1 to July 15, Republicans were quoted in news reports 44% more often than Democrats, and negative coverage of President Barack Obama was 17% higher than such coverage for Republican presidential candidate Mitt Romney." Michael Howe, 4th Estate's chief technology officer, told Dzwonkowski, "Media bias is certainly the perception, but it's based on a lot of anecdotal evidence and people talking about 'What I think. . .' We hope to change the nature of the debate."[10]

As we can see, whether the mainstream media is liberal, conservative, or centrist depends on who is being asked. Each side can point to studies and opinions that support its claims. My own take is that the conservative mantra of the liberal bias of the mainstream media is overblown and used as a way to rally its base. I think that, although more journalists identify themselves as liberal rather than conservative, most of them identify themselves as moderate. Many might bend over backward to make sure that they give the conservative viewpoint as a balance due to the concern that they will be criticized or dismissed as a biased liberal. I also think that the companies that own mainstream media outlets strive to be as neutral, balanced, and objective as possible, so as to not alienate viewers and diminish their ratings. They also see balance, objectivity, and neutrality as a means to demonstrate that they are honest brokers of the news and should be considered trusted news sources. If there is any bias, there might be a slight, subtle bias in the selection of which news stories to cover. Compare Fox News, conservative talk radio, and MSNBC to CBS, ABC, and NBC to assess blatant versus subtle bias. Even if we assume that the mainstream media is liberally biased, Fox News and talk radio go overboard the other way.

A Pew Research survey of 585 American reporters in 2008, as cited in stateofthemedia.org, reported that 53 percent of national journalists identified themselves as moderate, 32 percent described themselves as liberal, and 8 percent described themselves as conservatives. Although 585 persons might not be a large enough survey to adequately canvass the entire body of reporters, it does indicate that many journalists do consider themselves to be independent, moderate, and middle of the road. This rebuts the Republican conservatives blanket assertion that all of the mainstream media is liberally biased and shows that they are ignoring the bulk of reporters who are moderate. But it also indicates that more reporters do consider themselves to be liberal as opposed to conservative.[11]

Cass R. Sunstein, a Harvard University professor, wrote on the financial website *Bloomberg View* that the media is not liberally biased against Republicans. He cited a 2010 study by Matthew Gentzkow and Jesse Shapiro of the University of Chicago, which didn't find much evidence of liberal bias. Regarding the study, Sunstein said, "Its central conclusion is that readers have a strong preference for like-minded news—and that newspapers tend to show a slant in a direction that is consistent with the preferences of their readers."[12]

Mark Bowden, journalist and bestselling author, said in an e-mail interview that even if the media is liberal that might actually be a good thing:

I believe there is something inherently liberal in reporting new information and in thinking differently about what is known. The act of reporting and thinking and commenting concerns *change.* Conservatism is about upholding tradition and preserving the existing social structure. Good reporters tell us things we did not know, and in my experience, when I learn something new, it more often changes what I think than it reaffirms what I already believe—although not always. So I think conservatives are correct when they identify journalists as Liberal. Journalists are most often agents of change.[13]

Likewise, the American Press Institute has argued that reporters having a bias can be a good thing: "One can even argue that draining a story of all bias can drain it of its humanity, its lifeblood. . . . A bias, moreover, can be the foundation for investigative journalism. It may prompt the news organization to right a wrong and take up an unpopular cause. Thus, the job of journalists is *not* to stamp out bias. Rather, the journalist should learn how to manage it."[14]

Some believe that media bias is not ideological, but rather about economics. Kyle Whitmire, state political commentator for the Alabama Media Group, writes, "There is media bias, but it's not the liberal or conservative kind most folks look for. It's the need for conflict and the lust for the freak show. It favors the weird, the outlandish and the out of place—all those things that make [Donald] Trump Trump. The reason he's a front-runner [in the Republican race for that party's presidential nomination] is because those cameras point at him."[15]

However, the profession of journalism does have its inherent rules and safeguards that encourage truthful and fair reporting, as opposed to advocacy. In 1996, the Society of Professional Journalists eliminated the word "objectivity" from its code of ethics, but it stated that journalists should distinguish between advocacy and reporting and should seek the truth and report it. The *Washington Post* also put "fairness" in place of "objectivity" in its code.[16] Most newspapers have a philosophy that separates opinion articles from the rest of the newspaper. Opinion articles are usually limited to the editorial page, the op-ed page, movie reviews, book reviews, music reviews, and restaurant reviews. As we have seen, the editorial boards of newspapers meet separately from the rest of the newspaper and should therefore have no input into what is reported on its pages. Reporters are generally discouraged from giving—and disinclined to give—their own personal opinions when reporting on stories.

Does ideology and bias trump the pursuit of fairness, balance, objectivity, and truth? Is it acceptable for a journalist to be an activist in support of a cause? Likewise, it is permissible for a partisan activist to act like a journalist in reporting a story? Can news reporting be truly objective? Matt Taibbi of *Rolling Stone* says that it can't, no matter whether the bias is hidden, subtle, or out in the open, because every report advances someone's point of view:

The advocacy can be hidden, as it is in the monotone narration of a news anchor for a big network like CBS or NBC (where the biases of advertisers and corporate backers like GE are disguised in a thousand subtle ways), or it can be out in the open, as it proudly is with [Glenn] Greenwald [a journalist, columnist, and author], or graspingly with [Andrew Ross] Sorkin [a *New York Times* financial columnist and co-anchor of CNBC's *Squawk Box*], or institutionally with a company like Fox. . . . "Objectivity" is a fairy tale invented purely for the consumption of the credulous public, sort of like the Santa Claus myth. Obviously, journalists can strive to be balanced and objective, but that's all it is, striving.[17]

According to Roy Peter Clark of Poynter, finding bias in reporting is not unusual for people on both sides of the political spectrum, even when it wasn't intended or the evidence of bias was scarce: "This bias toward bias—seeing the other as the enemy and their language as lies— becomes magnified in times of war, or when political powers are polarized and gridlocked, as they are now. In such an environment, 'neutrality' or 'non-partisanship' becomes seen by some as either obsolete or vicious. This raises the question of whether a reporter can be—to use a word that has fallen out of fashion—'disinterested,' that is, not a mouthpiece for a special interest?"[18]

The concept of objectivity in journalism is a tricky one. It is true that there is no such thing as pure objectivity, since reporters bring their own beliefs and conscious or unconscious biases to each story. The Society of Professional Journalists' Code of Ethics no longer lists objectivity as a core value. Much more emphasis is now being put on the concepts of balance and transparency.[19] Transparency is very important and is a good thing, but I don't think it is enough to satisfy a reader who wants to find out accurate information. Being transparent actually alerts readers that the information they are viewing or reading might be slanted, biased, or unbalanced, meaning that they're clearly taking one side or not giving both sides' positions. Just because readers or viewers know what perspective the media outlet is coming from, though, doesn't mean that they are getting a fair, balanced, objective, or impartial presentation of the news. I believe that even though pure and perfect objectivity cannot be accomplished, reporters should strive to be objective. The term "impartial" might be a good choice instead of "objective." Impartiality indicates that the reporter is not taking sides, not being prejudiced against a point of view, and being fair and balanced in presenting the various sides' positions.

Most news wire services, such as the Associated Press and Reuters, try to emphasize straightforward, nonpartisan, and balanced reporting that gets picked up and used by media outlets around the world. There are straightforward news stations, such as KYW1060 AM in Philadelphia, which report the news without a bias. Generally, they go out and observe, describe what takes place, corroborate facts with multiple reliable and official sources, and give varied viewpoints on the issue. Some view this approach as dry and dull, but it is still the traditional news formula. Traditionally, most news outlets have discouraged reporters from stating an opinion or perspective. Given the reputation (deserved or otherwise) of the media as being too liberal, some news outlets will go out of their way to try to avoid reportage and viewpoints that confirm this view. The media's coverage of the lead up to the Iraq invasion in 2003 was an example, with the media failing to aggressively question the government's justifications for the invasion.[20]

There is no such thing as generic bias; instead, different levels of bias exist. The liberal bias of a newspaper like the *New York Times* is less obvious and more subtle than the blatant liberal bias of most of MSNBC's news shows. Similarly, the conservative bias of the *Wall Street Journal* is less obvious and more subtle than the blatant conservative bias of Fox News. In many cases, the bias comes across much more on the editorial pages, as opposed to in the other parts of the newspaper.

Recent allegations of liberal media bias came to a head during one of the Republican presidential primary debates in 2015, broadcast by the business cable channel CNBC. Several candidates angrily complained about the alleged mean-spirited tone and the content of the biased, inaccurate, and offensive questions they were asked.[21] A few days later, the Republican National Committee announced that it was suspending its partnership with NBC News and Spanish-language network Telemundo for a future debate in February 2016. Republican candidates Donald Trump, Marco Rubio,

Chris Christie, and Ted Cruz were particularly critical. During the debate, Cruz said that "The questions asked in this debate illustrate why the American people don't trust the media." And Rubio quipped that Hillary Clinton was exposed as a liar during the Benghazi hearings, but that she was being helped by her own Super PAC: the media. At first, the Republican candidates requested new rules for future debates and threatened boycotts, but eventually they dropped their demands. Cruz later called for a GOP debate hosted by Rush Limbaugh, Sean Hannity, and Mark Levin, all of whom are conservative media stars.[22]

Pollster Frank Luntz of Luntz Global tweeted that Cruz's focus group rating hit a record score of 98 after he made his debate criticism of the liberal media, the highest ever for a Republican focus group.[23] During the debate, the Republican audience booed many of the moderators' tough questions. Perhaps surprisingly, popular conservative commentator and author Ann Coulter defended CNBC, tweeting, "GOP's media bashing is getting boring. CNBC Qs not measurably different from CNN or FNC."[24] Blaming debate moderators from every network has proven to be successful for conservatives. It worked for Donald Trump in his criticism of Fox News's Megyn Kelly and for Newt Gingrich, who in 2012 criticized CNN debate moderator John King's question about open marriage, which Gingrich's ex-wife had said he had sought.[25] Trump even went as far to boycott the last debate before the 2016 Iowa caucus due to the fact that he thought that Kelly wouldn't treat him fairly during the debate.[26] In general, the Republican approach of blaming the liberal media and liberal moderators has been an effective way to dodge probing, difficult questions. It also plays well with the conservative base, who strongly believes that the mainstream media has a liberal agenda.

It's important for media outlets to fact-check candidates' debate statements, both during the debate and after the event. In the 2016 Republican Presidential Primary race, a controversy arose about alleged media bias regarding then Republican front runner Dr. Ben Carson. The media discovered inconsistencies in Carson's published memoir regarding many of his claims regarding incidents in his past about how he had overcome a troubled and rage-filled childhood to find salvation in God, which turned his life around. He had allegedly tried to kill a friend and to hit his mother, and had allegedly been offered a scholarship to West Point, claims that turned out not to be true.

Carson attacked the media, claiming it was lying and trying to distract from what was important through gotcha questions. In a press conference, Carson said, "People come up to me and say 'Don't let the media get you down.' They understand this is a witch hunt." The media was desperate to find scandals, he said, and some week they would find his kindergarten teacher to testify that he had peed in his pants. "We'd be Cuba if there were no Fox News," he said at another time.[27]

Carson's claims played well with the Republican base. He wrote to donors asking for contributions after the controversy broke. His followers love the fact that he fought back against the media. Only a week later, Carson claimed to have raised over $3.5 million, and ironically he thanked the media for it.[28]

Conservatives tend to believe that the mainstream media has a double standard, purposely attacking conservative Republicans, trying to tarnish their reputations and destroy them, while treating liberal Democrats with kid gloves. Many say that it's perfectly acceptable to ask Republicans legitimate tough questions but that the media should ask tough questions to liberal candidates as well. They claim that Fox News, Breitbart, and TheBlaze exist because they cover stories that the mainstream media ignores. They also believe that the mainstream media is geared toward elite liberals and that these media don't understand the average person in middle America.

In contrast, as former Republican presidential nominee Mitt Romney said, "Politics ain't bean bag." President Obama joked that if Republicans couldn't handle CNBC moderators, how would they be able to handle Russia and China? Candidates should be questioned and confronted about lies, inconsistencies, and policy issues. This is especially the case when an individual is the front runner in the polls. Republicans often use the media-bias shield to try to avoid answering legitimate and challenging policy questions. Political candidates must be subjected to rigid scrutiny, and their past troubles need to be exposed, especially in a party primary race, so that similar issues don't arise for the first time in a general election campaign.

Ben Carson focused much of his campaign on his character and over-coming a tough childhood to become a religious person and successful medical professional. If he fabricated or embellished this information, voters should know about it. In Carson's case, this was the first time that he had run for political office, so he hadn't been scrutinized in the past like presidential candidates who have previously held political office. Media outlets like CNN tried to independently confirm Carson's specific claims about his childhood but could not.[29] Throughout the campaign, Carson had raised eyebrows with a number of his comments—his belief that the pyramids had been built by the biblical patriarch Joseph to store grain, his advice that those threatened by a potential mass shooter should rush the shooter, his suggestion that the Holocaust might not have happened if Germany hadn't taken away people's guns, his opinion that Muslims should not be allowed to run for president, and his claim that Obamacare was the worst thing since slavery.[30]

Republican candidate and New Jersey governor Chris Christie talked to Howard Kurtz of Fox News about his advice to his fellow Republican candidates dealing with media criticism: "This is what it's like to run for president of the United States, and it's time to buck up and deal with it." He also indicated that the *New York Times* criticism of him over Bridgegate and other matters was like a badge of honor because he does not "carry their liberal banner."[31]

Despite complaints from Carson and other conservatives, journalists and debate moderators have asked tough questions of Democratic candi-dates as well. Hillary Clinton was asked about the Benghazi attack, her use of a private e-mail account for official e-mails, her close relationship with Wall Street, whether she had underestimated the Russians when she was secretary of state, her views on the death penalty, whether she had flip-flopped on various issues, and why she was viewed by many in national polls as not trustworthy. CNN's Anderson Cooper bluntly asked Clinton, "Will you say anything to get elected?" MSNBC's Chuck Todd asked her if she would be willing to release the transcripts of all of her paid speeches, such as the ones to Goldman Sachs.

During a CNN debate, Vermont senator Bernie Sanders, running against

Clinton for the Democratic nomination, was asked to explain his position as a democratic socialist as well as his position on gun control. Debate moderator Anderson Cooper asked Sanders, "How can any socialist win a general election in the United States?" Cooper then asked former Maryland governor and Democratic candidate Martin O'Malley why Americans should trust him to run the country when they could see the chaos that took place in Baltimore over the death of a black man in police custody, an unrest that O'Malley allegedly sowed the seeds for when he was mayor there.

Michael Dukakis's 1988 Democratic campaign unraveled after his rambling, bland answer to CNN moderator Bernard Shaw's hypothetical question about whether someone who had raped and killed his wife should receive the death penalty. In 1992, Democratic candidate Bill Clinton and his wife, Hillary, were grilled by CBS's Steve Kroft of *60 Minutes* in an interview that focused on Bill Clinton's alleged marital infidelities with Gennifer Flowers when he was governor of Arkansas. In 1960, the media raised questions about John F. Kennedy's religious beliefs and how they might impact his decision-making if he became president. In 2004, then Democratic presidential nominee John Kerry was asked about his flip-flopping on policy positions.

In an April 2008 Democratic primary debate, the moderators asked Obama about his relationship with former Weather Underground radical Bill Ayres. Obama was also questioned about why he didn't wear an American flag pin, why he made a statement that small-town Americans bitterly cling to guns and religion, and about the controversial statements made in sermons by the Obamas' pastor, Rev. Jeremiah Wright. And for several years, the media continued to ask him about his birth certificate and whether he was actually an American citizen eligible to be president.

Should debate moderators give their opinions and should media pundits opine as to which candidate came out on top in various debates? Republicans criticized CNN's Candy Crowley for interrupting Mitt Romney to correct him as to whether President Obama had referred to the Benghazi attack as an act of terror. Transcripts of the president's Rose Garden speech showed that Crowley was partially correct; Obama had said, "No acts of terror will ever shake the resolve of this great nation."[32] Personally, I don't think that it is the moderator's job to give their opinion or dispute facts during the debate. They should wait until afterward to do so. It's fine to ask tough questions and ask about inconsistencies in positions, but the moderator shouldn't be saying who is right and who is wrong as the debate is taking place. The moderators shouldn't make the debate about themselves.

After a debate, media pundits will give instant analysis about which candidates were the biggest winners and losers. Critics say that the media is often out of touch with the public in this analysis. As noted by the *New Yorker*, after the first Democratic Primary debate in 2015, most media outlets and pundits praised Hillary Clinton and declared her the clear winner; however, most focus groups and polling of Democratic voters showed that Sanders had won.[33]

Some skeptics believe that Republicans' and conservatives' frequent claims of media bias is done to play to their base and to fund raise. Just as coaches in basketball and other sports work the referees and complain about calls in order to get favorable calls later on, Republicans play the media-bias card to try to get more favorable coverage in the future.

Some people argue that the mainstream media should have a stronger voice, take sides, and be more entertaining, like the cable news shows. However, it's important that the mainstream media not become like MSNBC or Fox News. The broad base of the media shouldn't be part of any partisan bickering. It should strive to act as an impartial, neutral, objective, and balanced arbiter focused on factual reporting and let the readers, listeners, and viewers reach their own conclusions.

It can be argued that there has been so much criticism of the mainstream media for being liberally biased that these media sometimes bend over backward to show that their reporting is not skewed in any way. An analogy might be that of a father who coaches his child's Little League team and who is much tougher on his own child just to show the other parents that he isn't guilty of favoritism.

As noted by Paul Farhi of the *Washington Post*, "When all is said and done, left-leaning reporting is balanced by reporting more favorable to conservatives."[34] David D'Alessio, a communications sciences professor and author, told Farhi that the net effect was zero. D'Alessio told Farhi that news reporting tends to point toward the middle, "because that's where the people are, and that's where the [advertising] money is. . . . There's nuance there, but when you add it all and subtract it down, you end up with nothing."[35]

This supports what I said earlier about how media companies want to be as centrist as possible because doing so leads to more viewers and higher advertising revenue since they are alienating fewer people in this way. Therefore, the net effect of any perceived bias is minimal.

Eric Alterman, a journalist, college professor, and author, told Farhi, "Reporters have heard the criticism from the right so often that they lean over backwards to be fair to them."[36]

In addressing why the mainstream media is perceived as biased, Farhi mentions factors such as the changing media landscape—which now has more partisan media outlets, more watchdog groups, satirical television programs, and blogs that seek to expose bias; people perceiving slanted media outlets as news organizations; an increased access to news that lets the audience second guess the source; and people who think their own news sources are objective and fair, while the other side's media are spreading lies.[37]

The media has been called the Fourth Estate (following the legislative, executive, and judicial branches of government). It has also been described as serving a role as a watchdog on government and important institutions, acting as the eyes and ears of the public. However, both sides of the political spectrum often charge the mainstream media with being lapdogs manipulated by the federal and state governments.

There is often a sharp divide between the perceptions of mainstream traditional media outlets and those of new journalism outlets such as YouTube, websites, bloggers, alternative weeklies, and entrepreneurial journalism. Many in the mainstream media, especially older members, strongly believe that traditional media such as newspapers are essential and indispensable and that other forms of media, including blogs, could not survive without relying on mainstream media reports. They claim that mainstream media outlets are the ones going to city council and school board meetings and focusing on community reporting with experienced beat reporters. They believe that traditional media is more reliable, credible, and trustworthy.[38]

In contrast, supporters of new media claim that newspapers are dying—going bankrupt, buying out or laying off veteran reporters and replacing them with young and inexperienced reporters right out of college. There is no doubt that many, if not most, newspapers in America are struggling: some, such as the *Detroit News*, the *Detroit Free Press*, *The Oregonian*, the *Harrisburg Patriot News*, the *Syracuse Post Standard*, the *New Orleans Times-Picayune*, and the *Birmingham News* in Alabama, are resorting to reducing home delivery or publishing print versions of the newspaper only three days a week in order to cut costs.[39] The supporters of new media contend that their media has a stronger, more passionate voice that tends to be less restrained or encumbered. They probably don't see how this passion and lack of restraint could result in less truthful and balanced reporting; they just want to receive information in a more interesting manner.

Disclosures of mistakes and scandals are partially to blame for the common mistrust of the media by the average person. Surveys frequently indicate that trust in journalists has reached the low level of trial lawyers, politicians, and used car salesmen. For instance, as noted by Lymari Morales on the Gallup website, a Gallup poll conducted in 2012 showed that 60 percent of Americans had little or no trust in the media to report the news fully, accurately, and fairly.[40] Julie Moos of Poynter writes that a 2011 Pew poll revealed that 75 percent of Americans believe that journalists don't get the facts straight, and 72 percent said that journalists try to cover up their mistakes.[41] There have been many incidents of plagiarism, fabrication, and embellishment by reporters, which have caused people to question their trust in the media.

In one infamous example, Janet Cooke won a Pulitzer Prize in 1981 as a *Washington Post* reporter for her compelling article about an eight-year-old heroin addict. The problem is that she made it all up. Eventually her ruse was exposed and she resigned; the *Washington Post* relinquished the Pulitzer for her story.[42] In 2003, the *New York Times* announced that one of its reporters, Jayson Blair, had frequently fabricated information in his articles and plagiarized from other writers. Blair resigned from the paper.[43] One of the positives of the Jayson Blair scandal was that it caused newsrooms to take plagiarism, fabrication, and accuracy much more seriously in terms of ethics codes and ethics training. Stephen Glass, a staff writer for the *New Republic*, was exposed as a serial fabricator in 1998. His story was made into a movie titled *Shattered Glass*.[44]

Jack Kelley, a star reporter for *USA Today* for two decades, had been a Pulitzer Prize finalist in 2002. Kelley resigned from the paper when it was determined that he had made up twenty stories and plagiarized over one hundred quotes or passages from other publications, according to the *Washington Post*.[45] Columnist Mike Barnicle resigned from the *Boston Globe* in 1998 over allegations of plagiarism and fabrication, according to CNN.[46] NBC's Brian Williams was suspended and lost his nightly news anchor position due to his numerous claims that his helicopter had been attacked while he was reporting in Iraq.[47]

Roger Yu of *USA Today* reported that, according to "State of the First Amendment 2015," a study by the Washington, DC–based Newseum Institute's First Amendment Center, only 24 percent of Americans believe that the media tries to report without a bias, which is the lowest percentage in the eleven-year history of the poll. The study said that the respondents' feelings may have been negatively influenced by recent controversies involving NBC's Brian Williams, who was suspended and demoted for lying, and George Stephanopoulos of ABC, who was criticized for his contribution to the Clinton Foundation.[48] Citing the study, Yu said, "Older audiences are more likely to buy into the media's mantle of objectivity, with 26% of those 50 or older agreeing with the claim. Only 7% of 18–29 year olds agree. Democrats are much more likely to believe (36%) that the news media try to report without bias as opposed to Republicans (19%)."[49]

Contrary to what some might believe, it is possible for allegedly liberal debate moderators and television hosts to put aside their biases and act professionally. Reporters and hosts like Jake Tapper (CNN) and the late Tim Russert (NBC) have proven that you can interview people fairly. John Hawkins, a conservative columnist for Townhall.com, acknowledged Russert and Tapper as reporters who made an effort to be impartial.[50] Some Republicans have been hired from the political world, including Diane Sawyer (ABC) and Michael Smerconish (CNN), to work as news hosts and reporters and have succeeded admirably at it. Chuck Todd of NBC worked for Democratic senator Tom Harkin's 1992 presidential campaign.[51]

Ways do exist to prevent bias. One way is for news and media outlets to adhere to a strict codes of ethics, as we will discuss in chapter 14. Hiring minorities and encouraging gender, racial, and cultural diversity in their employees is also a way to ease bias. Some believe that media outlets should make an effort to have diversity in ideology as well, by hiring more reporters and news managers from conservative, liberal, libertarian, and other ideological stripes. Having a mixture of staff from rural as well as urban settings may also prove useful. The Society of Professional Journalists noted that nonmedia companies have successfully incorporated diversity into their management framework: "They value diversity as a means to support creative exchange, stimulate ideas, and enhance competitiveness."[52] I believe that having a diverse newsroom can improve balance and objectivity because the reporters and editors would be coming from different backgrounds and experiences and can learn from each other. For instance, it would be valuable to be able to consult minorities on the staff to get their opinion as to whether a certain article or editorial cartoon could be seen as being culturally insensitive to that particular minority group.

Where does CNN fall in the spectrum of advocacy journalism? Probably somewhere in the middle. At least its reporters strive to be noncommittal and balanced. According to Harvard University's Nieman Journalism Lab, which investigates future models of quality journalism, while other cable news networks favor opinion and advocacy journalism, "CNN has emphasized its non-ideological approach, billing itself as 'the only credible, nonpartisan voice left.' That approach has been criticized by some for creating a forced, false balance between viewpoints or as lacking an identity. Others have praised CNN's fact-based philosophy."[53] There are times when the network does get criticized for mistakes or questionable news judgment. Bill Carter of the *New York Times* described how CNN and other media outlets had erroneously reported that a suspect in the 2013 Boston Marathon bombing had been arrested.[54] Many people also criticized and even mocked CNN for its 24/7 coverage of the missing Malaysian Airlines plane over several weeks in 2014.[55] Comedian Bill Maher posted on Twitter, "Ted Turner wishes he was dead so he cld roll over in his grave." Despite the criticism, CNN's ratings increased during those weeks.[56]

Many people turn to CNN because they consider it an honest broker of news for the most part. The network typically features balanced panels, and its program hosts aren't as bombastic or opinionated as those found on Fox News or MSNBC. A March 2015 poll of media buyers and planners conducted by *Media Life* magazine showed CNN to be the most reliable of the three major cable news networks, slightly edging out Fox News.[57] I've noticed that CNN is usually the network of choice for doctors' offices, fitness centers, and other public areas, since it's the least objectionable news outlet. Personally, it's the television media outlet that I turn to if I want a balanced analysis of an issue or controversy.

In 1979, the Cable-Satellite Public Affairs Network (C-SPAN) was started by the cable industry as a public service, and it strives for objectivity and balance. It provides separate phone numbers for liberals, independents, and conservatives to call to comment during its daily call-in shows. Its critics describe it as bland and boring because it features programming such as congressional hearings and speeches. Nevertheless, it provides a public service for political junkies and concerned citizens who want thorough, detailed, unfiltered, and insightful coverage of Congress and other political functions.

The Public Broadcasting Service (PBS) and National Public Radio (NPR) are also important organizations in the media landscape. NPR features popular news shows like *Morning Edition* and *All Things Considered*. PBS features shows like the *PBS NewsHour*, *Washington Week*, and *Frontline*. Conservatives and libertarians find fault with these networks because they see those networks as liberal and they have to pay to support them with their tax dollars. Many have urged the end of government funding of public broadcasting. Republican Presidential Candidate Mitt Romney ruffled some feathers during a 2012 debate when he said that even though he loved Sesame Street's Big Bird, he didn't want to spend public money on public broadcasting. Despite the Republican assertions of liberal bias, NPR and PBS tend to fare well in terms of public trust. David Carr of the *New York Times* wrote, "In terms of assignments and sensibility, NPR has always been more blue than red, but it's not as if it has an overt political agenda."[58] According to a Pew Research Study in 2014, NPR and PBS had some of the highest ratings for news sources with respect to the ratio of trust versus distrust. Of the respondents, 38 percent said they trusted PBS and 12 percent distrusted it, while 29 percent trusted NPR and 9 percent distrusted it.[59]

Should reporters just report facts or should they also state opinions? Journalist and author Mark Bowden wrote that "It depends on the venue. Smart media (newspapers, networks, webpages, blogs, etc.) differentiate between opinion and pure reporting. It is hard to be persuasive when your audience cannot trust your reporting."[60] And Bill Reed of the *Philadelphia Inquirer* offered this observation:

> Every reporter brings personal experiences and perspectives to the job, which often help in the fact gathering and writing, but it is his or her responsibility to maintain objectivity and fairness. Relevant reporting goes beyond the facts not by including the reporter's opinion or bias, but by including context, such as the history or background of the event or issue, and divergent viewpoints or explanations by sources *with expertise*. Newspapers, magazines, radio and TV stations, and websites can round out their coverage with columnists' viewpoints, commentaries, analyses, and editorials, so readers can make informed decisions. So, there are many layers of coverage, but they are all built on a foundation of straightforward, fact-based, objective news, feature, and sports stories.[61]

Is it acceptable for reporters to give editorial perspective or does that count as presenting a biased view? According to Mark Bowden, "Again, it depends. If I am an independent journalist writing a long piece for *The Atlantic*, then I might decide to do either, depending on my goals for the piece. If I am a newspaper editor, I would try to adhere to the line between fact and opinion."[62] But, in the view of James B. Steele, "Reporters need to do more than just report. They need to connect the dots so that the reader can know the meaning of the facts. If the reporter collects information and it leads to a conclusion, you should make it. But if your reporting is driven by an agenda, that's improper. You go with what the facts show you. You generally don't push an agenda unless you have a series of articles and at the end you explain how to correct the problem. You want to shine a light on what people don't know and explain the problem."[63]

Is there a future for traditional, straightforward media? Bowden believes there is: "I believe journalistic institutions (if that's what you mean by 'Traditional Journalism') will survive and prosper in a great variety of forms. In a world awash in unreliable information, the need for reliable, independent, trustworthy reporting and opinion becomes ever more important. Good journalism is always interesting, by definition. We are always interested to learn something new, and to be offered new ways of thinking about what we already know."[64]

Many see a need for change in traditional media. Catherine R. Squires, a professor of communications studies at the University of Minnesota, wrote in the *New York Times* that there are valid reasons why many young African Americans distrust mainstream news media. She gave examples of double standards, such as the famous Hurricane Katrina photo of a black male carrying bags of food being captioned as "looting," while a white couple photographed in a similar situation was described as searching for food. Squires also observed that Amber Alerts for white children get more media attention than minority children's deaths. "They see journalists asking, with a straight face, if #BlackLivesMatter is a hate group. Given these patterns and incidents, why would young black people want to trust the mainstream news media with stories about their lives?"[65]

Chris Hayes of MSNBC told Trevor Noah, the new host of the *Daily Show*, that every reporter has certain biases, but that it isn't partisan: "I think the mainstream media is biased but not in any partisan way. We have bias towards spectacle. We have a bias towards someone just blew something up. . . . One hundred thousand people marched for something somewhere else."[66]

Thus, Hayes implies, and as I note in the next chapter, the media has a bias toward covering certain stories, such as crime, tragedies, and controversies, whether these stories involve liberals or conservatives.

Irrespective of the news outlet, there are some commentators and pundits who are considered to be independent and centrist, including David Gergen, Michael Smerconish, Kathleen Parker, David Brooks, and Harold Ford Jr. Perhaps one of the reasons why there are so few prominent centrist commentators is that the media, especially the advocacy media outlets, likes to present conflict between a liberal expert and a conservative expert.

Another issue related to bias is the extent that media outlets fact-check and act as watchdogs of government and politicians. After Donald Trump faced media scrutiny for asserting that Muslims in New Jersey had celebrated openly during the 9/11 Twin Tower attack, Matt Taibbi wrote in *Rolling Stone* that politicians can say almost anything and get away with it because America is now "too dumb for TV news":

> Along with vindication, apology and suffering, there now exists a fourth way forward for the politician spewing whoppers: Blame the backlash on media bias and walk away a hero. . . . We in the media have spent decades turning the news into a consumer business that's basically indistinguishable from selling cheeseburgers or video games. You want bigger margins, you just cram the product full of more fat and sugar and violence and wait for your obese, over-stimulated customer to come waddling forth. The old Edward R. Murrow, eat-your-broccoli version was banished long ago. . . . Right-wing and liberal media in this country are really just two different strategies of the same kind of nihilistic lizard-brain sensationalism. The ideal CNN story is a baby down a well, while the ideal Fox story is probably a baby thrown down a well by a Muslim terrorist or an ACORN activist.[67]

New York University journalism professor Jay Rosen wrote on his website *PressThink* that it's difficult for Washington, DC, reporters to be effective watchdogs on the government because they need to keep their insider status with access to government sources. In criticizing the White House Correspondents' Dinner, Rosen opined that access journalism doesn't work. He noted that the Washington press corps was too close to the Bush administration during the lead up to the Iraq war, and it failed to sufficiently investigate the faulty case for war: "After a maximal failure like 2002–04 there needed to be a critical reckoning with the whole idea of 'access to inside sources as a reliable route to scoops.' You can't maintain that idea *and* think of yourself as a watchdog, an adversarial force."[68]

I think that part of the problem is that reporters might not want to alienate their sources. It is human nature for reporters to want to give favorable coverage to people who treat them well and to criticize people who don't. This could apply to any beat, ranging from politics to sports, but political candidates and government officials who are accessible and media friendly might be treated more favorably.

In arguing that the mainstream media's ability to punish politicians for lying has been diminished in two ways, *Vox*'s David Roberts wrote:

> First is the unceasing attack on "liberal media bias," which has left journalists terrified of passing judgment on any matter of controversy. And second is the development of a parallel intellectual infrastructure, a network of partisan think tanks, advocacy organizations, and media outlets that provide a kind of full-spectrum alternative to the mainstream. . . . The establishment media has largely proven feckless in the face of this assault, clinging to the view-from-nowhere model even as an unabashed arm of the GOP became the highest-rated "news network." Now there are so many outlets, so many voices, that the old guard has very little control over the narrative. They have less and less power to penalize a politician for lying even if they want to; there's always another outlet with a more congenial perspective.[69]

I believe that the conservative Republican mantra of liberal media bias is overblown and overplayed. While I agree that sometimes the mainstream media might show a subtle bias in selecting and portraying stories, generally they give a fairly balanced portrayal of news coverage. Despite the allegation that the mainstream media is liberally biased, most of them do strive to be primarily fair and balanced. Obviously, there are times when they fall short of this ideal goal, since there is no such thing as perfect objectivity. The clear cases of media bias are instead reflected in cable news networks like MSNBC and Fox News, as well as talk radio and politically biased websites.

We have been considering whether the media is liberally biased, but how is bias displayed by a media outlet? How do media outlets select which stories to report on? There are many factors considered in deciding which stories to report. It's not an exact and precise formula, but there are certain elements that the media generally considers when making this decision.

CHAPTER 13

WHAT'S NEWS?
WHAT ARE THE FACTORS USED BY THE MEDIA IN DECIDING WHAT TO REPORT? HOW IS BIAS DISPLAYED IN THE SELECTION PROCESS?

So what is news? That's what reporters have to decide. Every day, the news editors will sit around a table and discuss what stories they will cover that day. In some cases, the stories are planned in advance or they will be covering planned events. In other cases, the choices are obvious because the reporters need to respond to and cover breaking news. For instance, on September 11, 2001, the main news story of the day was supposed to be the New York mayoral Democratic primary. Reporters had to shift their focus instantaneously. In other cases, reporters may engage in enterprising original reporting, where the journalist digs up information and doesn't just cover events, as well as investigative, feature, or issue-related stories. There is no magic rubric or formula in deciding what counts as news and which stories should be covered, but there are certain factors that will be weighed. Sometimes bias can be a factor, but there are many other factors that also influence a media outlet's decision to cover certain stories.

The media don't have a perfect formula and system. I often get frustrated when news outlets cover frivolous stories (celebrity journalism, for example) or overlook important stories. Editors and reporters have to decide what stories are worth reporting on and important enough to cover. There are hundreds, if not thousands, of stories that could be covered in a given day, but reporters need to sort out what is important and then develop stories around those decisions. As a freelance journalist, I often have to create and come up with article ideas that will interest an editor. As a university journalism professor, I've had some of my classes sit in on the *Philadelphia Inquirer* editors' meetings in which the editors of the various departments will brainstorm and discuss which topics and articles they plan to write about that day. Editors have a key role to play in determining what gets published or aired on a broadcast and what doesn't. The classic example is from journalist Charles Dana, who edited the *New York Tribune* and then the *New York Sun*, and who saw news as coming from the ordinary events of the day. He said, "When a dog bites a man, that is not news, but when a man bites a dog, that is news."[1]

Deciding what should count as news is often not easy. Sometimes it's obvious, such as when there is a natural disaster or an act of terrorism. Even when a major news story occurs, though, reporters still have to come up with different angles and story ideas for the event and its aftermath. I give my journalism classes a picture of a flood scene and have them come up with various story angles and ideas—maybe a profile article of a rescue worker or an article about what happens to pets during floods.

One important factor in determining when something is news and deserving of coverage has to do with its likely impact. Does the story have, appear to have, or possess the potential to have a huge impact on the media outlet's audience? These stories can include natural disasters like floods, earthquakes, tornadoes, wildfires, major snowstorms, and hurricanes. They also include tragedies like mass shootings, plane crashes, or acts of terror. They can also include stories that can affect people's lives in the long term, such as a new cure for cancer, a hike or cut in tax or interest rates, or a controversial school board decision affecting an entire community's children. Readers and viewers care about stories that will directly affect them, whether on a local, state, regional, or national level.

Due to the sheer number of potential stories to be covered, many important stories can and will get overlooked. In 2005, Latoyia Figueroa, a five months pregnant mother in Philadelphia, went missing. After news media ignored the story, local bloggers took up the cause and demanded that the local media give the story coverage, especially in light of the extensive coverage of the disappearance of Natalee Holloway in Aruba. Sadly, Figueroa was eventually found dead.[2] Many international stories can and will also get overlooked, especially those that appear, at least in the judgment of the editors and reporters, not to have an impact on the American public. Journalist Neil Clark observed in his RT article that terrorism in Africa receives minimal media attention in the West. He mentioned the dozens of churches in Kenya and Tanzania that were attacked and bombed in 2013; bomb attacks by al Shabaab militants in Uganda in 2010, at venues showing the soccer World Cup final, which killed over seventy people; and the sixty-seven people killed in a bombing in a Kenya shopping mall in 2010. At around the same time as the *Charlie Hebdo* terror attacks in Paris in January 2015, over two thousand people were killed by Boko Haram terror attacks in Nigeria, but this was mainly ignored by western media outlets.[3]

In general, stories that originate in Africa or South America tend to get ignored. In lamenting the lack of coverage of Madagascar's declining rain forests, Thomas Friedman of the *New York Times* wrote that the media doesn't focus enough on covering "big *trends*—trends that on any given day don't amount to much but over time could be vastly more significant than we can now imagine. Too bad we'll never see this news story: 'The U.N. Security Council met today in emergency session to discuss the fact that Madagascar, one of the world's most biodiversity-rich nations, lost another percentage of its plant and animal species.'"[4]

Some see the disparity in coverage as having a racial element. As noted by *Salon*, tragedies and terrorism in Africa tend to get less American media coverage: "In the wake of terrorist attacks in France, many asked why the mass slaughter of civilians in Lebanon the day before or Nigeria the Tuesday after (or in the six non-European sites which faced deadlier terrorist attacks this year), wasn't given similar coverage. The implication was that media attention skewed in the direction of lost white lives."[5] Personally, I don't see it as racial; I just think that this focus confirms the concept that American news media will focus on stories that have more impact on the United States. Stories from Africa get overlooked, but so do stories from Australia, Norway, and Sweden.

Most media outlets strive to present a centrist position because they don't want to alienate half of the population they serve. The mainstream media cherishes its watchdog role of exposing corruption and keeping the government and business interests honest. It is the eyes and ears of the public, and they will choose to cover topics that best fit that objective. They should do that for Republican and Democratic administrations at all levels. For media outlets that cater to a specific viewpoint or ideology, stories will be selected that cater to that audience's desires. Both types of media outlets make these decisions for economic reasons, in order to get better ratings, increase circulation, and improve advertising revenue. I think that this is a good business decision, especially for many media outlets that serve a broad population.

Another factor determining what to report on is the scoop mentality, the attitude that it is important to be first with the story. Whether it's Oprah Winfrey getting an exclusive with international cyclist Lance Armstrong regarding his admission of using performance-enhancing drugs or Diane Sawyer interviewing Bruce Jenner just before he became Caitlyn, media outlets want to be first, especially in today's twenty-four-hour news cycle. There is still prestige in being the first media outlet to report breaking news or the first to get a coveted interview. Oftentimes, this need for speed leads to mistakes and inaccurate reporting. This is especially the case for live on-air reporting. Accuracy must always trump speed, even if it means getting scooped.

Philadelphia Inquirer reporter John Timpane, in an e-mail interview regarding whether the media is making sense of breaking stories or engaging in advocacy journalism, said,

> I'm almost alone in thinking that the media as a whole, and that's a big, big whole, do pretty well with breaking stories. First reports are always prone to inaccuracy, garbled relays, and hysteria, but those generally do get corrected as the story runs on. The Paris attacks of November 2015 were a good case: body counts; accounts of terrorists caught, killed, or at large; and accounts of police activity had some inaccuracies that were corrected within hours or days. And sometimes the media were reporting inaccurate stuff given by authoritative sources. The police and government, too, are often wrong at first, but get better information with time. When we pass that wrong info along, as we will, it's the best anyone has. No one can be blamed on that account. It's how this game works.[6]

Another factor in determining which stories to cover is how current the data is. If the article intends to discuss legal cases and issues, it's important to have updated information about whether certain court cases were affirmed, vacated, remanded, or reversed. Medical and technological information also needs to be as current as possible before embarking on a story, especially in light of the speed at which this data can change.

Another factor has to do with story-choice as a purely business decision. Media outlets want to choose stories that will captivate their readers or viewers and don't want to choose stories that will drive them away. Generally, a Chicago newspaper will not write articles about Guatemalan copper mining, since its readership doesn't care about Guatemalan copper mining, unless there would be a human interest story or a tragic story such as one about trapped miners after an explosion.

An example of this is when the media chose to extensively cover the Natalee Holloway disappearance in Aruba. This was a sad, tragic story, but many people go missing. For whatever reason, the media latched on to the story and covered it nonstop for weeks. The decision paid off for many reporters and shows, including Nancy Grace (CNN) and Greta Van Susteren (Fox News), who got their best ratings of the year when they covered the story extensively. Many viewers related to Holloway's situation and identified with her family's tragedy. I know that it was a sad and tragic story, but it also made me feel sorry for the family members of other missing relatives who weren't getting such extensive coverage.

Many media critics objected to the saturation coverage given to Holloway's disappearance. Noted commentator Arianna Huffington wrote, "If you were to get your news only from television, you'd think the top issue facing our country right now is an 18-year-old girl named Natalee who went missing in Aruba. Every time one of these stories comes up, like, say, Michael Jackson, when it's finally over I think, what a relief, now we can get back to real news. But we never do."[7] There was also an allegation of "missing white woman syndrome" by some who criticize the fact that the media tends to ignore the disappearance of people of color.[8] I have to admit that I've noticed this trend, and it makes me wonder, even though I don't think it's intentional. It's a trend that should be changed.

Another example of news coverage as a business decision to increase ratings would be the extensive media coverage of Donald Trump's campaign during the 2016 presidential primaries. This occurred even before he shot up in the polls and dominated the primary field throughout 2015 and early 2016. Most cable news outlets cut into their live coverage by running almost every speech that Trump made. It was entertaining to many to see such an unconventional approach to politics, and he often became a political lightning rod for his controversial statements. Trump's approach led to higher than usual television ratings for the Republican debates.

Timeliness is another news factor. Media outlets will cover timely stories. If an annual car show takes place in January, the media won't write about it in June or September. It will write about the show the week before, the week of the show, and the week after the show. The media will cover current criminal and civil trials and current tragedies. They will cover current sports events and games, not games that took place months ago. This is precisely why radio and TV networks will cut into regularly scheduled programming to offer "breaking news."

Related to the concept of timeliness is the aspect of media convergence, or the fact that news outlets are distributing news via a variety of multimedia platforms, including cell phones, social media, podcasts, and photo slideshows. This has led to the concept of the 24/7 news cycle, where news is posted right away. The days of waiting for the next day's newspaper to read about a story are long over. Within thirty minutes after a sporting event is over, the initial game summary story will be posted on many newspaper websites. I know that I will scour the Internet for articles minutes after one of my favorite teams wins a big game to read the reporters' game analysis. People want and expect news to be provided right away. A friend told me that his two teenage kids were going crazy when they were on a camping trip without cell phone access and couldn't find out who the Philadelphia 76ers had drafted that night. This need for speed has led to more deadline pressure for reporters and the need to be first to break a story. *Los Angeles Times* social media editor Stacey Leasca told Jonathan Kuperberg of the Twitter media team in June 2014, "We want to make sure our followers get the latest, most accurate information as quickly as possible. Once we have independently confirmed information, we will tweet to let our followers know we are on top of the story and to continue to follow us as the news develops. Once we have a story to link to, we will tweet that link."[9]

Prominence is yet another news factor. Who is involved in the story? If an average person gets in a car accident and breaks a leg, it won't get on the local TV nightly news or the local paper. But if Justin Bieber, Snooki of the MTV television reality show *Jersey Shore*, Paris Hilton, Prince Harry of Great Britain, LeBron James, or the presidential motorcade has a similar accident, it will be covered extensively. That makes sense from a business perspective: people have more of an interest in what happens to well-known persons or government leaders.

Proximity can also be a factor in news judgment. The local TV nightly news' first ten minutes will normally focus on national and local stories. The sports segment will focus on major national and local sports teams. Most of the weather forecast will focus on the local weather, unless there is a significant national weather story. The exception is when there is a local angle to an international or national story, such as a local doctor going to Haiti to aid earthquake victims. Thus, most local media will cover major national news first if it is really significant. Otherwise, it will lead with the local stories.

There's an old news saying, "If it bleeds, it leads." This news philosophy goes back to the 1800s, meaning that stories involving crime will be highlighted. It's in the nature of the news media to sensationalize coverage in order to boost ratings and circulation. That often happens in crime coverage reporting. Shootings, drug busts, and serious traffic accidents are viewed as being in everyone's interest; there is a bias toward showing negative news. The "if it bleeds, it leads" approach demonstrates that tragedies, murders, serious crime, or natural disasters will get more coverage than other stories. Positive news is not generally emphasized, resulting in negative perceptions of certain vicinities or neighborhoods—bad news usually gets better ratings than good news. Some people just shrug off watching the nightly news because it's too negative or depressing. I've known a lot of people like that. They would rather immerse themselves in diversions such as sports or entertainment news. I remember that my grandmother used to lament how sad it was to watch the first ten minutes of the local newscast—fire, murder, hurricane, etc.—and that it made her want to change the channel.

In response, some media outlets are trying to put more of a focus on positive news. Most nightly news programs will have at least one positive, inspirational story at the end of the newscast. The *Huffington Post* has a section titled Huff Post Good News, which focuses on positive, inspirational stories. Other websites, such as the Good News Network, the Optimist, *Positive News*, and DailyGood focus on positive stories. I think that this is a good idea as long as important negative news isn't being whitewashed or ignored.

The media also like to portray bizarre and unusual stories. When the soccer World Cup occurs, it is not unusual to see videos of hamsters and elephants playing soccer or an octopus that predicts the game winners. Other examples might be taking a dog to yoga class, bears that invade a backyard swimming pool, a rat dragging a slice of pizza in a New York subway, kangaroos fighting in the street in Australia, the world's tallest man meeting the world's shortest man, and a two-year-old who can recite all of the United States presidents in order. I've had friends question these stories and ask something like, "Why are they focusing on a rat running loose on the New York subway? Don't they have more important things to cover?" Generally, these offbeat stories have no great impact, but they're often used as a change of pace to lighten things up in the midst of all the depressing news.

Trends often become news stories in and of themselves. Reporters need to follow trends in their beat, such as new developments in medicine and technology. They will read specialized magazines, books, and journals and cultivate sources to keep themselves up to date. Trends can also be a factor in coverage of certain neighborhoods, such as an increase in carjackings, robberies, DUIs, or murders. The same is also true with pop culture trends. I've noticed that my students tend to be about a year ahead of middle-aged people when it comes to current trends. Examples would be "twerking" (a sexually provocative dance move),[10] "sizzurp" (using cough syrup to get a high),[11] "the cinnamon challenge" (the dangerous trend of trying to swallow a spoonful of ground cinnamon),[12] the "choking game" (a dangerous trend that involves strangulation and fainting),[13] and abuse of Adderall as a recreational drug or to help students study.[14]

Media coverage is often driven by scandals and controversies. The media thrives on covering scandals, whether they involve Democrats or Republicans, especially when personal conduct is a factor. Whether it was extramarital affairs or other scandals involving President Bill Clinton, presidential candidate John Edwards, Senator Gary Hart's monkey business, Senator David Vitter, Idaho senator Larry Craig's wide stance in a bathroom stall, Congressman Anthony Weiner's sexting, Congressman Newt Gingrich, Congressman Henry Hyde, New Jersey Governor Jim McGreevey, South Carolina governor Mark Sanford (who temporarily disappeared after an affair), the media will not shy away from salacious stories. Generally, they mean better ratings. The media has become much more aggressive in covering wrongdoing by political figures and officials. In the past, they tended to avoid negative coverage of politicians and their flaws, such as Woodrow Wilson's incapacity due to his stroke while in office, Franklin Delano Roosevelt's polio and partial paralysis, and John F. Kennedy's Addison's Disease and rumored extramarital affairs. Watergate and the Gary Hart incident were some of the turning points when the media stopped covering up or ignoring politicians' wrongdoings and flaws.

There is a frequent bias or perceived bias in sports coverage. ESPN's college sports coverage focuses predominantly upon the Power 5 conferences, while it gives minimal attention to the so-called lesser Group of 5 conferences. Sports talk radio thrives on colorful personalities who lambaste the local teams' coaches, players, owners, and general managers when the teams aren't doing well. Many sports teams and leagues own media outlets, such as the MLB Network (Major League Baseball), the NFL Network (National Football League), NBA TV (National Basketball Association), the Big Ten Network, the SEC Network, and the Longhorn Network (University of Texas). Local network affiliates that carry a hometown team's games are often likely to be "homers" and don't give an objective, even-handed broadcast of the game, and often being in denial that the referee made a good call against their team. Many people believe that there is an East Coast bias in favor of East Coast sports teams. People often also believe that college athletes should not be criticized harshly by the media for poor performance on the field, since they aren't paid professionals. Although representation and coverage of women in sports has improved by leaps and bounds over the last forty years, many people believe that there is still inadequate coverage of women in sports. In some cases, whether it is justified or not, some fans of certain teams believe that certain national announcers have it out for them. In October 2015, some Kansas City Royals fans started a change.org petition demanding that Fox Sports remove Joe Buck from announcing the Royals playoff games due to his alleged bias against the Royals.[15]

The *Pittsburgh Post-Gazette*, in an article by editorial page editor Tom Waseleski titled "Inside the Opinion Page," explained its editorial philosophy and point of view to its readers: "Although *Post-Gazette* editorial positions have some consistency . . . they are not doctrinaire. The editorial board's outlook is generally liberal on social issues and more moderate on economic topics. We endorse both Republican and Democratic candidates. We like efficiency and consolidation in government. We like the public sector to be as modern and forward-looking as a young, high-tech business. More specifically, the newspaper has championed civil rights and civil liberties, separation of church and state, reproductive freedom, protection of the environment, strong schools and government as a benign catalyst for economic development and regional vitality."[16]

Candidates' past speeches, statements, and writings are public record and fair game for the media to examine. Political reporting is often poll driven and viewed as a horse race. During presidential primaries and election years, at least one new poll regarding the presidential campaign is released literally every day. At times, this can come across as repetitive, especially if there is no big change in the polling. Politicians from all sides of the political spectrum have issues and problems with the way that elections are covered. Independent senator Bernie Sanders criticized political coverage as being too superficial and not focused enough on important issues. In 2015, Sanders told Brian Stelter of CNN's *Reliable Sources*,

"There is more coverage about the political gossip of a campaign, about raising money, about polling, about somebody saying something dumb, or some kid works for a campaign sends out something stupid on Facebook, right? We can expect that to be a major story . . . when you have ABC, CBS, and NBC not devoting one minute to the most significant trade agreement in the history of the United States of America, help me out, help me out. Give me an explanation."[17]

Many liberals believe that, in the beginning, the mainstream media didn't give Sanders's campaign sufficient coverage. For the most part, the media had reached the conclusion that Hillary Clinton would be the Democratic nominee, and they focused their coverage on Donald Trump and the Republican primary contenders. David Schultz, a Hamline University political science professor, wrote in *MinnPost*, "What if Sanders received as much coverage as Trump? The fact that he does not ought to be proof of a media bias against real liberals or those on the left. He is marginalized by the mainstream media despite the fact that his poll numbers within the Democratic Party are better than Trump's in the GOP, and that there are more people identifying as Democrats than Republicans. . . . But Sanders is not media savvy and he offers a message that challenges the corporate media."[18] Even when Sanders pulled even with or ahead of Clinton in the polls in early 2016, his campaign was still less well covered despite the fact that many of his speeches drew thousands of enthusiastic people.

In some cases, reporting on sensitive issues or negative information can be difficult for beat reporters because they will be investigating and criticizing experts and sources that they count on regularly, and they don't want to alienate them to the point that they won't talk to the reporter anymore. A famous sports example was "silent" Steve Carlton, a Hall of Fame major league baseball pitcher who refused to speak to the press or be interviewed during the last decade of his career after feeling he had been betrayed and misquoted by the media during a couple of mediocre seasons. *Seattle Times* columnist Larry Stone mentioned Carlton when discussing Seattle Seahawks running back Marshawn Lynch's refusal to talk to the media.[19]

Selecting which stories to cover is only part of the picture, however, how reporters go about the business of reporting can also affect bias.

CHAPTER 14

THE PROCESS OF REPORTING AND HOW IT CAN AFFECT BIAS

The methods and manner in which reporters practice their craft can have an effect on bias. Generally, it's important for reporters to keep an open mind in their reporting. In 2002, Poynter described how important it is for reporters to check their premises: "Every writer ought to question his [or her] own assumptions and so-called conventional wisdom. When we look closely, we may find that our premises are wrong or too simplistic. This kind of questioning can lead to stories that are fresh and interesting, stories that cut against the grain, instead of stories that are predictable and boring."[1] Author and journalist Mark Bowden contends that "Reporters should always be fair and balanced, especially if they hope to persuade. To the extent that they are not, smart readers dismiss them as cheap salesmen."[2] And Bill Reed, a professional journalist for more than forty years (including thirty-two with the *Philadelphia Inquirer* and currently a member of the editorial board of that paper), points out that "Journalism and a democratic society are based on citizens formulating informed opinions on issues and who to elect to represent them. Those opinions require basic facts, which the mainstream media has a responsibility to provide, though that media also should provide all sides of the issues both in their straight news reports and in clearly identified analyses, commentaries and editorials."[3]

Should reporters just report facts or should they also give their opinions? Sometimes, in rare circumstances, opinions are warranted. In Will Bunch's view, "It's fine to give opinions. Walter Cronkite, the respected anchor and correspondent for CBS, went to Vietnam and concluded in 1968 that the war wasn't winnable and that the United States should get out of it. History looked back kindly on his judgment in weighing in with his wisdom. That shouldn't always happen, but sometimes it's OK when it's warranted."[4]

Is it acceptable for a reporter to push an agenda when covering an event? "That makes me uncomfortable," Bunch says. "I think it's OK to be energized and take a position for certain core values, like favoring the First Amendment or supporting democracy or voting access. What bothers me is where reporters have an agenda that they are personally involved in, such as a protest or advocating for the Audubon Society, even if it is wonderful. Supporting political candidates also makes me queasy. It might be clear who you like, but you shouldn't endorse or take an upfront position in pushing for a candidate. Politicians eventually let you down, and you need to be free to see that. If you were pro-Obama, you shouldn't look the other way for something like not closing Guantanamo and should criticize that, not excuse it."[5] Mark Bowden points out that "There are no laws that govern such things. If you wish to be trusted and believed, you should not push an agenda while reporting facts. No effective argument begins with a clearly distorted statement of the facts."[6] Bill Reed tries to look at the issue from the standpoint of the consuming public: "Readers and listeners should not be forced to sift through biased reports to ascertain the facts. And news reporters should not inject their opinions or bias in their stories. That is why it is dicey to assign a reporter who has an extensive knowledge of a subject or issue to also write an analysis and/or to write about it less formally on a blog or in the social media. Once the reporter expresses an opinion or personal perspective, it becomes difficult to ascertain whether his or her 'straight' news reports are objective and strictly based on facts."[7]

Usually, I am not in favor of injecting opinion into news reports. Generally, mainstream media reporters should just stick to providing facts and information and not insert biased opinions. It makes the reporting more credible when reporters avoid playing favorites. Providing some context and analysis might be fine, but it's important to be as fair and balanced as possible. Failing to do so results in the loss of trust among many readers and viewers.

Most media outlets require that reporters confirm their information through multiple sources. This has become much easier in our Internet age. "The ability to verify information today is greater than it's ever been," says Pulitzer Prize–winning journalist James B. Steele:

> I would say it's the golden age. The sheer volume of information that you can get instantaneously is huge. A few decades ago, to get public information about a corporation might take weeks or months. You could get the corporation to send you a report, try to get it from a library, or buy the reports from a company in Washington, DC. By the time you got the information, the issue might have passed. Today, at any time, you can check reports or policies. You can access copies of records, hearings, and federal court dockets. You can immediately pull up the case and analyze it. The access is breathtaking. It's a great resource. But in light of this instant information is the pressure to be first. You can't succumb to that pressure. Most reporters try to put accuracy first. A lot depends on who you work for and the standards of the institution. That's always been the case. If you can't verify the information, you shouldn't go with it. If you make a bad mistake, it affects your career. The *Rolling Stone* coverage of the alleged UVA [University of Virginia] rape was a textbook case of how not to do a story. They ignored the fundamental processes of verifying information. It's one of the better examples of where advocacy journalism can go wrong.[8]

When I interviewed John Timpane of the *Philadelphia Inquirer* on this topic, he was firmly of the belief that it is not the role of the reporter to change peoples' minds: "The only thing reporters can do is to be *honest* about what they find in the field. If their reporting uncovers things they themselves dislike, they have to suspend that dislike, unease, or disagreement and report honestly what they have found. They must have the discipline to write what they find and not allow personal preferences to shadow or color it. While you probably can't catch all, you can get 90 percent of it, I am very sure, and then work hard on the other 10 percent, which your editor should catch anyway."[9]

Reporters generally do not show emotion and do not express their opinions on news stories. Some reporters don't like this philosophy. There are exceptions, such as during national tragedies like 9/11 or during natural disasters like Hurricane Katrina, or historic moments, such as when Walter Cronkite got emotional during his coverage of the Kennedy assassination and the moon landing. No one expects reporters to be automatons or robots, but reporting on tragedies and sad stories is a regular part of their job. It's fine to use a more somber tone to report such stories, but generally it's best if reporters keep their composure.

How can reporters be objective, fair, and balanced in this polarized media environment? For that matter, should they be? "The philosophy that I've accepted is that I have two main responsibilities as a reporter—to be accurate and fair," observes Will Bunch. "Report the facts and don't make things up. For fairness, talk to everyone and do research related to the story. Listen to what the evidence says, even if it doesn't back up your view going into the assignment. If the issue is climate change, you don't have the obligation to create a false balance to reflect the 2 percent of scientists who challenge climate change. You listened to both sides and were fair and thorough, but the evidence points in one direction. [Adherence to] balance is not a horrible concept, but sometimes it leads to an artificial balance."[10]

The choice of which experts to rely on for information and quotes also displays bias. If a media outlet relies on James Carville for political perspective, they're going to get a liberal slant. If it interviews Karl Rove, it will get a conservative slant. If they interview the head of the National Rifle Association, they know they will be getting a pro-Second Amendment viewpoint. If they interview the president of Planned Parenthood, they know they will be getting a pro-choice viewpoint.

There are many ways of displaying bias. It can come through in the content of a speech or the tone of the speaker—academic and straightforward, snarky and sarcastic, or bitter and nasty. Bias can also be reflected by which stories the media outlet chooses to publish or to emphasize. The size or length or time spent on a story can reflect bias. Will a story be featured in a prominent article on page one of the newspaper or will it be hidden in a very short article on page eight? Will it be ignored or barely mentioned by a television anchor, or will it get five minutes of time featuring several reporters. Furthermore, the practice of frequently interrupting a guest to insert one's viewpoint can display a bias. Chris Matthews and Bill O'Reilly are both well known for this.

It's important to show statements in their full context. That doesn't always happen in a sound-bite society. Examples would be Jeb Bush saying "stuff happens" after a mass school shooting in Oregon,[11] Mitt Romney saying "corporations are people,"[12] or President Obama saying that businesses didn't create this or that.[13] Another example is Shirley Sherrod, who was forced to resign as a state rural development director for the USDA in 2010 after conservative blogger Andrew Breitbart and others posted video snippets online from a speech that Sherrod had given at an NAACP event. The edited videos made her appear to be racist since they left an inaccurate impression that she had deliberately refused to help a white farmer in 1986 when she worked for a Georgia nonprofit. The secretary of agriculture immediately fired Sherrod but later apologized and offered to reinstate her job after the fuller context of Sherrod's remarks was shown.[14]

There is also the bias of a pack mentality, in which media outlets report the same stories that others are reporting. In addition to which, the mainstream media tends to avoid stories that they believe would offend certain people or groups. Biases can exist regarding race, gender, ethnicity, sexual orientation, religion, educational background, disability, intelligence, foreign accents, age, and physical attributes such as height and weight. Reporters should be trained in and be aware of multicultural sensitivity. They should seek advice from other employees, especially other minorities, when writing about a racially charged incident. Gender-neutral terms such as firefighter and mail carrier are preferred, and reporters should remember that words like ghetto or inner city can have negative connotations. Some people view this concept as political correctness gone amuck, but it makes sense to be sensitive to various groups. For years, sports commentators would frequently call white quarterbacks smart and heady while referring to black quarterbacks as athletic, and today's reporters try to avoid such disparities.

There have been many incidents in which media reporters and commentators have been fired, criticized, or suspended for their controversial statements, especially for derogatory or insensitive remarks about minorities. Don Imus was fired due to complaints, outrage, protests, and threatened boycotts of sponsors after his "nappy headed hos" remark.[15] A *New York Post* cartoonist was criticized for his cartoon depicting two white police officers shooting a monkey (interpreted to be President Obama) regarding the stimulus bill.[16] An ESPN headline writer was fired when he wrote "A Chink in the Armor" after a loss by Asian American Jeremy Lin and his then team, the New York Knicks.[17] Jimmy "The Greek" Snyder was fired from CBS Sports in 1988 after giving statements during an interview that blacks were better athletes than whites because they were bred that way.[18]

There are hidden biases in corporations and hiring practices, and media corporations are no exception. Many people criticize the media for their lack of diversity, noting that their employee base is still predominantly white and male. The critics claim that media outlets should have diverse employees, in terms of race, gender, ethnicity, and sexual orientation, in order to reflect the views of the entire community. Subtle bias can be seen in the diversity or lack of diversity in the news reporters, as well as in the people and experts who are interviewed. Women, minorities, various ethnic groups, poor people, and gay people are not focused on as much as white males. This is an area where reporters and media outlets can improve.

Bias can also be demonstrated the way in which interviews are conducted. Sometimes, if a host agrees with a guest, the questioning is a friendly lovefest and features many easy or softball questions. If the host disagrees with the guest, on the other hand, the questioning can often be hostile, confrontational, and adversarial. As a result, some politicians and government officials might choose to avoid hostile media environments and go to more friendly media outlets, or hosts that they presume will take it easy on them. For example, conservatives and Republicans tended to shy away from appearing on the *Rachel Maddow Show* after she aggressively interviewed Kentucky senator Rand Paul concerning his views on the Civil Rights Act and whether businesses should be allowed to refuse to serve minorities.[19] There are often allegations that a reporter used the technique of "gotcha" questions in order to prove a point or throw the interview subject off guard.

In 2007, vice-presidential candidate Sarah Palin and her supporters alleged that Katie Couric had done this when Couric asked Palin what newspapers she read on a regular basis and Palin couldn't name one.[20] During the 2000 presidential campaign, candidate George W. Bush alleged that the media was using gotcha questions when they were asking him about alleged past cocaine abuse. He raised the same objection about an interview during which he was asked to name the leaders of Chechnya, India, Taiwan, and Pakistan. Bush could only correctly identify one.[21] During the 1992 presidential campaign, Bill Clinton said in an interview with *60 Minutes*, regarding questions about his marital infidelity, "I think what the press has to decide is, are we going to engage in a game of 'gotcha'?"

The allegation of gotcha questions was also raised by many Republicans when presidential candidate Governor Scott Walker of Wisconsin stated in an interview that he did not know whether President Obama was a Christian. Walker spokeswoman Jocelyn Webster subsequently told the *Washington Post* that Walker was trying to make a point of principle rather than trying to cast doubt on Obama's faith: "'Of course the governor thinks the president is a Christian,' she said. 'He thinks these kinds of gotcha questions distract from what he's doing as governor of Wisconsin to make the state better and make life better for people in his state.'"[22]

In 2015, Donald Trump alleged that radio talk show host Hugh Hewitt was using gotcha questions when Hewitt asked Trump about several key figures in the Middle East. Trump appeared to be confused and was unfamiliar with the names. At one point, Trump responded, "Well, that is a gotcha question, though," he told Hewitt of one detailed question. "I mean, you know, when you're asking me about who's running this, this this, that's not, that is not, I will be so good at the military, your head will spin."[23] Defenders of these questions would allege that they are relevant inquiries into presidential candidates' depth of knowledge or judgment.

President Bill Clinton and Hillary Clinton would disagree with the assertion that the media is liberally biased. The mainstream media has not been reluctant over the years to investigate in detail alleged scandals involving the Clintons. What's more, even liberal commentators criticized President Obama for being tone deaf after the Paris terrorist bombings, saying that he didn't speak out strongly enough against ISIS and the terrorists who were behind the attacks and didn't sufficiently address the American public's fears about terrorist attacks. They also criticized him on issues such as civil liberties, foreign intervention, economic inequality, and for his push for approval of the TransPacific Partnership, the newest global trade agreement.

Bias can be demonstrated in the phrasing of poll questions asked by pollsters employed by large media outlets. Responses would be different if a poll question asked, "What do you think about Obamacare, which is denying people their choice of doctors, killing jobs, hurting businesses, and raising the national debt?" versus "What do you think about the Affordable Care Act, which is giving millions of people access to healthcare, ending denial of benefits based on preexisting conditions, and ending lifetime limits on medical care?"

There can be bias reflected in the way race, gender, ethnicity, religion, and sexual orientation are presented in the press. Bill O'Reilly and Fox News emphasize the nation's cultural war on Christmas, ridiculing and criticizing companies that required their employees to say "Happy Holidays" instead of "Merry Christmas." MSNBC had an ongoing theme of the Republican Party's alleged "War on Women," with examples including the GOP attack on Planned Parenthood, its opposition to pay-equity for women, and attempts to restrict abortion rights and access to contraception.[24]

Word choice and labeling, such as how people are identified and described, can show bias. Newspaper headlines and teasers in radio and television can reflect a bias, either intentionally or unintentionally. A classic example of bias cited by many people occurred during the Hurricane Katrina aftermath, when two similar photos received substantially different labeling. One photo, taken for Getty Images and distributed through Agence France Presse, showed a white couple wading through murky water holding bags of food, with the caption identifying them as "finding bread and soda from a local grocery store." A similar photo distributed through the Associated Press showed a black man wading through murky water carrying a case of soda and pulling a floating bag, and the caption read that he had "been looting a grocery store."[25] Rapper Kanye

West criticized the apparent double standard during an NBC concert for hurricane relief, saying, "I hate the way they portray us in the media, You see a black family, it says they're looting. You see a white family, it says they're looking for food."

The AP's Jack Stokes defended the caption, stating, according to the *New York Times*, "Mr. Stokes said that Mr. Martin had seen the man in his photograph wade into a grocery store and come out with the sodas and bag, so by AP's definition, the man had looted."[26]

Headlines for news stories and newspaper covers can indicate bias. As pointed out by Matt Stopera of *BuzzFeed*, Fox News took a *Washington Times* story with the headline "USDA Gay-Sensitivity Training Seeks Larger Audience" and reprinted the article with its own headline "Obama Bureaucrats Imposing Radical Homosexual Sensitivity Training?"[27] In response to complaints about National Public Radio's allegedly biased headlines, NPR's Edward Schumacher-Matos described headline writing as an art form: "They must accurately reflect the story while at the same time grab your attention with either catchiness or the obvious importance of their content—all in a few words." He observed that headlines are usually written by the editor, not the reporter, and that online headlines must have keywords favorable to search engine optimization. He noted that NPR has evolved "to have extremely good headlines in the art form sense. I leave it to you to pass political judgment."[28]

Some publications prefer more straightforward and serious headlines, while others, especially tabloids like the *New York Post*, the *New York Daily News*, and the *Philadelphia Daily News*, like to have headlines and covers that are edgy, humorous, and controversial. One example occurred when presidential candidate Ted Cruz criticized Donald Trump and his "New York values"; the *New York Daily News* cover the next day had the Statue of Liberty giving the middle finger, with the words, "Drop Dead, Ted (Hey, Cruz: You don't like N.Y. values? Go back to Canada!)."[29]

Bias need not be expressed in words at all. It can be shown by the images that a media outlet chooses to publish or broadcast. Photos can make a person look good or bad. Showing them laughing when they should be serious might imply cold-heartedness or indifference, while showing them frowning or scowling at something most would view as positive could be interpreted as complete disapproval. The bias is in the context of the choice of image and the audience interpretation. The images that the media chooses to show or is allowed to show can reflect bias. There was a long-time ban on reporters taking photos of coffins of dead soldiers returning to Dover Air Force base because the government felt that it could sour the public on the popularity of the conflict in question. During World War II, most of the media did not show photos of graphic war scenes. During Vietnam, reporters had more access and were able to take photos and videos of burning villages and children running from napalm. Showing or not showing these types of photos can have an influence on how the public views a war.

Media outlets have to decide whether to show graphic photos or videos. Fox News showed the video of a hostage who was burned to death by ISIS. *TIME* magazine was criticized for having a cover featuring an Afghan girl with her nose and ears cut off. Some media outlets were criticized for showing photos of the charred bodies of American contractors who were killed by a car bomb in Fallujah, Iraq. Their dead bodies were dragged to a bridge and hung. Many media outlets that chose to show the graphic photos were criticized as being insensitive or opportunistic.[30] Thus, a frequent debate among journalists and reporters is whether to show graphic images, videos, and photos. Should they show ISIS beheadings, hangings, 9/11 jumpers, soldiers' coffins returning from war, dead soldiers in the battlefield, and the like?

I wrote an article for the *Huffington Post* on this topic, after *Time* magazine was criticized for running the cover photo of the young Afghan woman whose nose and ears were chopped off as a result of a Taliban decree because she had fled her abusive in-laws. Critics alleged that the cover photo was too graphic and disturbing, especially for children to see. Hofstra University anthropology professor Daniel Martin Varisco had stated that the cover photograph was "startling, haunting, disturbing and an unfortunate example of sensationalized news reporting."[31] I felt at the time and still believe that *Time* made the right decision because it was necessary to show how badly the Taliban would treat women if the American soldiers left the country.

This issue pops up frequently in journalism. The *New York Times* and other media outlets were criticized for running photos of people who had jumped from the World Trade Center buildings during the 9/11 attack. As mentioned above, another publicized incident took place during the Iraq War when government contractors were killed by a bomb and their dead bodies were then dragged through the streets and hung on a bridge in Fallujah. Many American newspapers declined to show the graphic photos of the charred bodies hanging from the bridge, but a few of them, including the *Philadelphia Inquirer* and the *New York Times*, chose to show the images on their front pages. Other papers showed the graphic photos but placed them on the inside pages. During the Iraq War, debates also arose as to whether the media should show the Abu Ghraib prison abuse photos and the coffins of dead soldiers returning to the United States. During the Winter Olympics in 2014, media outlets were criticized for showing the video of the Georgian luger who was killed during a trial run. While it was newsworthy, many people criticized the networks for sensationalizing the story by showing the actual crash.

These media debates about displaying graphic images aren't new. Matthew Brady shocked Americans by publishing his staff photographers' photos of dead bodies at the Battle of Antietam during the Civil War. During the Vietnam War, several graphic yet iconic photos were taken, including Kim Phuc, a crying naked young girl fleeing from a napalm attack, a South Vietnamese General executing a Viet Cong prisoner on a Saigon street, and dead bodies of My Lai massacre victims after they were shot. During the war in Somalia, photos and videos were shown of a dead American soldier being dragged down the street.

In addressing the issue of whether news outlets should show a photo of a man stepping over dead bodies in the aftermath of the Haiti earthquake, Terry Eiler, a photojournalist and director of Ohio University's school of visual communication, told Alicia C. Shepard of National Public Radio, "Can I run this dead body in my publication without offending, harming, hurting, or disturbing the audience? When you are looking at the scale of destruction in Haiti you can't tell that story without showing dead bodies."[32]

That same thought process applies to *Time* magazine's cover. The point of *Time*'s article was to show that Afghan women would suffer if deals were cut with Taliban leaders. Showing the picture of the Afghan teen with her nose cut off displayed the gravity of the problem. In defending his decision to run the cover, *Time*'s managing editor, Richard Stengel, said in the magazine that it's the publication's job to give an explanation when violence occurs: "The image is a window into the reality of what is happening—and what can happen—in a war that affects and involves all of us. I would rather confront readers with the Taliban's treatment of women than ignore it. I would rather people know that reality as they make up their minds about what the U.S. and its allies should do in Afghanistan."[33] If a photo or video sheds light on an important issue or conveys a powerful message then it generally should be shown. Of course, there are certain exceptions, such as a beheading or a live execution, for example.

There are certain ways that media outlets can forewarn readers and viewers. Television networks often run graphic video but add a disclaimer beforehand warning the viewers that they are about to see disturbing footage. This at least gives viewers the option of turning away or temporarily changing the channel. Newspapers and magazines can put graphic photos on the inside pages or on their website with a warning on the front page or cover.

Another factor in favor of showing the *Time* magazine photo of the brutally disfigured young woman was that the woman willingly cooperated and wanted to pose for the photo to get the message out about how she and other women were being treated. Some people prefer the "would it spoil someone's breakfast?" test as to whether to run graphic photos. However, the media has an obligation to bring important stories and images to the public, even if it makes them uncomfortable.

Generally, I would lean toward showing graphic photos and videos if they are important news stories and if warnings and disclaimers are given. But there are exceptions and times when media outlets should show restraint. Fox News received some criticism in 2015 when it showed video of an ISIS prisoner, a Jordanian pilot, being burned alive. It gave the disclaimer WARNING, EXTREMELY GRAPHIC VIDEO.[34] There was also criticism when local television stations replayed video of Pennsylvania state treasurer R. Budd Dwyer fatally shooting himself in the mouth with a gun during a press conference after he had been convicted of bribery, mail fraud, and racketeering.[35]

War reporting can reflect bias. Many liberals criticized the mainstream media for failing to ask probing questions of the Bush administration during the lead up to the second Iraq war. They also criticized the media for failing to focus on civilian casualties in Iraq during the course of the war.

There is also an issue regarding the policy of embedding reporters with troops and whether journalists' independence will be sacrificed.[36] On one hand, it may be deemed essential to keep reporters safe by having them embedded with troops. However, there may be concern that these reporters become too close to the troops and will sanitize their coverage and not report any negative information about the troops' conduct or performance. There is a concern about the reliability of embedded war reporters who are not free to roam wherever they want and must travel with the military to get access. Journalists might fear reporting negative information about the troops and their activities because that might alienate the people who are protecting them and make them less likely to cooperate and give information to reporters in the future. For instance, as a hypothetical situation, a reporter who observes rampant drug abuse among soldiers might feel reluctant to report such a story.

There is also the hostile media effect, in which both sides of an issue feel that the media coverage is skewed against them. According to Nieman Lab, both pro-Israeli and pro-Arab viewers believed that coverage during the 1982 Lebanese civil war of the massacre of Palestinian refugees by Christian militias while Israeli soldiers stood by was biased against them: "This effect—where both sides feel that a neutral story is biased against them—has been replicated so many times, in so many different cultural settings, with so many types of media and stories, that it has its own name: hostile media effect. The same story can make everyone on all sides think the media is attacking them. . . . We might like to think of ourselves as impartial judges of credibility and fairness, but the evidence says otherwise. Liberals and conservatives can (and often do) believe the same news report is biased against both their views; they aren't both right."[37]

To what extent is the media portraying war protests or other types of protests? Are they being ignored or marginalized by the media outlet, or are they complimented and praised. Right after the Iraq war invasion in 2003, many protesters were not shown in a positive light and dissenting voices were marginalized. In some cases, protesters were portrayed as unpatriotic traitors. Years later, some mainstream media outlets portrayed Tea Party protesters as being fringe kooks and crazies.

There are times when bias has been demonstrated through the use of Photoshop to manipulate photos. One well-known example took place during the Israel-Hezbollah conflict, when Adnan Hajj, a freelance photographer for Reuters, manipulated and enhanced the smoke in a photograph of the aftermath of an Israeli airstrike in suburban Beirut. The doctored photo showed more and darker smoke than the actual scene. Hajj also altered another photo to show three flares dropped from an Israeli jet fighter instead of one. Reuters fired Hajj after the incident and instituted stricter photo editing measures for the future.[38] *Time* magazine was criticized for its cover that made O. J. Simpson look darker and more sinister.[39] During the 2004 Presidential election, a picture of John Kerry at an anti-war rally with Jane Fonda digitally added next to him was widely circulated.[40]

Traditional news media outlets aren't the only ones facing scrutiny for the use of digital manipulation. There is a debate as to whether magazines, especially celebrity magazines, should use digitally edited photos of models.

I wrote an article for *Philadelphia Magazine*'s website in 2012 regarding *Seventeen* magazine's pledge to stop using digitally retouched images of young female models in the magazine.[41] In one of its editions, an editor's note announced in its "Body Peace Treaty"—a list of vows regarding how young women would be portrayed in the magazine—"We vow to . . . never change girls' body or face shapes." The magazine's decision was sparked by a campaign led by Julia Bluhm, a fourteen-year-old girl from Maine, who started a Change.org petition that was signed by more than 84,000 people. The petition urged the magazine to stop showing photos that were air brushed and made the models look thinner and with perfect skin. "I know how it affects girls and . . . my friends," Bluhm told CNN. "We don't realize it sometimes when we're just looking at the magazine and having fun. It can lower self-esteem."[42] In general, media outlets have a strict policy against digitally manipulating photos. The readers should have an expectation that the photos that are published are real and not altered.

Several journalists have been fired or suspended for using computer programs like Adobe Photoshop to alter images. A *Charlotte Observer* photographer was fired for changing the color of the sky in a picture of fire-fighters. A *Toledo Blade* photographer was fired for altering images, with tricks like inserting a basketball into a game photo or deleting a tree limb or utility pole. Some people might not think that such minor changes are a big deal, but they distort reality.[43] Sometimes the issue is more serious. Reuters fired a freelance photographer who manipulated the aftermath of an Israeli airstrike in suburban Beirut, Lebanon, to show enhanced and darker smoke rising from the buildings. In 2008, the media arm of the Iranian government altered a photo of missiles that it had fired. In reality, one of the four missiles failed to fire, but the altered image showed the launch of four missiles. In 2008, a freelance photographer for *The Atlantic* took photos of Senator John McCain, doctored some of them to make him look sinister, and then put them on her website. *The Atlantic* later reported that the photographer had been dropped by her photo agency as a client.[44]

Altering images is prohibited in news journalism, but should it be allowed in celebrity magazines? I think it's a close call, but I would still say no. Some well-known celebrity incidents involving digital manipulation include a *Redbook* cover of Faith Hill that made her arm much skinnier than it actually was, a *TV Guide* cover that imposed Oprah Winfrey's head onto Ann-Margret's body, a *Redbook* cover that combined three photos of Jennifer Aniston into one, a British *GQ* cover that gave Kate Winslet thinner legs, and a *Men's Fitness* cover that super-enhanced the arm muscles of tennis star Andy Roddick.[45]

Some argue that fashion or celebrity magazines should have a different standard, in that the average reader has an expectation that the photos are being altered to make the subject look better, if not perfect. However, many people have said that doctored photos in celebrity magazines have led to some readers to experience eating disorders, low self-esteem, and depression because they portray unrealistic body images.[46]

Magazines geared toward teenagers should be held to a higher standard and should be accurately portraying people in their photos. They should see that models and their peers have pimples, freckles, moles, blemishes, birthmarks, glasses, braces, and a few extra pounds if that is how the person actually looks. Sure, young people should be encouraged to be physically fit, but all body types should be celebrated, not just super-skinny ones with carrot-stick arms and legs. Although celebrity, fashion, and teen magazines are often a guilty pleasure and an escape from reality for their readers, their content should still be based on reality.

It would be one thing if a doctored photo appeared in a satirical publication like the *Onion* or in the old tabloid *Weekly World News*, which had doctored photos of heaven from the Hubble Telescope, Hillary Clinton holding her adopted alien baby, and Bat Boy. In such satirical or tongue-in-cheek publications one hopes readers know what they're getting.

There was hope that other, similar publications would follow *Seventeen*'s lead and stop digitally altering its models. Two other teen girls trying to get *Teen Vogue* to change its image policy had gotten more than 33,000 petition signatures. However, those teens told various publications that the *Teen Vogue* editors were rude to them and unreceptive. In May 2012, *Vogue* did agree not to use models under age sixteen who appear to have an eating disorder.[47] Knowing that teens try to emulate what they see in their magazines, these magazines should keep it real. *Seventeen*'s new image policy was a good start.

Unfortunately, using digitally altered models is still the norm in 2016. Requiring disclosure of techniques used to manipulate each image could be a possible remedy. According to CBS News, Israeli law requires that digitally altered print ads must have a disclaimer indicating that it was altered.[48]

While digitally altering a photo or video can play into bias, bias can also be shown through emphasis on unaltered photos or videos, with news stories that ridicule a politician, organization, or public figure. Even though President Gerald Ford was an outstanding athlete and an All-American football player at the University of Michigan, his reputation as an uncoordinated klutz was cemented by the media and *Saturday*

Night Live focusing on his accidental trips and falls.[49] MSNBC and others loved showing bloopers from President Bush, including his botching a popular adage and instead saying, "Fool me once . . . shame on you. Fool me. . . . You can't get fooled again."[50] Fox News and conservative websites gave extensive coverage of President Obama's "latte salute," in which he gave a lazy salute to Marines at the bottom of Marine One while holding a cup.[51] Oftentimes, the media plays into and perpetuates stereotypes, such as Obama being aloof and Bush being a dim bulb.

Sometimes, bias is evident due to the closeness of the reporter or commentator to the issue. In some cases, they are just as much an advocate as they are a reporter. Sometimes the lines get blurred. This was evident in the reporting by conservatives James O'Keefe and Hannah Giles, who dressed up as a pimp and prostitute in a sting to catch ACORN giving illegal tax advice and then distributed their video through conservative Andrew Breitbart and his website. While O'Keefe and Giles were right-wing activists attempting to put ACORN in a bad light, their techniques were similar to those used by mainstream media reporters who go undercover.

When Jorge Ramos of Univision confronted Donald Trump at a press conference about his immigration policies, he had a specific agenda and bias. In this situation, Ramos was clearly acting as an advocate rather than an impartial journalist.[52]

Al Sharpton frequently gets involved in social issues regarding race and then "reports" on them on his MSNBC show. This was evident during the Trayvon Martin killing and during the Ferguson riots after the fatal shooting of Michael Brown by a police officer. Sharpton's bias was evident in that he was interviewing the families while advocating on their behalf at the same time.[53]

To what extent do journalists' personal feelings about an issue reflect their coverage of a story? Is it appropriate for them to cover stories that they have a particular personal connection to? Should a reporter who was a rape victim report on an alleged rape victim? Should a reporter who is a parent of a young child do an investigative series on the quality of local day cares? Should a reporter who homeschools her children do a story about the success claims for homeschooling? There is a concern that these reporters might feel so passionate about the issue that they won't be able to report the story in a fair and balanced manner.

One of the problems of examining media bias is the fact that the organization or people examining the bias are likely to have their own personal biases that would affect the research. Liberal analysts are more likely to conclude that the media outlet has a conservative slant, while conservative analysts are more likely to conclude that the media outlet is liberal. Media bias analysis by liberal outlets like Media Matters and FAIR will focus on different things than conservative bias analysts and research think tanks like Bernard Goldberg or the Heritage Foundation.

There are many conflict of interest restrictions for journalists that are instituted to prevent the appearance of bias or favoritism. Mainstream news outlets have these policies so that they don't alienate portions of their viewership and so that people don't question their ability to be fair and balanced. Reporters are not allowed to volunteer for political campaigns, cannot wear campaign buttons or have political bumper stickers or lawn signs, and can't receive free tickets or trips. A local newspaper reporter might not be allowed to cover the police and crime beat if he or she is married to the police commissioner, a prosecutor, a trial lawyer, or a police officer.

Financial connections or conflicts could also influence bias. George Stephanopoulos of ABC came under fire after it was determined that he had contributed $75,000 to the Clinton Foundation. Despite an outcry from some media analysts, Stephanopoulos was not fired or suspended. He later admitted that he should not have made the donation to the foundation and that he would not moderate an upcoming Republican presidential primary debate in February 2016 in New Hampshire, as previously planned. He apologized to viewers for failing to disclose his contributions to the foundation, especially because he failed to make that disclosure during his aggressive interviewing of Peter Schweizer, author of the book *Clinton Cash*, which alleged that donations to the foundation may have influenced her decisions as secretary of state.[54] I wrote in a *Huffington Post* op-ed that the Stephanopoulos incident not only hurt his credibility but hurt the credibility of the many mainstream media professionals who do take objectivity and fairness seriously.[55]

I did note that it is possible for political operatives to become objective journalists. Diane Sawyer was a press aide for the Nixon administration from 1970 to 1974. Tim Russert was a counselor to Governor Mario Cuomo in the early 1980s. Michael Smerconish was heavily involved in the campaigns of Senator Arlen Specter and President George H. W. Bush and became a regional housing director in the Bush administration. David Gergen was an advisor in the Nixon, Ford, Reagan, and Clinton administrations. All of them became well-respected fair, neutral, and objective reporters and commentators. For most of his time at ABC News, Stephanopoulos has been fair and objective. The Clinton Foundation incident damaged the reputation that he had spent so long building. He should have known better. He knew that many people were suspicious of his potential bias because of his affiliation with the Clinton administration when he worked as the White House communications director. ABC News should have suspended him for a period of time as a message to other journalists that they need to be careful when it comes to conflicts of interest.

Other reporters have not been as fortunate when they violated conflict of interest policies. In 2010, Keith Olbermann was suspended and nearly fired for violating an NBC News policy by donating to three political campaigns, including the congressional campaign of Arizona Rep. Gabrielle Giffords.[56] Henry Norr, a *San Francisco Chronicle* technology reporter, was fired, in part, due to his participation in a rally against the Iraq war. Like most other media outlets, the *Chronicle*'s ethics code required that reporters not participate in political activities or express controversial opinions.[57] In 2007, a TV reporter in Omaha who posted a photo of herself on Facebook with a congressional candidate, urging her friends to vote for him, was dismissed.[58] An *Allentown Morning Call* reporter was suspended in 2006 after he served as grand marshal in a gay pride parade. The paper contended that he had violated the company's ethics policy, which prohibited employees from participating in demonstrations in favor of or opposing a cause.[59]

Timing and geography could have an impact on these conflicts of interest cases. When Norr participated in the anti-Iraq war protest, the war was popular and many people speaking out against it were deemed as unpatriotic. Conservative parts of the country, like Allentown, Pennsylvania, might view participation in a gay rights parade as advocating for gay rights and speaking out on a controversial issue, but in liberal areas it might be viewed as the equivalent of participating in an ethnic parade, such as a St Patrick's Day, Columbus Day, Pulaski Day, or an NAACP event. Also, views toward gay marriage have changed considerably since 2006. Fifty years ago, a reporter marching in civil rights protests in Alabama might have been deemed as advocating a controversial cause. Times change, and conflict of interest rules should evolve as well.

One of the most blatant incidents of financial conflict of interest took place in 2004 when the Bush administration paid columnist Armstrong Williams $241,000 to write positive articles about its No Child Left Behind policy. According to Howard Kurtz of the *Washington Post*, "In taking the money, funneled through the Ketchum Inc. public relations firm, Williams produced and aired a commercial on his syndicated television and radio shows featuring Education Secretary Roderick R. Paige, touted Bush's education policy, and urged other programs to interview Paige. He did not disclose the contract when talking about the law during cable television appearances or writing about it in his newspaper column." In light of the scandal, Tribune Media stopped distributing Williams's column.[60] Tribune Media Services released a statement, saying, "Accepting compensation in any form from an entity that serves as a subject of his weekly newspaper columns creates, at the very least, the appearance of a conflict of interest. Under these circumstances, readers may well ask themselves if the views expressed in his columns are his own, or whether they have been purchased by a third party"[61]

In commenting on reporters' conflicts of interest, Bill Reed of the *Philadelphia Inquirer* said in an e-mail interview, "Journalists should not forfeit their right to vote, but many register as Independents to avoid the appearance of political bias."[62]

Reporters' own race, ethnicity, and sexual orientation can influence their opinions and potentially inject bias into their reporting. Jose Diaz Ballart of MSNBC chooses to focus much of his program on issues related to Hispanics and Latinos, such as immigration and normalization of relations with Cuba. Al Sharpton and Melissa Harris Perry of MSNBC tended to focus on issues related to African Americans, such as voting rights and police abuse. Rachel Maddow often features stories on gay rights. Many Fox News hosts focus on issues important to Christians, such as abortion.

Should reporters have to disclose their own personal connections to issues that they are reporting on? Where should the line be drawn? If a sports reporter covers University of Alabama football, would it be necessary for the reporter to divulge that she graduated from that school? Do they have to disclose whether they are a gun owner if they write about the NRA? Do they need to disclose that they had an abortion if they are writing on that topic? Do they have to disclose that they are gay if they are writing about the debate on gay marriage? Many people suggest that transparency is key. Some journalists believe that the media should abandon its philosophy of achieving balance, fairness, and objectivity, and replace it instead with the philosophy of disclosure or transparency.

According to Christopher Harper, journalism professor at Temple University, in an e-mail interview, transparency regarding reporters' biases is essential:

Transparency is the characteristic of providing access to information particularly about business practices. As applied to journalism, transparency needs to be addressed in a variety of ways. First, journalists need to answer questions to demonstrate their biases and that information must be published by the news organization and easily available to the public. Second, a news organization must provide the public access to the manner in which a story was reported, including primary documents. Third, if complaints of bias occur against a journalist, the news organization must begin an outside evaluation of a sample of the content produced by the journalist, with the results of the inquiry easily available to the public. In journalistic parlance, confirmation bias translates into not letting the facts stand in the way of a good story, which has been an ongoing problem that will not be corrected until news organizations provide more transparency about how stories are reported.[63]

Harper adds,

I wrote a column for the *Washington Times* in which I divulged my biases. I am pro-life, anti-euthanasia, anti-death penalty. I am a conservative from flyover country who has lost a job because of my political views. I have donated to conservative causes and candidates. I called upon other journalists to divulge their biases. I think the American public would think better of the media if we admitted our biases rather than believe they do not affect what we do.[64]

Harper also repeated to me what he stated in one of his columns in the *Washington Times*:

Journalists need to give more information to the public about who they are, what they think and how much money they receive from speaking engagements. Media companies need to break out details about specific advertisers and revenues, money spent on journalistic endeavors and profits or losses from news programming.[65]

Are there certain reporting methods that can lead to more fairness? Is transparency a sufficient substitute or replacement for objectivity? Can a media outlet report fairly on itself when it is in the news, such as during a labor strike or when the media outlet or its reporters are being criticized for their content or comments? Media outlets that have a certain bias or viewpoint should make their bias clear and transparent. In the "About Us" section of the website or the front page, the outlet should describe and explain that bias so the reader knows what he or she is getting. It should explain its mission and whether it is independent, nonprofit, or who supports it financially.

Is the transparent disclosure of a bias as a preferred goal enough? Is it sufficient? Journalist Will Bunch thinks it is: "Journalists should let readers know as much as possible up front. Where they grew up, what their values are, and where they stand politically. It's not OK to endorse candidates, but it's OK to say who you voted for. It's better to say where you're coming from. Readers are smart and can make their own judgments. Reporters can't have Dalai Lama objectivity and they will be influenced."[66] Mark Bowden agrees: "To the extent that a journalist has a bias . . . she ought to be transparent about it. It goes to trustworthiness."[67] Honesty and transparency about one's personal biases is essential for John Timpane: "When a writer surfaces his or her biases, it always helps secure the trust of the audience. I can't imagine a news organization allowing reporters either to state personal biases or to let them exist unaddressed in a news piece."[68] Advocacy journalists who put their views out there openly and clearly do their audiences a service, says James B. Steele: "As long as advocacy journalists, such as a columnist, are clear about what they're doing, it's fine. There's no problem if the reader or viewer knows that it's an opinion. Beyond that, it's a problem if a reporter or news outlet tries to cloak their opinions as news."[69] As Chris Hayes tells Terri Gross of NPR, "I think that having a very clear transparent evaluative framework, like I do, which is I'm coming from the left . . . that lets people know where I'm coming from so there's no trickery, there's no bait-and-switch; and also I think allows people to put sets of facts into an evaluative framework that can be very useful for them to make their own judgments."[70]

I believe that transparency is an admirable and essential principle in journalism, especially for media outlets that have an admitted bias. It's essential for a skewed media outlet and host to be upfront about their biases in reporting. However, transparency still doesn't diminish the fact that their reporting might not be giving a fair and balanced presentation of the issue. Even if viewers and listeners know that MSNBC, Fox News, and Rush Limbaugh are biased, they are still receiving skewed information and "news" from those sources. There should be transparency, but there needs to be more than that in order to obtain better accuracy. In some cases, it might be useful for media outlets to specify opinion and commentary. Bill O'Reilly has his talking points at the beginning of each show. When Keith Olbermann was on MSNBC, he had a regular series of special comments at the end of the show that ran several minutes and were often very passionate opinions. Chris Matthews ends most of his shows with a two minute opinion commentary titled "Let Me Finish." Many people don't mind reporters giving their opinions, as long as it's an opinion they agree with.

Another concern is the relationship between public relations professionals and media outlets. In some cases, media outlets will simply reprint press releases as news items. Or they might rely heavily on the press release without doing any independent fact-checking. This is a concern since the organization writing the press release would be biased in favor of itself.

Beware of self-serving media content. A television network will often have its news division run stories about one of its new programs or a focus on one of the show's stars. These are often puff pieces chock-full of soft-ball questions. A network announcing Emmy awards might focus almost exclusively on its own network's shows that were nominated or won.

Journalists report, investigate, advocate, and explain issues. Facts are objective and can be verified, while opinions are subjective interpretations of information. Stating that a college linebacker is the best in the country is an opinion, while stating that the linebacker led the nation in tackles and interceptions would be a verifiable fact.

Journalists are trained to do all they can to put their personal feelings aside and not express their beliefs. The Society of Professional Journalists' code of ethics states that journalists should seek the truth and report it.[71] They should also show balance by presenting different sides.

Can there be true, 100 percent objectivity? Probably not, since reporters, their editors, and their publications have their own personal perspectives on issues. Is it possible for the media to be objective in a polarized environment? Alex S. Jones, a journalist and director of Harvard University's Shorenstein Center for Media, Politics, and Public Policy, defended the concept of objectivity in *Nieman Reports*, stating, "But journalistic objectivity is an effort to discern a practical truth, not an abstract, perfect truth. Reporters seeking genuine objectivity search out the best truth possible from the evidence that the reporter, in good faith, can find. To discredit objectivity because it is impossible to arrive at perfect truth is akin to dismissing trial by jury because it isn't perfect in its judgments."[72]

Some people claim that the goal of objectivity should be abandoned because it is impossible to achieve due to the inherent biases of reporters. However, just because perfect objectivity may not be attainable doesn't mean that reporters shouldn't try to be fair and balanced and as objective as possible, presenting both or as many sides of a story as need to be told.

Media-literacy expert Tessa Jolls isn't so sure that such a goal is attainable:

Objectivity is impossible because, inevitably, some points of view will be omitted and others will be included. People bring their own knowledge and point of view to what they produce, whether they want to or not. You can only see through your own eyes and present that point of view to others. You can try to balance the information and get other points of view, but that representation will be limited, and you can't report it all or include everyone. You only have so much time and space. You represent, to the best of your ability, a variety of points of view, but it's important to recognize the limits of what you can do. It's good for people to look at different sources and points of view. Balance is a better word. It's possible to be more balanced and represent more points of view. Sometimes journalists think they are being "objective" by presenting points of view that are polar opposites, but this is taking a short cut that provides a false dichotomy that doesn't serve readers.

Jolls sees this concept of objectivity as a deficit of media literacy: "I've spoken to many journalism and education groups. I don't believe that media literacy is being adequately taught, if at all. It's really shocking, especially, that journalism students have no exposure to media literacy. It's sad; it's a disservice to every citizen in the United States. After all of these years, to see journalists talk about objectivity is appalling. It's no wonder that journalism has so little credibility; claims of objectivity automatically set up unrealistic expectations that can't realistically be met."[73]

James Taranto of the *Wall Street Journal* writes, "Perfect objectivity is an unattainable goal, but objectivity is a worthy aspiration, its pursuit a discipline that makes for better journalism. It is the source of whatever authority journalists still enjoy."[74] My own viewpoint aligns more with Jones's and Taranto's perspectives. Every reporter has his own experiences and biases that make perfect objectivity impossible. However, reporters should always strive to be objective.

As I pointed out earlier, objectivity is no longer listed as one of the factors in the code of the Society of Professional Journalists. It's more a question of being fair and balanced as well as being transparent about bias and agenda.

The SPJ code states that reporters should "Seek Truth and Report It." That portion of the code states, in part:

Journalists should: Take responsibility for the accuracy of their work. Verify information before releasing it. Use original sources whenever possible. . . . Provide context. Take special care not to misrepresent or oversimplify in promoting, previewing, or summarizing a story.[75]

Another section of the SPJ code states that journalists should "Act Independently." Part of that section states:

Journalists should: Avoid conflicts of interest, real or perceived. Disclose unavoidable conflicts. Refuse gifts, favors, free travel, and special treatment, and avoid political and other outside activities that may compromise integrity or impartiality, or may damage credibility.[76]

Another minefield for mainstream media reporters who wish to avoid displaying bias is the explosion of social media and the expectation that reporters use Twitter and Facebook on a regular basis to be interactive with their viewers and readers. It can be difficult for reporters to keep an objective, neutral voice in these outlets.

PBS host Gwen Ifill was criticized by many when she responded to a White House tweet that outlined the positives of the Iran nuclear deal by tweeting, "Take that, Bibi." Critics said that she was taking a shot at the Israeli prime minister. Ifill defended herself by saying that she was merely paraphrasing the White House tweet. She wrote in a subsequent tweet and e-mail, "I was [re-tweeting] a @TheIranDeal tweet. Should have been clearer that it was their argument, not mine."[77]

I see reporters' use of social media as a double-edged sword. On one hand, it can be helpful to humanize the reporters and give them a voice. On the other hand, it can easily lead to expressions of bias that can alienate readers or viewers. And as we have seen, there are also debates as to whether reporters and news anchors should even give commentaries or their opinions.

Bias can be reflected in which political party is blamed or criticized for certain events. During the government shutdown of 2013, liberal media outlets such as MSNBC blamed the shutdown on congressional Republicans and focused their stories on people who were adversely affected by the shutdown, such as government workers who were furloughed. They also focused on the tensions between House Speaker John Boehner and the Tea Party. The media had a tendency to portray this as a crisis that would bring America to a catastrophic standstill. Conservative media outlets like talk radio and Fox News blamed President Obama and Senate Majority Leader Harry Reid for their failure to compromise with congressional Republicans. They also claimed that the liberal media was being too alarmist and that the effects of a government shutdown would not be catastrophic.

Another factor is the interactivity of the presentation of news, especially through social media. Rumors seem to gain credibility the more they are retweeted or posted on Facebook. Because of this, some news outlets choose to vet or edit their reporters' tweets before they go out.

It is essential for reporters to corroborate information and double-check their facts and sources. It is required that reporters quote people accurately and not out of context. Reporters are trained to verify people's names (Jimmy, Jimmie, or Jimi? James or Jaymes? Michael, Micheal, or Mychal?), people's ages, statistics, and math calculations. They are trained to carefully track research; avoid relying on assumptions and memory concerning dates, quotes, and physical descriptions; verify claims with multiple credible sources; verify information in headlines; check the accuracy of photo identification, grammar, spelling, and adherence to the Associated Press style guide; among other things. Most media organizations have a policy that requires reporters to confirm information through at least two reliable sources, though there are exceptions during breaking news stories.

The owners or publishers of a media outlet can strongly influence the bias that a publication will have. We discussed this when reviewing the history of American journalism during the colonial period, as well as during the days when multiple newspapers were collected under the ownership of a single person, such as Horace Greeley, Joseph Pulitzer, and William Randolph Hearst.

These days, there is a new trend of journalists, photojournalists, and documentary makers using crowdfunding websites such as Kickstarter, Sponsume, Beacon, Contributoria, CrowdNews, Patreon, and Uncoverage in order to raise money for their projects. *New York Times* public editor

Clark Hoyt was scrutinized on the issue of journalistic independence after he donated $50 to a crowdfunding website to support a freelance writer who was trying to raise money for a trip to cover a story for the *Times* as a freelancer.[78] There also is a concern that journalists who used this method to pay for their story expenses would not want to take positions or reveal information that might go against the beliefs and values of those who contribute financially to their projects.

Although reporters should strive for neutrality, fairness, balance, and objectivity, they still need to engage in fact-checking to report accurate information and to debunk inaccurate claims. To their credit, media outlets are expected to admit their mistakes prominently and print or broadcasts corrections when they make mistakes. Mistakes made on social media should not be ignored or whitewashed. They should be prominently acknowledged.

Ideally, media outlets would use more centrist non-ideologues as experts since they would be less predictable. Reporters should be like Mr. Spock of *Star Trek*—as logical and unemotional about their reporting as possible. It's natural for reporters to have a viewpoint, value system, and assumptions about issues, but it's important that they be open minded enough to change their viewpoint or kill or revise the story if the evidence does not confirm their assumptions. A good example of this was the *Rolling Stone* reporting on the alleged University of Virginia rape, as discussed in an earlier chapter.[79] In order to be accurate, it's important to seek out, examine, and consider facts that might challenge or rebut your viewpoint.

Dr. Neil Levy, a Research Fellow at the University of Melbourne, stated in *On Line Opinion*, Australia's e-journal of social and political debate, that reporters should try to not let their political biases influence their reporting: "When they are reporting the news—that is, informing us of the day's events, rather than editorialising—journalists ought to refrain, so far as possible, from allowing their personal opinions to influence what they say and how they say it. Some do a remarkably good job: I have sometimes been surprised to learn that a journalist whose reports I have heard or read many times, has strong political leanings to the right or to the left. Some are less good at it, and some news services, more or less openly, discourage objectivity."[80]

One of the concerns about having network news anchors give commentaries is that they would presumably play it safe and give bland and uninspiring opinions that don't have much value. They would want to be careful so as to not alienate segments of their wide-ranging, diverse audience.

There is a great tradition of Sunday news shows like *Meet the Press*, *Face the Nation*, ABC's *This Week*, *Fox News Sunday*, and CNN's *State of the Union*. Among the notable hosts have been Tim Russert, David Brinkley, Bob Schieffer, Howard K. Smith, Leslie Stahl, Chuck Todd, Jake Tapper, Chris Wallace, Cokie Roberts, Sam Donaldson, and George Stephanopoulos. Are these Sunday news shows fair and balanced? Most people believe that the hosts are fairly nonpartisan, although conservatives have an issue with George Stephanopoulos, who they feel is too closely aligned with the Clintons. Most of the shows do have balanced guest-expert panels and do present both sides' points of view and interview guests from both political parties. I'm a big fan of these shows because they do attempt to provide balance and varied points of view and the hosts don't have a personal agenda. The hosts ask their guests tough questions, but they do it in a respectful manner, and they ask tough questions of members of both political parties.

Throughout the years, there have been a number of television news programs and news magazines, such as *Dateline NBC*, *60 Minutes*, *Nightline*, *20/20*, *Larry King Live*, *48 Hours*, *Primetime Live*, *Frontline*, *Crossfire*, the Capitol Gang, *This Week in Washington*, *Washington Week in Review*, the *McLaughlin Report*, *Jim Lehrer*, and *Charlie Rose*. In 2004, there was a huge controversy involving *60 Minutes* and Dan Rather using a forged memo during its reporting of President Bush's Vietnam War record. Despite the controversy, the underlying story was accurate—the fact that Bush's family had used its influence to get him into the National Guard and that he failed to satisfy many of the requirements of his service. The *Boston Globe*'s analysis of Bush's war record showed significant gaps in his Guard service.[81] However, even though the underlying story was likely true, the fact that *60 Minutes* relied on a forged document overshadowed the rest of the true story.[82]

As I wrote in the *Philadelphia Metro* in 2004, the mainstream media makes mistakes, but citing the Internet as a bastion of credibility is laughable. I observed, "Do you really want to rely on 'Joe's Blog for Freedom' for your news, when Joe is a part-time real estate agent or a substitute first-grade teacher blogging in his pajamas at home, without any training or real experience in journalism?" Not much was made of right-wing Internet gossip columnist Matt Drudge's embarrassing blunder earlier in 2004 when he erroneously alleged that John Kerry had had an extramarital affair with a former intern. Reporters are trained on libel and slander and are much more cognizant as to what standards must be met to constitute reliable sources. In many cases, mainstream media outlets have more resources, editors, proofreaders, and fact-checkers than most Internet site operators and bloggers. I stated, "If Internet sites, talk radio, and bloggers were under as much scrutiny as the mainstream media, there would be many more examples of falsehoods and mistakes."[83]

Most of the time, the mainstream media gets the story right. I expressed my hope that "Rathergate" wouldn't cause major news outlets to pull back from investigative journalism, which serves a valuable public service. Also, I noted that this controversy shouldn't stop the media from asking legitimate questions about Bush's gaps in his National Guard service, just as the *Boston Globe* did.

The public takes a much bigger risk when it relies on the alternative media and advocacy media as its primary source of news. These outlets might be exciting and entertaining, but in the long run, an informed person would rather rely on something like CBS, in the mainstream media.

Anonymity is a major issue in journalism. Traditionally, the concept of anonymity is raised when media outlets want to use anonymous sources in a story. There is an ongoing debate as to whether journalists and media outlets should use anonymous sources to break and cover stories. Some media outlets have instituted higher standards as to whether to use them and some have a policy of not using them at all. Some media outlets choose not to use anonymous sources because it is more credible to have sources to go on the record. However, many major stories have been broken through the use of anonymous sources, including Watergate. Nevertheless, reporters should use anonymous sources as a last resort. Generally, reporters should try to get the information from other sources, such as from public documents, Freedom of Information Act searches, or disgruntled former employees.

One of the approaches that media outlets use to combat the perception of bias is to provide conflicting viewpoints to offer readers, listeners, and viewers a broader spectrum of opinion. Newspaper op-ed pages will frequently run opposing views, such as pro-Iran deal vs. anti-Iran deal, pro-Affordable Care Act vs. anti-Obamacare, or pro-choice vs. pro-life. However, this is not done all of the time, and sometimes opposing viewpoints are given weeks and months apart.

On television, expert panels are often balanced with guests who have opposing viewpoints. However, especially on cable, many panels are stacked in favor of one view. For instance, on MSNBC, the host and three of the panelists may have pro-Affordable Care Act viewpoints, while the one token conservative on the panel has an anti-Obama Care viewpoint and is drowned out by the others. The same thing happens on Fox News, where panels are often stacked with predominantly conservative voices. Oftentimes, the host will interrupt the guest with the opposing viewpoint and won't let them complete their thoughts. Or the host and the majority of the panel will mock the lone dissenter and try to make him or her look like a buffoon or an out-of-touch radical.

Advocacy journalism doesn't just appear in newspapers, magazines, websites, radio, or television, of course. It can also be presented in the form of nonfiction books, such as Rachel Carson's *Silent Spring* and Ralph Nader's *Unsafe at Any Speed*. Movie and television documentaries can also act as advocacy journalism, such as Michael Moore's works, like *Bowling for Columbine, Roger and Me, Sicko,* and *Fahrenheit 9/11*, with their clear liberal, progressive bias and point of view.

Dan Gillmor refers to advocacy organizations like the ACLU and Human Rights Watch as performing "almost-journalism." Gillmor contends that these groups should apply the journalism principle of fairness to their work and that they should "a) listen hard to people who disagree with you; b) hunt for facts and data that are contrary to your own stand; and c) reflect disagreements and nuances in what you tell the rest of us."[84]

Reporters should be wary of "trial balloons," intentional news leaks by politicians or government officials who want to judge public reaction and opinion on certain issues. Modern-day presidents frequently float ideas,

names, foreign policy approaches, proposed decisions, potential nomina-
tions, and potential policies to members of the press in order to see what
the public thinks and to assess support or opposition.

There is often a bias regarding reporting on disabled people. Shawn
Burns writes in *MediaShift*, "Professor Beth Haller is a world leader in the
field and helped develop the 'media models of disability.' Haller and colleagues claim the news media is still, despite decades of disability activism,
inclined to represent people with disabilities as tragedies or heroes, and to
use language and imagery that serves to embed stereotypes and put at risk
members of an already vulnerable community."[85]

Bias in the coverage of criminal trials is common. The coverage often
reflects a "presumed guilty" slant, partially because the prosecution is free
to give facts, information, and statements to the media that can skew public
perception, while the defendant is often limited as to what he or she can say
before trial because what they say can be held against them. Prime examples of criminal defendants who talked too much to the media and hurt
themselves at trial were convicted child molester Jerry Sandusky, former
Illinois governor Rod Blogoivich, and convicted murderer Drew Peterson.
Often, pundits will try the case on television and in the media, but the end
result turns out to be surprising because the jury can only consider evidence that is admissible and presented to them at trial. Many pundits were
proven wrong in their assessment of high-profile trials such as those of O.
J. Simpson, Michael Jackson, Casey Anthony, and George Zimmerman
trial, as well as about things such as the grand jury's decision not to press
charges in the Michael Brown shooting in Ferguson, Missouri.

Television hosts can sometimes give biased presentations of criminal
trials. Nancy Grace, a former prosecutor, is well known for her pro-pros-
ecution stance.

Bias is a frequent part of media coverage, but media outlets can and
should try to minimize it. Most of the mainstream news outlets do strive
to be impartial and fair. They won't succeed in perfect objectivity, but it is
something that they can strive for. Advocacy journalism, in which objectivity is less of a goal, has been a major factor in America's polarized political and social climate. That will be the focus of the next chapter.

CHAPTER 15

THE POLARIZING EFFECT OF ADVOCACY JOURNALISM ON POLITICS AND SOCIETY

The United States government is in gridlock. Our Constitution intended to create an executive branch and two chambers of the legislative branch that would serve in part as checks on each other's legitimate powers. But what we have today is not shared government but a divided government, in which there has been little legislative action during President Obama's administration. According to the Pew Research Center, "As part of a year-long study of polarization, the Pew Research Center has conducted the largest political survey in its history—a poll of more than 10,000 adults between January and March of this year (2014). It finds that Republicans and Democrats are further apart ideologically than at any point in recent history."[1] Part of this intense partisanship is a result of the gerrymandering of voting districts. In 2015, President Obama told Steve Inskeep of NPR that gerrymandering (or political redrawing) of congressional districts had helped to polarize the country: "I think political gerrymandering has resulted in a situation in which, with 80 percent Democratic districts or 80 percent Republican districts and no competition . . . that leads to more and more polarization in Congress, and it gets harder and harder to get things done."[2] With more representatives in districts where they are practically guaranteed to win reelection, there is no incentive for these elected officials to compromise with their colleagues in the other party. With such "safe seats," these politicians can be as partisan as they want without fear of losing their seat in the next election.

This leads to a Congress that is extremely polarized. There are fewer moderate Republicans or conservative Democrats than before. The members of Congress do not want to alienate their voter base. They also do not want to be ridiculed or vilified by partisan media outlets of their own party, and they don't want to risk being primaried (i.e., losing their seat in a primary election to a member of their own party who is viewed as being more in tune with the constituency). Working with members of the other party, even on just one key issue, could be seen as a sign of weakness or betrayal. Even though members of both parties do hold similar views on many issues, it doesn't behoove them to act in a bipartisan manner. Therefore, House and Senate votes tend to fall predictably along party lines.

There is little bipartisan cooperation in government compared to that found during the era of President Ronald Reagan and Speaker of the House Tip O'Neill or the period of President Bill Clinton and Speaker of the House Newt Gingrich. In both those instances, the president and the speaker of the house disagreed on policy but were able to get things done. Now, logic, civility, and cooperation have given way to strict, unyielding ideology in which the other party is viewed as the enemy that can never be trusted. While Ronald Reagan was able to work with Tip O'Neill on many issues and Bill Clinton could work with Newt Gingrich, it proved to be more difficult for George W. Bush, and especially harder for Barack Obama, to come to agreement on legislation with their respective Congresses. When Obama was elected, Sen. Mitch McConnell told the *National Journal* that "The single most important thing we want to achieve is for President Obama to be a one-term president."[3] During President Obama's State of the Union address in 2009, South Carolina Rep. Joe Wilson shouted "You lie!" when Obama stated that the Affordable Care Act would not give illegal immigrants free healthcare.[4] Congressional Republicans tried to repeal Obamacare dozens of times in a five-year period. Conservative critics blame Obama for the polarization, saying that he pandered to his Democratic base on issues like not approving the Keystone Pipeline that would bring oil from Canadian oilfields to the Gulf of Mexico for shipping and processing; and that he didn't reach out to congressional Republicans to get their input on the healthcare debate.

The United States Supreme Court is highly polarized as well. Consistently conservative, the late justice Antonin Scalia and Justices Samuel

Alito and Clarence Thomas were pitted against consistently liberal justices Ruth Bader Ginsburg, Stephen Breyer, Sonia Sotomayor, and Elena Kagan. Those justices' votes are fairly predictable in most major Supreme Court cases. Justice Anthony Kennedy is the most consistent swing vote and Chief Justice John Roberts shows an occasional independent streak, most notably in the Obamacare cases. This has led some conservatives and conservative commentators to label Roberts a traitor and a disappointment, even though most of his decisions lean conservative. Polarization continued in the aftermath of Justice Scalia's death with the debate as to whether President Obama should nominate Scalia's replacement or hold off and let the next elected president handle the nomination.

Many people believe that advocacy journalism has contributed significantly to this adversarial political and cultural climate. A Quinnipiac University poll from March 2015 showed that Fox News had the most trusted network and cable news coverage in the United States, but that responses varied significantly depending on one's political party. Overall, 29 percent responded that they trusted Fox News the most, followed by CNN (22 percent), CBS News and NBC News (10 percent each), ABC News (8 percent), and MSNBC (7 percent). Republican voters trusted Fox News the most, at 58 percent, with the next trusted being CNN at 13 percent. Democrats trusted CNN the most, with 32 percent, while only 3 percent trusted Fox News most.[5]

And an e-mail interview I conducted with Rob Kall, operator of *OpEdNews*, reinforces this view: "The country IS polarized. I'd say that is primarily because of right wing media—Fox News, Clear Channel, and the right wing Radio echo chamber."[6] Of course, conservatives would put much of the blame of polarization on President Obama and the liberal mainstream media, such as major newspapers like the *New York Times*.

The polarization of America in general and of the media in particular has been reflected in coverage of and commentary on many issues, including the Iraq War, Obamacare/the Affordable Care Act, nuclear negotiations with Iran, education policy and funding, rights of labor unions, whether to invade Libya or Syria, the government's handling of the Benghazi attack, abortion and the funding of Planned Parenthood, race relations, the alleged war on women, national security, the right to privacy, religious freedom, gay rights and gay marriage, income inequality and raising the minimum wage, immigration, government spending and the national debt, and normalizing relations with Cuba, among other subjects. This pervasive and wide-ranging political and cultural animosity has Thomas Carsey and Geoffrey Layman observing in the *Washington Post* that, although Democrats and Republicans have almost always disagreed deeply on some policy issues, the two major political parties are more polarized and divided on major issues and policies than they have been in the last fifty years: "However, what may be different is the emergence of party polarization across all major dimensions of domestic political debate. That political polarization seems, to most people, to be worse now than in prior eras may be due partly to this conflict extension. Where parties in earlier periods may have found many areas of agreement even as they fought bitterly over some issues, parties today disagree on virtually everything."[7]

The politics and messages of "us versus them" or "you're with us or against us" leads to crippling gridlock and the tendency to view the other political side as the enemy. The rise of cable news channels, talk radio, and Internet opinion websites has led to a self-reinforcing echo chamber in which if enough talk show hosts and pundits repeat each other's views often enough, they become gospel even if they are completely or partially false. Both sides are content to yell at each other and refuse to engage in constructive dialogue that could, if attempted, actually lead to bipartisan solutions. Conservatives get their talking points for their family dinners from the likes of Rush Limbaugh and Sean Hannity, while liberals get their talking points from talking heads like Rachel Maddow and Chris Hayes. In many cases, the ensuing heated political arguments at holiday meals across the country supports the long-held viewpoint that talking about religion and politics at family gatherings should be discouraged. Your liberal Uncle Joe argues with your conservative Aunt Esther. I've been there and done that. It gets to the point where several relatives have to chime in and yell, "Stop talking about politics!"

Growing numbers of rank-and-file Republicans and Democrats express extremely negative views about the opposing party, mainly because of what they see on cable news, listen to on talk radio, and read on slanted websites, blogs, newspapers, and magazines. Conservative media portray Obama as an elite and aloof socialist who wants to destroy America, while liberal media blame the obstructionist Congress for what ails America. During the administration of George W. Bush, liberal media outlets mocked incurious George and his reckless cowboy diplomacy, while conservative media outlets painted those who opposed the Iraq war as unpatriotic. Both sides use rhetorical hyperbole, or loose figurative language in the form of insults, epithets, and name calling, to disparage their opponents. Granted, I've been guilty of this at times in my op-eds, criticizing Republicans and conservatives as being insensitive and cold-hearted in their policies regarding poor people. All this is protected by the First Amendment and part of the political and media game, but at some point it becomes tiresome to watch and listen to, especially on cable news and talk radio, where the views tend to be predictable and repetitive.

Is advocacy journalism tearing America apart? "I think so," Will Bunch answers:

> We're leaning more toward advocacy journalism due to the economics of the news industry. Fewer and fewer news organizations have the money to afford original reporting. For instance, I recently went to a Bernie Sanders campaign rally and was surprised how small the press corps was compared to similar events around sixteen years ago. Fewer people are doing that kind of reporting, as well as overseas reporting or focusing on big issues such as poverty. The Internet makes it easier to find information. You get more advocacy journalism because is easiest to do. It's generally not field reporting, and they can rely on field reporting to [then] add their own opinion and give their hot take of the day or rant about whatever is in the news. People then self-select what they want to read. Liberals will go to Daily Kos, Talking Points Memo, or Eschaton. It's easier to do advocacy journalism and easier for people to find information that matches their own points of view. That tends to reinforce extreme opinions and people don't get exposed to views that challenge their own. I don't want to go as far as blaming journalism for all of this. There are other factors. But advocacy journalism is a factor.[8]

John Timpane, former op-ed page editor for the *Philadelphia Inquirer* concurs:

> Advocacy itself is polarizing the country. Since advocacy journalism is part of that universe, it's part of the dynamic causing the increasing (and increasingly vituperative) political split in the United States. Advocacy deforms discourse. If the only thing you hear or read is advocatorial—pitching for the home team, zero-sum argument, casting the "other side" as bad guys always and your side as always right and truthful, while urging extreme arguments yourself in scorched-earth rhetoric—you'll get a distorted picture of the true state of the world. And since the folks who scream loudest and have the biggest bucks get into print and before the cameras, that's too often what you do hear or see: advocacy at all costs, well-paid, fast-talking, articulate, desperate, and extreme.[9]

Mark Bowden believes that "advocacy journalism reflects a divided country and somewhat amplifies that divide."[10]

My impression is that advocacy journalism is a major factor in the current polarization of the country. It's as though we are living in parallel universes. When major news breaks, we go to our separate corners in the ring and get our information and talking points from skewed media outlets so that we're ready for verbal sparring with friends and family. Liberals bought into MSNBC's portrayal of President George W. Bush as a blundering, war hungry, stubborn moron, while conservatives were convinced by talk radio and Fox News's portrayal of President Obama as a feckless anti-American socialist weakling.

It is not uncommon for members of each political party to refer to one another as enemies. When Hillary Clinton was asked during a Democratic presidential primary debate in October 2015 to name her enemies, she included "Republicans" in her list. Vice President Joe Biden chided her a few days later during his announcement at the White House that he would not run for president in 2016. Biden said that he did not "think we should look at Republicans as our enemies. They are our opposition; they're not our enemies. And for the sake of the country, we have to work together."[11]

Conservative Republican congressman Louis "Louie" Gohmert had this to say during an Ohio Christian University's *Faith & Liberty* radio program regarding President Obama's failure to allow Israel to bomb Iran's nuclear facilities: "Those are the kind of things that an enemy does. . . . An enemy within. There will be consequences for the betrayals of this administration, as the leaders of our country. And it is just a little scary the kind of betrayals there have been."[12]

The polarized media landscape frequently feeds into this narrative by choosing to publicize the efforts of liberals and conservatives to degrade and demean one another. Both sides often use Nazi and Hitler analogies when discussing members of the other political party, and the media is on hand to provide these views wide circulation. During the 2008 presidential contest, conservative columnist Thomas Sowell offered the observation that people assume "change" will make them better, and that they care more about inspiring rhetoric and confidence than specifics: "But many twentieth century leaders with inspiring rhetoric and great self-confidence led their followers or their countries into utter disasters. These ranged from Jim Jones who led hundreds to their deaths in Jonestown to Hitler and Mao who led millions to their deaths. What specifics do we know about Barack Obama's track record that might give us some clue as to what kinds of 'changes' to expect if he is elected?"[13] Sowell wrote in another column about the German crowd's adulation and enthusiastic reception for Obama when he was visiting in 2008 as a presidential candidate: "To find anything comparable to crowds' euphoric reactions to Obama, you would have to go back to old newsreels of German crowds in the 1930s, with their adulation of their fuehrer, Adolf Hitler. With hindsight, we can look back on those people with pity, knowing now how many of them would be led to their deaths by the man they idolized."[14]

According to the *Arizona Capitol Times*, Republican state legislator Rep. Brenda Barton of Payson, Arizona, compared President Barack Obama to Adolf Hitler on a Facebook post urging county sheriffs to revoke authority from the National Parks Service to enforce the federal shutdown on national parks lands: "Someone is paying the National Park Service thugs overtime for their efforts to carry out the order of De Fuhrer. . . . [W]here are our Constitutional sheriffs who can revoke the Park Service

Rangers authority to arrest? Do we have any sheriffs with a pair?" she wrote.[15]

Liberal writers are just as good at slinging mud as conservatives. Columnist Dave Lindorff of *CounterPunch* linked President George W. Bush's governing style to Hitler's when he wrote, "It's going a bit far to compare the Bush of 2003 to the Hitler of 1933. Bush simply is not the orator that Hitler was. But comparisons of the Bush Administration's fear mongering tactics to those practiced so successfully and with such terrible results by Hitler and Goebbels on the German people and their Weimar Republic are not at all out of line."[16] In 2015, after candidate Donald Trump announced his proposed ban on all Muslims entering the United States, some individuals and news outlets compared him to Hitler. On its cover, the *Philadelphia Daily News* showed a photo of Donald Trump, right arm extended at a 45 degree angle similar to the Nazi salute, over the caption: "The New Furor."[17]

Democratic congressman Keith Ellison of Minnesota made a Hitler/ Nazi analogy during the Bush administration in a speech to members of Atheists for Human Rights by comparing 9/11 to the destruction of the Reichstag, the German parliament, in 1933, which was possibly burned down by the Nazis in order to justify Hitler's later seizure of emergency powers. He said, "After the Reichstag was burned, they blamed the Communists for it, and it put the leader [Hitler] of that country in a position where he could basically have authority to do whatever he wanted." Ellison told the group that he wouldn't accuse the Bush administration of planning 9/11 because "that's how they put you in the nut-ball box."[18]

I think the Hitler comparisons from both sides of the political spectrum are inappropriate and offensive and shouldn't be made. I understand the concept of rhetorical hyperbole, exaggeration, and attempts at humor, but the Hitler/Nazi analogies just don't apply. As bad as President George W. Bush was as far as Democrats were concerned or as bad as President Obama was as far as Republicans were concerned, neither of them rounded up mass numbers of people and killed them in concentration camps.

Because many people get their news from such biased sources, an outsider might think that he or she is living in two parallel universes. During the negotiation and aftermath of the Iran nuclear deal in the summer of

2015, advocacy media sources framed the issue in vastly different ways. Conservative media unanimously condemned the deal and compared President Obama to Neville Chamberlain handing Czechoslovakia to the Nazis during the 1938 Munich Accords. Liberal media outlets put a more positive spin on the deal, comparing Obama's outreach to Iran to Nixon's historic trip to China and Reagan's negotiations with the Soviet Union. During that time, it was hard to find balanced perspectives on the deal, thus making it more difficult for average people to make a reasoned, informed assessment as to whether the deal was a good one for the United States and Israel.[19] I know that I found myself frustrated by the biased and skewed coverage that cable news outlets had during this time period. Most of the experts were either strongly for the deal or decidedly against it, depending on which network you were watching. I wanted to maintain an open mind and get perspectives from experts who didn't have an agenda, in the hope that I could assess whether it was a good deal or not. The coverage for this issue, like many other issues, was predictable.

In September 2015, Kim Davis, a county clerk in Kentucky, was sent to jail by a US District judge for refusing to issue marriage licenses to couples (both gay and straight) after the US Supreme Court ruled that gay couples had a constitutional right to marry. Liberal media outlets condemned Davis, arguing that she had an obligation to comply and follow the law as a government worker. In a *Washington Post* op-ed, George Washington University professor Jonathan Turley compared her to George Wallace, the Alabama governor who defied the government by trying to block desegregation.[20] However, Conservative media outlets hailed her as a hero and a martyr, even comparing her to Rosa Parks.[21]

There was a slight lull in partisanship after the 9/11 attacks, but it revived with a fervor after the aftermath of the Iraq invasion and then during the Obama administration.

When the country celebrated the announcement of the killing of Osama bin Laden in May 2011, you would have thought that the media coverage might have been unifying. However, that wasn't the case. Many conservative pundits and news outlets criticized President Obama for taking credit for the bin Laden killing and argued that it was a "no brainer" decision and was mostly a result of President Bush's foreign policies and interrogation policies. For instance, the headline for Larry Elder's Creators Syndicate article read: "Bush Led, bin Laden Dead. Where's the Credit?"[22] According to Pew Research Center, only two weeks after the raid that killed bin Laden, 21 percent of news outlets were focused on the debate as to whether Bush or Obama deserved more credit.[23]

One of the best examples of the use of advocacy journalism as a divisive tool was the coverage of the George Zimmerman case in Florida in early 2012 and thereafter. People who watched MSNBC's coverage were exposed to the consistent viewpoint that Zimmerman was a racist who gunned down an innocent black teenager named Trayvon Martin and that he should be found guilty. Fox News's coverage urged viewers to have an open mind about the case and portrayed Zimmerman in a positive light as a neighborhood watch captain on patrol trying to protect his neighbors, while painting Trayvon Martin as a bad kid.[24] *Salon* criticized Fox News's negative portrayal of Martin, noting how ridiculous it had become on occasion, as the network "speculated that Martin could probably kill someone with the Skittles bag and Arizona Iced Tea bottle he was carrying. Meanwhile, conservative blogs set to work painting Martin as a dangerous thug. The *Daily Caller* obtained Martin's Twitter feed, selecting tweets that made him look most intimidating. For George Zimmerman, his lawyers are not his only defense team."[25]

For its part, the *Weekly Standard* criticized Rev. Al Sharpton, civil rights activist and host of the MSNBC show *Politics Nation*, for his coverage of the Zimmerman trial, which it claimed was skewed and portrayed Martin as a victim of racism: "Despite scant evidence that race was a factor in Martin's death—George Zimmerman . . . is Hispanic and claims the killing was self-defense—Sharpton came to Florida to tape on location, thundering that Martin was a victim of racial injustice."[26]

NPR commentator and television critic Eric Deggans criticized cable punditry and how it covered race issues. After denouncing Fox News and CNN, he criticized MSNBC and Sharpton, stating that Sharpton "has been a strong advocate for families at the heart of these cases, speaking for the parents of slain Florida teen Trayvon Martin in 2012 and leading a rally on [Eric] Garner's case. . . . That tracks with MSNBC's status last year as most-watched among black cable news viewers. These are all ways in which news outlets' drive from conflict and their target audiences are side-tracking the conversation during a crucial moment. It may be time for an educated public to demand better coverage from an industry that is some-times too wrapped up in its own priorities to get it right."[27]

According to Brett LoGiurato of the publication *Business Insider*, Sean Hannity unfavorably compared Obama and Martin on his program "by wondering if Obama was admitting that both he and Martin 'smoked pot and did a little blow' in comparing himself to the slain teenager."[28]

Doug Spero's op-ed in the *Christian Science Monitor* criticized all sides of the media spectrum for their unfair coverage of the Trayvon Martin–George Zimmerman incident and the lack of balanced coverage: "The media's pro-Martin agenda was quick to highlight rallies, marches, and protests in defense of Martin while choosing to ignore similar news coverage from the pro-Zimmerman crowd. . . . Fox News was airing mostly pro-Zimmerman interviews. . . . MSNBC appeared to be in total support of a guilty verdict." Spero argued, "A rush to judgment, info-tainment, agenda reporting, and a push to increase the bottom line at the expense of solid reporting, creates the perfect storm for journalism—and democracy. The frustration and aftermath of the George Zimmerman trial are precisely the circumstances in which thoughtful, balanced coverage is most needed"[29]

The *Miami Herald*'s Marc Caputo pointed out the absurdity of the par-tisan coverage by noting a poll showing that Republicans had a much more favorable opinion of George Zimmerman than of President Obama: "That's right. The Democratic occupant of the White House is held in less favor-able regard by Republicans than the guy who shot an unarmed teenager and successfully pleaded self-defense." Caputo cited a Fox News poll indi-cating that 18 percent of Republicans had a favorable opinion of Obama, while 45 percent of GOP voters had a favorable opinion of Zimmerman.[30]

The shooting of Michael Brown in Ferguson, Missouri, offers another example of the media fanning the flames of political and social discord. Liberal media outlets condemned the police officer who shot Brown and adopted the mantras "Hands up, Don't Shoot" and "Black Lives Matter." Conservative media outlets portrayed Brown in a negative light, repeatedly showing him shoving a store clerk, and also painted the officer in a more favorable light, saying he acted in self-defense. Writing in the *Columbia Journalism Review*, Alexis Sobel Fitts pointed out that, in addition to discussion of racial bias as to how black victims are portrayed in the media, there is racial bias in the selection of crimes the media chooses to cover: "In a survey of broadcast news . . . Media Matters for America found that television coverage of crime suspects' race doesn't match up to the raw data of who is actually arrested—black suspects receive disproportionate coverage for their alleged crimes."[31]

On MSNBC's *Morning Joe*, cohost Joe Scarborough criticized the media's Michael Brown coverage, expressing his anger at the media narrative of police officers looking to shoot and kill people and of Michael Brown as the face of black oppression. He compared that narrative to those of right-wing "nut job" conservatives who embraced George Zimmerman, a "nasty, thuggish guy that chased a young black man through a neighborhood simply because he was black." In arguing that Michael Brown should not be embraced as a hero, Scarborough said, "There are so many great people to embrace as heroes in the black community, that deciding you're going to embrace a guy that knocked over a convenience store, and then, according to grand jury testimony, acting in ways that would get my children shot on Staten Island or in Queens or in Brooklyn, that's your hero? That's the reason you want to burn down black businesses?"[32]

At the end of 2015, the *Washington Post*'s "Fact Checker" column listed "Hands up, don't shoot" as one of the top Pinocchio's, or false statements, of the year. It noted that "various investigations concluded this did not happen—and that Wilson acted out of self-defense and was justified in killing Brown."[33]

I think that media outlets on both sides of the political spectrum do their viewers a tremendous disservice when they provide slanted coverage of emotionally charged criminal trials. It's as though the networks and their hosts have rooting interests in guilt or innocence. MSNBC's coverage reflected a bias that there should have been guilty verdicts for George Zimmerman and for the police officer who shot Michael Brown. Fox News's coverage reflected a bias in favor of acquittal for the defendants in those cases. Television host Nancy Grace demonstrated a prosecutorial bias when she said, "The devil is dancing tonight," after Casey Anthony was acquitted of killing her young daughter, Caylee, in a highly publicized trial. There have been numerous times when pundits act more like prosecutors or defense attorneys and end up predicting the wrong verdict or outcome. Yes, news outlets have to provide coverage, but they need to give more balanced portrayals and be open to evidence that contradicts their beliefs. The American justice system is supposed to operate under the assumption that defendants are "innocent until proven guilty," but in the media it's often "guilty until proven innocent."

In the past, liberals and conservatives had a limited number of news outlets and tended to get their news from the same newspaper, radio, or television sources. As of forty years ago, there were only three major commercial television networks: NBC, ABC, and CBS. Viewers would get the nightly news from either Walter Cronkite on CBS, Harry Reasoner on ABC, or John Chancellor on NBC. With the explosion of cable TV, the Internet, and social media, liberals and conservatives now get their news from different sources, which present the news in different fashions and with different objectives, agendas, and points of view. These news outlets cater to what their audiences want and don't want. Fox News viewers don't want to hear positive opinions and statistics about Obamacare or the Iran nuclear deal. MSNBC viewers don't want to hear positive statistics and opinions about the IRS scandal or the Keystone Pipeline.

In 2004, conservative media accused John Kerry of flip-flopping due to his change of opinion regarding his Senate vote authorizing President Bush to use force in Iraq: "I voted for the 87 billion, before I voted against it." Liberal media outlets, on the other hand, defended Kerry for being able to change his mind and adapt to new information and different circumstances.

There is an implicit media bias in the way that election coverage is framed due to the almost exclusive focus on the two major political parties. Very rarely is any credence given to other political parties or candidates, such as the Green Party or Libertarian Party. Independent voters and candidates are mostly ignored by the media. Third-party candidates are rarely invited to participate in televised presidential debates (John Anderson in 1980 and Ross Perot in 1992 are the notable exceptions). As of 2015, there were only two Independents who were congressmen or senators, Bernie Sanders (from Vermont) and Angus King (from Maine). Most Americans are probably unaware of political third parties such as the Green Party, the Libertarian Party, or the Constitution Party. As long as the media continues to ignore third parties, the current state of two-party dominance and political wrangling is unlikely to change.

As John Timpane of the *Philadelphia Inquirer* said in an e-mail interview,

> We should remember that there does not have to be only two parties. Too much investment, however, resides in there being only two, so all political battles can be nice and tidy and clear, that all political conversations be *only and exclusively* "us" and "them." The two private clubs have too much money and clout invested in keeping it that way. Meantime, everyone knows, or should know, that many other possible political viewpoints exist, or could exist, on almost all issues worth discussing. True socialism doesn't exist to any great extent in this country as of 2015, really, which is why Bernie Sanders is seen as such a refreshing outlier. True environmentalism doesn't either, despite widespread sympathy for aspects of the environmentalist stance.
>
> As long as we assent to the notion that there always are only two parties, we condemn ourselves to factitious "balance," to a tit-for-tat notion of "fairness," until such time as waves of ineluctably bad news overwhelm one side or the other, and then we are forced to report bad news as the bad news that it is, with no other side.
>
> Yes, that's right: the whole notion that there are "sides" is a fiction, a piece of marketing. There are many sides—we hear about only two, because they have the clout and bucks.[34]

A 2015 Washington State University study published in the *International Journal of Opinion Research* found that the federal Telecommunications Act of 1996 and its deregulation of the television industry led to increased political polarization in the United States. One of the study's co-authors, Darin Watkins, explained that "having more TV news choices means programmers can target particular consumers and consumers can pick news they prefer. Also, corporate consolidation of TV news resulted in drastic cuts to newsroom budgets, reducing coverage and variety."[35]

I know plenty of people who just get their all of their news from partisan sources, simply because that's who they trust. That was much harder twenty-five to thirty years ago, but due to the proliferation of niche media outlets it's much easier today.

Deanna Zandt in *Forbes* acknowledges this rise of political and social extremism, noting the concept of confirmation bias in light of her observations of a ramp-up in ideological spewing in social media. Zandt said that confirmation bias "works like this: If I see evidence that supports what I already believe, I will support that evidence. If the evidence is neutral, I will interpret it in a way that supports what I believe. And, if the evidence completely contradicts what I believe, I will discount the evidence, dig my heels in deeper and keep believing what I want."[36]

Michael Kranish of the *Boston Globe* indicates that the rise of democratized and personalized media sources has been a factor in heightened political partisanship:

> What was once billed as the greatest democratization of information in the world's history has helped land us where we are now. The growing personalization of media sources has yielded a world of competing commentators who, with few exceptions, stake out the rigid edge of their piece of the political spectrum. The profit is in extremity. Any remark can catch fire, and each channel or site can have outsized impact. The result: an explosion in the availability of information has coincided with historic levels of political polarization—the starkest divide since the early 1900s, according to a Duke University study released this year [2013]. While many factors have fed this trend, analysts believe that ideological media outlets have contributed significantly and hardened the battle lines.[37]

John Diaz, columnist and editorial page editor of the *San Francisco Chronicle*, advocates for people being open-minded and listening to what the other side is saying, even if it goes against what they typically believe: "Americans on the right should be open to evidence that the Affordable Care Act is working, or that concern about climate change is something other than a pretext for government taxation and regulation. Americans on the left must not foreclose the idea that the miscalculations in Benghazi truly were egregious, or that Social Security does need fixing so it will be there for future generations. Sometimes, it really is healthy to change the channel, and to listen."[38]

I agree with Diaz. I force myself to watch Fox News and listen to conservative talk radio, even though I know that it will frustrate me, make my blood boil, and make me want to change the channel. Nonetheless, it's important to get the perspective of the other side, and conceivably there might be times when they make some sense or make me think in a different way about an issue.

Research by Jonathan M. Ladd, a Georgetown University political scientist, showed that media unpopularity has promoted political polarization by making voters disconnected from reality and leading them to vote based on partisan ideology. Ladd found that "General economic conditions had less of an impact on the voting preferences of voters who had more negative views of the news media, while party identification had more. Voters tend to fall back on their party identification as a baseline for making choice," Ladd writes. "I expect voters who distrust the media to rely more on their party to make voting decisions."[39]

Nicholas DiFonzo, psychology professor at the Rochester Institute of Technology, wrote in the *New York Times* that relying on like-minded sources for news, including liberal or conservative blogs, can lead to false rumors. People confirm rumors through sources they trust, he noted, and they trust their own social group more than they trust the media. For example, he said, liberals widely spread false rumors about Sarah Palin and conservatives are inclined to believe the "birther" rumor that President Obama was born in Kenya.[40]

It is this like-minded echo chamber that makes many Republicans believe not only that President Obama was born in Kenya but that he is a Muslim. Presidential candidate Senator John McCain of Arizona in

2008 received boos from the audience when he corrected a woman in the audience who stated that she didn't trust Obama because he was an Arab. McCain shook his head and said, "No ma'am, no ma'am. He's a decent family man." In contrast, many conservative pundits fed into the false narrative of Obama as a Muslim and repeatedly used his middle name "Hussein" in a pejorative manner. During the 2008 presidential campaign, there was a popular e-mail being circulated alleging that Obama was a Muslim who would not recite the Pledge of Allegiance. As noted by Snopes, a fact-checking website, this claim was false.[41]

According to Caitlin Dewey of the *Washington Post*, social media is a significant factor in this polarization: "The anti-Twitter cohort just scored a big point: According to a fascinating audit of Congressional Twitter accounts by *New York* magazine's Dan Amira, our politicians overwhelmingly follow only people and news sources that align with their views."[42]

The Brookings Institute, a think tank in Washington, DC, reports that data scientists at Facebook published a study that confirms the existence of political polarization on the social network because people tend to befriend others with similar political beliefs. The study found, generally, that "A Facebook user has five politically likeminded friends for every one friend on the other side of the spectrum. In a democracy it's generally a value add for citizens to encounter a variety of political opinions. This fact does not enumerate the 'right' number of friends to have from across the political aisle."[43]

Personally, I've noticed a reluctance of my social media friends to criticize other people's posts, even when they disagree with them politically. I know that I generally try to follow that philosophy as well. I tend to "Like" social media posts that I agree with politically and not comment on those that I disagree with. My social media friends tend not to criticize my opinionated, politically oriented social media posts, even though I know many of them disagree with me. Therefore, most of the opinions on my social media outlets tend to echo each other as well.

National Public Radio's *On the Media* quotes Harvard Law School professor Cass Sunstein, who warns about the inherent risks of the media echo chamber: "The greatest danger of the echo chambers is unjustified extremism. So it's a well-known fact that if you get a group of people who tend to think something, after they talk to each other, they end up thinking a more extreme version of what they thought before. And the danger of that is [that] you can make a situation where people demonize those who disagree with them. And that's an ongoing threat to our democracy."[44]

Michael Barone argues in the *Washington Examiner* that liberals are less likely to be exposed to the other side, because conservatives cannot avoid the liberal views of the mainstream media, Hollywood entertainment, and President Obama, which makes them aware of the other side's arguments and helps them respond: "Liberals can protect themselves better against assaults from outside their cocoon. They can stay out of megachurches and make sure their remote controls never click on Fox News. They can stay off the AM radio dial so they will never hear Rush Limbaugh." Because of this, Barone argues that this leaves liberals "unprepared to make the best case for their side in public debate. They are too often not aware of holes in arguments that sound plausible when bandied between confreres entirely disposed to agree."[45]

I would respectfully disagree. I think that both sides are guilty of staying in their own comfort zones.

Political consultant James Carville states in *The Hill* that media fragmentation means that people don't challenge themselves by being exposed to opposing points of view, since conservatives access news from conservative media outlets and liberals get news from liberal media outlets: "And you can spend your whole life never being challenged, never having to hear or think about or confront viewpoints that are different from your own . . . a big part of the media industry now exists in large part to confirm your beliefs. People have figured out that there's a lot of money to be made telling you that you were right in the first place. It makes both sides more dug in."[46]

As I've noted, I try to engage in such exposure as much as possible, no matter how painful it can be. I want to know how talk radio and Fox News are framing the controversial issues of the day. It might make me angry, but it's important to know how others think and feel about important issues of the day. Knowledge of opposing arguments helps each of us to better frame and support our own arguments for the ideas we believe in.

Referring to the October 2015 CNBC Republican presidential primary debate, CNN's Brian Stelter offered this observation to fellow CNN host Anderson Cooper regarding conservatives' distrust of the liberal mainstream media, "Now, most journalists will tell you they try very hard to expunge any and all bias from their stories, but many conservatives laugh at that. . . . The result? More political polarization. According to Pew Research Center, the more conservative you are, the fewer mainstream media sources you trust. Fox News has benefited from that and so have some candidates. On Thursday, several of them declared war on the liberal media, e-mailing supporters asking for money while mocking the moderators and they're not the only ones doing that."[47] Candidates follow this playbook because they know it works with the base. It's become a common technique for Republicans to avoid tough questions or criticism by responding that they are the victim of a liberal media crusade against them.

Matthew Levendusky, associate professor of politics at the University of Pennsylvania, writes that research has shown that partisan media affects news consumers' vote choice, participation, and attitudes toward bipartisanship and compromise. Research "finds that while there are effects, they are concentrated primarily among those who are already extreme. This suggests that these programs contribute to polarization not by shifting the center of the ideological distribution, but rather by lengthening the tails (i.e., moving the polarized even further away from the center)."[48]

Journalist, author, and filmmaker Steven Beschloss e-mailed the following to me during an interview: "There's no question that the divisiveness in the political sphere and the growing toxicity and hostility in public discourse has been fueled by advocacy media (print and broadcast). Politicians and their media allies are rewarded for polarizing comments and praised for analyses that seek to burn and bury the opposition." Noting that Americans used to view their enemies as outside the United States, such as during the Cold War, Beschloss said, "But these days the enemies are identified as those who hold alternate political views. While cable TV, political blogs and other online outlets are helping fuel this, the political class has also embraced it as a method to attract attention and raise money. Taken together, this shift not only has created parallel worlds defined by different narratives, but also a climate where facts matter less than the ideological ideas and storylines that fuel their respective audiences. This is bad for the country at a time when cohesion and finding solutions is so critical. Many of our problems are national and global in scale; when advocacy journalism heightens our divisions and differences, it makes solving problems that much harder."[49]

Beschloss added, "That said, there's also no question that people are not only entitled to their opinions, there's a benefit to having advocates that can clearly articulate a worldview and offer ideas and solutions that can lead to productive change. Editorial perspective has always served this purpose. But we all are in trouble when advocacy undermines our capacity to tell the difference between fact and opinion, between truth and lies, between reasonable differences that can lead toward finding solutions and angry skirmishes that only heighten antagonisms and spur hatred. This is especially dangerous at a time of escalating fear and paranoia."[50]

Recognizing this polarization, some organizations are trying to bridge the gap to find common ground and to decrease polarization, antagonism, and confusion, both politically and in the media. No Labels is an organization that is attempting to bring the country together politically and to break the partisan gridlock in Washington by finding common ground and common solutions. For example, the organization developed the concept of "No Budget, No Pay," which would suspend pay for members of Congress if they failed to pass the annual budget and spending bills on time. The idea was incorporated into proposed legislation introduced by Senator Dean Heller (R-NV) and Representative Jim Cooper (D-TN). A modified version of the bill was passed by Congress and signed into law by President Obama in 2013. Language for another No Labels initiative regarding improving healthcare for veterans was incorporated into the 2013 Defense Appropriations legislation.[51] And there is the website All Sides, established in 2012, which sets out to decrease polarization and confusion in the news media by presenting news stories that reflect all the various sides of the political spectrum. Their main news page features three columns of major news, labeled in order: "From the Left," "From the Center," and "From the Right." It also provides rotating news feeds from liberal-leaning, centrist, and conservative media outlets.[52]

From my perspective, I think it would help ease polarization if more people were willing to expose themselves more to what others are saying instead of being locked up in their safe little echo chamber that doesn't challenge them. Granted, those who do so might just get annoyed or angry watching or listening to another side, but conceivably there could be times when doing so might alter one's opinion on an issue.

There are many causes for the increased polarization in the United States in recent years. Political gerrymandering is one cause, but partisan media outlets have also contributed significantly to the rancor and distrust that liberals and conservatives have toward each other.

Despite the polarizing effect of advocacy journalism, it remains a major force in today's media landscape, and it isn't going to go away.

CHAPTER 16

THE POPULARITY OF ADVOCACY JOURNALISM AND ITS INFLUENCE

Peter Johnson, long-time media writer for *USA Today*, wrote that "The 'social journalism' that made Oprah Winfrey an international fairy godmother is the new rage in network and cable news, and it's expanding to other media. Increasingly, journalists and talk-show hosts want to 'own' a niche issue or problem, find ways to solve it and be associated with making this world a better place, as Winfrey has done with obesity, literacy, and, most recently, education by founding a girls school in South Africa."[1]

Many media outlets are practicing advocacy journalism. Why is this such a popular news presentation model? One factor is that advocacy journalism allows the reporters and commentators to have a strong voice, use humor, and put forth a forceful opinion or point of view. This is in contrast to the straightforward delivery of more traditional network news, which many people perceive as boring. Some audiences find the new approach interesting and thought-provoking. They also like to hear hosts and experts who confirm or verify their own opinions. Such audiences enjoy when the hosts or commentators demonize and mock the other side and expose their alleged flaws, hypocrisies, and falsehoods. They are eager to hear what outrageous thing the host will say during his or her next show.

Exposure to news, information, and opinion can influence how people view the world, the country, politics, and social issues. Liberals will praise muckraking advocacy journalists who expose societal ills and propose solutions, while conservatives will praise reporters and hosts who advance pro-capitalist, low-tax, and minimalist government agendas. Radio and television host Glenn Beck has held a number of well-attended rallies for a variety of conservative causes. His "All Lives Matter" march drew over 20,000 supporters in Birmingham, Alabama, in August 2015, according to the Alabama Media Group,[2] and his "Restoring Honor" march in Washington, DC, in August 2010—in which he advocated religious patriotism and traditional values—drew thousands of people on the National Mall, according to the *Washington Post*.[3] MSNBC host and liberal activist Rev. Al Sharpton has organized many protests on social issues, including a series of rallies across the country protesting the fatal police shooting of Michael Brown and the fatal shooting of Trayvon Martin by George Zimmerman. These hosts try to influence their audiences to act differently in certain ways or to see the world in a different way. In recent years, MSNBC has been substantially involved in creating and televising the annual Global Citizen Festival in New York's Central Park, which encourages people to get involved in issues such as environmental sustainability, eradicating poverty, women's empowerment, education, and climate change. Fox News's Sean Hannity has hosted Freedom Concerts since 2003 to raise money for veterans and their children.

The amount and extent of media coverage for a particular topic, issue, or candidate can influence politics by making it seem far more important and meaningful than it may actually be. The initial nonstop coverage of Donald Trump's presidential primary campaign helped to catapult him to a substantial lead in state and national polls of likely voters during the summer and fall of 2015. The media gravitated toward Trump for a reason—he was loud, funny, entertaining, bombastic, said outrageous things, openly advocated actions that were considered by many to be radical and even offensive, and insulted people who objected to his views or his methods. And the disaffected members of the Republican Party felt he understood them, their frustration with politics as usual, and their plight. Plus, covering Trump would bring readers, listeners, and viewers to the media outlets airing him. Other candidates complained that Trump was getting too much attention and taking all the oxygen from the room. The media didn't pay as much attention to other candidates because they weren't as captivating as Trump and they weren't doing anything to steal his political thunder.

Another example is the extensive media coverage that was given to the

Ebola crisis in 2014. As noted by *The Hill* and Media Matters, there were around one thousand mentions of the Ebola virus in the four weeks leading up to the 2014 midterm elections in November and only forty-nine mentions in the two weeks following the elections.[4]

The continuous high ratings for Fox News and conservative talk radio reflects their audience's deep mistrust of the perceived traditional mainstream media and a desire to receive news, information, opinions, and commentary that reflect their conservative viewpoints. Dominic Patten, legal editor and writer for *Deadline Hollywood* wrote in March 2015 that Fox News's ratings had climbed back on top of all cable television networks in terms of prime-time ratings for the first time in a year: "FNC had 1.934 million viewers on average between 8 PM and 11 PM during the March 2–8 frame. That's 9 percent ahead of the number 2 ranker of TBS [Turner Broadcasting System], which had 1.767 million."[5] According to Al Weaver of the *Daily Caller*, Fox was the most-watched cable news network for the thirteenth straight year in 2014: "Although the network dropped four percent this year in its total day viewers in both the demo and in overall numbers, Fox came in second among all cable networks in overall primetime numbers, only behind ratings behemoth ESPN, according to Nielsen ratings."[6]

Jim Angle, who left ABC News to join his former colleague Brit Hume for the channel's launch and later became Fox's chief Washington correspondent, told Mike Allen of *Politico* in 2012 that Fox News "really turned the corner with the coverage of the [presidential vote] recount in Florida in 2000. . . . That's when we passed up CNN, and we have never looked back."[7] David Zurawik of the *Baltimore Sun* wrote that one of the main reasons for Fox News's popularity in recent years might be that it served as a much better watchdog on the Obama administration than any other television network, despite taking extensive heat and blowback from the administration that showed enmity towards the press: "[Fox] stayed the course. And now with viewers seeing the contempt this administration had for them and the truth, they respect what Fox did the last six years. Or maybe, it's what some critics of Fox say: That those who watch the channel only want to hear one side of the story, and that's all that Fox gives them."[8]

Michael Harrison, publisher of *Talkers* magazine, told Joanne Ostrow of the *Denver Post* that he believes conservatives dominate talk radio "because the conservative audience is easier to target than the liberal audience." Conservative listeners are alienated and disenfranchised by big media, Hollywood, and academia, Harrison said, and represent "a perfect mind-set for radio, a niche medium, to target an audience that will be loyal. They're seeking validation. . . . [T]he conservative audience mind-set is much more cohesive and uniform, whereas 'liberal' is a broader term that takes in many different political philosophies, ethnicities, voting habits, socio-economic classes. It's not as cohesive a unit."[9]

Liberals aren't as cohesive as conservatives, but they do have many common interests and causes—abortion rights, minority rights, equal pay, women's rights, distributive justice, welfare, social security, etc. However, they tend to get their news and information from more of a variety of sources than conservatives.

Because advocacy media outlets are so popular with segments of the public, they can get their loyal followers riled up to take action. When Rush Limbaugh or Sean Hannity says the audience should bombard their Congressmen with protest letters or angry tweets about an issue, there is a tangible impact on the phone calls, mail, e-mails, and tweets that legislators receive. People have sometimes even called Limbaugh the real leader of the Republican Party. According to Nicole Hemmer of *U.S. News & World Report*, in 1992 President George H. W. Bush was concerned that Limbaugh's support for Bush's Republican primary opponent Pat Buchanan would cost him conservative votes, so he invited Limbaugh to the White House for an overnight stay in the Lincoln bedroom.[10] Brad Woodhouse, president of Americans United for Change, a liberal advocacy group, told the Associated Press, "Rush Limbaugh is the leader of the Republican Party—he says jump and they say how high."[11] According to the *London Telegraph*, after the Republicans made decisive gains in the 2002 midterm elections, many American politicians credited talk radio as a major factor in the GOP's success. Senate minority leader Democrat Tom Daschle blamed Limbaugh and other conservative talk show hosts for promoting hatred, and Democratic senator Dick Durbin credited the "right-wing screamers" on the radio who had drowned out the Democrats' message. On the other hand, "Senator Orrin Hatch, a Republican, told Sean Hannity, another prominent talk show host, 'I thank my Father in heaven every day for people like you, Rush Limbaugh and others.'"[12]

Both liberal and conservative viewpoints are represented by popular and influential websites. According to eBizMBA, there are fifteen political news websites that have over 5.5 million unique monthly visitors each, including *Huffington Post*, TheBlaze, *Drudge Report*, Newsmax, *Politico*, *Salon*, Infowars, Breitbart *News Network*, *Daily Caller*, *Washington Times*, *Christian Science Monitor*, *WND*, *Daily Kos*, *ThinkProgress*, and Townhall.com.[13] Many of these websites are cited as reliable sources by mainstream media outlets, and many of their writers, such as Sam Stein and Howard Fineman of the *Huffington Post*, appear as regular guests and commentators on television talk shows.

As this chapter demonstrates, advocacy journalism is extremely popular and influential and is a major part of the media landscape. But what are the pros and cons of advocacy journalism?

CHAPTER 17

WHAT'S GOOD ABOUT ADVOCACY JOURNALISM?

Advocacy journalism can be tremendously entertaining for some consumers. Many people find television news to be too matter-of-fact, lacking in drama or humor, and essentially boring. Noted media critic Jim Romenesko talking about a book written by University of Texas journalism professor Paula Poindexter, which researched news consumption among millennials, quoted her as saying that "millennials describe news as garbage, lies, one-sided, propaganda, repetitive and boring."[1] In suggesting a replacement for Brian Williams on NBC Nightly News, Mark Whittington, a television writer for the *Houston Examiner*, suggested that the network leave its stolid and boring style of news broadcasting and hire entertainer Craig Ferguson.[2] Jessica Toonkel wrote in Reuters that the Virginia-based broadcast company Tegna was trying to develop new ways to make local television news more interesting to younger people.[3] Having energetic, funny, and entertaining personalities with strong opinions and voices appeals to many people. They like cable news and Internet web writing because it is free-wheeling, opinionated, passionate, and has a strong, entertaining voice. Bloggers are not restrained by editors and are free to have strong opinions and use humor. In some cases, readers can relate to the personality of the blogger or cable television host, who often use plain, conversational language that doesn't appear to talk down to the reader. These bloggers and hosts choose stories that their niche audience will care about and can relate to.

These forms of news reporting give audiences another option aside from network news and other straightforward news outlets that don't (and shouldn't) strive to entertain. The traditional forms of news media are there to present the major news and information of the day and get the facts across to consumers. Being informative doesn't require journalists to be stuffy, stilted, or overly formal, but it is hard for the network news anchors to be entertaining when they are trying to fit as many news stories as possible into a half-hour newscast.

Advocacy journalism outlets can be places people turn to reinforce their viewpoints and values and to hear from like-minded experts and average people. These outlets can cover stories that the mainstream media does not cover or has been able to cover briefly. An example would be the Flint, Michigan, contaminated water crisis in 2015. All major news outlets gave the story extensive coverage for about a week and then moved on to cover the presidential race. MSNBC's Rachel Maddow was among the first to report the story, and she stayed with it, traveling to Flint to host a televised town hall on January 27, 2016.[4] Another example would be Sean Hannity touring the Mexican border with Texas governor Rick Perry in July 2014 and airing a report on the immigration crisis at the southern border.[5]

For many conservatives, Fox News and talk radio serve as places where they can get news and information without the perceived liberal bias of the mainstream media. Liberals who distrust the corporate media can turn to liberal websites and MSNBC. Most viewers know that they are getting news that is skewed, but that's what the viewers of these networks want. They're not tuning in for objectivity. Other viewers might have trouble knowing whether they are getting news that is accurate rather than conservative or liberal opinions or views that are simply masquerading as news.

Advocacy journalism can shed light on important stories and causes. It can lead to social or government change. John Timpane of the *Philadelphia Inquirer* writes, "It gets the message out. You can't say it hasn't been very effective. The word 'homeless,' for example, was seldom uttered before the early 1980s, when a concerted effort arose to make people aware, especially in the neglected cities. You could make a long list of terms and ideas created by advocates who used journalism, for better or worse, to get their ideas into the world: reproductive rights, partial-birth abortion, reverse racism, weapons of mass destruction, #BlackLivesMatter, sex positivity, and so on. Many of these put their finger on a social change or issue that really was happening; some of them sought to create that change or issue."[6]

In some cases, objective and balanced reporting is not appropriate. The Holocaust would be such an issue, for example, or the promotion of racial or religious hatred, sexual exploitation, torture, human slavery, and the like. Reporters wouldn't and shouldn't give credence or equal time to such ideas. People and groups are allowed to have controversial and offensive views. The Ku Klux Klan and Nazi supporters are allowed to march, demonstrate, and have rallies in public places. They have that First Amendment right, and the news media is free to cover these events. However, covering such events doesn't mean that the media has to give credence and credibility to Holocaust deniers and treat their viewpoints seriously.

Sometimes, the objective, neutral, and balanced approach of reporters giving both sides' points of view without stating what they themselves believe doesn't give audiences enough information; readers or viewers are left without any perspective as to what is really going on or what is the accurate viewpoint. A reporter or news host who offers his or her personal thoughts on a story can be seen as providing perspective or insight on a story, but it's something that is generally prohibited. Most reporters are constrained by their employers or their sense of professionalism from being allowed to say what they really think about an issue. Should the United States and its allies invade Iraq to oust Saddam Hussein? Is the Affordable Care Act/Obamacare good for the country? Is the nuclear pact with Iran a good deal or is it a catastrophic mistake? Most reporters aren't permitted or expected to say but instead will just be reporting both sides' viewpoints and spin. But they can call out the spin to viewers and make them aware that this is just a particular side's attempt to convince people of its case.

In contrast, bloggers and advocacy journalists do not have such filters that restrain them from giving their opinions and perspectives. They are not hamstrung by editors who might be concerned about alienating their audience with controversial opinions. Bloggers are not expected to be objective, and so they can bring passion and concern to a story in the news while highlighting issues or opinions that they and their audience care deeply about.

It is this passion and opinion-saturated approach that attracts many readers and viewers who are less enthused by the more straightforward news offered in newspapers and on network television. Advocacy journalists often have a strong voice, equally strong opinions, colorful facial and body expressions, and an edgy approach that appeals to many. They are often entertaining, funny, and sarcastic. They make the consumption of news and information fun and interesting, instead of being a chore. Many people have suggested that the mainstream media abandon its neutral, balanced approach and allow their experienced, knowledgeable reporters to give their informed perspective and opinions. That doesn't necessarily mean that traditional media can't be entertaining, interesting, and colorful while still being informative and balanced. But it can be difficult given the nature of thirty-minute nightly news programs. The networks and local affiliates need to cover as many major stories of the day as possible, as quickly as possible, and they don't often have time to go into depth on many of them. This holds true for straightforward news radio stations, as well. In contrast, hour-long cable television news shows and three-hour-long radio shows have more time to be creative.

Advocacy journalism is also reflected in many popular magazines. On the liberal end, there are, among others, the *Progressive*, *Rolling Stone*, *Sojourners*, *Utne Reader*, *Washington Monthly*, *Mother Jones*, the *New Republic*, *The Nation*, *Harper's* magazine, and the *American Prospect*. Among conservative magazines are the *National Review*, the *Weekly Standard*, the *American Spectator*, the *American Conservative*, *FrontPage* magazine, *Reason* magazine, *Commentary*, and *Human Events*. Most of these publications do identify their philosophies up front and have columnists with a clear liberal or conservative point of view. It's a case-by-case determination as to whether these magazines are more or less extreme than talk radio or cable television. Some publications come across as more learned, reasonable, or academic, while others present a more snarky or humorous tone.

Where does investigative journalism fall on the nonpartisan versus partisan spectrum? This type of journalism, often practiced by mainstream media, aims to serve the public's interest and the public's right to know about important issues. Investigative journalists are interested in issues that may appear to have been hidden from public awareness, public or private attempts to escape transparency, or criminal or unethical actions by government officials, corporations, or organizations. Sometimes this is also called accountability reporting. Media reporter and critic Dean Starkman writes that this type of investigative, public service, and accountability journalism is a practice that has served as an effective advocate and true watchdog since Ida Tarbell, but that not everyone is in love with it and it has had to fight for its existence for decades:

> Confrontational and accusatory, it provokes the enmity of the rich and powerful as a matter of course. When Theodore Roosevelt dubbed it "muckraking" in 1906, he didn't mean it as a compliment. Risky, stressful, expensive, and difficult, it perennially faces resistance within news organizations and tries the patience of bureaucrats, bean counters, and hacks. News corporatists, such as the late *USA Today* founder Al Neuharth and mogul Rupert Murdoch, deride public-service reporting—or anything that resembles it—as a form of elitism, an affectation of prize-mongering and self-important reporters, journalists writing for "other journalists," as one Murdoch biographer puts it. Withholding resources for public-interest reporting . . . is invariably couched as opposition to "long" and "pretentious" stories foisted on the public by "elitist" reporters. But opposing long and ambitious stories is like fully supporting apple pie but opposing flour, butter, sugar, and pie tins. In the end, there is no pie.[7]

Advocacy journalists and investigative journalists often set out to expose the problems of the poor, the suffering, the disadvantaged, or the oppressed. They will set out to challenge the status quo, especially when government and corporate policies are not working for people who are struggling—financially and otherwise. Oftentimes, the mainstream media tends to focus on the same stories, and many important stories go unreported because they aren't deemed "sexy" or interesting enough to keep readers' or viewers' attention. Supporters of advocacy journalism claim that they are acting in the great tradition of muckrakers or whistle blowers who have long shed light on important issues and controversies. They believe that, too often, the mainstream media shies away from controversial issues due to economic issues, such as fear of alienating the audience and the relatively high cost of funding such detailed stories. When asked to describe the value of advocacy journalism, Rob Kall of *OpEdNews* pointed out that such journalism, "Offers voices and casts light on issues and stories that the mainstream corporate media ignores or misleads on."[8]

I believe that advocacy journalism can inspire readers or viewers to wake up and care about an issue and convince people to get involved or to speak out against injustice. It can serve as an educational rallying cry and as a call to action. Supporters of independent bloggers and websites unaffiliated with the mainstream media claim the benefit of these sites is that they are not restrained by corporate media owners who want to play it safe and avoid alienating an audience, losing circulation or ratings, or offending advertisers—keeping audience numbers up is important to retaining advertising dollars. That isn't as big a concern for bloggers and websites that enjoy a niche audience.

As we discussed previously, there has been a great tradition of advocacy journalism for many decades, which has led to social change and awareness of important political, economic, and public health and safety issues. The muckraking journalists of the early 1900s shed light on food safety, substandard housing, poor working conditions, and much more. This tradition continued later in the century with important work on auto safety by Ralph Nader, environmental concerns raised by Rachel Carson, the plight of the nation's working people brought to public awareness by Studs Terkel, and the political disclosures of writers like I. F. Stone and Bob Woodward and Carl Bernstein, among others. According to Mark Bowden, "Good advocacy journalism informs, educates, and changes peoples' minds."[9]

How does advocacy journalism change minds? In some cases, the facts of a particular issue are presented as clearly as possible, letting news consumers decide for themselves the value of what they are being exposed to. Other, more partisan, media outlets or hosts view their work as an effort to get an issue resolved in a very particular way.

Will Bunch offers a slightly different approach when assessing the positive aspects of advocacy journalism. He refers to the insufficient reporting before the Iraq war, in which the government did not fact-check the claims about weapons of mass destruction (among other claims), as well as the media coverage of global warming:

> Balanced reporting has its limitations. For instance, it failed to cut through the baloney that the government gave us about the lead up to the Iraq war. You get situations where reporters strive too hard to create an artificial balance when they know that one side's position doesn't hold water. For instance, oil companies have funded the minority of the climate scientists that deny the severity of global warming and that it is manmade. They push to get equal time in news coverage even though 97 percent of the scientists are convinced that global warming is happening and that it is serious. Opinion or advocacy journalists who understand the environment can say "this theory is bunk." They will identify the need for something and will provide evidence that supports that view. There has been a rise in advocacy journalism due to the failures of balanced journalism.[10]

Many argue that there is a difference between advocacy journalism and investigative solutions journalism. In defending its approach of using investigative solutions journalism to focus on important local problems that affect residents and taxpayers, George Rodrigue of the *Cleveland Plain Dealer* stated that such an approach adds extra focus, inquiry, and effort to traditional journalism: "Advocacy journalism intentionally adopts a non-objective viewpoint, generally to achieve a political or social end. It is fact-based, so it's not propaganda. But it does advocate a cause. . . . Solutions journalism is different. Our work will be fully consistent with the core values of traditional journalism. We will remain as objective as human nature allows us to be, and use all the normal professional techniques to correct for bias. We will vet our facts carefully and present multiple sides of the story."[11]

In his opening speech at a conference on advocacy journalism, American University's School of Communications dean Larry Kirkman argued that advocacy journalism fills a void: "What can replace the cutbacks in investigative reporting, the cutbacks in explanatory reporting, the cutbacks in global reporting? Advocacy journalism can speak up and talk back to the powers that be—whether defending human rights abroad and civil liberties at home, supporting the struggles of the poor to improve their lives, explaining climate change or denying a call to war."[12]

Despite my many critiques and criticisms of advocacy journalism and its various techniques in other parts of this book, as a media consumer I am a big fan of this type of news presentation, and I enjoy watching cable news, listening to talk radio, and reading articles that have a slanted, biased viewpoint. I like to hear various viewpoints on the important issues of the day, and I appreciate the passion and strong voice of the presenters, even if I disagree with the positions they espouse. It can be edgy, funny, and entertaining. Admittedly, I like advocacy journalism much better when it is giving me information and opinions I agree with and that are consistent with my beliefs. This gives me information and positions that I can use when arguing social issues and politics with other people. It exposes me to issues and causes that I'm not going to hear about by watching the local or national network news. In other cases, it can inspire me to want to get involved in some way.

Despite the positives of advocacy journalism, however, such journalism also poses some risks.

CHAPTER 18

WHAT'S BAD ABOUT ADVOCACY JOURNALISM?

The rise of advocacy journalism has led to a nation in which many people get their news in a self-selective, self-reinforcing echo chamber from biased, agenda-driven sources. When these media, on whatever end of the advocacy spectrum they may be positioned, report the news, they do so with a clear bias that favors one side over the other. For important issues—such as Obamacare/the Affordable Care Act, the nuclear deal with Iran, racial issues, immigration, economic policy, taxes, freedom of religion/separation of church and state, gun control and gun rights, and pro-choice and pro-life conflicts—consumers of advocacy media are getting skewed presentations and selective facts on the issues from the sources they choose to provide them with news. Many find comfort in getting their news from biased sources that confirm, validate, and echo their own personal viewpoint. For this reason, many skewed news sources are just preaching to the choir rather than convincing opponents or the uncommitted with firmly grounded arguments and the evidence to support them.

Given the partisan nature of so much of what passes for journalism these days, many people wonder where they can obtain reliable news. A 2014 Pew Research Poll of 2,901 web respondents revealed that the ten most trusted news sources were the *Economist*, the BBC (British Broadcasting Company), NPR (National Public Radio), the *Wall Street Journal*, ABC News, CBS News, NBC News, CNN, and *USA Today*, while the ten least trusted news sources were *BuzzFeed*, the *Rush Limbaugh Show*, the *Glenn Beck Program*, the *Ed Schultz Show*, Al Jazeera America, the *Sean Hannity Show*, *Daily Kos*, the *Drudge Report*, the *Daily Show*, and *ThinkProgress*.[1]

One of the flaws of advocacy journalism is that information is presented out of context. Fox News hosts and guests criticized President Obama for being aloof, apathetic, cavalier, and "a pathological illness of a president" for allegedly calling the Paris attacks "just a setback" or "just a little setback."[2] In fact, Obama had called the attacks "heinous attacks" and said that "the terrible events in Paris were a terrible and sickening setback."[3] Erik Wemple of the *Washington Post* noted an incident where critics of MSNBC's Andrea Mitchell alleged that she presented a video of Mitt Romney out of context, portraying him as being an aloof rich person because he seemed to be amazed at the convenience store/gas station chain Wawa's sandwich-ordering kiosk. Romney was using the Wawa appearance to emphasize the wonders of private industry, but Mitchell suggested that it was evident that he hadn't been in too many roadside Wawas.[4]

Name calling, personal attacks, and vitriol are other negative elements of advocacy journalism and numerous cable news shows. This can be a turnoff to many people. In December of 2015, Fox News suspended two of its regular on-air contributors for two weeks for using crude language regarding President Obama. After Obama's nationally televised Oval Office address on terrorism, Lt. Col. Ralph Peters, in an interview on Stuart Varney's show on the Fox Business Network, called Obama a "total pussy" when describing the president's remarks. While speaking on the Fox News show *Outnumbered*, Stacey Dash said that the president didn't "give a shit" about terrorism.[5] Martin Bashir resigned from his MSNBC show in 2013 after he suggested that Sarah Palin deserved to be punished by having someone defecate into her mouth.[6] MSNBC suspended host Ed Schultz when he called conservative pundit Laura Ingraham a "right wing slut."[7]

The hosts and guests of these television and radio programs often yell at each other, rudely and persistently interrupt each other, and talk over one another—to the point that viewers or listeners can't understand what any of them are saying. Sometimes, the host simply loses control of moderating the discussion. In such situations, while the passion of the participants is fully evident, their intended objective of trying to reinforce the opinions of their audiences may well be hampered when the views expressed are garbled by a failure to engage in a more orderly give and take of ideas. Entertaining the audience doesn't necessitate appealing to the baser instinct to debase, malign, or insult those whose views you consider wrongheaded.

Many people rebut the assertion that a journalist being transparent about his or her bias and particular viewpoint should replace the concept of objectivity because it leads to more realistic reporting. Detractors allege that the traditional model of journalism, when carried out effectively, is more authoritative, reliable, and credible. Once media outlets or reporters set out to report on a story in a manner that merely confirms a preconceived notion or viewpoint, it will be natural for them to gather only the facts that support their position and to leave out facts that counter their viewpoint. There is a temptation to leave out facts that go against one's own predisposition on an issue and to stack the deck in favor of the preferred position.

One method of sensationalizing issues is to label them with a pejorative term like "gate" or "scandal," in order to compare the incident to the now notorious Watergate political scandal that resulted in a president's resignation and several major prosecutions. Liberal media outlets harped on New Jersey governor Chris Christie's alleged potential involvement in the closing of the George Washington Bridge, leading to huge traffic tie-ups and problems for the Fort Lee, New Jersey, mayor who had not endorsed Governor Christie in his election. The incident was termed "Bridgegate." The term "gate," when used to label a scandal, implies unethical behavior that involved a cover up. "Nipplegate" was a term that some used to describe Janet Jackson's wardrobe malfunction during the halftime of the 2004 Super Bowl. The news magazine *60 Minutes*'s use of a forged document in a report by Dan Rather was referred to as "Rather-Gate." And "Contra-Gate" was used to refer to the Iran Contra arms scandal that plagued the Reagan administration. "Monica-Gate" was used to describe President Bill Clinton's sexual relations with the White House staffer Monica Lewinsky. Other Clinton-era scandals included "Travelgate," "Filegate," and "Whitewatergate." "Nanny Gate" related to the nomination and considered nomination to the United States Supreme Court of two women who allegedly hired illegal aliens as nannies. "DeflateGate" was used to describe the allegation that the New England Patriots football team intentionally used deflated footballs during an NFL playoff game.[8] Coverage of these scandals becomes relentless, sensationalized, and often partisan. Media outlets dwell on them in order to increase ratings and circulation. Some continue their coverage because they feel that if they don't others will, and they will be left out in the cold with fewer readers, listeners, or viewers. They may well recognize a story as silly or as one that does not warrant extensive coverage but still decide that they have to continue covering it just to keep up with competing media outlets.

A precursor to today's toxic media environment was the series of debates between conservative William F. Buckley Jr. and liberal Gore Vidal on ABC during the 1968 Republican convention in Miami. These debates were highlighted in the 2015 movie documentary *The Best of Enemies*. During the debates, Vidal called Buckley a "pro-war crypto-Nazi," while Buckley called Vidal a "queer" and threatened to punch him in the mouth.[9] Other precursors to the toxic cable news shout-fests include the shows of Morton Downey Jr., Phil Donahue, and Jerry Springer. Granted, none of these, including the Buckley/Vidal debate, were actual news programs. They were human-interest programs that discussed social and political issues, among other things, but they were never viewed by anyone as news sources. However, their sensationalized style was adopted and emulated to some extent by the cable news outlets.

There are times when the guests fight back against an aggressive host. Chris Matthews had one notable exchange with Zell Miller during the Republican convention in 2004. Miller, a Democratic senator from Georgia, gave a scathing criticism of Democrats in a prominent speech at the convention. After his speech, he appeared for an interview with Matthews on MSNBC. They sparred contentiously for over six minutes. Matthews repeatedly questioned Miller's statement during his speech that John Kerry and Ted Kennedy wanted to defend America with spitballs. Miller said, among other things, "This is a bunch of baloney," "Get out of my face, let me answer," "You're hopeless," "Are you gonna shut up and give me a chance to answer," "Don't pull that stuff on me," and, most notably, "I wish we lived in the day where you would challenge somebody to a duel." Miller is the one who lost his temper, but he felt it was a justified backlash and response to

Matthews's aggressive and confrontational interviewing style, which often doesn't let his guests get a word in edgewise. It's because of this style that many conservatives and Republicans wouldn't want to appear as a guest on his show, since they know they would be interrogated vigorously and might not be able to state their case due to constant interruption by the host. That same rationale would apply to Democrats and liberals being reluctant to go on, say, Bill O'Reilly's show.

Members of Congress seem to be afraid to buck their party or their voting base, even if they think a piece of legislation would be in the general public's interest; they seem to believe (perhaps correctly) that they will incur the wrath of their respective advocacy journalism outlets. This has been shown by the recent trend of mainstream Republican incumbents being primaried by outsiders. This means that if a congressman doesn't toe the party line and vote the way his or her constituent base, party, or partisan media want, he or she is likely to be challenged by a more conservative opponent in the Republican primary, one backed by conservative organizations. As radio host and journalist Michael Smerconish writes, "There is the effect of a polarized media, itself a creation in the last three decades. This is where those ideologically driven voters who dictate the nomination process in hyperpartisan districts within closed primary states [in which only party members can vote for their candidate] go for their news and opinion, and where the members of Congress who are elected strive to stay in good stead."[10]

There is a concern that the consumers of biased media outlets will blindly accept the facts, spin, and opinions that are presented in these outlets and will consider them to be providing objective, fact-based reporting that they can rely on. This can lead to audiences being uninformed and unaware of certain important issues and controversies, especially as the facts may well have been selected for their ability to support the reporting venue's particular bias. A 2014 Pew Research poll showed that 47 percent of consistent conservatives and 31 percent of those with mainly conservative views cited Fox News as their main source of political and government news. Local radio was cited by 11 percent of consistent conservatives as their main source, while 6 percent of mostly conservatives cited local radio. For liberals, 12 percent cited MSNBC as their main source.[11] A July

2013 Gallup Poll of over two thousand respondents revealed that 8 percent of respondents cited Fox News as the main place they turn to for news, 1 percent cited MSNBC, 18 percent cited the Internet, 2 percent cited social media, and 1 percent cited talk radio. The poll also showed that 20 percent of Republicans surveyed cited Fox News as their main news source.[12] I remember being disappointed when I heard a woman call Sean Hannity's radio program to tell him that his show was the only place that she got her political news. I would also be disappointed if someone just relied on Rachel Maddow for news, because she, like Hannity, is presenting news and opinion with a biased slant. Pew Research's 2013 overview of television news indicates the opinionated and biased nature of cable news reporting: "Separate analysis of cable in late 2012 finds that, over all, commentary and opinion are far more prevalent on the air (63% of the airtime) than straight news reporting (37%). CNN is the only channel to offer more reporting (54%) than opinion (46%), though by a small margin. By far the highest percentage of opinion and commentary is on MSNBC (85% to 15% reporting). Fox was in between at 55% commentary and 45% reporting."[13]

There is also concern about traditional media outlets letting their reporters express their own opinions. This practice can lead to alienating the audience and can result in people being suspicious of the reporting because of the viewpoints expressed. In Margaret Sullivan's January 5, 2013 *New York Times* article, she quoted Philip B. Corbett, the *Times*'s associate managing editor for standards as saying, "I flatly reject the notion that there is no such thing as impartial, objective journalism—that it's some kind of pretense or charade, and we should just give it up, come clean and lay out our biases. We expect professionals in all sorts of fields to put their personal opinions aside, or keep them to themselves, when they do their work—judges, police officers, scientists, teachers. Why would we expect less of journalists?" Veteran NBC special correspondent Tom Brokaw was criticized by some in 2015 for giving his opinions, when he called Donald Trump's proposed ban on Muslims entering the United States "dangerous" and compared it to the internment camps for Japanese Americans in World War II, the Holocaust, Senator Joseph McCarthy's anti-communist witch hunt, and racial discrimination against blacks during the 1960s.[14]

Another problem with advocacy journalism is that it makes it hard for the consumer to figure out the pros and cons of a complex issue. During the recent debate about the international nuclear treaty with Iran, it was clear that conservative talk radio and Fox News were against the deal and that liberal outlets like MSNBC mostly supported it. Granted, people who select liberal shows for news would expect that the pro-treaty view would be offered and conservative consumers would select media venues for the antitreaty position. But many people who rely on those biased news sources as their main sources of news won't be exposed to the full picture, to the full range of debate.

A Fairleigh Dickinson University survey in 2012 revealed that people who watched only cable television news sources were the worst informed group with respect to current events and answered fewer questions correctly on that subject than those in other groups. People who only watched Fox News performed worse than people who said they watched no media at all and those who said that they watched only the *Daily Show*. Among the questions asked were ones related to the Iowa and New Hampshire primaries, unemployment rates, the Keystone XL Pipeline, the composition of Congress, sanctions on Iran, the economic bailout of Greece, and uprisings in Egypt and Syria.[15] Poynter also reported on the above study, pointing out that reliance on partisan news sources can have an adverse effect on people's knowledge of current events: "NPR and Sunday morning political talk shows are the most informative news outlets, while exposure to partisan sources, such as Fox News and MSNBC, has a negative impact on people's current events knowledge."[16]

Will Bunch has this to say about the problems posed by advocacy journalism: "The problem is that too many reporters start with a point of view. They might overlook the other side or countervailing facts that an objective journalist might include. For instance, you might start with the premise that raising the minimum wage to $15 an hour is good. Maybe you would find a city that tried that and it led to increased unemployment. Or that a well-intentioned program to fight poverty backfired. You need to recognize that other view. Reporters might need to reconsider their positions. That happens less in advocacy journalism."[17] Mark Bowden writes that "bad advocacy journalism simply affirms and hardens peoples' preconceptions,"[18] while Rob Kall notes that advocacy journalism tends to indulge in "siloing [separating or isolating from others]—they tend to preach to the choir."[19]

In considering the dangers of such highly partisan reporting, John Timpane is concerned that presenting skewed information can seek to create a need or a feeling, a tension or a polarity. He writes that while some needs—such as homelessness—were genuine, other controversies and terms are created by advocates. For example, he says, current controversies such as "fetal organ donation" and "anchor children" were nonexistent until they were whipped up:

> The oft-debunked notion of the "anchor child" is a great example. Doubtless some immigrants have had children here and later used that fact to leverage longer stays [for themselves] in the country. But it's not widespread, and next to no one has babies for the express purpose of staying here. But thanks to the success of the term as an advocacy tool, many people think these things are all but universal. . . . Since forever, political advocates have used the available marketing tools to drive their message into social discourse . . . packaging is everything—you can sell almost anything if you package the product correctly and target it to the right audience. It's both inevitable (rhetoric is, after all, packaging, and all use of language involves rhetoric) and amoral, meaning it's a tool and not a system of betters and worses [sic]. And, much like many business practices, it shouldn't matter what the product is or whether it's right, true, better, or good. And that's the terrible moral problem.[20]

Regarding Timpane's analogy and connection between selling a product and selling an idea or concept, I would add that conservative media outlets and personalities were able to establish language and phrases such as "death panels" and "drive-by media" as part of the language of the right, while liberals were able to establish phrases like "the war on women" and "Incurious George" (referring to President George W. Bush) on the left. Advocates know that such catchphrases and terms will play well with their base.

James B. Steele makes this observation about the risks of skewed journalism: "I consider advocacy journalism to be more like opinion, but it comes off as [ordinary] journalism to the average person. I've seen cable news hosts ask the dumbest questions. It often gives the press a black eye. The twenty-four-hour news cycle and social media can be a problem in that people read false information, which leads to polls showing that 40 percent of Americans believed that Saddam Hussein had brought down the World Trade Centers. I'm not sure how to counteract that. Once the false information is out there, it's hard to turn it around." He then adds, "I've listened to Rush Limbaugh at times where he made some really good points, but then he blames liberals. The problem is that it might not be a liberal or conservative issue. Advocates like to link issues to politics, but journalists shouldn't do that."[21]

Undercover techniques for gathering information are a powerful tool, but they can be misused while engaging in advocacy journalism. In one incident, two conservative bloggers visited the offices of ACORN, a community advocacy group that worked to register voters and serve low-income persons, and allegedly asked about how their income from prostitution might be hidden from taxation. When the undercover operation was made public, Congress eventually voted to defund ACORN.[22] Another incident occurred when a different conservative group made undercover videos claiming to show that Planned Parenthood representatives were discussing the sale of fetal body parts. Again there were congressional hearings, and Planned Parenthood's president insisted that the video was edited and statements were taken out of context. Nonetheless, there have been further congressional hearings and continuing calls to defund the organization.[23] It can be debated whether these two cases were instances of undercover reporting or just undercover work by groups attempting to discredit the organizations involved. Sometimes the lines get blurred as to whether journalists are activists or whether activists are attempting to be journalists. How does advocacy journalism fit into it? I would say that the groups who made these videos used journalism techniques to do their reporting and that by posting their videos on websites, blogs, or YouTube they were at a minimum engaging in citizen journalism. They were reporting their allegations and offering a position with an agenda.

As Joe Strupp of *Editor & Publisher* reported in 2005, some major newspapers have banned the practice and technique of undercover journalism. He quotes Amanda Bennett, editor of the *Philadelphia Inquirer*, as saying, "I don't permit deception; I would not allow it. We go into reporting in a straighter way. We are not private investigators, we are journalists. Undercover is a method of the past."[24]

Some people believe that there are times when advocacy journalism crosses the line. Many journalists have criticized Emily Miller, a television reporter in Washington, DC, for Fox affiliate WTTG, for being an outspoken advocate for gun rights while at the same time being an investigative reporter who often reports on issues related to guns. As noted by Erik Wemple of the *Washington Post*, Miller has given speeches at rallies advocating Second Amendment gun rights. Wemple objects to her conflict of interest, writing, "Miller's appearance puts WTTG in a bind vis-a-vis Maryland politics. Her presence directly assisted several groups in advancing their causes in the statehouse. Attendees were urged to take the message from the morning's speakers to their representatives in the surrounding buildings. Should the gun-rights proponents prevail in their policy agenda, WTTG anchors may want to beat their chests on air."[25] Lou Dobbs, as a news host at CNN, became a vocal advocate against illegal immigration, and he included angry diatribes in many, if not most, of his newscasts. According to Brian Stelter and Bill Carter of the *New York Times*, this led Dobbs to resign from CNN after the network told him that he "could vent his opinions on radio and anchor an objective newscast on television, or he could leave CNN."[26] Stelter and Carter's article reported that Jonathan Klein, CNN's president, said in a statement that "Lou has now decided to carry the banner of advocacy journalism elsewhere."[27] Dobbs ended up as an anchor on the Fox Business News network. Earlier I have mentioned other incidents of advocacy journalists being criticized for going too far, among them Univision anchor Jorge Ramos confronting Donald Trump about his positions on immigration during a press conference in Iowa in 2015 and the *Rolling Stone* magazine reporting of an alleged rape at the University of Virginia.

Peter Johnson of *USA Today*, noted that Brian Ross, who runs the investigative unit at ABC News, worries about the growth of "agenda" reporting: "Ross says the practice 'clouds your vision and makes it sometimes difficult to see all sides.'"[28]

The Ramos incident at the Trump press conference drew national attention and much media scrutiny. Juan Castillo of NBC News said that while he admires and respects Ramos, he feels that Ramos was acting too much like an advocate: "He looked more like a man who knew the answers before even posing the questions, declaring that Trump could not deport 11 million people and could not build a fence along the entire U.S.-Mexican border. . . . But Ramos has called Trump's attacks on Mexico and Mexican immigration 'personal,' and . . . he looked like a man offering opinions and ready for a confrontation. . . . [A]t times I'm slightly uncomfortable with his advocacy journalism, however well-meaning it may be."[29]

I believe that even though Trump had long before stated that most Mexican illegal aliens were criminals and rapists and Ramos was a journalist for a Latin American network, Ramos should have handled the situation differently. He was perfectly entitled to ask Trump tough questions about his controversial and inflammatory comments, but he shouldn't have dominated and filibustered the press conference. The job of journalists is to ask questions that solicit informative answers from those being questioned, so that readers, listeners, and viewers have more information with which to reach their own conclusions about the issue at hand. Journalists are not supposed to be generators of news, or subjects of the news themselves.

According to Patricia Mazzei of the *Miami Herald*, Ramos had engaged in advocacy journalism in the past and had been critical of both political parties: "Yelling out questions is far from unusual in news conferences, especially in Miami, where Ramos lives and where a bilingual press corps routinely jostles to get in a question. Ramos, who . . . called the immigration issue 'personal,' began addressing Trump with a lengthy statement about Trump's past remarks, rather than with a question. . . . Ramos's brand of advocacy journalism has pitted him against both Republicans and Democrats in the past—he memorably chided President Barack Obama for breaking his promise to push for immigration reform in his first term in office—but it has grated on Republicans in particular because of Univision's ties to Democrats."[30]

According to Jack Martinez of *Newsweek*, both sides bore some blame in breaking the rules of press conference etiquette and customs: "Generally, at political press conferences, the politician calls on reporters, the reporters ask their questions, and the politician answers them. . . . But in general, what Ramos did is considered out of bounds, not because his questions were inappropriate (they weren't) but because filibustering at a presser, and speaking out of turn, is rude to other reporters. . . . Still, the escorting of Ramos out of the room is rare and very worrisome to reporters."[31]

Although Jorge Ramos was widely criticized for interrupting Donald Trump's press conference, his supporters believe that he appropriately confronted Trump's inflammatory comments about illegal immigrants. In defending Ramos, Bankole Thompson of the *Detroit News* compared him to great advocacy journalists of the past, such as Ida B. Wells-Barnett, who documented racial lynchings and crusaded against them in the South, in addition to fighting for women's rights, and Frederick Douglass, whose emancipation campaign would lead to President Lincoln's Emancipation Proclamation. Thompson argued that Ramos, an immigrant with millions of viewers on his weekly Univision television program, was "advocating for an issue that some say will define this nation's character for a long time."[32]

What should be done when reporters create stories and controversies that don't really exist or when they exaggerate a perceived problem? Many people, especially liberals, felt that this is exactly what took place regarding Fox News's coverage of the New Black Panthers' alleged voter intimidation cases. Fox News gave extensive coverage in separate incidents in 2008 and 2012 to Jerry Jackson, a member of the New Black Panthers, a small fringe black supremacist hate group. In 2012, Jackson was shown standing by himself outside a Philadelphia polling place as a designated poll watcher. Fox made it a lead story and gave the narrative that this was an example of extensive, ongoing voter intimidation by the New Black Panthers. In 2008, Jackson and two other men, including a man holding a nightstick, had stood outside a polling place in Philadelphia. Civil charges against Jackson and the others arising from the 2008 incident were dropped, but Sean Hannity noted that they were dropped by the black attorney general Eric Holder's Justice Department. Fox emphasized this case and gave it extensive air play because it fit their narrative that Democrats were engaging in voter intimidation and causing white voters to stay away from the polls, which they believed demonstrated how the Democrats were responsible for the hostility and incivility in today's political culture. Using one or two isolated incidents, Fox News made it appear as though voter intimidation was a pervasive, ongoing problem that the Obama administration was ignoring.[33]

David A. Graham of *Newsweek* argued that, as in the ACORN case, the Black Panther scandal was minimal but became great fodder for the conservative media. He quoted Abigail Thernstrom, a white conservative member of the Commission on Civil Rights, as saying, "Get a grip, folks. The New Black Panther Party is a lunatic fringe group that is clearly into racial theater of minor importance. . . . This case is a one-off. There are plenty of grounds on which to sharply criticize the attorney general—his handling of terrorism questions, just for starters—but this particular overblown attack threatens to undermine the credibility of his conservative critics." Graham noted, however, that "Like the ACORN case, it's not about a real investigation; it's about staging an effective piece of political theater that hurts the Obama administration."[34]

Another problem with advocacy journalism is that it has become too predictable. Whenever breaking news about a major social issue occurs, you pretty much know where Fox News and other conservative media outlets will stand, along with where MSNBC and liberal media venues will stand. They will both go to their respective corners and come out fighting along predictable party lines and take sides. Whenever a school shooting or mass shooting takes place, liberal media outlets will passionately advocate for gun control and background checks, while conservative media outlets will advocate Second Amendment rights and the importance of people arming themselves to combat mass shooters.

Robert Samuelson wrote in the *Washington Post* that polarization in the media is partly due to economic factors, not just ideological competition, as websites and cable news stations want to attract more members of their core audience with their content. These outlets "feature stories and guests that please their core audiences and help to maximize viewers, unique page visits. . . . Cable and the Internet have splintered media audiences and, thereby, created ferocious fights for ever-larger shares of ever-smaller fragments of the old mass market. The logic is powerful that the commercial imperatives of the new technologies will deepen the country's political divisions."[35]

In a podcast interview on *The Mike O'Meara Show*, Chuck Todd, MSNBC host and current *Meet the Press* moderator, was critical of advocacy journalism, saying it isn't healthy for politics. He gave his analysis of how cable news has affected political discourse and stated that *Meet the Press* did not have a point of view. He also discussed how he deals with criticism from the right that he works for the "liberal media": "I probably get more heat from the left than the right these days because the left gets just as aggressive at trying to work the refs [referees]. They think that we in the, quote, 'mainstream media,' overcompensate to the criticism. . . . Of course, the right says we're never [overcompensating to the criticism]. . . . I think advocacy journalism, sort of the Fox and what MS[NBC] primetime, those models, that hasn't been healthy for politics."[36]

As much as I like advocacy journalism, I know that I need to always remind myself that the information is presented with a skewed bias and might not be trustworthy. Sometimes, the hosts make the shows more about themselves rather than about reporting information. The demonizing of the other side, while often funny, can quickly get old and stale.

So what is the future of advocacy journalism? Will it continue to grow and thrive? We will discuss this in the next chapter.

CHAPTER 19

The Future of Advocacy Journalism and Balanced Journalism

There is likely to be an ongoing demand and need for both advocacy journalism and balanced, impartial journalism in the future. The public will always have a desire to be informed, to be aware of breaking news, and to know what's going on in their communities. But they will also want context, interpretation, analysis, opinion, and passionate and entertaining commentary. Some media analysts believe that advocacy journalism should be the predominant model for journalists in the future. But will it continue to grow and thrive? "It will continue to thrive as long as people have opinions," says Mark Bowden.[1] John Timpane believes "it will remain strong and ubiquitous."[2]

In 2014, former NBC correspondent Beverly Kirk spoke to students at Campbellsville University in Kentucky about the rising popularity of advocacy journalism and whether it constitutes the future of journalism. She said, "It's certainly going to have a bigger place at the table in the future. The reason behind the surge is money and resources. Traditional journalism outlets continue to shrink because of budget cuts and the fact that no one has quite figured out how to make as much money from the Internet as advertising dollars provided to newsrooms in the past."[3] Why is advocacy journalism more likely to bring in more money? Just look at the cable news ratings and the popularity of conservative talk radio hosts and news websites with edgy commentary. These media outlets have capitalized on the concept of niche media and giving their audiences exactly what they want.

Is it possible for the media to be objective, balanced, fair, and impartial in such an adversarial and polarized environment? How should the media address itself to such an environment? Michelle Ciulla Lipkin, executive director of the National Association for Media Literacy Education (NAMLE), believes that "It's not possible given the financial model of media. They tell a story in a certain way to get viewers. With all the pressure, there's no ability to be objective. It's sad that news outlets are money-making entities. You're supposed to tell people information, not depend on ad sales. It's a cycle with the pressure to stay number one, to bring money in, and to be powerful. I feel so negative, but one day hopefully it will change. Social media has apps that allow for many different points of view. But everyone's [web] feeds look different. There's still polarization."[4]

News outlets should seek centrist commentators. Former presidential advisor David Gergen of CNN, along with radio and CNN host Michael Smerconish, blogger Andrew Sullivan, former congressman Harold Ford Jr., John Avlon (editor in chief of the *Daily Beast* and a CNN political analyst), Joe Klein of *Time* magazine, and syndicated columnist Kathleen Parker, are among the few commentators who tend to give balanced opinions, at least based on my observations, as well as according to the *Daily Beast*'s John Avlon's list of top centrist commentators.[5]

When asked about the future of advocacy journalism, Will Bunch of the *Philadelphia Daily News* said, "It's not going to go away. But in the last couple of years there has been a flood of explanatory journalism, such as Vox.com and Nate Silver's 538 blog. It has set the stage for better advocacy journalism that takes strong positions but makes sure it is factual. It reflects a desire to go back to reporting more factual information. But it's presented in a more entertaining way than the traditional inverted pyramid. People are hungry for background information in news reporting, especially for complicated issues like gun rights and Syria. It's an implied backlash against too much opinion without the underlying facts."[6]

If skewed media presentations of the news are to be even more prevalent in the future, what is to become of straightforward, balanced journalism? Bunch believes that "It won't die off. People crave to know what happened, but we're just changing the way we get information. We've gone from newspapers to television to cell phones. Whether it's traditional media or new media, the goals are to get factual information to people quickly while being able to make money and support themselves."[7] But if biased and opinionated reporting is to be a permanent part of our future as a society, then won't the more boring and bland approach of the mainstream media have to transform itself into something more like cable news or the Internet and engage in advocacy journalism, at least to some extent, if it is to survive at all? Bunch sees this as "a complicated question. I agree that it's too boring, but it shouldn't replicate cable news and be who shouts the loudest. It has to find new ways to be provocative. A good outlet is the *New York Times Magazine*, which has provocative cover stories. People crave long-form journalism, which is the opposite of cable news. Cable outlets, such as CNN and MSNBC, haven't been doing well. A large pool of people crave interesting and provocative information about the world."[8]

As to what the future holds for traditional, straightforward media, John Timpane is a bit unsure: "God, I wish I knew. We need and want it, but the collapse of the business model makes it increasingly unlikely that it can keep going in anything like its present form." But he does not think that journalism should try to avoid being boring or ordinary: "Who cares if it's boring? Let it be boring. And why do what anyone else does? I hope people continue to have the money to pay reporters to find out the truth."[9] James B. Steele is concerned that the traditional media will feel the need to jump on the advocacy bandwagon and lose their identity in the process: "The mainstream media shouldn't engage in advocacy journalism just to be more opinionated or entertaining. It should write crisp, powerful stories. Newspapers are better than they were years ago. They are presented better and the reporters bring more knowledge to the subjects. They connect the dots and explain what the information means. You see where the chips fall and can be honest about it."[10]

Journalist Philip Meyer wrote that news reporting should emphasize data-intense methods: "Investigative reporters like Barlett and Steele in Philadelphia and Steve Doig in Miami practice objectivity of method, not objectivity of result. Barlett and Steele are mad as hell about the way things are going in America, and their writing shows it. A piece of Doig's roof was torn off by [Hurricane] Andrew, and he wasn't happy about that. But both reporting projects followed the objective scientific standard of replicability. They informed their investigations with theories about the underlying causes of events. They developed operational tests of those theories. And they documented the steps in executing their tests with a paper trail that any other investigator could find and follow and come out with the same results."[11]

Stanford University's Center for Internet and Ethics states that journalists should abandon the concept of objectivity while at the same time not engaging in advocacy. It argues that reporters should challenge their biases, examine opposing views, and be skeptical: "But abandoning the myth of the press as a neutral bystander to world events will go a long way toward reconnecting journalists with their audiences and with reality. Contrary to popular wisdom, it is possible to give up on the doctrine of objectivity without resorting to partisanship or advocacy. The best reporting tells a story rather than making an argument or attempting to persuade. It is authentic and human without being emotional and one-sided. These qualities are critical to maintaining an audience of people with diverse backgrounds and perspectives."[12]

In a *Guardian* article, Kellie Riordan writes that journalism can have a viewpoint, if it is based on evidence, and still be impartial: "And it should equally be possible to write a passionate piece of journalism that is impartial where the audience is left to draw its own conclusions. What has changed in the digital era is not so much the need for impartiality but the method to achieve it. New media prefer transparency and plurality to achieve impartiality, old media achieve it with objective methods. . . . Maybe what we do need to recognize is that a third form of publishing is emerging. In the *Columbia Journalism Review*, *Washington Post* reporter Marc Fisher asks 'as the lines between old and new increasingly blur, are the two schools of journalism's core values blending into a hybrid?'"[13]

Riordan cites *Quartz*, *Vice News*, and *Vox* as examples of media outlets that are successfully using an approach of reporting with a viewpoint while being impartial. I think that Matthew Yglesias's *Vox* article on April 20, 2016, could fall into that hybrid category because it stated the point of view that Bernie Sanders represents the future of the Democratic Party in that young democrats want a more ideological and more left-wing party.

The article cites statistics showing the overwhelming support that Sanders has from young people, but it did acknowledge his weaknesses and flaws, including his age and his being out of step culturally with his young supporters, his lack of rigorous policy proposals, his declarations about being a socialist, his reliance on a mostly white constituency, and his lack of interest in discussing foreign policy. Therefore, the article had a point of view, but it also had statistics and balance.[14]

Many people lament the decline of investigative journalism that serves as a watchdog on the government as well as the private sector. As Laura Frank wrote for PBS, "When faced with cuts, investigative reporting is often the first target. Investigative journalism takes more time and more experienced journalists to produce, and it often involves legal battles. It's generally the most expensive work the news media undertakes."[15] Jonathan Stray, reporter, editor, and director of the Associated Press's Overview Project, which helps investigative journalists, advocates the use and value of contextual journalism. Contextual journalism involves greater analysis and interpretation by the reporters. In describing truth as a tricky concept, Stray says, "Much easier to say that there are objective facts, knowably correct facts, and that that is all journalism reports. The messy complexity of providing real narratives in a real world is much less authoritative ground. Nonetheless, we all crave interpretation along with our facts. Explanation and analysis and *storytelling* have become prevalent in practice. We as audiences continue to demand certain types of experts, even when we can't tell if what they're saying is any good. We demand reasons why, even if there can be no singular truth. We demand narrative."[16]

Tim Rowland of Herald-Mail Media complements the celebrity gossip channel TMZ for its reporting of breaking news and cites this as an encouraging trend in reporting: "Mostly, TMZ reporters are obsessed with which stars wore the same hideous dress to the ball, but when they want to get a news story, give them credit, they go out and get it. With all due respect to traditional news outlets, when it comes to breaking stories, their reporters are just plain better."[17]

Like others, I have a mixed view of TMZ. They do break many accurate stories involving celebrities and famous people, such as football star Ray

Rice's abuse incident in a casino elevator,[18] *Seinfeld* star Michael Richards' angry, racist rant at black hecklers at a nightclub,[19] Los Angeles Clippers' owner Donald Sterling's racist rants,[20] and the Jahlil Okafor altercation in Boston.[21] And they also do it in an entertaining way. But they have also posted false stories, such as stories about rapper Lil Wayne being in a coma and in critical condition[22] and about Janet Jackson slapping and verbally abusing her niece.[23]

Advocacy journalism and balanced journalism can continue to coexist as successful media presentation models, and I hope that they continue to exist, even thrive. People will always crave reliable, trustworthy, balanced news sources that can give them an overview of what's going on locally, nationally, and around the world. However, consumers also want opinions, commentary, and perspective on the news, and they will often gravitate toward the passionate, biased voices that give it. My hope would be that mainstream media outlets that strive to practice balanced and objective journalism continue to do so and resist the temptation to become advocacy journalists with a clear agenda or bias.

Thus far, this book has focused on the journalism profession and how it reports the news. But what about news consumers? How do we navigate all of this information that we receive from news outlets with their various points of view and perspectives? How can we become savvy news consumers?

CHAPTER 20

The Importance of Being a Savvy Media Consumer

In light of the polarized media and the plethora of venues for news, we consumers need to be more savvy about how we get our information. Ideally, each of us should reach beyond our own echo chambers and seek news from a variety of media outlets and perspectives. We should be wary of facts and information that we receive from biased sources, and we should verify that information through other reliable sources. Therefore, if you're liberal, you should certainly continue watching MSNBC and reading the *New York Times* editorial page to get opinions that confirm your views. But, if you really care about being objective and fair-minded, you should attempt to determine for yourself which of the conservative news media sources are considered the best and then expose your beliefs to arguments expressed by Fox News, conservative talk radio, and publications like the *Wall Street Journal* editorial page. Finally, any desire to be well-rounded and thoroughly informed should include exposure to sources such as CNN, PBS, C-SPAN, the network nightly news, and a variety of newspapers to get more balanced reporting without an agenda. For international news, Reuters and the BBC are often considered good options. Likewise, if you're conservative, go ahead and watch Fox News, listen to Rush Limbaugh, and read the *Wall Street Journal*, but expose yourself to news and opinions from mainstream media outlets, MSNBC, and the *Huffington Post*.

But who has time for all of this? How can socially and politically concerned people, who are often quite busy with their own lives and professions, make sense of this vast array of information and conflicting ideas? Unfortunately, most people aren't thinking critically about what they hear, watch, or read. They need to be careful about what sources they are relying on.

We are all bombarded daily—hourly, in fact—with information from all types of sources. This is especially the case with millennials, who frequently engage in media multitasking, meaning that they will be involved in varied media use at the same time. For example, they might be doing their homework on their laptop while simultaneously watching television and texting a friend every twenty seconds or so. In 2015, a study conducted by Common Sense Media, which provides information, advice, and tools to help parents and teachers harness the power of media and technology as a positive force in children's lives, revealed that 26 percent of American teens spent up to eight hours a day on entertainment media, including music, videos, video games, and social media.[1] Their cell phones might as well be glued to their hands. A 2010 study by the Kaiser Family Foundation, a nonprofit organization that focuses on national health issues, found that young people aged eleven to fourteen spent an average of seven hours and thirty-eight minutes per day using media.[2] Younger millennials (age 18 to 24), labeled "the Unattached" by the American Press Institute's Media Insight Project, have low motivation about news. Older millennials, between the ages of 25 and 34, labeled "the Distracted," also lack a strong interest in news: "Like the younger Unattached Millennials, the Distracted mostly get their news and information by bumping into it in the course of other activities. Their reasons, however, tend to be different from those of younger more accidental news consumers. Where the Unattached may be too young or inexperienced to care about general news, the Distracted are likely too busy."[3] This multitasking and lack of interest in news could reflect young people's ability to select and integrate news and make up their own minds about issues of the day. As noted by Janna Anderson and Lee Rainie of the Pew Research Center, an online survey of over one thousand technology experts revealed that many predicted "that the impact of networked living on today's young will drive them to thirst for instant gratification, settle for quick choices, and lack patience. A number of the survey respondents argued that it is vital to reform education and emphasize digital literacy. A notable number expressed concerns that trends are leading to a future in which most people are shallow consumers of information, and some mentioned George Orwell's *1984* or expressed their fears of control by powerful interests in an age of entertaining distractions."[4]

It should take only thirty minutes or so to get an overview of what's going on locally, nationally, and in the world. Put the TV cable stations or the local or network news on in your house or apartment, and let it run in the background even if you can't physically watch it. Go to Google News to get a basic summary overview of the major stories of the day, and then click on stories that interest you. Monitor your Facebook and Twitter feed for news, but make sure that you verify stories via other media outlets. Don't just rely on what Aunt Mary or your friends send you via Facebook—verify it by going to several respected media outlets to see if they are reporting the same facts. You should also follow more reputable, traditional media outlets and reporters on social media.

At the beginning of all of my journalism courses, I go around the class and ask my students where they get their news. They give a wide range of responses, including local and national print newspapers, online newspapers, the Internet, local and national television broadcasts, Twitter, Facebook, word of mouth, and shows like the *Daily Show* and the former *Colbert Report*. As one might expect, the number of students who read print newspapers or magazines is not very high unless they are provided online. I also give news quizzes to some of my classes in which I ask them questions about events that took place locally, nationally, and internationally during the past week. The topics range from politics, breaking news, entertainment, sports, international news, etc. At times, the results are disappointing; they might only be able to answer a few of the sports and entertainment questions and have no clue about what major events took place in politics, national news, or international news.

We live in a sound-bite society. The local and national news television broadcasts only have thirty minutes to present the news (actually less, due to commercials). On the local level, there is even less time because these news sources include segments on sports and weather. Sound bites can reflect a bias simply due to their brevity. The nature of broadcast news is to focus mostly on providing information quickly in short chunks, as opposed to offering detailed explanations. Many typical broadcast segments on radio and television only last thirty to forty-five seconds. Given these extreme time constraints, it's difficult, if not impossible, for broadcasts to provide context, interpretation, and analysis. People should try to go beyond these news chunks to read more in-depth articles about important topics.

Why is it hard to get accurate information in a sound-bite society? Eugene Kiely, Director of FactCheck.org, writes, "This is opinion, not based in any scientific research, but I personally think that the weakening of traditional journalism combined with the rise of the Internet and cable TV has made it more difficult for people to get accurate information. It is available but sometimes overwhelmed by bloggers and political pundits."[5]

I tell my students that it's important to verify information that comes from any source, but most particularly from their friends on Twitter or Facebook. To rework a phrase of former president Ronald Reagan: Don't trust, and verify. Check a few established, credible news sources to confirm the information that your friends send you. A couple of years ago, I remember a few students in my class talking about an apparent incident involving an NBA player punching out Justin Bieber in a fight. "Dude, did you hear that Blake Griffin slapped Bieber in a Starbucks?" one student asked another. It turned out to be a false Internet rumor, much to the dismay of some of them. Pretty much every week, social media trolls and pranksters kill off celebrities who are in fact still alive, ranging from Bill Cosby to Betty White to James Earl Jones. In 2013, Mark E. Anderson of the *Daily Kos* talked about some of the false social media rumors circulating—that Wisconsin governor Scott Walker hated Labor Day and thought it should be replaced by Patriots Day, that the Beatles' sons would be forming a band, and that Led Zeppelin would reunite and go on tour.[6] In 2012, Samantha Murphy Kelly of *Mashable* listed eight social media hoaxes that people fell for that year, which included fake pictures of Hurricane Sandy, the rumor that Justin Bieber had been diagnosed with cancer and was encouraging his fans to shave their heads in support, and the story that CEO Mark Zuckerberg planned to shut down Facebook on March 15.[7]

There are many instances in which people have been duped by satirical stories in the *Onion*. China's *People's Daily* and South Korea's *Korea Times* picked up a fake *Onion* story that satirically declared North Korean leader Kim Jong Un had been voted the world's sexiest man. Two Bangladesh news outlets picked up an *Onion* story that made up quotes from astronaut Neil Armstrong in which he purportedly admitted that the moon landing was faked and was actually filmed at a studio in New Mexico. A Louisiana congressman became outraged by an *Onion* story that touted the building of a major $8 billion abortionplex facility, and he posted the *Onion* article on Facebook.[8]

I have developed a healthy skepticism when I hear breaking news. When a friend told me that TMZ had posted a video of a Philadelphia 76ers rookie apparently getting into an altercation outside a Boston bar, I immediately went to other sources (ESPN, the *Philadelphia Inquirer*, the *Boston Globe*, CNN, and Google News) to try to confirm the information, which did in fact turn out to be true.

All of us need to be careful about rumors, speculation, and hasty conclusions. During the coverage of the 9/11 tragedy, events were happening at a frantic pace, and the media were scrambling to keep up and to sort fact from rumor. At first, there was speculation that it was a small plane that had hit the first tower. The media relayed an unconfirmed report that a Palestinian organization had taken credit for the attack. There was an initial report of a car bomb that went off near the State Department, but that turned out to be false. More recently, there were false rumors that the missing Malaysian airplane had landed safely in China. Readers should verify and check out rumors and initial news reports by checking a variety of traditional media sources. I personally would go to the *Philadelphia Inquirer* and KYW1060 News Radio for local Philadelphia stores. For national and international stories, I would go to CNN, the *New York Times*, the *Washington Post*, and Google News.

In situations where news is spotty, the flow of information is fast-paced, and many versions of a news event are occurring at once, outlets are almost forced to rely initially on speculation, assumptions, and rumors. But these media outlets have an obligation to specify when information is unconfirmed and has yet to be verified. If viewers or listeners are not hearing that sources of information are yet to be confirmed or are still being checked during a rapidly occurring news event, this should be a clue that another news source needs to be checked—preferably one that does clarify the speculative nature of the information being conveyed until multiple sources confirm it.

It is important for media outlets to confirm and verify the original source or provider of the information, as well as the content and context of the information being given. Activists of one type or another may try to hijack the coverage by providing information with a bias toward their own agenda, the possibility of which should cause media outlets to be careful in their verification process. Many people believe that the heavily edited Planned Parenthood videos, which purported to show Planned Parenthood illegally making arrangements to sell fetal tissue, was a good example of this. The two antiabortion activists had used fake driver IDs when they made the undercover video; in January 2016, a Houston grand jury indicted them for tampering with a government record.[9]

Another barometer of credibility is whether reporters rely on biased sources. As noted earlier, this occurred when *60 Minutes* and Dan Rather relied on forged memos provided by Lt. Bill Burkett, who was known to be a Bush critic and Kerry supporter. This should have raised a red flag and indicated that strict verification was needed. It is important to assess whether the source, witness, or person being interviewed has something to gain from what he or she says. As noted by the American Press Institute, "If the best information a journalist has comes from a potentially biased source, naming the source will reveal to the audience the possible bias—and may inhibit the source from attempting to deceive you as well."[10] There should always be a preference among media outlets and reporters to have sources go on the record to enhance credibility, as opposed to citing anonymous sources. Generally, it is preferred that reporters be transparent and pursue on-the-record information. Many times, however, sources do not want to go on record for fear of losing their jobs or being physically threatened. Relying on anonymous sources can be dangerous. In a lecture, John Christie, editor in chief of the Maine Center for Public Interest Reporting, warned that the false god of relying on anonymous sources to break a story has been problematic for many reporters. Noting mistakes made in reporting about the Newtown, Connecticut, and Washington Naval Yard shootings due to reliance on anonymous sources, Christie said, "That's one problem with anonymous sources: They often get it wrong because why make sure you have it right when you will not be held accountable for what you say? And even if it is accurate, readers cannot judge the value of the material for themselves if they don't know the source. Many sources hide behind anonymity to take cheap shots without anyone knowing they have an axe to grind or a dog in the fight."[11]

News consumers should always approach the information they receive with a healthy bit of skepticism. I am not suggesting that we all be perpetual doubters but rather that we should exercise caution about accepting a news story as fact without giving it some serious thought. Are there questions about the event that remain unanswered or even questions that have yet to be posed? Reporters were guilty of speculating during the West Virginia coal mine tragedy on January 2, 2006, when it was reported that twelve of thirteen miners at the Sago Mine in Tallmansville had been found alive, when in fact twelve of the thirteen were dead. Reporters failed to get specific details from mining officials as to how they "knew" that the miners were alive instead of relying on assumptions. They interviewed regular people who ran up to the cameras and announced that the miners were alive, even though their assertions were based on false rumor.[12] Other examples of the media being misled or failing to check sources include reporting on the causes behind the downing of the commercial airliner in the Ukraine, the missing Malaysian airliner, and the downing of the Russian airliner in Egypt, as well as the accidental bombing of a hospital in Afghanistan. When covering major political or military stories, reporters should rely on public, political, and military officials, but should be skeptical about how the event is being described, interpreted, or "managed" by these sources. Each side hopes to present its analysis of the situation in the most favorable light, while discrediting those who have opposing views. Coverage of military conflicts, global tragedies, and international incidents are frequently susceptible to broad interpretation, requiring careful media and public scrutiny regarding the facts involved.

Albeit rare, people should be wary of news hoaxes, especially around April Fools' Day. Perhaps the most famous media hoax was Orson Welles's radio adaptation broadcast of H. G. Wells's *War of the Worlds* in October 1938, which led many listeners to believe that the earth was being invaded by Martians.[13] On April 1, 1985, *Sports Illustrated* ran a fake fourteen-page story about Sidd Finch, a twenty-eight-year-old rookie for the New York Mets who could throw a 168 mph fastball.[14] Over the years, as recently as 2015, there have been hoaxes and false stories about needles and razor blades in Halloween candy.[15] In 1996, Taco Bell bought full-page ads in six major newspapers on April Fools' Day, "announcing" that it had purchased the Liberty Bell and would be renaming it the Taco Liberty Bell. In 1992, famed Richard Nixon impressionist Rich Little and NPR's John Hockenberry teamed up to air a hoax story on NPR's *Talk of the Nation* program that Richard Nixon would be running for president in 1992. A 1957 BBC April Fools report alleged that there were spaghetti trees in Switzerland. In 1976, the BBC was at it again on April Fools' Day when its radio astronomer told people that the earth's gravity would be diminished temporarily due to an unusual alignment of Pluto and Jupiter. In 1998, Burger King bought a full-page April Fools' Day ad touting its "left handed Whopper." These false rumors and fake stories are even more abundant in social media.[16]

Few of us have difficulty dismissing obvious and blatant attempts to skew the news in one direction or another, but how can we determine hidden bias? How can we distinguish facts from opinions? What is media literacy and why is it important? How can readers ferret out kernels of truth in advocacy journalism articles? How do readers determine accuracy in this age of advocacy journalism? What are the signs of bias in media outlets that purport to be objective? How can we learn to read between the lines to get accurate information?

Media-literacy experts can shed important insight on those questions. Michelle Ciulla Lipkin, executive director of the National Association for Media Literacy Education (NAMLE) offered this observation: "It's important to wait until the whole story is constructed. Take time to pause. Be careful with your words. Don't just believe what you read or watch at first, see the story unfold and get the full picture. Don't just go by the initial report. Find other sources to corroborate the information before you believe it's true."[17] She goes on to say,

Look at the facts of the story. How was the story covered? What is the bias? Who was the source? The same story on Fox or CNN is told from a totally different point of view. If you understand the different biases, you can make your own assessment. The problem is that people reinforce their own ideology. If you're conservative, you watch Fox and believe what's regurgitated. Same thing with liberals and MSNBC. It's troublesome that people aren't willing to hear other points of view, so there's less dialogue. We choose what we want to hear. Millennials who will be voting for the first time get their news from Twitter and never consider watching the twenty-four-hour news programs. Where we get the news affects what we learn about the story.[18]

In advising on how to separate fact from opinion, Eugene Kiely said,

That's not as easy as it may seem. Opinions can be fact-based, so it is not always easily separated. During the recent recession if you said "the economy's lousy" you certainly had enough facts on your side to support that opinion. The stock market and the GDP [Gross Domestic Product] were down and unemployment rates, bankruptcies and foreclosures were all up. But if you said that now then that would be an opinion. The stock market has recovered, the unemployment rate is down, the GDP is up and bankruptcies and foreclosures are receding. But the labor participation rate is low and median wages have not increased much. It now becomes an argument over whether the economy has SUFFICIENTLY recovered and to me that's a matter of opinion. But, generally, facts are concrete things—hard data—that do not change regardless of one's belief, while opinions are subjective and must be supported by facts in order to be true.[19]

Media-literacy expert Kathleen Tyner of the University of Texas had this to say about the whole effort to seek the truth: "The word 'truth,' is in itself a biased perspective. And so again, I think that logical thinking, based on evidence, can be accomplished through more understanding of research and more opportunities for dialogue. In contentious arenas, it helps to initiate dialogue in a more structured and moderated way. An example would be managed comment sections in online news outlets. But public dialogue is imperative and everyone should have opportunities to engage in it. And so access is still important. In addition to technology access, people must be welcomed into the dialogue with strong literacy skills and respectful spaces for civic engagement."[20] Similarly, I believe that dialogue is imperative and that it is important for everyone to be able to participate in that dialogue but that, in addition to heated, personal attack-filled online comments, it's important to also have other opportunities to have a higher level, more thought-out discussion on issues. For instance, in 2007, the University of Pennsylvania hosted a Public Conversation Series exploring dimensions of urban poverty and economic development. Town halls, public forums, and moderated discussion forums lend themselves to more thoughtful discussions.

What is objective, informative journalism? What is slanted, biased journalism? What is outright propaganda? Is the information from a public-relations perspective or sponsored content paid for by an organization? Sometimes, it can be hard to tell. Michelle Ciulla Lipkin described the public's awkward position in relation to the news in this way: "It's become increasing difficult to appreciate the difference given the way we receive messages. There's so much noise and so many media outlets. It's more difficult to determine what's objective and what's subjective, what's truth and what's story. The lines have become blurred. For this election [2016], the debates and conversations haven't been substantive. There's blurring between entertainment and news. Media literacy is the answer. People need to have literacy skills."[21]

According to Leann Davis Alspaugh of Pearson's Online Learning Exchange (a website that helps teachers build customized lessons), media bias can be hard to detect because it usually isn't announced openly by the media outlet: "There are clear cases where bias is expected, such as in opinion pieces or editorials. Learning to detect bias means hunting for clues. It also means becoming familiar with different kinds of writing and considering context. Developing the ability to detect bias enables students to weigh the evidence and form their own opinions rather than simply following the lead of others."[22]

Assessing the source of the information is among the ways to detect and assess bias. Who is the writer or the media outlet? Who owns and operates the media company? What is their purpose, goal, or ideology? What type of story construction do they use? Do they present a diverse range of viewpoints? What qualifications are possessed by the experts surveyed?

One key factor used to evaluate the credibility of a source is the authority of the publication. Is it a peer-reviewed journal article written by an expert in the field and reviewed by other experts before being published? Or is it written by the sole operator of a website who has no authority or expertise in the field? Is the author qualified to write the article through his or her education and professional experience? Are you getting information about the medical effects of marijuana from the Mayo Clinic's website or from Joe's Weed page (whoever Joe is)?

It is important to rely on primary sources as much as possible. Primary sources are original, first-hand accounts that are factual and not filtered through interpretation, such as diaries, letters, historical and legal documents, journals, newspaper and magazine articles, government records, photos, videos, recorded speeches, and interviews with participants or witnesses. Secondary sources are second-hand accounts that analyze or interpret primary sources, such as biographies, commentaries, and criticism. In order to analyze a speech by Abraham Lincoln, it would be better to read the original transcript of the speech to see exactly what he said, instead of a secondary source that paraphrased what he said or gave commentary on it. Don't just rely on what a secondary source like *Wikipedia* says. The reader should click on the link in the citations provided at the end of the *Wikipedia* entry to read the original source and assess the credibility of the original article and source. Readers should treat *Wikipedia* more as a search engine than a primary source. Since *Wikipedia* is crowdsourced, with entries produced by members of the public, and can be agenda-driven, people need to be suspicious. To its credit, *Wikipedia* lists warnings and disclaimers for some *Wikipedia* topics. As far as filtering sources, government websites, peer-reviewed journals, and educational websites with a ".edu" domain are considered to be more authoritative by many academics.

Unfortunately, far too many young people and adults limit their research to secondary sources like *Wikipedia* or Google. Mind you, I think Google is great; I use Google, Google News, Google Scholar, and Google Books frequently. However, the search results that I get, especially on Google or Google News, aren't always reliable or authoritative. Certain research databases are more likely to consistently guide readers to more credible, authoritative sources. These would include WestLaw, Lexis Nexis, Proquest, Academic Search Premier, FirstSearch, MedLine, PubMed, Wilson Select Plus, OMNI Select, and JSTOR. Some of these sites are better for general information, while others are special sources for specific types of topics, such as MedLine for medical conditions and WestLaw for recent Supreme Court decisions.

All of us as news consumers should be skeptical about the information we are receiving. We should do our own research to confirm information as best we can on respected media and government websites that provide information, statistics, and data, such as the CDC or Census Bureau. In the end, it is our responsibility as news consumers to be well informed. Most of these government websites are universally considered to be trustworthy and nonpartisan in nature.

Another key factor in evaluating bias focuses on who the news writer or program host is. What is his or her religion, political party, race, gender, age, or socioeconomic status? If readers, listeners, or viewers are unfamiliar with a website or media outlet, they should research the outlet to determine whether it might have an ideological slant. You can click the "About Us" button on the website or use the website ICANN's WHOIS Lookup to find the registered domain owner. Consider the thoroughness of the article or program segment and whether certain facts could have been omitted or whether only one side of the story was presented. Sometimes a media outlet will have a consistent ideology or philosophy. *Salon*, Pacifica Radio, and *Democracy Now!* are liberal examples, while Breitbart, the *Washington Times*, and Newsmax are conservative examples. It is important for readers or viewers to know about a media outlet's ideology in order to assess the reliability of the information provided.

Just like readers and consumers, reporters need to be aware of potential bias and be careful to avoid it. If the reporting is to have value for the news consumers, it is important for reporters to secure information from a wide variety of what they know to be reliable sources. And it is fine to include material from social media, but those who report the news should be skeptical of information sent via such open-access sources.

We are well aware, based on discussions in previous chapters that writing or programming with a bias or agenda is geared toward influencing the audience to think a certain way about an issue. When assessing a news report, we need to ask ourselves whether alternative or opposing points of view are offered in the article or the program. If they are, is the writer or host favorable or open-minded to the opposing point of view? Or is he or she dismissive, snarky, or cynical toward it? Sometimes the opposing viewpoint is drowned out by the host or by other panelists, who repeatedly interrupt the person giving a dissenting view. At times, the panels are stacked in favor of one side or the other, which can make the dissenter, who is in the minority, look like he or she is wrong or out of touch. If this appears to be the case with respect to a particular program, then viewers need to question its newsworthiness.

Is there a way to evaluate accuracy in the age of advocacy journalism? Kathleen Tyner contends that there is: "The reader must look for references to credible sources of information and evidence, the reporter's data collection methods (usually interviews), and the reporter's (or newspaper's) previous record with accuracy in reporting are a few ways to 'clock' accuracy in reporting."[23] The various fact-checking organizations and media watchdogs could also be a way to check the previous record of the reporter or news outlet. News consumers should fact-check what partisan news sources report against more nonpartisan sources. FactCheck.org's Eugene Kiely adds, "Check what you hear from advocacy journalists against reliable and credible nonpartisan sources. Advocates are not always wrong, but they should be viewed with skepticism until proven right."[24]

Dan Giancaterino has been a law librarian at Jenkins Law Library in Philadelphia, the oldest law library in the country, since 2000. He has given Internet presentations at meetings hosted by county bar associations, community legal services, the Municipal Court of Philadelphia, the Pennsylvania Bar Institute, and the Philadelphia *Daily News*. On many occasions, Giancaterino has discussed web searching on the *Michael Smer-*

conish Morning Show, the *Glenn Beck Program*, and Bill O'Reilly's *Radio Factor*. Regarding evaluation of accuracy, Dan Giancaterino points out that there are three things he looks for:

- Descriptive words—These can alert you to a bias right away. Is Edward Snowden a "fugitive traitor"? Or is he a "whistleblower"?
- Quotations—Do you really have the complete picture if a story on the economic effects of Obamacare contains comments exclusively from administration officials or Democratic lawmakers? Would you trust an article on climate change that only quotes a conservative think tank?
- Data cited—Does the Obamacare article mentioned above point to a report from the Congressional Research Service? Are there citations to refereed journal articles in the climate change article?[25]

Giancaterino also suggests that we "Build a toolbox of Web reference tools. Obviously Google. But also Wolfram|Alpha, a 'computational knowledge engine' that can calculate an answer to queries such as *U.S. GDP growth 2008–2010*. The Annenberg Public Policy Center's fact-check.org is great for political claims. And snopes.com for urban legends and the like. NewsBank is an excellent archive of newspapers, some going back more than 30 years. The Internet Archive's WayBack Machine lets you look at older versions of websites—some all the way back to 1996!—to see how information presented on them has changed. Even Wikipedia has value for fact-checking, in certain applications."[26]

Another question to ask is whether the content was written by an organization or person who has a clear agenda. Was it written by a conservative think tank or a liberal think tank? There has been a rise in think tanks, often corporate-fronted, that provide experts who give biased opinions. Think tank organizations such as the Cato Institute, Heritage Foundation, Brookings Institution, the Center for American Progress, the American Enterprise Institute, Manhattan Institute, and Hudson Institute will likely have a bias. For instance, the Heritage Foundation identifies itself as conservative and holds an annual Conservative Policy Summit. The Brookings Institute is known as liberal leaning. In some cases, these organizations identify their philosophy in an "About Us" or "Mission Statement" online, or in their annual reports posted online. Other times, you can check for ongoing, consistent topics or themes that they focus on, such as reproductive rights or second-amendment rights. You can also check the background of the organizations' directors and who their donors are. Writers for these think tanks will frequently write and publish op-eds for major newspapers and be interviewed as experts on radio and television. In most cases, the titles of these organizations don't reflect any bias, and often the media outlet that publishes their work or interviews them does not identify the bias of the organization. In many cases, they identify themselves as nonideological or independent even though they have an agenda. Readers and viewers need to be aware of that bias so they can evaluate the credibility of the writer or speaker.

A bias is likely to occur in cases where the publication is produced by an organization that is writing about itself. University alumni magazines will focus on positive aspects of the school, like increased enrollment or higher SAT scores, but will be unlikely to focus on scandals or news that embarrasses the school. A professional football team that has its own magazine or website is unlikely to be highly critical of management, coaches, or players, even if the team has never won a game all season. The same is true of corporations, associations, societies, and the like. Articles written on an organization's website are likely to be biased in favor of the organization or the organization's viewpoints. Similarly, with sponsored content (as described in chapter 8), organizations and corporations will pay media outlets for placement of articles that are in reality public-relations pieces.

Sometimes, reporters qualify their remarks by stating "I think" or "I believe" or "In my opinion," which makes it easy to determine that a bias, however slight, is present. More often than not, opinions are slipped into the reporting in a subtle manner such as in headlines, teasers for upcoming television program segments, topics covered, phrasing of questions, or choice of experts interviewed.

Beware when media outlets engage in cheerleading. Many people criticized MSNBC's Chris Matthews's overexcitement when he stated after a speech by presidential candidate Barack Obama in 2008 that "I felt this thrill going up my leg."[27] In 2010, Fox News contributor Dick Morris said that instead of just going after Democratic "pawns" in the midterm elections, the Republicans should also go after the rooks, bishops, and knights (higher targets) such as Congressman Barney Frank of Massachusetts.[28] On election night of 2012, Fox News contributor Karl Rove refused to admit that President Obama had carried Ohio, even though Fox had called the race for Obama.[29]

Does the writer or host use pejorative language, insults, or name-calling to diminish or ridicule the source, the subject of discussion, or the guest on the show? Pejorative language that demonizes a person or group reflects a clear bias. Similarly, if a source or subject is heaped with praise or described with numerous superlatives, this, too, signals a positive bias on the part of the writer or host. Use of such words as "great," "stupid," "worst," "best," "moronic," "idiotic," "bloviating," and "unpatriotic" can demonstrate the skewed nature of the discussion or reportage. Beware of labels that pigeonhole the other side, such as "bloviating ignoramus," "damaged goods," "ethically challenged," or "high maintenance."

Use of hyperbole and exaggeration should set off red flags in consumers' minds, telling them that what they are being exposed to may not be reliable information. Many media outlets sensationalize the news and use shock value to report it. While discussing President Obama's reaction to the arrest of Henry Louis Gates on *Fox & Friends*, Glenn Beck called Obama a racist and said that he "has a deep-seated hatred for white people."[30] Conservative radio host Mark Levin called President Obama a disgrace and an anti-Semite and stated that he had more blood on his hands than any modern president.[31] In one of his MSNBC Special Comments, Keith Olbermann called President Bush a bald-faced liar and said that he had no business being president.[32]

For many people, reading blogs, Facebook pages, and Twitter feeds is still a relatively new way to obtain information. It is important to be mindful that most people posting this information were not trained in journalism and are not bound by journalistic ethics codes. In some cases, they might not even be fully aware that any such ethical principles or guidelines exist. This is especially the case for social media forums, even though the sponsoring venue has explained its code of conduct in a digital document that those posting on the venue must attest that they have read and will comply with the stated rules for participation. In many cases, these forums are open-ended venues for the expression of beliefs, feelings, frustrations, anger, fear, and the like. As legitimate sources of news or credible information, they should be viewed as highly suspect. Simply because these comments are available to anyone who seeks out the venue does not mean that they have in any way been vetted for accuracy, truth, or fairness.

If consumers are seeking information from news venues outside their own country, it is important to know if the media outlet is privately owned or if it is state owned. In various countries, the primary media—newspapers, magazines, radio stations, and television networks—are owned and operated by the government. This can lead to serious credibility and trust issues. When reporting on major news events that impact the nation, these government-run media outlets may be used for propaganda purposes or to spin a news story to the advantage of the state. There is a difference between bias and outright propaganda. Information from countries with state-controlled media should be viewed with considerable suspicion. This is different than something like PBS, which receives government funding but strives to be informational. In contrast, North Korea does not have freedom of the press. All of the radios and televisions in that country are pretuned to government stations that give government propaganda and do not criticize the government. All reporters are under government control and are mandated to praise the country's leader and not report on the suffering of average North Korean people.[33]

Al Jazeera, which is partly owned by the country of Qatar, claims to be independent of the Qatar government, but some skeptics disagree. Al Jazeera's director, Al Anstey, defended the network's independence in an interview with Ian Burrell of the *Independent* on November 5, 2014, stating that Qatar does not dictate or censor its content, that it reports negative and embarrassing stories about Qatar—such as the allegations of bribery over granting the 2022 World Cup—and that its coverage of ISIS and other contentious stories was not controlled by Qatar.[34] In general, Al Jazeera is widely respected for its independent voice. However, there have been times when that independence has been called into question. For example, in 2012, Dan Sabbagh of the *Guardian* wrote, "Al-Jazeera's editorial independence has been called into question after its director of news stepped in to ensure a speech made by Qatar's emir to the UN led its English channel's coverage of the debate on Syrian intervention."[35]

In some cases, the lines of state-run or state-sponsored media can be blurred. An example of that would be Russia Today, or RT, which is officially backed by the Russian government and was established to be a balance against US media coverage. Although the network is technically described as being independent, it consistently provides positive coverage of the Russian government. In 2013, Russian president Vladimir Putin told RT's Margarita Simonyan, "We never expected this to be a news agency or a channel which would defend the position of the Russian political line. We wanted to bring an absolutely independent news channel to the news arena. Certainly the channel is funded by the government, so it cannot help but reflect the Russian government's official position on the events in our country and in the rest of the world one way or another. But I'd like to underline again that we never intended this channel, RT, as any kind of apologetics for the Russian political line, whether domestic or foreign."[36] Critics and skeptics would disagree vehemently with Putin's statement. Count Elizabeth Wahl as one of those skeptics. She was a former RT reporter who quit on live television after the Russian invasion of the Ukraine. "I cannot be part of a network funded by the Russian government that whitewashes the actions of Putin," she said. "I am proud to be an American and believe in disseminating the truth. And that is why, after this newscast, I am resigning."[37] She later explained her decision in an article she wrote for *Politico*, saying that the network was used as a tool to push Putin's agenda, that it was spewing lies to justify Russian military intervention in a sovereign country, and that it was a sketchy organization that posed as legitimate news.[38]

Beware when media outlets are just repeating or reprinting a story written by another medium without doing its own reporting or verification. Many media sources quote Reuters, the *New York Times*, or the Associated Press, or reprint stories that come over the newswire. Generally, this is accepted, but sometimes media outlets might quote or reprint articles from other sources that might not be as credible, don't have an extensive fact-checking or editing operation to monitor accuracy, or have a clear bias or agenda.

In terms of following politics, news media and news consumers need to be skeptical of politicians' statements and claims. Some candidates are less scripted than others. When quoting or citing a candidate's or politician's words, media outlets should be on guard to fact-check the claims and statements. The consumer needs to be able to judge the media outlet's success or failure at doing so. The nature of fact-checking by media outlets is evolving. The traditional model of in-house fact-checkers started in the 1920s with major newspapers and magazines. Now, there is a trend of public fact-checking by individuals and by organizations. According to Federica Cherubini of Poynter, in July 2015 there were sixty-four websites worldwide dedicated to fact-checking.[39] Some have rating meters to assess the accuracy of statements. Most major news outlets engage in some form of public fact-checking, however. Duke University's Reporters' Lab website has a map that helps people locate fact-checking websites in the United States and around the world. The website AllSides has a bias rating that calculates bias, including the bias of several major media outlets.[40]

But how do we separate truth from spin? What is hyperbole and what is sheer nonsense? What is fact and what is fiction? When do people go too far in stretching the truth? Many fact-checking organizations have arisen. Some monitor politicians, while others analyze the media. Media outlets fact-check candidates' statements made during political debates. Some organizations focus on fact-checking journalist's claims.

In January 2012, Arthur S. Brisbane of the *New York Times* raised the issue of whether and when its reporters should act as truth vigilantes, challenging facts asserted by the newsmakers they cover.[41] Oftentimes, it's a mixed bag when assessing accuracy. No one's statements are always true or always false, and there are grey areas as well. Some of Donald Trump's claims proved to be valid, while others were not, or were borderline, regarding birthrates, deportations during the Eisenhower administration, citizenship, crime rates of immigrants, his initial opposition to the Iraq war, and whether celebrations by Muslims occurred in New Jersey after the attack on the World Trade Center on September 11, 2001.

PolitiFact, established as a project of the *Tampa Bay Times*, is an independent fact-checking journalism website that focuses on exposing truth in politics, looking at statements made by local and national politicians, government officials, political parties, political action committees, advocacy groups, and members of the media, including columnists, bloggers, and radio and television hosts and their guests. PolitiFact has a feature called the Truth-O-Meter, which features ratings like true, false, half-true, mostly true, and pants on fire—reflecting the most ridiculous falsehoods. Another feature, called the Flip-O-Meter, indicates whether politicians have changed their opinion on an issue. In 2009, PolitiFact won the Pulitzer Prize for its coverage and fact-checking of the 2008 presidential election. It has affiliates and state partners with news organizations, including New Hampshire's *Concord Monitor* for the 2016 presidential primary. While PolitiFact has a staff of nine reporters and editors, average people and news consumers can also e-mail the organization to suggest a fact-check.[42]

FactCheck.org is part of the University of Pennsylvania's Annenberg Public Policy Center. It is nonprofit and nonpartisan. It analyzes trending topics, looks through transcripts, videos, and source material from C-SPAN and others. It goes through government speeches, candidate speeches, and talking points to see if they are being distorted.[43] The director, Eugene Kiely, said, "Our mission is to reduce the level of deception and confusion in U.S. politics. We monitor the factual accuracy of what is said by major U.S. political players in the form of TV ads, debates, speeches, interviews, and news releases. Our goal is to apply the best practices of both journalism and scholarship, and to increase public knowledge and understanding." He emphasized that the organization is independent and nonpartisan: "We are independent because we accept no money from advertisers and no contributions from labor unions, corporations or any individuals actively involved with politics. We are funded by foundations with no political agendas (Annenberg Foundation and Stanton Foundation are two of our major funders), and individuals who are not politically active. We publish the names of any individuals who give us more than

$1,000 in a fiscal year. We are nonpartisan because we write critically of both major parties."[44]

Snopes is a nonpartisan and independent website founded in 1995 that focuses on investigating and debunking rumors, myths, and urban legends. It has been featured on news programs such as CNN and NPR, as well as in the *New York Times*, the *Washington Post*, the *Wall Street Journal*, and *Reader's Digest*. It covers an eclectic range of topics, including politics, media, medical, military, religion, science, movies, September 11, and old wives' tales.[45]

The *Washington Post*'s "Fact Checker" uses a rating system of Pinocchios to assess the truth or falsity of politicians' statements, ranging from one Pinocchio for some shading of the truth to four Pinocchios for outright whoppers. In explaining the website's goals, Glenn Kessler wrote, "The purpose of this website, and an accompanying column in the Sunday print edition of the *Washington Post*, is to 'truth squad' the statements of political figures regarding issues of great importance, be they national, international or local. As a presidential election approaches, we will increasingly focus on statements made in the heat of the presidential contest. But we will not be limited to political charges or countercharges. We will seek to explain difficult issues, provide missing context and provide analysis and explanation of various 'code words' used by politicians, diplomats and others to obscure or shade the truth."[46] In an e-mail interview, Kessler said that the goal and purpose of Fact Checker is "To vet the accuracy of public statements by politicians and public figures and to inform voters about issues." He emphasizes that it is independent and nonpartisan: "We play no favorites and go only where the facts lead us. A study a few years ago found the Fact Checker split pretty evenly between the parties."[47]

It is important for these fact-checking organizations to be neutral and nonpartisan. Bias can be demonstrated if a media outlet does more fact-checking on one political party, candidate, group, or type of information than another. Fact-checkers serve as a validating service in pointing out mistakes, but readers should be aware that even fact-checking can be subject to bias. Not everyone agrees that some of these fact-checking organizations are fair and balanced. A George Mason University Center for Media and Public Affairs survey discovered that PolitiFact found that Republicans were more dishonest in their claims three times as often as Democrats.[48] Some viewed this finding as showing that PolitiFact was guilty of selection bias, however, some media outlets, such as *Salon*, viewed the three-to-one ratio as proof that the Republicans were less credible than Democrats.[49]

Media watchdog groups, which are intended to monitor the accuracy of media organizations, include Media Matters, Accuracy in Media, Fairness and Accuracy in Reporting (FAIR), Media Research Center, and PR Watch. Some of these organizations have a specific focus and so may also demonstrate a bias toward or against various of the media outlets they monitor. For example, Media Matters will focus primarily on catching mistakes and bias reported in conservative media. In the "About Us" section of its website, the group identifies itself as being "a progressive research and information center dedicated to comprehensively monitoring, analyzing, and correcting conservative misinformation in the U.S. media."[50] Conservative media watchdogs will focus on catching mistakes and biased reporting by liberal media outlets and the mainstream media. These partisan media watchdogs are unlike the more objective watchdog groups that ferret out inaccuracies no matter who commits them, such as FactCheck. org, Snopes, PolitiFact, and Fact Checker.

Fact-checkers and watchdog groups serve a valuable purpose in showing news consumers what statements are true, false, or skewed a certain way. Most people don't have enough time in their busy day to do extensive research as to what is true, so these fact-checking organizations do it for them. It's helpful to know if a politician is lying through his teeth during a debate, a campaign rally, or a television interview. It helps voters in assessing whether the candidate is genuine and trustworthy.

The more the public knows about how journalists verify and confirm information, the better we will be at determining the veracity and accuracy of the news we consume. Some institutions of higher learning, such as Columbia University and Toronto's Ryerson University, have begun teaching courses in verification strategies.[51] In light of reliance on user-generated content (such as *Wikipedia*), many media outlets have created policies regarding the process of verifying information. In some cases, the media outlets provide a disclaimer that the user-generated content cannot be verified as being authentic or accurate. This happens frequently in reports from war and disaster scenes in foreign countries. According to Craig Silverman of Poynter, it is difficult to explain how the verification system works because there has been little academic research on the topic. A Canadian study was one of the first on this topic and concluded that, while journalists value accuracy and verification, there is no one standard since "the methods for achieving accuracy vary from one journalist to the next. There is no single standard for verification, and not every fact is treated the same." Silverman argues that there needs to be better and clearer guidance and practices on verification for reporters.[52]

A subsequent study, published in *Journalism Practice* in 2015, cites several online verification tools, but notes that there are no common practices: "At present, there are multiple online tools, such as SocialMention, Storyful, PolitiFact, Fastfact, Topsy, Sulia, TinEye, FotoForensics, and Trackur, to name but a few that journalists may apply for social media research and verification. However, the extent to which journalists actually use such tools is unknown, and no commonly shared practices exist. At present, there is also no single tool to track and verify all social media sources, satisfying the totality of journalistic verification needs. The verification process in social media is arguably rather complex, due to large amounts of user generated content, real time information flow and various forms of sources and content modalities, such as video and images."[53]

Social Mention is a social media search and analysis program that monitors over one hundred social media outlets like Twitter, Facebook, and YouTube, and allows users to search any topic. Storyful is a website that verifies social media content and can help users identify the source, corroborate the location, and establish the date. According to Joseph Lichterman of the Nieman Journalism Lab, "Storyful, which was bought by News Corp in 2013, uses a mix of software and a team of journalists to find, verify, and license videos and other social media content. Though Storyful has recently expanded by working with brands and highlighting viral content, breaking news remains the core of its business."[54] It has also integrated with the messaging app Slack,[55] which gave Storyful users even more access to breaking news stories. Topsy had provided Twitter data, such as tweets, sharing of posts, hashtags, and demographics, but it was acquired by Apple and then shut down in 2015.[56] Sulia was a curation service that aggregated and organized online content by specialized topics, but it shut down in 2014.[57] Trackur is relied on by media outlets to get insight on social media and reputation management monitoring, as a journalist can track what is said about a keyword online and through social media.[58] TinEye is an image search and recognition company, which helps journalists verify user-generated content and adhere to copyright protocols.[59] FotoForensics is a photo analysis website that can detect fake or modified photos.[60] These social media tools help journalists find, monitor, filter, verify, curate, and source online content. They can also help them monitor and cover breaking news that is being reported through social media and citizen journalists, such as the Boston Marathon bombing, the Hudson River plane landing, or a school shooting or hostage crisis.

The American Press Institute in Arlington, Virginia, started a fact-checking program in 2014 that examines the quality of fact-checking in media organizations, studies best practices, provides training, evaluates fact-checking ratings, and gives updated news on fact-checking related to the 2016 election. The project is partially funded by the Democracy Fund, the Rita Allen Fund, and the William and Flora Hewlett Foundation.[61] The transparency in naming these foundations as funding sources adds to the fact-checking program's goal of being impartial and objective. Furthermore, the stated goals of these foundations include increasing political transparency and raising the level of civic literacy, according to the website *Inside Philanthropy*.[62] In the institute's press release announcing the program, Tom Glaisyer of the Democracy Fund said that fact-checking was a growing and essential practice in political reporting: "The American Press Institute will use its extensive networks within the news media, along with its credibility as a research group, to advance, refine, and defend this vital journalistic practice."[63]

Duke University, also, has created a Reporters Lab, which has a fact-checking website that provides news related to fact-checking and offers a database that lists fact-checking websites around the world.

Quality news reporting relies on access to sources. During recent wars, for example, this access has been limited in light of the requirement that reporters be embedded with troops, meaning that they are attached to a specific military unit and accompany them on their missions into combat zones. Embedded reporters can only go where the military lets them go. Part of the reason for this is the safety of the reporters. However, a consequence is that sometimes reporters might pull their punches and self-censor themselves, not wanting to alienate sources. They also are likely to bond with soldiers and feel as though they are part of the group and would not want to publish negative information about them. As Patrick Cockburn observed in the *Independent*, "Over-reliance on 'embedding' as the primary method of gathering information may have been inevitable, but it produces a skewed picture of events. Journalists cannot help reflecting to some degree the viewpoint of the soldiers they are accompanying. The very fact of being with an occupying army means that the journalist is confined to a small and atypical segment of the political-military battlefield." And Cockburn adds, "Perhaps the most damaging effect of 'embedding' is to soften the brutality of any military occupation and underplay hostile local response to it."[64]

Going back to ways people can use to judge the credibility of a news item, the publication or air date of a report is very important to note. Older articles and broadcasts on topics pertaining to medicine, law, psychology, technology, or political science may be out of date and therefore the facts may have changed. Consumers should be seeking the most timely information they can secure on topics that interest them, although information changes quickly when it comes to breaking news.

Another consideration for readers, listeners, and viewers is the commitment of a media outlet to spend the resources to hire quality reporters and travel to scenes to report on important stories. Many media outlets cannot afford to engage in detailed investigative reporting due to budgetary restrictions, which means that they often aren't delving deeply into important policy issues. This means that the public is often only getting sound bites and only a partial overview of important issues. As noted by Mary Walton in the *American Journalism Review* in September 2010, the fact that investigative reporters are a vanishing species means that there are fewer watchdogs of democracy. When Walton asked Tom Dubocq, a *Palm Beach Post* investigative reporter who took a buyout knowing that he would eventually get laid off due to budget constraints, what would happen when people like him vanished from American newsrooms, he replied, "The bad guys get away with stuff."[65]

Whether a story is published or aired by a traditional media source or one that engages in advocacy journalism, are the opinions or the reporting supported by facts, solid data, statistics, or specific examples? And if the support is definitely there, one has to ask how the statistics are presented. One of the ways to do this is to compare stories on the same issue with other media outlets to see if the facts and statistics are being reported consistently. Also, it helps to determine whether the source of the statistics is well respected or whether it is known for its bias.

Despite the criticisms made of traditional mainstream media, many people who are alerted to breaking news stories via social media will often turn to traditional media sources to confirm the information. Websites and bloggers themselves often rely on the mainstream media for information that they then comment on. This shows that, despite the ongoing criticisms of mainstream media bias, people will and should still turn to it to get important news and information. It's best to get the news and information from the more credible and objective mainstream media and then turn to the advocacy journalism outlets to get opinions and perspectives about that news.

Consumers need to be able to recognize the presence of a motive or an agenda that may skew the message being delivered by media sources. This can be tricky because, as we know, the bias may be quite subtle or even intentionally hidden. Tessa Jolls, president and CEO of the Center for Media Literacy, points out that "It is up to us as consumers to determine what bias is. We should try to determine what the possible motive might be of the producer of the information we are receiving. All media are geared toward gaining profit and/or power. We use the term 'power' broadly—in the sense of ideology or influence. People have to discern motive and purpose; they need to look at the text and context of the media message."[66] Are all of the relevant facts being provided? Is there context given? How do we recognize fact from fiction, from false or misleading information?

What are the signs of bias? Dean Howard Schneider of the State University of New York at Stony Brook offers this advice:

> First, there's a lot of confusion about bias. Lots of people confuse bias, for example, with opinion when it comes from a columnist or a commentator. That's not bias. Opinion journalists are supposed to have a point of view. As long as it is properly labeled, opinion journalism is fine. Other people confuse a legitimate journalistic error with bias or a "news media agenda." Reporters get things wrong all the time, but mostly because of time pressures, sloppiness, or because sources give them inaccurate or incomplete information. It's not excusable, but it's *not* bias. Nor is one example of unfairness, such as what appears to be a one-sided story, an automatic sign of bias. That can occur for lots of reasons, including bad editing and lazy reporting. In News Literacy, we define news media bias *as a pattern of unfairness.* Is there a pattern of stories that quote only one point of view? Is there a pattern of stereotypical language or the use of stereotypical images?[67]

Beware of conspiracy theories. Many people buy into these theories even though they seem obviously ridiculous to many. It's hard to figure out what pushes people to believe them, aside from partisanship and bias. Many conservative Republicans still believe that President Obama is a Muslim who was born in Kenya, for example.[68] There were also conspiracy theories regarding the government's and President Bush's involvement in the 9/11 attacks. Some people asserted that the Twin Towers and 7 World Trade Center were brought down by a controlled demolition, as opposed to the impact of the planes hitting the buildings and resulting explosions and fires. Others allege that the Pentagon was not hit by a plane, but was instead hit by a missile launched in the United States. Others claim that high-level government officials had advance knowledge of the specific pending attack but deliberately ignored the warnings. The 9/11 Commission debunked these conspiracies as being false.[69]

I've asked my students whether they've received any training or education in media literacy and the overwhelming general consensus is that they have not. Too often, students will cite obscure websites as sources instead of authoritative government documents or respected news sources. I also give current news events quizzes to some of my classes, and I am astonished at how disappointing the results are. Given this lack of understanding when it comes to media messaging, reliability, sorting information, and potential bias, many educators are making an effort to improve students' news and media literacy.

So what is media literacy? Tessa Jolls makes the point that "Media literacy is the ability to access, analyze, evaluate, and react to media in all of its forms. It explores the role of media in society. It is important in the work of journalists and citizens alike to understand that a free media contributes to democracy." She goes on to say, "All media have bias. Media literacy helps people recognize bias and helps people understand how global media works. People watch news on television, read it in newspapers, and see it on social media, and they accept it as gospel. The first step is to question that dangerous assumption. Readers have to dig and have the skills to be able to discern and recognize bias. It's easier to do that if you can compare more than one source."[70]

Michelle Ciulla Lipkin points out that we need to be more critically aware of the media we consume: "Media literacy is an expansion of the definition of traditional literacy from text to all media. It means your ability to access, analyze, construct, evaluate, and act using all forms of communication. If you asked twenty media literacy experts, they would tweak the definition a little bit. The purpose of media literacy education is to build critical thinking, effective communication, and active citizenship. Education can build these skills for people. It's not just thinking; action is part of it."[71]

Kathleen Tyner sees media-savvy and critically aware consumers as people for whom a wider array of possible ideas and social actions present themselves: "Media literacy involves print, oral, visual, and interactive modes of communication. Media literacy offers a broader pathway to 'read the world,' as [noted Brazilian educator] Paolo Freire would say. The more ways to do this, the better. How you read the world and the steps you take to interact with the world are shaped by society, but in the end, the uses of literacy are various and it's up to you. A wider range of literacy offers a wider range of choices."[72]

Dean Howard Schneider clarifies the difference between media literacy and news literacy as follows:

> As an academic discipline, Media Literacy is far broader than News Literacy. Media Literacy emphasizes a student's ability to analyze, evaluate, and create media, as a way of understanding how media works. In exploring the impact of media messages on society, Media Literacy can examine everything from gender bias in advertising to violence on television to media ownership and control. News Literacy is a very well-focused tributary of Media Literacy. We focus, like a laser beam, on news and how news consumers can discern what news is reliable and why. We focus on evaluating news because we believe news is the currency of citizenship. No democracy is really safe without an informed citizenry, and unfortunately it is harder and harder for that to happen today, in an environment that spawns a tsunami of information—and misinformation.[73]

NAMLE publishes the *Journal of Media Literacy Education*, with the goal of supporting the development of research, scholarship, and teaching media-literacy education. The journal is geared toward educators, scholars, and media professionals as part of an attempt to educate people to become critical thinkers and news consumers.[74]

Are we doing enough to teach media literacy in our K–12 classrooms and to adults? Michelle Ciulla Lipkin believes that we are trying but we haven't reached nearly enough people: "There is incredible media literacy being taught, but not enough. The challenge is to get districts, schools, and teachers passionate [about it]. There are minimum state standards and no national mandates. Common core generally mentions critical thinking and technical knowledge, but education laws and policies differ state by state, district by district, and school by school. It's very hard to infiltrate. It needs teachers and districts to recognize the importance of media literacy. It's not happening enough. Media Literacy Week [which takes place the first week of November] is helping to put a spotlight on the issue and that it should be taught. It's helped raise awareness. It's not just one class, it's a way to teach within a discipline."[75] And Tessa Jolls adds,

Media literacy is not being taught enough to schools and adults. The advertising industry spends billions for consumers. The school systems spend a lot of money, but not on media literacy. Media literacy is not being valued as it should be. There is a big disconnect. We learn everywhere, not just at temples of learning. We need a process to understand information and the media. The goal is not to bash the media or complain. The goal is to help people learn how the media works and what we can do about it. Media literacy addresses the new media world and how it affects attitudes and behaviors. We see media literacy as a holistic methodology. . . . Media literacy teaches an internal process of inquiry and teaches people how to be more discerning and responsible.[76]

Samuel Reed III, a Philadelphia educator who attended NAMLE's 2011 conference in his city, praised the turnout of over 350 worldwide educators, but lamented that few educators from Philadelphia and surrounding areas attended. He wrote in the *Philadelphia Public School Notebook*, "[Local committee chair Allison] Stuart reflected that NAMLE is fighting a perception that media literacy is reserved for the collegiate level. She questioned why so many of the attendees were college professors and research associates, and not elementary school teachers." Reed added, "With pressures from scripted curriculum and high stakes tests, I understand why some local administrators and district officials did not show up for a media literacy conference. But why so few?"[77]

Kathleen Tyner writes that the main problem of inadequate media-literacy education is the nature of public education, which emphasizes high-stakes testing, content delivery, debatable assumptions that education leads to workforce development in a changing and global labor market, industrial-era models of seasons, class times, disciplinary content, and traditional power relationships between learners and teachers: "In this context, educators introduce media literacy when they can, but it is idiosyncratic. Some teachers in elementary and secondary education incorporate media analysis into their lessons. And ed-tech programs offer support to learn about devices and software. But few teachers have the time or expertise to incorporate project-based work in creative media production." Tyner also laments the reduction in art and design classes and other opportunities for project-based work. These offer an alternative to the use of technology for "content delivery" by the teacher: "Without a bridge between critical analysis and production, it is difficult to teach media literacy. In higher education, courses can be found in education, communication and other humanities courses. . . . In particular, teacher education programs have a number of requirements that often do not provide much time or space for innovation and creative, project-based experiences."[78]

The critical awareness that media literacy can provide is vital to our social survival, for without it we will be doomed to be tossed and thrown about in a vast sea of competing ideas until we drown from sheer exhaustion. Michelle Ciulla Lipkin vividly captures this point:

People create and consume media 24/7. Media helps create and affect who we are and what we become. It has a huge influence on our thoughts and actions. We want to create educated citizens who make judgments and assessments from an educated place. This is especially the case in the saturated media environment and sheer volume of media messages. We want people to hone their skills to become educated citizens and think about what they consume and create in a smart way. It's important and it affects us as to issues like climate change, LGBT issues, gun control, sports, etc., things that matter to us. People need to do a better job of being critical thinkers. It's especially important during a presidential election where the information affects our votes and who leads us.[79]

Why is news literacy important? For Dean Howard Schneider,

It's more than important. We think News Literacy is a core competency of the Digital Age. How will we as a society make crucial, collective decisions and how will individuals make life choices? Will decisions be made on the basis of viral rumor, crowd-sourcing on social media, assertions masquerading as verifiable facts, propaganda, self-promotion, or advertising masquerading as independent journalism? (We have to go no further than the explosion in "native advertising.") I think this is a growing danger as lines blur and information hucksters get more and more sophisticated in peddling their deceptive wares, whether it be about presidential politics, climate change, the efficacy of medications, or in spreading toxic comments about our neighbors or fellow-citizens. I think the danger is exacerbated in an age when we are all more than just news consumers. Every time we send a text or e-mail, or post a video or a photograph, or share a story, we also act as news distributors and producers. And as innocent an act as that might seem, when executed by people who don't understand the principles of news literacy—who don't understand it is *their* responsibility to check the veracity of information before they share it—these simple acts can have disastrous consequences.[80]

Being able to navigate media effectively and assess its content and value for our own lives is critically important in today's fast-paced society. Internet librarian Dan Giancaterino offers this observation: "The media landscape has changed dramatically in the last ten years. Not too long ago you got your news from the Big Three TV networks or your local newspaper. The reporting didn't differ substantially from channel to channel or from paper to paper. Information homogeneity disappeared with the rise of social media. Now anybody can get news from anybody else. For example, more than 40 percent of the adult US population says it gets news from Facebook. Since that news is coming from people and organizations you've chosen to follow, you're probably going to experience a filter bubble. That's when the news you see only serves to reinforce the views and beliefs you already have."[81] And Tessa Jolls adds,

Media is an important part of everyone's life, with uses ranging from social media and new technology to traditional media such as radio and billboards. Media is global. We as consumers must understand how media operates as a system to help us navigate the media world and become active participants and informed citizens. Our society has traditionally viewed access to media content as being scarce. You needed to go to school, have a teacher, or have a printed text to access information. Now content is plentiful and can be accessed anywhere and anytime. Also, in the past, adult guidance in the form of teachers, parents, and librarians was plentiful and essential for young people to learn. Today, that guidance is scarce, as there is no one to look over kids' shoulders to help them navigate the online media. What was once scarce is now plentiful; what was plentiful is now scarce. Today's educational system uses the old model—the view that schools, adults, and "temples of learning" are essential to get information. That old model is changing, and "seat time" will no longer be the measure of whether learning is occurring or not. There needs to be a profound shift in how we teach and learn. The whole structure of the media industry is changing, and that is a big factor as to why media literacy is important. It's not just having access to social media and being able to reach millions of people. You need to understand how the system works. The perception is that the new media, such as Facebook, Twitter, and Instagram are free. They're not free. We pay for it through clicks and providing data. The business model has shifted. We are producers as well. We are the product. People don't understand their relationship with the media. We aren't able to actually make decisions on how to use media.[82]

It is important for K–12 students and college students to be educated about media and news literacy if we are to give them tools to evaluate the news and information that bombards them every hour of every day. Teachers need to be given extensive media literacy training so they can pass on that knowledge to their students. Kathleen Tyner suggests that "One promising trend can be seen in strategic partnerships between formal education teachers and practitioners and community-based organizations with youth media production experience. This can be seen mostly in after-school and summer programs. The partnerships provide cross-training for teachers and practitioners in critical analysis and creative production that bridges this gap between analysis and production and goes beyond the usual ed-tech programs taught in public schools. Production can be used to inform critical analysis of various media. Analysis can be used to inform critical production. These work together to support critical literacy, just as reading and writing worked together in the past."[83]

Katie Donnelly of *MediaShift*, which focuses on analyzing digital media, acknowledges that media-literacy programs are insufficient at this point but indicates that this is changing: "Strong, national support for digital and media literacy initiatives is currently lacking—both in the public broadcasting and educational sectors. However, innovative programs are popping up across the country, sometimes in unexpected locations."[84] Donnelly writes that initiatives are being produced from diverse sources, including public broadcasting stations, nonprofit organizations, museums, schools and federal agencies. Some examples that she cites are the United States Holocaust Museum, which established its *State of Deception: The Power of Nazi Propaganda* exhibit to teach digital and media-literacy skills, and the PBS NewsHour Reporting Labs, which pair high schools with media professionals and combine digital and media literacy, media production, and news, current events, and journalism education.[85]

According to NAMLE, in 2007 there were twenty-one universities that had media-literacy programs, and four with postgraduate degrees in the field, including Appalachian State, Webster University, and Southern Illinois University. American universities with undergraduate programs include MIT, the University of Texas, the University of California at Berkeley, the University of Pennsylvania, the University of Southern California, Rutgers University, Temple University, the University of Massachusetts, and New York University. NAMLE also cited major organizations, faith-based groups, providers of curriculum resources, and activism groups that focused on media literacy.[86]

In describing its Media Literacy Education Specialization Program, the University of Florida website states that students are rarely asked to question texts or think critically about media's role in American culture. It notes that a change is taking place, as all states now include media-literacy skills in curriculum standards: "The Media Literacy Education specialization provides an opportunity for graduate students to investigate the processes of using popular media culture and Internet texts to support literacy growth."[87]

Apart from offering degrees in media literacy, some high schools, universities, and nonprofit organizations are trying in other ways to help people sort out reliable news from unreliable information.

In 2006, the State University of New York at Stony Brook created the Center for News Literacy, which is the only center in the United States to teach undergraduate students how to use critical thinking skills to judge the reliability and credibility of news reports and news sources.[88] The center is also developing curricula for high schools and the public through the Digital Resource Center, funded by the Robert R. McCormick Foundation, whose

CEO, David D. Hiller, was described by *Inside Philanthropy* magazine as being a social liberal with a conservative view on economic issues. The Center for News Literacy has organized national conferences on news literacy and started a high school teacher training program in order to bring news literacy courses to classes across the nation.[89] Stony Brook's Dean Howard Schneider described to me the goal and success of the Center for News Literacy: "We created our News Literacy course to be relevant to *every* student on campus, not primarily to journalism students, although they are all required to take the course. Since the inception of the course in 2007, we have taught more than 10,000 students at Stony Brook, across all disciplines. One sign of our success is that the course has spread to several dozen other American campuses and now overseas. Currently, elements of the course are being taught in Russia, Poland, China, Vietnam, Australia, and Israel."[90]

Is news literacy being taught enough in schools and to adults? Schneider's answer is no: "But it's a relatively new discipline. I don't think, by the way, that the ideal way to teach news literacy is necessarily to introduce it to nineteen-year-old college students. Ideally, we should begin teaching News Literacy to middle school and high school students. And it's starting to happen. At IS 303 in Coney Island, Brooklyn, sixth through eighth graders are being taught a news literacy lesson each week for three years. The principal, Carmen Amador, has become an evangelist for teaching these skills to her students. I think IS 303 could be a model for New York City and the country."[91]

Amador told Rory O'Connor, director of the Digital Resource Center at Stony Brook's Center for News Literacy that "We're proving to a lot of middle schools that our students can delve into these articles, they can interpret, they can become meta-cognitive and understand what is going on. Before news literacy, they really couldn't tell you what was happening in their communities or the world at large. Now they're talking to you about the latest news reports, and why they believe or don't believe them."[92]

The Center for Media Literacy, headquartered in California, has spent over thirty years providing guidance and information about media literacy and methods of teaching it. The center has created a MediaLit Kit for teaching critical thinking about media, as well as fact sheets, media interviews, blogs, articles, and publications on the topic of media literacy.[93] In explaining CML's instructional approach, Tessa Jolls says, "I have problems with the concept of objectivity. All media represent a bias, a set of beliefs. You can try to have balance and present—or represent—other points of view, but it is impossible to represent all points of view. . . . We have a method for teaching media literacy that rests with the CML Five Core Concepts of media literacy, the most important of which is 'All media are constructed.' The other four concepts flow from that big idea of construction."[94]

The CML Five Core Concepts of Media Literacy (© 2002–2015 Center for Media Literacy) are:

1. All media are constructed.
2. Media messages are constructed using a creative language with its own rules.
3. Different people experience the same media messages differently.
4. Media have embedded values and points of view.
5. Most media messages are organized to gain profit and/or power.[95]

The CML Five Key Questions (© 2002–2015 Center for Media Literacy) in interpreting these five core concepts are:

1. Who created this message?
2. What creative techniques are used to attract my attention?
3. How might different people understand this message differently than me?
4. What lifestyles, values, and points of view are represented in, or omitted from, this message?
5. Why is this message being sent?[96]

Regarding the concept of media being constructed and the question of who created the message, CML's website states that media messages are written by people and images are captured and edited by a talented creative team that put them all together. As to creative language and techniques, CML says that this "examines how a message is constructed, the creative components that are used in putting it together—words, music, color, movement, camera angle and many more."[97] Regarding people understanding the same media messages differently, CML explains that "Each audience member brings to each media encounter a unique set of life experiences (age, gender, education, cultural upbringing, etc.) which, when applied to the text—or combined with the text—create unique interpretations. A World War II veteran, for example, brings a different set of experiences to a movie like *Saving Private Ryan* than a younger person—resulting in a different reaction to the film as well as, perhaps, greater insight."[98] As to lifestyles, values, and point of view represented in or omitted from messages, CML points out in its classroom guide that "Media messages are like onions. Whether words, pictures, audio, or all three together in a multimedia experience, each message consists of many layers of meaning made up of ideas, attitudes and opinions that can either be obvious or subtle. Key Question #4 helps to peel back the layers to reveal how the choices made in constructing a message inevitably communicate values, lifestyles and point of view."[99] As to media messages being sent to gain profit and/or power, CML gives several guiding questions, including "What's being sold in this message?" "Who profits from this message?" and "Who is served by or benefits from the message?"[100] These concepts and questions are all significant to the overall analysis and interpretation of advocacy journalism. Readers, listeners, and viewers can use and apply these concepts to help them analyze the viewpoint or bias of the publication that they're reading, the radio show they're listening to, or the television show they're watching.

According to Jolls, "We teach core concepts and key questions using a consistent process of inquiry. The CML Five Key Questions are only the beginning—we want to give a starting point to learn a process of inquiry, and then use it over and over, to apply the process to all media. Once people understand the inquiry process and acquire the ability to discern, they have a lifelong way of acquiring knowledge."[101] She adds that "It is up to us as consumers to determine what bias is. We should try to determine what the possible motive might be of the producer of the information we are receiving. All media are geared towards gaining profit and/or power. We use the term 'power' broadly, in the sense of ideology or influence. People have to discern motive and purpose; they need to look at the text and context of the media message."[102]

Jolls talks about how there are signs of bias in all kinds of media, even in what would appear to be balanced programs: "There is bias in all media. One of the CML Five Core Concepts of media literacy is that 'Media have embedded values and points of view.' All reporters have values and points of view."[103] But can't some step outside their personal values to report in a nonpartisan way? Is this really an impossibility? Jolls says, "Someone must make the media product, and they will bring their embedded values to the content they create. It is important for people to turn to different channels and see how they portray the news differently, to compare how websites or newspapers frame the same events or the same subjects differently. Each reporter brings different interpretations to reporting."[104]

Starting in November 2015, NAMLE, headquartered in New Jersey, spearheaded the effort to establish Media Literacy Week in the United States. The effort was inspired by Canada's Media Literacy Week, which has taken place annually in the first week of November for the past ten years.[105] Michelle Ciulla Lipkin, director of NAMLE, offers a brief mission statement:

> Our mission is broad. We want to expand and enhance media literacy in the United States. We're an umbrella organization for media literacy. We are a membership of organizations, with members including K-12 teachers, librarians, higher education professors, and students, and organizations engaged in media practice. We're an eclectic group. Our goal is to connect people and to share resources and best practices. We connect media literacy organizations in different states. We have an academic conference every two years and produce a media literacy education journal three times a year on a rolling basis. Our website shares six core principles and beliefs. This year, we launched Media Literacy Week in the United States, which was inspired by the Canadian version. It was a great success and we plan to continue it annually.[106]

According to the Canadian Media Literacy Week website, "Media Literacy Week highlights the importance of teaching children and teens digital and media literacy skills to ensure their interactions with media are positive."[107] Among the questions that they suggest in analyzing information are: "Who is the audience of a media production and why? From whose perspective is a story being told? How do the unique elements and codes of a specific genre affect what we see, hear or read? How might different audiences interpret the same media production?"[108] NAMLE's Media Literacy Week website gives the following ideas to encourage involvement:

- Gather teachers for a professional development workshop.
- Organize a screening and panel discussion at your school or in your community.
- Create a film festival of youth media projects developed in your classroom.
- Take your students on a tour of a local television station.
- Host a webinar about news literacy.
- Explore a community issue and have children come up with civically minded creative solutions.
- Debate the ethical opportunities and challenges of what "free" or "private" means online.[109]

Educational approaches and actions like this that can help to create critical thinkers of media.

How can news consumers appreciate objectivity over ideology? How can they recognize the characteristics and qualities of objective, even-handed reporting amid the media landscape of opinion, agenda furthering, advocacy, and mudslinging? Eugene Kiely of FactCheck.org offers this answer: "For the most part, ideologues have trouble appreciating objectivity—and that's too bad. I believe that others can learn to appreciate objectivity by keeping an open mind. By that I mean, don't automatically assume that a candidate or party that is aligned with your beliefs is always right and the other party is always wrong. There are good ideas and good people in both major parties."[110] He continues, "Look at the body of work. Does the reporter or organization apply the same standards to both sides? Look for sources. What sources are they using? Are they credible sources? Does the publication provide links so I can check the source of information? Look at funding. Where does this group get its funding and do the funders have any influence over the editorial content?"[111]

Due to the 24/7 nature of reporting news and the need to break stories quickly, all of us should be aware of the potential for the media to make mistakes in their initial reporting, and so we should avoid instantaneous reactions and conclusions to breaking news that has been reported. We should always follow up on the story to see if the initial reporting was accurate. "How to know if information is credible is harder to answer," Ciulla Lipkin observes. "People need to develop skills to try to figure it out. They should avoid knee-jerk reactions to hearing initial news reports. Until you read three legitimate news sources, you shouldn't believe the information is true. Find the information in more than one place. See how the issue develops. Often, news outlets start with the wrong information. People often don't follow up on the story and just remember the initial news report even if the facts change. You should constantly question and be in the habit of inquiry. Beware when you share information and when information is shared with you."[112]

Kathleen Tyner, associate professor in the Department of Radio-Television-Film at the University of Texas at Austin, teaches and writes extensively on the topic of media literacy. When I contacted her by e-mail, she offered this insight:

Objectivity is in the eyes of the beholder, but beyond that, people will do what is in their own best interest and this is often directed by their communities in a kind of cascade effect of information flow. Even if the information is based on bad evidence, it is difficult to reverse the flow. Presenting a simple dichotomy of arguments for social and political topics cannot override the social pressures of self-interest and "community think." Nuanced arguments are even more difficult and take more time to evolve in an era when people have little time for relaxed dialogue.

Ideology begins at the local level and so when people have an opportunity to meet and dialogue with people "across the aisle," it opens up possibilities for innovation. . . .

Respectful dialogue, critique, argumentation, and listening skills should be established early. In education, one way to establish this is through traditional debate clubs, opportunities to participate in scenarios with game-based learning and more reinforcement of research methods and skills so that people can make sense of evidence-based decision-making by understanding the way that research works to support (or not) arguments. Teaching about research methods and analysis could start at a very early age and reinforces interdisciplinary learning goals like math, logic, communication, self-expression and even perhaps opportunities for creative work in big data and data visualization. I don't think it's idealistic to begin to introduce an understanding of research and the way it works for decision-making as early as elementary school.[113]

How can readers uncover hidden bias? Dan Giancaterino observes that "The *Washington Post* is owned by Amazon's CEO Jeff Bezos. Would you expect it to publish the same kind of investigative journalism on the workplace culture at Amazon.com that the *New York Times* recently did? Would you expect a balanced story on Net Neutrality from NBC, which is owned by Comcast? Readers have to ask themselves, 'Who has skin in this game?'"[114]

How can readers separate facts from opinion? Tessa Jolls insists that "Most people don't have that skill to separate facts from opinion. It's a sad fact that this skill is not well taught." She continues, "All media are biased. What is the bias? Are other points of view represented or omitted? That's part of the questioning process. Readers have to look at more than one source to verify information. It's part of the process of inquiry. We have different checklists on our website [medialit.org] to help readers discern between different content and websites and gives ways to help readers assess credibility. We have a checklist that is a tool to assess website quality and to give people guidelines."[115]

Regarding the need to evaluate accuracy in the age of advocacy journalism, Dean Howard Schneider thinks we should "Choose reliable news outlets. Get news from multiple sources. Pay close attention to how information is labeled. (Always read the 'about' section of a website.) Evaluate a source's self-interest or independence. Examine if other points of view are totally left out of a story. In summary, always ask three questions before reaching a conclusion: What do I *know*? *How* do I know it? What *don't I* know?" Schneider also adds, "I don't buy the impression that the media can't be objective, fair, and neutral."[116]

In its online introduction to one of its videos on media literacy, the Newseum Digital Classroom urges readers to dig deeper to assess bias and credibility. It notes that most media organizations try to be fair and accurate, but that presidential campaigns often lead to allegations of media bias and favoring one party or perspective. However, there are other types of bias, including "information bias," in that how a story is reported can color news content: "Journalists sometimes seek to personalize and dramatize stories to make them more compelling, but the results may jeopardize the ability of their readers or viewers to grasp the complete context in favor of a focus on a few people or ideas. Limited space and airtime also lead to the fragmentation of stories."[117]

Reporters are expected to verify information through multiple sources, and news consumers, including students, should do the same. According to Lynh Bui of the *Washington Post*, "With information so readily available via social media, the Internet, and traditional news sources, educators say news literacy—teaching students how to identify credible information and good journalism—is increasingly important."[118] Bui notes that news literacy programs are expanding nationwide, which require students to read and analyze more nonfiction texts. "Younger students might feel that all information is created equally," Alan C. Miller, president of the News Literacy Project and a Pulitzer Prize-winning journalist, told Bui. "If something is put on the Internet, they tend to believe it."[119]

According to technology journalist Larry Magid, young people need to be critical thinkers when assessing and producing media messages. In his CNET article honoring Walter Cronkite, who had died a few days prior in July of 2009, Magid noted that, unlike their parents, young people didn't have to worry about the information they were receiving being filtered by a small, elite group of journalists working for one of the three broadcast networks or one of the two local newspapers. Magid noted that producing and receiving information is now a two-way street, and that the diversified media landscape brought new challenges to news consumers and producers: "Today's news consumers can also be producers thanks to blogs, social-networking sites, YouTube, podcasting, and microblogs like Twitter. . . . Not only must young people learn to 'consider the source' of what they take in but also think critically about what they post in a world where just about every young person is now potentially an author, photographer, and videographer."[120]

Dean Howard Schneider indicates that there are two crucial barriers to assessing objectivity: "Before consumers can appreciate 'objective' information—I would prefer to characterize it as information that is verified, independent, and accountable—they need to learn how to *find* reliable news amidst a flood of information that is self-interested, deceptive, or ideologically skewed. This is not always easy. Early in our [News Literacy] course, we introduce the concept of 'information neighborhoods.' We tell students they won't find what you refer to as 'objective' news unless they can find the three qualities I've mentioned above—VIA (is it verifiable, independent, and accountable?). If not, they are in the wrong information neighborhood."[121] Schneider says that the second barrier is even more of a challenge: "News consumers will never find 'objective' news if they don't *want* to find it. In other words, many readers are not open to information that challenges their own preconceived ideas. Audience bias can be as toxic, if not more so, than news media bias, and a greater challenge. In our course, we work hard to overcome this challenge, first by having students recognize their own biases and then by having them ask a series of hard questions when they find themselves reacting emotionally to what they read or watch."[122]

Schneider indicates that readers can separate facts from opinions "by paying close attention to the use of language and tone by those providing the news. Here are some red flags: The use of the word 'I.' The use of personal attacks. The presentation of 'facts' without any supporting evidence. Pay close attention to labeling so you know if you are in the 'opinion neighborhood' or the conventional news neighborhood. For instance, are stories labeled 'commentary' or 'opinion'?"[123]

It's important that people become aware of the concept of media literacy and demand that schools teach their children well on this topic. Michelle Ciulla Lipkin contends that the more media coverage that is given to media literacy and how to attain it the better: "Media literacy is an essential life skill in the twenty-first century. Schools need to work toward it. There need to be more conversations and books about it."[124] Schneider concludes, "In the end, students and adults must be trained on how to become their own editors. We're not born with those skills. They must be learned and applied. We can't slow down the news cycle. It will only get even faster, if that's possible. But we can slow down the way we *think* about the news."[125]

Conclusion

Although I realize that perfect objectivity in journalism is impossible due to reporters' biases, I still believe that news outlets can and should strive for that elusive standard of objectivity. I believe that most mainstream media outlets are trying to do this and most should and will continue to do so, whether their attempts use the words *impartiality, balance, fairness, straightforward, neutrality, transparency,* or *objectivity*. While there might be a slight liberal skew in reporting by the mainstream media, especially with respect to the selection of stories, it is my firm conviction that the conservative mantra of "the mainstream liberal media" is overblown to serve a political purpose.

Furthermore, the straightforward mainstream media outlets need to be the adults in the room. They need to be the places where people look to get accurate information. While the temptation is there for them to be more entertaining, outrageous, controversial, edgy, and opinionated, in order to get better ratings and higher circulation, they should leave that to those who practice advocacy journalism.

As for advocacy journalism, it has its pros and cons. While it is popular, entertaining, provocative, and serves to reinforce people's opinions, it is often less credible due to the bias and agenda-driven reporting. It has also been a major factor in creating the toxic politically polarized red state/blue state nation that America has become.

What are the issues of the future that could bring skewed media yet again to the forefront? What kind of a society will we risk facing if we are not educated to be critically aware of the media we watch, listen to, and read—and, for the journalists among us—create? On one hand, the explosion of media outlets and information providers is great for average people, in that news and information can be accessed almost anywhere and at any time, on a multitude of platforms. In theory, this should make us all well informed. However, that's not always the case since, as we have learned, much of this information flying at us is not provided in a balanced and objective manner. The recent emergence of media-literacy education will be essential in creating media-savvy consumers who will be able to sift through skewed and biased news presentations and make educated and reasoned evaluations about the accuracy of the information that fills their every waking hour. For all of us who must attempt to navigate the incessant waves of news and information that penetrate our awareness from all sides, it is vital that we remain alert, strive to be open-minded but stay aware of the sources of the information we are considering, expose ourselves to diverse points of view—especially those with which we may disagree, check facts (including ones we believe to be accurate), think through the arguments being offered, and reach our own independent conclusions, all while recognizing that new, more compelling facts and better-grounded arguments could find us altering our conclusions in the future. Being savvy and critical consumers of news and information won't guarantee that we have reached a correct conclusion, but it will help to ensure that we have done all we can to counter the effects of skewed and biased "news."

NOTES

INTRODUCTION

1. Brent Cunningham, "Re-Thinking Objectivity," *Columbia Journalism Review*, July/August 2003, http://www.cjr.org/feature/rethinking_objectivity.php (accessed July 24, 2014).

2. Margaret Sullivan, "When Reporters Get Personal," *New York Times*, January 5, 2013, http://www.nytimes.com/2013/01/06/public-editor/when-reporters-get-personal .html (accessed July 24, 2014).

CHAPTER 1: GOING INSIDE THE ECHO CHAMBER

1. A small percentage of this chapter consists of text from a 2014 *Huffington Post* op-ed that I wrote on this topic: Larry Atkins, "Advocacy Journalism Is Polarizing Our Country," *Huffington Post*, August 24, 2014, http://www.huffingtonpost.com/larry-atkins/ advocacy-journalism-is-po_b_5526745.html.

2. Eric Hananoki and Julie Millican, "2009: A Year of Fox News Political Activism," Media Matters for America, December 22, 2009, http://mediamatters.org/ research/2009/12/22/2009-a-year-of-fox-news-political-activism/158412 (accessed July 27, 2014).

3. Greg Pollowitz, "Ed Schultz and His Bogus Apology to Rick Perry," *National Review*, August 17, 2011, http://www.nationalreview.com/media-blog/274848/ed-schultz -and-his-bogus-apology-rick-perry-greg-pollowitz (accessed July 27, 2014).

4. Rebecca Riffkin, "Americans' Trust in Media Remains at Historical Low," Gallup, September 28, 2015, http://www.gallup.com/poll/185927/americans-trust-media -remains-historical-low.aspx (accessed December 12, 2015).

5. "Political Polarization in the American Public," Pew Research Center, June 12, 2014, http://www.people-press.org/2014/06/12/political-polarization-in-the-american -public/ (accessed July 27, 2014).

6. Andrew Beaujon, "Study Says Fox News May 'Harden Conservative Views' of Its Audience," Poynter, June 10, 2014, http://www.poynter.org/2014/study-says-fox-news -may-harden-conservative-views-of-its-audience/255114/ (accessed July 28, 2014).

7. Robert P. Jones, Daniel Cox, Juhem Navarro-Rivera, E.J. Dionne Jr., and William A. Galston, "What Americans Want from Immigration Reform in 2014," Brookings Institution, June 10, 2014, http://www.brookings.edu/research/

reports/2014/06/10-americans-immigration-reform-2014-survey-panel-call-back
(accessed July 28, 2014).

8. Tom Zeller, "Ideas & Trends; One State, Two State, Red State, Blue State," *New York Times*, February 8, 2004, http://www.nytimes.com/2004/02/08/weekinreview/ideas -trends-one-state-two-state-red-state-blue-state.html?_r=0. See also: "Origin of Red States, Blue States," Baruch College, 2008, http://www.baruch.cuny.edu/library/alumni/ online_exhibits/pres_election_08map/page2.htm (accessed January 14, 2016).

9. Howell Raines, "The Romenesko Empire," *Upstart Business Journal*, June 16, 2008, http://upstart.bizjournals.com/companies/media/2008/06/16/Jim-Romeneskos -Impact-on-Journalism.html?page=all (accessed July 28, 2014).

10. Richard W. Rahn, "The Sensational Giles and O'Keefe," *Washington Times*, September 16, 2009, http://www.washingtontimes.com/news/2009/sep/16/the-sensational -giles-and-okeefe/ (accessed July 28, 2014).

11. Chris Ariens, "O'Reilly: I Am Exhausted by These Ideologues Masquerading as TV Critics," *AdWeek*, September 28, 2009, http://www.adweek.com/tvnewser/oreilly-i -am-exhausted-by-these-ideologues-masquerading-as-tv-critics/28105 (accessed July 28, 2014).

12. Howard Kurtz, "How Al Sharpton Is Using Obama, Ferguson and MSNBC to Boost His Influence," Fox News, August 25, 2014, http://www.foxnews.com/ politics/2014/08/25/how-al-sharpton-is-using-obama-ferguson-and-msnbc-to-boost-his -influence.html (accessed September 2, 2014).

13. Malcolm Forbes, "Glenn Greenwald against the World," *Columbia Journalism Review*, July/August, 2014, http://www.cjr.org/critical_eye/glenn_greenwald_against _the_wo.php (accessed January 20, 2016).

14. Josh Gerstein, "Rogers: Greenwald Illegally Sold Docs," *Politico*, February 4, 2014, http://www.politico.com/story/2014/02/intelligence-chairman-argues-selling -snowden-docs-a-crime-103100 (accessed March 9, 2016).

15. Robert Scheer, "Edward Snowden Is Not a 'Traitor' and Glenn Greenwald Is Not an 'Accomplice,'" *The Nation*, February 18, 2014, http://www.thenation.com/article/ edward-snowden-not-traitor-and-glenn-greenwald-not-accomplice/ (accessed March 9, 2016).

16. T. Rees Shapiro, "Lawyers for U-Va. Dean: Jackie Lied to Rolling Stone, 'Invented' Story," *Washington Post*, January 8, 2016, https://www.washingtonpost.com/ news/grade-point/wp/2016/01/08/lawyers-for-u-va-dean-jackie-lied-to-rolling-stone -about-gang-rape-invented-story/ (accessed January 22, 2016).

17. T. Rees Shapiro, "U-Va. Dean Sues Rolling Stone for 'False' Portrayal in Retracted Rape Story," *Washington Post*, May 12, 2015, https://www.washingtonpost .com/local/education/u-va-dean-sues-rolling-stone-for-false-portrayal-in-retracted-rape -story/2015/05/12/2128a84a-f862-11e4-a13c-193b1241d51a_story.html (accessed January 22, 2016).

18. Paul Farhi, "On NSA Disclosures, Has Glenn Greenwald Become Something Other Than a Reporter?" *Washington Post*, June 23, 2013, https://www.washingtonpost .com/lifestyle/style/on-nsa-disclosures-has-glenn-greenwald-become-something-other

-than-a-reporter/2013/06/23/c6e65be4-dc47-11e2-9218-bc2ac7cd44e2_story.html (accessed January 22, 2016).

19. Jim Tankersley, "CNN Loves Donald Trump, Fox Loves Hillary Clinton, and It's All Less Strange Than It Sounds," *Washington Post*, December 30, 2015, https://www .washingtonpost.com/news/wonk/wp/2015/12/30/cnn-loves-donald-trump-fox-loves -hillary-clinton-and-its-all-less-strange-than-it-sounds/ (accessed January 24, 2016).

20. T. Becket Adams, "Did MSNBC's 'Bridgegate' Coverage Actually Bring Chris Christie Down?" *Washington Examiner*, March 17, 2015, http://www.washington examiner.com/did-msnbcs-bridgegate-coverage-actually-bring-chris-christie-down/ article/2561654 (accessed January 24, 2016).

21. Aaron Sharockman, "How MSNBC and Fox News Covered Chris Christie's 'Bridgegate,'" PolitiFact, January 14, 2014, http://www.politifact.com/punditfact/article/ 2014/jan/14/how-msnbc-and-fox-news-covered-chris-christie/ (accessed January 24, 2016).

22. James Fidlerten (Fidlerten), "MSNBC's Christie Bridgegate Wall-to-Wall Media Coverage Shows Obsession," *Daily Kos*, January 21, 2014, http://www.dailykos.com/ story/2014/1/21/1271365/-MSNBC-s-Christie-Bridgegate-Wall-to-Wall-Media-Coverage -Shows-Obsession (accessed January 25, 2016).

23. "Best of 2015," *Global Press Journal*, http://globalpressjournal.com/special -reports/best-of-2015/ (accessed January 25, 2016).

24. "'Hardball with Chris Matthews' for Thursday, May 15," transcript, *Hardball with Chris Matthews*, MSNBC, May 15, 2008, http://www.nbcnews.com/id/24664512/ns/ msnbc-hardball_with_chris_matthews/t/hardball-chris-matthews-thursday-may/ (accessed July 26, 2014).

25. "Exclusive: Hannity One-On-One with Imam Anjem Choudary on Rise of Radical Islam," *Hannity*, Fox News, August 27, 2014, http://www.foxnews.com/ transcript/2014/08/28/exclusive-hannity-one-one-imam-anjem-choudary-rise-radical -islam/ (accessed September 26, 2014).

26. Nora Daly, "Judy Woodruff to Aspiring Journalists: 'You Need to Care about the World around You,'" *PBS NewsHour*, PBS, January 29, 2015, http://www.pbs.org/ newshour/rundown/judy-woodruff-you-need-care-world-around-you/ (accessed January 25, 2016).

27. "Top 15 Most Popular Political Websites," eBizMBA, February 2016, http:// www.ebizmba.com/articles/political-websites (accessed March 2, 2016).

28. Hannah Karp, "Talk Radio's Advertising Problem," *Wall Street Journal*, February 3, 2015, http://www.wsj.com/articles/talk-radios-advertising-problem -1423011395 (accessed October 23, 2015).

CHAPTER 2: WHAT'S THE GOAL AND PURPOSE OF ADVOCACY JOURNALISM?

1. Comedy Central, "'The Daily Show with Jon Stewart' and 'The Colbert Report' Top the Competition During 1Q 2013 as the Most-Watched Late Night Talk Shows among Adults 18–49, Adults 18–34, Adults 18–24, Adults 25–34, Men 18–49, Men 18–34 and Men 18–24," press release, April 4, 2013, http://press.cc.com/press-release/2013/04/04/comedycentralrecords (accessed October 4, 2015).

2. Matthew H. Reavy, "Objectivity and Advocacy in Journalism," *Media Ethics* 25, no. 1 (Fall 2013), http://www.mediaethicsmagazine.com/index.php/browse-back-issues/179-fall-2013-vol-25-no-1/3999003-objectivity-and-advocacy-in-journalism (accessed October 4, 2015).

3. Robert Niles, "Why We Need Advocacy Journalism," *Online Journalism Review*, December 20, 2011, http://www.ojr.org/p2042/ (accessed October 4, 2015).

4. Bankole Thompson, "Advocacy Journalism Lacking in 2016 Campaign," *Detroit News*, September 10, 2015, http://www.detroitnews.com/story/news/politics/elections/2015/09/09/thompson-advocacy-journalism-lacking-campaign/71984330/ (accessed January 22, 2016).

5. Walter Cronkite, *A Reporter's Life* (New York: Alfred A. Knopf, 1996), p. 257.

6. Nikole Hannah-Jones, "A Prescription for More Black Doctors," *New York Times Magazine*, September 9, 2015, http://www.nytimes.com/2015/09/13/magazine/a-prescription-for-more-black-doctors.html (accessed October 23, 2015).

7. Mark Bowden, e-mail interview, November 15, 2015. Apart from *Black Hawk Down*, Mark Bowden's books include *The Best Game Ever*, *Bringing the Heat*, *Guests of the Ayatollah*, and *The Finish*. He has been a contributing editor for *Vanity Fair* and *The Atlantic* and has written for many other magazines, as well. He is currently the writer in residence at the University of Delaware.

8. Dan Gillmor, "In Praise of the Almost-Journalists," *Slate*, March 28, 2014, http://www.slate.com/articles/technology/future_tense/2014/03/human_rights_watch_and_other_advocacy_groups_doing_great_journalism.html (accessed October 25, 2015).

CHAPTER 3: THE EARLY HISTORY OF ADVOCACY JOURNALISM: THE LATE 1700s AND THE 1800s

1. "The Events Leading to Independence," *U.S. History: Pre-Columbian to the New Millennium*, chapter 9 (Philadelphia: Independence Hall Association, nd), http://www.ushistory.org/us/9.asp (accessed November 4, 2015). See also, Thomas Paine, *Common Sense*, http://www.ushistory.org/paine/commonsense/.

2. Thomas V. DiBacco, "Banned in Boston: America's First Newspaper," *Wall Street Journal*, September 24, 2015, http://www.wsj.com/articles/banned-in-boston-americas-first-newspaper-1443139281 (accessed November 4, 2015).

3. Allen Pusey, "August 4, 1735: John Peter Zenger Acquitted," *ABA Journal*, August 1, 2013, http://www.abajournal.com/magazine/article/august_4_1735_john_peter _zenger_acquitted/ (accessed November 4, 2015).

4. "About the Federalist Papers," Congress.gov, https://www.congress.gov/ resources/display/content/About+the+Federalist+Papers (accessed November 4, 2015).

5. Frank W. Scott, "Newspapers, 1775–1860: Partisan Bitterness; Administration Organs; *The Gazette of the United States*; *The National Gazette*," in *Early National Literature, Part II and Later National Literature, Part I* [American], vol. 16, *The Cambridge History of English and American Literature*, ed. A. W. Ward et al. (New York: G. P. Putnam's Sons, 1907–21; New York: Bartleby.com, 2000), http://www.bartleby .com/226/1206.html (accessed November 4, 2015).

6. Miller Center of Public Affairs, "Thomas Jefferson: Campaigns and Elections," University of Virginia, http://millercenter.org/president/biography/jefferson-campaigns -and-elections (accessed November 5, 2015).

7. Joanna Weiss, "Partisan Politics? Take a Look at the 19th Century," *Boston Globe*, October 9, 2012, https://www.bostonglobe.com/opinion/2012/10/08/partisan -politics-take-look-century/04FsP1WkuqPNEUioPSqpUP/story.html (accessed November 5, 2015).

8. Leonard Downie Jr., and Michael Schudson, "The Reconstruction of American Journalism," *Columbia Journalism Review*, November/December 2009, http://www.cjr .org/reconstruction/the_reconstruction_of_american.php (accessed November 5, 2015).

9. Paul Starr, "Governing in the Age of Fox News," *The Atlantic*, January/February 2010, http://www.theatlantic.com/magazine/archive/2010/01/governing-in-the-age-of-fox -news/307845/ (accessed November 5, 2015).

10. Dr. Carolyn Kitch, e-mail interview, December 16, 2015.

11. Ibid.

12. Jonathan Alter, "An Erosion of Trust," *Newsweek*, May 25, 2003, http://www .newsweek.com/erosion-trust-137509?rx=us (accessed November 5, 2015).

CHAPTER 4: THE RISE OF CORPORATE, OBJECTIVE JOURNALISM, AND THE INVERTED PYRAMID

1. Chip Scanlan, "Writing from the Top Down: Pros and Cons of the Inverted Pyramid," Poynter, June 20, 2003, http://www.poynter.org/2003/writing-from-the-top -down-pros-and-cons-of-the-inverted-pyramid/12754/ (accessed November 12, 2015).

2. Chip Scanlan "Birth of the Inverted Pyramid: A Child of Technology, Commerce, and History," Poynter, June 20, 2003, http://www.poynter.org/2003/birth-of -the-inverted-pyramid-a-child-of-technology-commerce-and-history/12755/. Excerpted from Christopher Scanlan, *Reporting and Writing: Basics for the 21st Century* (New York: Oxford University Press, 2000).

3. Jonathan Alter, "Just the Facts," *Washington Monthly* 31, no. 1 & 2 (January/February 1999), http://www.washingtonmonthly.com/features/1999/9901.symposium.alter.html (accessed November 12, 2015).

4. David T. Z. Mindich, *Just the Facts: How "Objectivity" Came to Define American Journalism* (New York: New York University Press, 2000); Alter, "Just the Facts."

5. Dr. Carolyn Kitch, e-mail interview, December 16, 2015.

6. Obituary, "Adolph S. Ochs Dead at 77; Publisher of Times Since 1996," *New York Times*, April 9, 1935, http://www.nytimes.com/learning/general/onthisday/bday/0312.html (accessed January 23, 2016).

7. Stephen A. Smith, "A Case against Boring," *Journalism Still Matters*, May 3, 2010, http://journalismstillmatters.blogspot.com/2010/05/case-against-boring.html (accessed January 23, 2016).

8. Neal Lulofs, "March 2014 U.S. Newspaper Data Now Available," Alliance for Audited Media, May 1, 2014, http://auditedmedia.com/news/blog/2014/april/march-2014-us-newspaper-data-now-available/ (accessed January 23, 2016).

9. Albert Oetgen, "Market-Driven Objectivity and the State of the Media," Poynter, January 12, 2005, http://www.poynter.org/2005/market-driven-objectivity-and-the-state-of-the-media/29737/ (accessed January 23, 2016).

10. John Timpane, e-mail interview, November 30, 2015.

11. Ibid.

CHAPTER 5: THE OP-ED PAGE, EDITORIAL PAGE, COLUMNISTS, EDITORIAL CARTOONS, YELLOW JOURNALISM, MUCKRAKING JOURNALISM, AND INVESTIGATIVE REPORTING

1. Kenneth Rystrom, *The Why, Who, and How of the Editorial Page* 4th ed. (State College, PA: Strata, 2003).

2. Sharon Shahid, "Editorials on the Front Page: New Spin on an Old Practice," Newseum, April 2, 2015, http://www.newseum.org/2015/04/02/editorials-on-the-front-page-new-spin-on-an-old-practice/ (accessed January 8, 2016).

3. Jack Shafer, "The Op-Ed Page's Back Pages," *Slate*, September 27, 2010, http://www.slate.com/articles/news_and_politics/press_box/2010/09/the_oped_pages_back_pages.html (accessed March 2, 2016); "End the Gun Epidemic in America," *New York Times*, December 4, 2015, http://www.nytimes.com/2015/12/05/opinion/end-the-gun-epidemic-in-america.html (accessed January 8, 2016); Ravi Somaiya, "Gun Debate Yields Page One Editorial," *New York Times*, December 4, 2015, http://www.nytimes.com/2015/12/05/us/gun-debate-yields-page-1-editorial.html (accessed January 8, 2016).

4. Jimmy Stamp, "Pioneering Social Reformer Jacob Riis Revealed 'How the

Other Half Lives' in America," *Smithsonian*, May 27, 2014, http://www.smithsonianmag.com/history/pioneering-social-reformer-jacob-riis-revealed-how-other-half-lives-america-180951546/?no-ist (accessed January 10, 2016).

5. James Smart, "Steffens Dumped on Philadelphia, but He Bad-Mouthed Other Cities," *Philadelphia Inquirer*, July 4, 1993, http://articles.philly.com/1993-07-04/news/25977056_1_corruption-lincoln-steffens-graft (accessed January 10, 2016).

6. Gilbert King, "The Woman Who Took on the Tycoon," *Smithsonian*, July 5, 2012, http://www.smithsonianmag.com/history/the-woman-who-took-on-the-tycoon-651396/ (accessed January 10, 2016).

7. Chris Bachelder, "The Jungle at 100," *Mother Jones*, January/February 2006, http://www.motherjones.com/media/2006/01/jungle-100 (accessed January 10, 2016).

8. "Ida B. Wells-Barnett," *Encyclopedia Brittanica*, http://www.brittanica.com/biography/Ida-B-Wells-Barnett.

9. Dr. Carolyn Kitch, e-mail interview, December 16, 2015.

10. Bill DeMain, "Ten Days in a Madhouse: The Woman Who Got Herself Committed," *Mental Floss*, May 2, 2011, http://mentalfloss.com/article/29734/ten-days-madhouse-woman-who-got-herself-committed (accessed January 8, 2016).

11. Amanda Foreman, "A Brief History of Media Muckraking," *Wall Street Journal*, July 25, 2014, http://www.wsj.com/articles/a-brief-history-of-media-muckraking-1406330669 (accessed January 8, 2016).

12. Office of the Historian, "U.S. Diplomacy and Yellow Journalism, 1895–1898," *A Short History of the Department of State*, United States Department of State, https://history.state.gov/milestones/1866-1898/yellow-journalism (accessed January 8, 2016).

13. Dr. Carolyn Kitch, e-mail interview, December 16, 2015.

14. Larry Atkins, "Newspaper Endorsements Should Stick to Local Races and Stop Endorsing Presidential Candidates," *Huffington Post*, November 3, 2012, http://www.huffingtonpost.com/larry-atkins/newspaper-endorsements-sh_b_1932030.html; Larry Atkins, "In the Era of Celebrity Politics, Newspaper Endorsements Are Irrelevant," *Philadelphia Magazine*, October 2, 2012, http://www.phillymag.com/news/2012/10/02/era-celebrity-politics-newspaper-endorsements-presidents/.

15. "Why We Endorse," *Chicago Tribune*, January 24, 2012, http://articles.chicagotribune.com/2012-01-24/opinion/ct-edit-endorse-20120124_1_tribune-endorsements-local-judicial-races-readers (accessed November 14, 2015).

16. "America's Choice, 2012: Election Center," CNN, http://www.cnn.com/interactive/2012/05/politics/celebrity.endorsements/; Lisa Mascaro, "Todd Akin Gains Support of Key Conservatives," *Los Angeles Times*, September 26, 2012, http://articles.latimes.com/2012/sep/26/nation/la-na-akin-support-20120927 (accessed November 14, 2015).

17. "The Oprah Factor and Campaign 2008," Pew Research Center, September 20, 2007, http://www.people-press.org/2007/09/20/the-oprah-factor-and-campaign-2008/ (accessed November 14, 2015).

18. Kathleen Hall Jamieson, *Everything You Think You Know About Politics . . . and Why You're Wrong* (New York: Basic Books, 2000).

19. Greg Mitchell, "EXCLUSIVE: Newspaper Endorsements for President since 1940 Show Wide GOP Edge," *Editor & Publisher*, October 23, 2008, http://www .editorandpublisher.com/news/exclusive-newspaper-endorsements-for-president-since -1940-show-wide-gop-edge/; "Inquirer Backs Obama; Not Unanimous," 6ABC, October 18, 2008, http://6abc.com/archive/6456797/ (accessed November 14, 2015).

20. Meteor Blades (Timothy Lange), "Here's Another Update of Newspaper Endorsements for President," *Daily Kos*, October 27, 2012, http://www.dailykos.com/ story/2012/10/27/1149243/-Here-s-another-update-of-newspaper-endorsements-for -president (accessed November 14, 2015).

21. Deirdre Edgar, "L.A. Times Endorses Obama—Does That Show a Bias?" *Los Angeles Times*, October 22, 2012, http://articles.latimes.com/2012/oct/22/local/la-me -rr-la-times-endorses-obama-does-that-show-a-bias-20121022 (accessed November 14, 2015).

22. John Timpane, e-mail interview, November 30, 2015.

23. David Francis Taylor, "Five Things We Learned from 'the Father of the Political Cartoon," CNN, June 1, 2015, http://www.cnn.com/2015/06/01/opinions/political -cartoon-james-gillray (accessed November 22, 2015); Dan Gilgoff, "Political Cartoonists Impact Presidential Races," *U.S. News & World Report*, February 28, 2008, http://www .usnews.com/news/articles/2008/02/28/political-cartoonists-impact-presidential-races; "Thomas Nast Biography," Billy Ireland Cartoon Library Museum, Ohio State University Libraries, http://cartoons.osu.edu/digital_albums/thomasnast/bio.htm (accessed November 22, 2015).

24. Sean Delonas, *New York Post*, February 18, 2009; Associated Press, "NY Post Cartoon Links Obama Stimulus Plan to Dead Chimp," 4NBC Washington, June 14, 2009, http://www.nbcwashington.com/news/archive/NYPost-Cartoon-Links-Obama-to-Dead -Chimp.html; Ashley Fantz, "Racism Row over Chimp Cartoon Sparks Debate," CNN, February 19, 2009, http://www.cnn.com/2009/US/02/19/chimp.cartoon.react/index .html?iref=24hours (accessed November 22, 2015).

25. Martin Asser, "What the Muhammad Cartoons Portray," BBC News, January 2, 2010, http://news.bbc.co.uk/2/hi/middle_east/4693292.stm; "Jyllands-Posten Won't Print Charlie Hebdo's Muhammad Cartoons," NBC News, January 9, 2015, http://www .nbcnews.com/storyline/paris-magazine-attack/jyllands-posten-wont-print-charlie-hebdos -muhammad-cartoons-n282801 (accessed November 22, 2015).

26. Larry Atkins, "Mainstream Media Outlets Showed Appropriate Restraint in Declining to reprint 'Charlie Hebdo' Cartoons," NewsWorks, WHYY, January 14, 2015, http://www.newsworks.org/index.php/local/essayworks/77295-mainstream-media-outlets -showed-appropriate-restraint-in-declining-to-reprint-charlie-hebdo-cartoons.

27. Rosie Gray and Ellie Hall, "Many Outlets Are Censoring Charlie Hebdo's Satirical Cartoons after Attacks," *BuzzFeed*, January 7, 2015, http://www.buzzfeed.com/ rosiegray/some-outlets-are-censoring-charlie-hebdos-satirical-cartoons#.era0RxmXe (accessed November 22, 2015).

28. Paul Farhi, "News Organizations Wrestle with Whether to Publish Charlie Hebdo Cartoons after Attack," *Washington Post*, January 7, 2015, https://www

.washingtonpost.com/lifestyle/style/news-organizations-wrestle-with-whether-to-publish
-charlie-hebdo-cartoons-after-attack/2015/01/07/841e9c8c-96bc-11e4-8005-1924ede
3e54a_story.html (accessed on November 22, 2015).

29. Judy Faber, "CBS Fires Don Imus over Racial Slur," CBS News, April 12, 2007,
http://www.cbsnews.com/news/cbs-fires-don-imus-over-racial-slur/ (accessed December
2, 2015).

30. Dean Schabner and Sheila Marikar, "Dr. Laura Says She's Quitting Radio after
N-Word Flap," ABC News, August 17, 2010, http://abcnews.go.com/Entertainment/
dr-laura-schlessinger-quits-radio-word-flap/story?id=11424039 (accessed December 2,
2015).

31. Irving DeJohn and Helen Kennedy, "Jeremy Lin Headline Slur Was 'Honest
Mistake,' Fired ESPN Editor Anthony Federico Claims," New York Daily News, February
20, 2012, http://www.nydailynews.com/entertainment/tv-movies/jeremy-lin-slur-honest
-mistake-fired-espn-editor-anthony-federico-claims-article-1.1025566 (accessed
December 2, 2015).

32. George Solomon, "'Jimmy the Greek' Fired by CBS for His Remarks,"
Washington Post, January 17, 1988, https://www.washingtonpost.com/archive/politics/
1988/01/17/jimmy-the-greek-fired-by-cbs-for-his-remarks/27536e46-3031-40c2-bb2b
-f912ec518f80/ (accessed December 2, 2015).

33. "Golfweek Fires Editor Responsible for 'Noose' Imagery," ESPN, January 20,
2008, http://espn.go.com/golf/news/story?id=3202573 (accessed December 2, 2015).

34. Tim Hume, "Outrage over Charlie Hebdo Cartoon of Dead Toddler Alan Kurdi
as Sex Attacker," CNN, January 14, 2016, http://www.cnn.com/2016/01/14/europe/
france-charlie-hebdo-aylan-kurdi/ (accessed February 3, 2016).

35. Bob Woodward and Carl Bernstein, "GOP Security Aide among Five Arrested in
Bugging Affair," Washington Post, June 19, 1972, https://www.washingtonpost.com/
politics/gop-security-aide-among-five-arrested-in-bugging-affair/2012/06/07/gJQAYT
dzKV_story.html (accessed February 3, 2016).

36. Donald L. Barlett and James B. Steele, "America: What Went Wrong?" Philadelphia Inquirer, http://www.philly.com/philly/opinion/inq_HT_WhatWentWrong
1991.html (accessed February 3, 2016).

Bartlett and Steele garnered two National Magazine Awards while writing for Time
magazine from 1997 to 2006. They subsequently were contributing editors at Vanity Fair.
Together, they have written eight books, including America, Who Stole the Dream? and
America, What Went Wrong?

37. James B. Steele, phone interview, December 13, 2015.

38. "About Us," ProPublica, https://www.propublica.org/about (accessed February
3, 2015).

39. Peter Osnos, "These Journalists Spent Two Years and $750,000 Covering One
Story," The Atlantic, October 2, 2013, http://www.theatlantic.com/national/archive/
2013/10/these-journalists-spent-two-years-and-750-000-covering-one-story/280151/
(accessed February 3, 2015).

CHAPTER 6: THE START OF THE BIG CHANGE:
THE RISE OF TALK RADIO IN THE LATE 1980S

1. Brian Rosenwald, "The Talk Radio Effect," *Politico*, June 17, 2014, http://www.politico.com/magazine/story/2014/06/the-talk-radio-effect-107942 (accessed November 14, 2015).

2. Michelle Malkin, "In Defense of Conservative Talk Radio," *National Review*, February 13, 2008, http://www.nationalreview.com/article/223655/defense-conservative-talk-radio-michelle-malkin (accessed November 14, 2015).

3. Jesse Singal, "Bill Clinton on the Connection between Rhetoric and Violence," *Boston Globe*, January 10, 2011, http://www.boston.com/bostonglobe/editorial_opinion/blogs/the_angle/2011/01/bill_clinton_on.html (accessed November 14, 2015).

4. Dan Shelley, "Secrets of Talk Radio," *Milwaukee Magazine*, August 24, 2009, http://www.milwaukeemag.com/2009/08/24/SecretsofTalkRadio/ (accessed November 14, 2015).

5. Simon Maloy, "Limbaugh's Unrivaled Influence on Republican Politics," Media Matters, March 13, 2012, http://mediamatters.org/blog/2012/03/13/limbaughs-unrivaled-influence-on-republican-pol/186630 (accessed November 14, 2015).

6. Ibid.

7. Alexa Keyes, "Rush Limbaugh Doubles Down on Sandra Fluke, Offering 'as Much Aspirin to Put between Her Knees as She Wants," ABC News, March 1, 2012, http://abcnews.go.com/blogs/politics/2012/03/rush-limbaugh-sandra-fluke-a-slut-and-prostitute/ (accessed November 15, 2015).

8. Lauren Moraski, "Bill Maher: Accept Rush Limbaugh's Apology," CBS News, March 7, 2012, http://www.cbsnews.com/news/bill-maher-accept-rush-limbaughs-apology/ (accessed November 15, 2015).

9. Al Franken, *Rush Limbaugh Is a Big Fat Idiot*, reprint ed. (New York: Dell, 1999).

10. "Limbaugh Resigns from NFL Show," ESPN, October 1, 2003, http://espn.go.com/gen/news/2003/1001/1628537.html (accessed November 15, 2015).

11. Kathleen McKinley, "Why Rush Limbaugh and Fox News Are so Popular," *Houston Chronicle*, October 20, 2009, http://blog.chron.com/texassparkle/2009/10/why-rush-limbaugh-and-fox-news-are-so-popular/ (accessed December 11, 2015).

12. Ryan Chiachiere, "Imus Called Women's Basketball Team 'Nappy-Headed-Hos,'" Media Matters, April 4, 2007, http://mediamatters.org/research/2007/04/04/imus-called-womens-basketball-team-nappy-headed/138497 (accessed December 11, 2015).

13. Paul Farhi, "Don Imus Is Fired by CBS Radio," *Washington Post*, April 13, 2007, http://www.washingtonpost.com/wp-dyn/content/article/2007/04/12/AR2007041201007.html (accessed December 11, 2015).

14. Dean Schabner and Sheila Marikar, "Dr. Laura Says She's Quitting Radio after N-Word Flap," ABC News, August 17, 2010, http://abcnews.go.com/Entertainment/dr-laura-schlessinger-quits-radio-word-flap/story?id=11424039 (accessed December 11, 2015).

15. Paul Farhi, "Talk Show Host Graham Fired by WMAL over Islam Remarks,"

Washington Post, August 23, 2005, http://www.washingtonpost.com/wp-dyn/content/article/2005/08/22/AR2005082201255.html (accessed December 11, 2015).

16. David Hinckley, "Bob Grant, Legendary Talk Radio Pioneer, Dead at 84," *New York Daily News*, January 2, 2014, http://www.nydailynews.com/entertainment/tv-movies/radio-icon-bob-grant-dead-84-article-1.1564561 (accessed December 11, 2015).

17. Caitlin Yilek, "Conservative Blogger Shoots Holes through *New York Times* Editorial," *The Hill*, December 5, 2015, http://thehill.com/blogs/blog-briefing-room/news/262223-erick-erickson-shows-bulletholes-nytimes (accessed January 25, 2016).

18. "Kathleen Hall Jamieson on Talk Radio's History and Impact," interview with William Brangham, *NOW on PBS*, February 13, 2004, http://www.pbs.org/now/politics/talkradiohistory.html (accessed December 11, 2015).

19. Larry Atkins, "Finally, Liberal Radio," *Philadelphia Inquirer*, October 3, 2003, http://articles.philly.com/2003-10-03/news/25465405_1_liberal-radio-anita-drobny -conservative-mantra.

20. Richard Corliss, "Why Air America Will Be Missed," *Time*, January 21, 2010, http://content.time.com/time/nation/article/0,8599,1955848,00.html (accessed December 20, 2015).

21. Mackenzie Weinger, "How to Rescue Liberal Talk Radio," *Politico*, November 28, 2013, http://www.politico.com/story/2013/11/liberal-talk-radio-rescue-100408 (accessed on December 20, 2015).

22. Ibid.

23. James B. Steele, phone interview, December 13, 2015.

24. The Fairness Doctrine was revoked in 1987 and then officially eliminated in 2011. See, Dylan Matthews, "Everything You Need to Know About the Fairness Doctrine in One Post," *Washington Post*, August 23, 2011, https://www.washingtonpost.com/blogs/ezra-klein/post/everything-you-need-to-know-about-the-fairness-doctrine-in-one -post/2011/08/23/gIQAN8CXZJ_blog.html.

25. Tamika Thompson, "Are We Better Off without the Fairness Doctrine," *Tavis Smiley*, PBS, August 23, 2011, http://www.pbs.org/wnet/tavissmiley/uncategorized/are -we-better-off-without-the-fairness-doctrine/ (accessed December 13, 2015).

CHAPTER 7: THE RISE OF FAKE ENTERTAINMENT NEWS AND CELEBRITY JOURNALISM

1. Mark Bowden, e-mail interview, November 15, 2015.

2. Journalism and Media Staff, "Journalism Satire or Just Laughs? 'The Daily Show with Jon Stewart,' Examined," Pew Research Center, May 8, 2008, http://www.journalism.org/2008/05/08/journalism-satire-or-just-laughs-the-daily-show-with-jon -stewart-examined/ (accessed December 10, 2015).

3. Kirsten Powers, "Powers: Ladies of 'The View' Should Think before Calling Carly Demented," *USA Today*, November 12, 2015, http://www.usatoday.com/story/

opinion/2015/11/10/hosts-view-carly-fiorina-joke-media-bias-column/75463660/ (accessed December 15, 2015).

4. Jesse Byrnes "Fiorina Spars with View Hosts over Her Looks," *The Hill*, November 6, 2015, http://www.msn.com/en-us/news/politics/fiorina-spars-with-view-hosts-over-her-looks/ar-CC2nx3 (accessed December 15, 2015).

5. Brian Steinberg, "Bill Maher Courts Danger by Working Live on HBO," *Variety*, April 13, 2015, http://variety.com/2015/tv/news/bill-maher-danger-live-real-time-hbo-1201471473/ (accessed December 15, 2015).

6. Thomas Kent, "Jon Stewart Was Important, but Balanced Journalism Is Valuable, Too," *New York Times*, August 6, 2015, http://www.nytimes.com/roomfor debate/2015/08/06/did-jon-stewart-have-a-serious-lesson-for-journalists/jon-stewart-was-important-but-balanced-journalism-is-valuable-too (accessed November 4, 2015).

7. Mark Silva, "THE NATION: Hannity Says Sorry for Using Wrong Rally Video," *Los Angeles Times*, November 13, 2009, http://articles.latimes.com/2009/nov/13/nation/na-hannity-crowd13 (accessed November 4, 2015).

8. Amber Phillips, "Many Millennials Are About to Lose Their Most-Trusted News Source: Jon Stewart," *Washington Post*, July 30, 2015, https://www.washingtonpost.com/news/the-fix/wp/2015/07/30/jon-stewart-will-leave-plenty-of-millennials-in-search-of-a-new-way-to-get-their-news/ (accessed November 4, 2015).

9. Stephen Collinson, "How Jon Stewart Changed Politics," CNN Politics, February 11, 2015, http://www.cnn.com/2015/02/10/politics/how-jon-stewart-changed-politics/ (accessed November 4, 2015).

10. Ibid.

11. Lisa Lambert, "Poll: Americans Favor Jon Stewart, Stephen Colbert over Conservatives for Punditry," Reuters, May 8, 2015, http://www.reuters.com/article/us-usa-politics-pundits-idUSKBN0NT0C620150508 (accessed November 4, 2015).

12. Howard Kurtz, "Fake News Rules: The Real Impact of Jon Stewart," Fox News, February 13, 2015, http://www.foxnews.com/politics/2015/02/13/fake-news-rules-real-impact-jon-stewart.html (accessed November 4, 2015).

13. Howard Homonoff, "Brian Williams, Jon Stewart, and News/Entertainment's 'Shocking' Blend," *Forbes*, February 11, 2015, http://www.forbes.com/sites/howard homonoff/2015/02/11/brian-williams-jon-stewart-and-newsentertainment-conflation/ #dc1499b70ee3 (accessed November 4, 2015).

14. Caitlin Dewey, "The 15 Worst Internet Hoaxes of 2014—and Where the Pranksters Are Now," *Washington Post*, December 18, 2014, https://www.washingtonpost.com/news/the-intersect/wp/2014/12/18/the-15-worst-internet-hoaxes-of-2014-and-where-the-pranksters-are-now/ (accessed October 20, 2015).

15. Kevin Fallon, "Fooled by 'The Onion': 9 Most Embarrassing Fails," *Daily Beast*, November 27, 2012, http://www.thedailybeast.com/articles/2012/09/29/fooled-by-the-onion-8-most-embarrassing-fails.html (accessed October 20, 2015).

16. Tim Hume, "Indicted Ex-FIFA Official Jack Warner Cites 'Onion' Article to Defend Himself," CNN, June 1, 2015, http://edition.cnn.com/2015/06/01/football/fifa-corruption-warner-onion/ (accessed October 20, 2015).

17. Alexander Marquardt, "Iranian News Agency Rips Off Satirical Onion Report," ABC News, September 28, 2012, http://abcnews.go.com/blogs/headlines/2012/09/iranian -news-agency-rips-off-satirical-onion-report/ (accessed October 20, 2015).

18. Tap Vann, "Five Classic Weekly World News Covers," *Weekly World News*, October 2, 2008, http://weeklyworldnews.com/headlines/3075/five-classic-weekly-world -news-covers/ (accessed October 20, 2015); Stephanie Clifford, "New Adventures for Bat Boy, and His Tabloid Creator," *New York Times*, October 21, 2008, http://www.nytimes .com/2008/10/22/business/media/22adcol.html (accessed October 20, 2015).

19. Stephenson Billings, "12 Reasons to Boycott 'Game of Thrones' in 2012," *Christwire*, January 3, 2012, http://christwire.org/2012/01/12-reasons-to-boycott-game -of-thrones-in-2012-2/ (accessed March 20, 2015) [site discontinued].

Mark Oppenheimer, "A Niche of the Unreal in a World of Credulity," *New York Times*, September 3, 2010, http://www.nytimes.com/2010/09/04/us/04beliefs.html? _r=0; Adam Pasick, "The Guys behind Christwire, Creating Parody from 'Glenn Beck on Steroids,'" *New York Magazine*, September 3, 2010, http://nymag.com/daily/ intelligencer/2010/09/christwire.html.

20. Jim Geraghty, "Liberals Can't Tell the Difference between 'Satire' and News, and GOP Presidential Campaigns Are Paying the Price," *National Review*, June 3, 2015, http://www.nationalreview.com/article/419224/real-problem-fake-news (accessed October 20, 2015).

21. Keely Herring, "'Teabagger' Group Makes Splash with Fake-Quote Memes," PolitiFact, May 28, 2015, http://www.politifact.com/truth-o-meter/article/2015/may/28/ teabagger-group-makes-splash-fake-quote-memes/ (accessed October 20, 2015).

22. Neal Lulofs, "Top 25 U.S. Consumer Magazines for June 2014," Alliance for Audited Media, August 7, 2014, http://auditedmedia.com/news/blog/2014/august/top-25 -us-consumer-magazines-for-june-2014.aspx (accessed October 31, 2015).

23. Darcie Lunsford, "Taming the Tabloids," *American Journalism Review*, September 2000, http://ajrarchive.org/Article.asp?id=269 (accessed October 31, 2015).

24. Ashley Lutz, "11 Crazy National Enquirer Stories that Turned Out to Be True," *Business Insider*, February 6, 2013, http://www.businessinsider.com/national-enquirer -stories-that-were-true-2013-2?op=1 (accessed October 31, 2015).

25. Michael H. Randall, "Tabloids," *Serials Review* 11, no. 2 (Summer 1985): 31–35.

26. "Media Credibility Declines," Pew Research Center, Washington, DC, June 8, 2004, http://www.people-press.org/2004/06/08/v-media-credibility-declines/ (accessed October 31, 2015).

27. Kate Knibbs, "Watch MSNBC Interrupt a Congresswoman to Break News about Justin Bieber's Arrest," *Time*, January 24, 2014, http://newsfeed.time.com/2014/01/24/ watch-msnbc-interrupt-a-congresswoman-to-break-news-about-justin-biebers-arrest/ (accessed October 31, 2015); Dorsey Shaw, "Bieber Coverage Proves that MSNBC Is Back in the Breaking News Business," *BuzzFeed*, January 24, 2014, http://www.buzzfeed .com/dorsey/bieber-coverage-proves-that-msnbc-is-back-in-the-breaking-ne#.iv1AyMVde (accessed October 31, 2015).

28. Larry Atkins, "Why the Media Will Always Cover Celebrities," *Huffington Post*, July 28, 2010, http://www.huffingtonpost.com/larry-atkins/why-the-media-will -always_b_662457.html.

29. Ariana Eunjung Cha, "Print Media's Hot New Star: Celebrity Mags," *Washington Post*, September 22, 2005, http://www.washingtonpost.com/wp-dyn/content/article/ 2005/09/22/AR2005092202156.html.

30. Nancy Leung, "After Media Frenzy, Lindsay Lohan Begins Life in Jail," CNN, July 22, 2010, http://insession.blogs.cnn.com/2010/07/22/after-media-frenzy-lindsay -lohan-begins-life-in-jail/ (accessed July 25, 2014) [link no longer active]. See also: "Welcome to the 'Lindsay Lohan Goes to Jail' Live-Blog," CNN Entertainment, July 20, 2010, http://marquee.blogs.cnn.com/2010/07/20/welcome-to-the-lindsay-lohan-goes-to -jail-live-blog/ (accessed July 25, 2014); Richard Winton, Sam Allen, and Abby Sewell, "Lindsay Lohan Is Booked into Jail," *Los Angeles Times*, July 21, 2010, http://articles .latimes.com/2010/jul/21/local/la-me-lindsay-lohan-20100721 (accessed July 25, 2014).

31. Andrew Grice, "Freeing Megrahi 'Wrong', Cameron Will Tell Obama," *Independent*, July 18, 2010, http://www.independent.co.uk/news/world/americas/freeing -megrahi-wrong-cameron-will-tell-obama-2029751.html (accessed July 25, 2010).

32. Kim Ghattas, "Clinton Defends US Strategy in Afghanistan," BBC News, July 20, 2010, http://www.bbc.com/news/world-south-asia-10692971 (accessed July 25, 2010).

33. Tami Luhby, "Senate Votes to Extend Jobless Lifeline," CNN, July 21, 2010, http://money.cnn.com/2010/07/21/news/economy/unemployment_benefits/.

34. Kyle Trygstad, "WV: Capito Out, Raese Expected In Today," RealClearPolitics, July 22, 2010, http://www.realclearpolitics.com/politics_nation/ (accessed July 25, 2010).

35. Carole Rich, *Writing and Reporting News: A Coaching Method*, 7th edition (Belmont, CA: Wadsworth Publishing, 2012).

36. Neal Lulofs, "Top 25 U.S. Consumer Magazines for December 2013," Alliance for Audited Media, February 6, 2014, http://auditedmedia.com/news/blog/2014/february/ us-snapshot.aspx.

37. Victor Merina, "Celebrities in Journalism: The Ethics of News Coverage," Poynter, January 20, 2004, http://www.poynter.org/2004/celebrities-in-journalism-the -ethics-of-news-coverage/20426/ (accessed October 31, 2015).

CHAPTER 8: THE RISE OF SPONSORED CONTENT

1. Matthew Flamm, "Readers Say They Distrust Ads that Look Like Real News," *Advertising Age*, July 10, 2014, http://adage.com/article/media/readers-distrust-ads-news -survey-finds/294075/ (accessed November 6, 2015); William Launder, "When Ads Look like Content," *Wall Street Journal*, December 1, 2013, http://www.wsj.com/articles/SB1 0001424052702303332904579228060901902566 (accessed November 6, 2015); Maria Shinkevich, "'South Park' Lampoon of Native Advertising Highlights Important Issues," *Advertising Age*, February 24, 2016, http://adage.com/article/digitalnext/south-park -lampoon-native-advertising-highlights-issues/302756/ (accessed February 27, 2016).

2. Anders Vinderslev, "The Top 10 Examples of BuzzFeed Doing Native Advertising," Native Advertising Institute, September 30, 2015, http://native advertisinginstitute.com/blog/the-top-10-examples-of-buzzfeed-doing-native-advertising/ (accessed November 6, 2015).

3. Michael Sebastian, "Media Brands Shy Away from the A-Word, When It Comes to Labeling Native Ads," *Advertising Age*, June 11, 2015, http://adage.com/article/media/media-companies-label-native-ads/298944/ (accessed November 6, 2015).

4. Jeff Weisberger, "5 Publishers Who Created the Best Sponsored Content in 2014," *New York Times*, http://blog.newscred.com/5-publishers-who-created-the-best-sponsored-content-in-2014/ (accessed November 6, 2015).

5. Benjamin Mullin, "The Boston Globe Begins Running Sponsored Content," Poynter, November 4, 2015, http://www.poynter.org/2015/the-boston-globe-begins-running-sponsored-content/382994/ (accessed December 5, 2015).

6. *Super Lawyers Magazine*, http://www.superlawyers.com/about/digital_magazine.html.

7. Sebastian, "Media Brands Shy Away From the A-Word."

8. Erin Griffith, "Sponsored Content Is the Holy Grail of Digital Publishing. But Does It Work?" *Fortune Magazine*, July 9, 2014, http://fortune.com/2014/07/09/readers-dislike-sponsored-content-native-ads/ (accessed December 5, 2015).

9. David Weinberger, "The Ethics of Using Paid Content in Journalism," *Harvard Business Review*, July 22, 2013, https://hbr.org/2013/07/the-ethics-of-using-paid-content-in-journalism (accessed December 5, 2015).

10. Edward Wyatt, "As Online Ads Look More like News Articles, F.T.C. Warns against Deception," *New York Times*, December 4, 2013, http://www.nytimes.com/2013/12/05/business/ftc-says-sponsored-online-ads-can-be-misleading.html?_r=0 (accessed January 8, 2016).

11. Sarah Shearman, "Edelman Outlines Sponsored Content Guidelines," *PR Week*, July 16, 2013, http://www.prweek.com/article/1275201/edelman-outlines-sponsored-content-guidelines (accessed January 8, 2016).

12. Sydney Ember, "F.T.C. Guidelines on Native Ads Aim to Prevent Deception," *New York Times*, December 22, 2015, http://www.nytimes.com/2015/12/23/business/media/ftc-issues-guidelines-for-native-ads.html (accessed January 8, 2016).

13. "Native Advertising: A Guide for Businesses," Federal Trade Commission, December 2015, https://www.ftc.gov/tips-advice/business-center/guidance/native-advertising-guide-businesses (accessed January 8, 2016).

14. Jeremy Barr, "The IAB Is 'Concerned' about the FTC's New Native Advertising Rules, but Publishers Play it Cool," *Advertising Age*, December 29, 2015, http://adage.com/article/media/iab-concerned-ftc-s-native-advertising-rules/301948/ (accessed January 8, 2016). See also, "IAB Concerned about FTC Guidance on Native Advertising," December 24, 2015, http://www.iab.com/news/iab-concerned-about-ftc-guidance-on-native-advertising/ (accessed January 8, 2016).

CHAPTER 9: THE RISE OF FOX NEWS

1. Frazier Moore, "Fox News Channel Chief Roger Ailes Looks Back on 15 Years," *Dallas Morning News*, November 6, 2011, http://www.dallasnews.com/entertainment/television/headlines/20111006-fox-news-channel-chief-roger-ailes-looks-back-on-15-years.ece (accessed September 23, 2015).

2. Kevin Coy, "Fox Business Network Fastest Growing Cable Channel of 2015," *News on News*, December 31, 2015, http://newsonnews.com/story/311215-1888 (accessed January 8, 2016).

3. Deborah Potter, "The Secrets of Fox's Success," *American Journalism Review* 82 (December 2006/January 2007), http://ajrarchive.org/Article.asp?id=4236 (accessed September 23, 2015).

4. Chris Mooney, "How the Iraq War Launched the Modern Era of Political BS," *Mother Jones*, June 25, 2014, http://www.motherjones.com/politics/2014/06/iraq-war -wmds-saddam-political-unreason (accessed September 23, 2015).

5. Bruce Bartlett, "How Fox News Changed American Media and Political Dynamics," Social Science Research Network, May 11, 2015, http://papers.ssrn.com/sol3/papers.cfm?abstract_id=2604679 (accessed September 23, 2015).

6. Ibid.

7. Ben Adler, "The Real Problem with Fox News," *Columbia Journalism Review*, March 25, 2011, http://www.cjr.org/campaign_desk/the_real_problem_with_fox_news .php (accessed September 25, 2015).

8. Greg Gutfeld, "Brian Williams and Advocacy Journalism," Fox News, February 9, 2015, http://www.foxnews.com/on-air/the-five/article/2015/02/09/gutfeld-brian -williams-and-advocacy-journalism (accessed on September 25, 2015).

9. Donna Freydkin, "Megyn Kelly Fired Up for First GOP Debate," *USA Today*, August 3, 2015, http://www.usatoday.com/story/life/people/2015/08/03/megyn-kelly -fired-up-first-gop-debate/30930439/ (accessed September 25, 2015).

10. Paul Bedard, "15 Years On, the Secret of Fox News's Success," *U.S. News & World Report*, October 7, 2011, http://www.usnews.com/news/blogs/washington -whispers/2011/10/07/15-years-on-the-secret-of-fox-newss-success (accessed September 25, 2015).

11. Justin Peters, "Rupert and Roger," *Slate*, June 12, 2015, http://www.slate.com/articles/business/culturebox/2015/06/rupert_murdoch_is_stepping_back_from_his _empire_why_that_won_t_mean_a_change.html (accessed September 25, 2015).

12. Erik Wemple, "Fox News All Day: Hard, and Conservative," *Washington Post*, March 27, 2013, https://www.washingtonpost.com/blogs/erik-wemple/wp/2013/03/27/fox-news-all-day-hard-and-conservative/ (accessed September 25, 2015).

13. Bernard Goldberg, "Conservatives Who Never Really Wanted Fair and Balanced," BernardGoldberg.com, August 10, 2015, http://bernardgoldberg.com/conservatives-who-never-really-wanted-fair-and-balanced/ (accessed September 25, 2015).

CHAPTER 10: THE RESPONSE OF MSNBC

1. David Akadjian, "15 Things Everyone Would Know If There Were a Liberal Media," *Daily Kos*, August 7, 2013, http://www.dailykos.com/story/2013/8/7/1229087/ -15-things-everyone-would-know-if-there-were-a-liberal-media (accessed September 7, 2015); "Bottom Line Pressures Now Hurting Coverage Say Journalists," Pew Research Center, May 23, 2004, http://www.people-press.org/2004/05/23/bottom-line-pressures -now-hurting-coverage-say-journalists/ (accessed September 7, 2015).

2. Eric Bohlert, "Katrina Jolts the Press," *Salon*, September 7, 2005, http://www .salon.com/2005/09/07/press_katrina/ (accessed November 20, 2015).

3. Emanuella Grinberg and the CNN Wire Staff, "Keith Olbermann Signs Off from MSNBC," CNN, January 25, 2011, http://www.cnn.com/2011/US/01/22/olbermann .msnbc/ (accessed November 20, 2015).

4. Jessica Pressler, "The Dr. Maddow Show," *New York Magazine*, November 2, 2008, http://nymag.com/news/media/51822/ (accessed November 20, 2015).

5. Howard Kurtz, "Rachel Maddow Seizes Her Moment," *Newsweek*, February 27, 2011, http://www.newsweek.com/rachel-maddow-seizes-her-moment-68611 (accessed November 20, 2015).

6. Ben Craw, "*The Daily Show* Takes Apart the Haiti Earthquake Reactions of Limbaugh, Robertson, and Maddow," *Talking Points Memo*, January 15, 2010, http:// talkingpointsmemo.com/news/em-the-daily-show-em-takes-apart-the-haiti-earthquake -reactions-of-limbaugh-robertson-and-maddow-video (accessed November 10, 2015).

7. Jack Coleman, "Suddenly Less Snarky Maddow Forced to Admit Rubio Did Well in Iowa," *NewsBusters*, February 6, 2016, http://www.newsbusters.org/blogs/nb/ jack-coleman/2016/02/06/suddenly-less-snarky-maddow-forced-admit-rubio-did-well -iowa (accessed February 17, 2016).

8. Clara Jeffrey, "Rachel Maddow's Star Power," *Mother Jones*, January/February 2009, http://www.motherjones.com/media/2009/01/rachel-maddows-star-power (accessed February 17, 2016).

9. Leslie Kaufman, "Seeking a Lead on News, Network Turns to Data-Mining Media Group," *New York Times*, February 23, 2014, http://www.nytimes.com/2014/02/24/ business/media/teaming-with-data-mining-security-firms-to-get-a-lead-on-news.html? _r=0 (accessed February 17, 2016).

10. Dylan Byers, "PEW: MSNBC More Negative than Fox News," *Politico*, November 2, 2012, http://www.politico.com/blogs/media/2012/11/pew-msnbc-more-negative-than -fox-news-148088 (accessed September 24, 2015); Dylan Byers, "Is MSNBC Worse than Fox News?" *Politico*, December 9, 2013, http://www.politico.com/blogs/media/2013/12/ is-msnbc-worse-than-fox-news-179175 (accessed September 24, 2015).

11. David Rutz, "Big Eddie's Big Questions," *Washington Free Beacon*, September 26, 2013, http://freebeacon.com/politics/big-eddies-big-questions/ (accessed March 8, 2016); Maxwell Strachan, "The 12 Most Absurdly Leading 'Ed Show' Poll Questions," *Salon*, November 20, 2010, http://www.salon.com/2010/11/20/ed_schultz_questions/ (accessed March 8, 2016).

12. Brian Steinberg, "MSNBC Spikes Three Hours of Afternoon Lineup," *Variety*, July 30, 2015, http://variety.com/2015/tv/news/msnbc-cancels-ed-show-cycle-alex-wagner-1201553699/ (accessed February 24, 2016).

13. Dylan Byers, "How to Read the MSNBC News," *Politico*, July 23, 2015, http://www.politico.com/blogs/media/2015/07/how-to-read-the-msnbc-news-211134 (accessed July 27, 2015).

14. Christian Datoc, "'Thanks, Andy!' Scarborough Praises MSNBC for Canning Liberal Hosts," *Daily Caller*, August 27, 2015, http://dailycaller.com/2015/08/27/thanks-andy-scarborough-praises-msnbc-for-canning-liberal-hosts-video/ (accessed December 2, 2016).

15. Steve Rendall, "With Fox News Liberals, Who Needs Conservatives?" FAIR, March 1, 2012, http://fair.org/extra-online-articles/with-fox-news-liberals-who-needs-conservatives/ (accessed December 2, 2015).

16. Larry Atkins, "MSNBC's Changes Are Needed, but It Needs to Keep Its Liberal Voice," *Huffington Post*, July 29, 2015, http://www.huffingtonpost.com/larry-atkins/msnbcs-changes-are-needed_b_7894602.html.

17. Rick Kissell, "Cable News Ratings: CNN, Fox News Continue to Grow at MSNBC's Expense," *Variety*, June 30, 2015, http://variety.com/2015/tv/news/cable-news-ratings-fox-news-cnn-continue-to-grow-at-msnbcs-expense-1201531595/ (accessed December 12, 2015).

18. Mark Joyella, "July 2015 Ratings: MSNBC Sees Viewer Growth, but Down in Prime Time Demo," *AdWeek*, July 29, 2015, http://www.adweek.com/tvnewser/july-2015-ratings-msnbc-sees-viewer-growth-but-down-in-prime-time-demo/268409 (accessed December 12, 2015).

19. Kissell, "Cable News Ratings."

20. *TV Week*, January 8, 2016, http://www.epageflip.net/i/624367-january-08-2016/15 (accessed March 8, 2016).

21. Alex Griswold, "MSNBC's Hayes Defends *Lockup* Reruns: Sometimes It's 'Highest Rated Show' on Network," *Mediaite*, October 20, 2015, http://www.mediaite.com/tv/msnbcs-hayes-defends-lockup-reruns-sometimes-its-highest-rated-show-on-network/ (accessed March 8, 2016).

22. Eric Kelsey, "Keith Olbermann Rejoins ESPN with Late-Night Sports Show," Reuters, July 17, 2013, http://mobile.reuters.com/article/idUSBRE96G1DM20130717 (accessed December 14, 2015).

23. Evan McMurry, "MSNBC Guests Have Awkward Moment over Whether They're Journalists or Advocates," *Mediaite*, October 23, 2013, http://www.mediaite.com/tv/msnbc-guests-have-awkward-moment-over-whether-theyre-journalists-or-advocates/ (accessed December 14, 2015). It was unclear whether McMurry was referring to October 16 or October 23.

CHAPTER 11: THE RISE OF BLOGGING, BIASED WEBSITES, YOUTUBE, SOCIAL MEDIA, AND CITIZEN JOURNALISM AND THEIR RELEVANCE TODAY

1. Clive Thompson, "The Early Years," *New York Magazine*, February 20, 2006, http://nymag.com/news/media/15971/ (accessed January 24, 2016).

2. Gregg Russell, "Pandora's Web," CNN, January 30, 1998, http://www.cnn.com/ALLPOLITICS/1998/01/30/pandora.web/ (accessed January 24, 2016).

3. Ana Marie Cox, http://anamariecox.typepad.com/; "Beyond Wonkette," *Time*, January 7, 2006, http://content.time.com/time/nation/article/0,8599,1147105,00.html (accessed January 24, 2016).

4. Rob Tannenbaum, "Bill Simmons' Big Score," *Rolling Stone*, April 29, 2014, http://www.rollingstone.com/culture/news/bill-simmons-big-score-20140429 (accessed January 24, 2016); "Bill Simmons '92 Is 'Boston's Sports Guy,'" College of the Holy Cross, June 1, 2001, http://news.holycross.edu/blog/2001/06/01/bill-simmons-92-is-bostons-sports-guy/ (accessed January 24, 2016).

5. Anthony Crupi, "Nate Silver Dumps New York Times for ESPN," *AdWeek*, July 20, 2013, http://www.adweek.com/news/television/nate-silver-dumps-new-york-times-espn-151344 (accessed January 24, 2016).

6. "YouTube Top 100 Most Subscribed News & Politics Channels List—Top by Subscribers," VidStatsX, http://vidstatsx.com/youtube-top-100-most-subscribed-news-politics-channels; "News and Politics Channels," YouTube, https://www.youtube.com/channels/news_politics (accessed January 26, 2016).

7. Eugene Scott, "Right to Left: Ex-Conservative Teen YouTube Star Backs Sanders," CNN, December 9, 2015, http://www.cnn.com/2015/12/09/politics/cj-pearson-youtube-endorses-bernie-sanders/ (accessed January 26, 2016); Tal Kopan, "Viral Teen YouTube Star Renounces Conservatism," CNN, November 28, 2015 (accessed January 26, 2016).

8. Blog Talk Radio, http://www.blogtalkradio.com/about.aspx (accessed January 26, 2016).

9. Lori Soard, "How Internet Radio Can Increase Your Site's Traffic," Web Hosting Secrets Revealed, October 13, 2012, http://www.webhostingsecretrevealed.net/blog/web-business-ideas/how-internet-radio-can-increase-your-sites-traffic/ (accessed January 26, 2016).

10. "Pulitzer Prize Winners by Year," The Pulitzer Prizes, http://www.pulitzer.org/prize-winners-by-year (accessed January 30, 2016).

11. Sierra Rayne, "The Top 40 Conservative Websites: June 18, 2015 Edition," *American Thinker*, June 18, 2015, http://www.americanthinker.com/blog/2015/06/the_top_40_conservative_websites_june_18_2015_edition.html (accessed January 30, 2016).

12. Blog Loblaw, "The Best Liberal Blogs Online," Ranker, http://www.ranker.com/list/liberal-blogs/blog-loblaw (accessed January 30, 2016).

13. Rob Kall, e-mail interview, November 29, 2015.

14. "About OpEdNews," *OpEdNews*, http://www.opednews.com/populum/faq
.php?fid=about.

15. Kall, e-mail interview.

16. "Digital Publishing Guidelines: Social Media," *Washington Post*, September 1,
2011, http://www.washingtonpost.com/wp-srv/guidelines/social-media.html (accessed
January 30, 2016).

17. Katie Takacs, "Newsrooms Grapple with How to Avoid Twitter Bloopers,"
American Journalism Review, January 8, 2015, http://ajr.org/2015/01/08/newsrooms
-grapple-avoid-twitter-bloopers/ (accessed January 30, 2016).

18. Angela Lee and Hsiang Iris Chyi, "The Rise of Online News Aggregators:
Consumption and Competition," *International Journal on Media Management* , January
22, 2015, http://www.academia.edu/10339781/The_rise_of_online_news_aggregators
_consumption_and_competition (accessed January 28, 2016).

19. Joe Pinsker, "The Covert World of People Trying to Edit Wikipedia for Pay,"
The Atlantic, August 11, 2015, http://www.theatlantic.com/business/archive/2015/08/
wikipedia-editors-for-pay/393926/ (accessed January 28, 2016).

20. Alyson Shontell, "Why You Should Care about Twitter," *Business Insider*,
September 21, 2013, http://www.businessinsider.com/why-you-should-care-about
-twitter-2013-9 (accessed January 29, 2016).

21. Ashley Ross, "Parisians Use #PorteOuverte Hashtag for Those Seeking Safety
from Attacks," *Time*, November 13, 2015, http://time.com/4112428/paris-shootings-porte
-ouverte/ (accessed January 29, 2016).

22. Jillian Sederholm, "#StrandedInUS: Americans Open Homes to Strangers Stuck
after Paris Attacks," NBC News, November 14, 2015, http://www.nbcnews.com/storyline/
paris-terror-attacks/strandedinus-americans-open-homes-strangers-stranded-after-paris
-attacks-n463431 (accessed January 29, 2016).

23. Mark Bowden, e-mail interview, November 15, 2015.

24. Larry Atkins, "Media and Consumers Must Be Careful in Relying on Twitter for
Breaking News," *Huffington Post*, August 4, 2011, http://www.huffingtonpost.com/larry
-atkins/twitter-reporting-pitfalls_b_914873.html.

25. Ian Tennant, "False Tweet about Piers Morgan Sparks Media Debate on Proper
Use of Twitter," *Journalism in the Americas* (blog), Knight Center, University of Texas at
Austin, August 2, 2011, https://knightcenter.utexas.edu/blog/false-tweet-about-piers
-morgan-sparks-media-debate-about-proper-use-twitter (accessed August 3, 2011).

26. Ibid.

27. Toni Fitzgerald, "Looking Ahead: It's Pulitzer Prize Day," *Media Life*, April 15,
2013, http://www.medialifemagazine.com/looking-ahead-its-pulitzer-prize-day/ (accessed
January 29, 2016).

28. Steve Safran, "How Incorrect Reports of Giffords' Death Spread on Twitter,"
AdWeek, January 9, 2011, http://www.adweek.com/lostremote/how-an-incorrect-report
-of-giffords-death-spread-on-twitter/15366 (accessed August 3, 2011).

29. Mandy Jenkins, "Accuracy and Accountability Checklist for Social Media,"

Zombie Journalism, January 18, 2011, http://zombiejournalism.com/2011/01/accuracy
-and-accountability-checklist-for-social-media/; Damon Kiesow, "Use an Accuracy
Checklist Before Sending Twitter and Facebook Updates" Poynter, January 19, 2011,
http://www.poynter.org/2011/use-an-accuracy-checklist-before-sending-twitter-and
-facebook-updates/115261/ (accessed August 3, 2011).

30. Mallary Jean Tenore, "Conflicting Reports of Giffords' Death Were Under-
standable, but Not Excusable," Poynter, January 10, 2011, http://www.poynter.org/2011/
conflicting-reports-of-giffords-death-were-understandable-but-not-excusable/113876/
(accessed August 3, 2011).

31. Heidi Moore and Dan Roberts, "AP Twitter Hack Causes Panic on Wall Street
and Sends Dow Plunging," *Guardian*, April 23, 2013, http://www.theguardian.com/
business/2013/apr/23/ap-tweet-hack-wall-street-freefall (accessed January 30, 2016).

32. David Knowles, "Lil' Wayne Says He's 'Good' Via Twitter, Despite Reports
He Was Being Read His Last Rites at a Los Angeles Hospital after Suffering Multiple
Seizure," *New York Daily News*, March 15, 2013, http://www.nydailynews.com/
entertainment/music-arts/lil-wayne-critical-condition-hospital-tmz-article-1.1290388
(accessed January 30, 2016).

33. Erik Wemple, "New York Post Settles 'Bag Men' Defamation Suit,'" *Washington Post*, October 2, 2014, https://www.washingtonpost.com/blogs/erik-wemple/wp/2014/
10/02/new-york-post-settles-bag-men-defamation-suit/ (accessed January 30, 2016).

34. Brian Stelter, "CNN and Fox Trip Up in Rush to Get the News on the Air," *New
York Times*, June 28, 2012, http://www.nytimes.com/2012/06/29/us/cnn-and-foxs
-supreme-court-mistake.html?_r=0 (accessed January 30, 2016).

35. Tom Rosenstiel and Amy Mitchell, "The State of the News Media 2011:
Overview," Pew Research Center's Project for Excellence in Journalism, http://www
.stateofthemedia.org/2011/overview-2/ (accessed August 3, 2011).

36. Bill Reed, e-mail interview, December 7, 2015.

37. Jessica Blais, "Poynter Receives $750,000 Ford Foundation Grant to Expand
Sense-Making Programs," Poynter, March 26, 2010, http://www.poynter.org/2010/
poynter-receives-750000-ford-foundation-grant-to-expand-sense-making-programs/
101675/ (accessed August 4, 2011).

38. Amanda Hess, "Is All of Twitter Fair Game for Journalists?" *Slate*, March 19, 2014,
http://www.slate.com/articles/technology/technology/2014/03/twitter_journalism_private
_lives_public_speech_how_reporters_can_ethically.html (accessed February 23, 2016).

39. Jerome R. Corsi, "Claim: Obama Hid 'Gay Life' to Become President,"
WorldNetDaily, September 11, 2012, http://www.wnd.com/2012/09/claim-obama-hid
-gay-life-to-become-president/ (accessed February 23, 2016); Kevin DuJan, "Is Barack
Obama Gay?" *HillBuzz*, http://hillbuzz.org/is-barack-obama-gay; John Craig, "Is
Obama Gay?" Free Republic, September 18, 2012, http://www.freerepublic.com/focus/
bloggers/2933126/posts (accessed February 23, 2016).

40. Neal Gabler, "What's Behind the Right's 'Obama Is Gay' Conspiracy?" *The
Nation*, October 23, 2012, http://www.thenation.com/article/whats-behind-rights-obama
-gay-conspiracy/ (accessed February 23, 2016).

41. David Mikkelson, "Sandy Hook Exposed?" Snopes, February 6, 2015, http://www.snopes.com/politics/guns/newtown.asp (accessed February 23, 2016).

42. Rob Lever, "Nastiness Threatens Online Reader Comments," Agence France Presse, Yahoo News, November 6, 2015, http://news.yahoo.com/nastiness-threatens-online-reader-comments-053929979.html (accessed February 23, 2016).

43. Ibid.

44. Larry Atkins, "The Sad Passing of Chris Squire Reminds Us that Yes Belongs in the Rock and Roll Hall of Fame," *Huffington Post*, July 1, 2015, http://www.huffingtonpost.com/larry-atkins/the-sad-passing-of-chris_b_7707798.html.

45. Steve Outing, "Objectivity: Questioning Journalism's Bedrock Principle," Poynter, February 19, 2004, http://www.poynter.org/2004/objectivity-questioning-journalisms-bedrock-principle/21112/ (accessed December 15, 2015).

46. Brian Stelter and Dylan Byers, "CNN Suspends Correspondent over Refugee Tweet," CNN Money, November 20, 2015, http://money.cnn.com/2015/11/20/media/elise-labott-cnn-suspended/ (accessed December 15, 2015).

47. Mathew Ingram, "Why CNN Was Wrong to Suspend a Reporter For a Tweet," *Fortune*, November 20, 2015, http://fortune.com/2015/11/20/cnn-tweet/ (accessed December 15, 2015).

48. "Atlanta Radio Host Suspended after Insulting ESPN's Mendoza on Twitter," *Sports Illustrated*, October 7, 2015, http://www.si.com/mlb/2015/10/07/mike-bell-radio-host-insult-twitter-jessica-mendoza-espn (accessed December 15, 2015); William Bigelow, "Radio Host Suspended for Criticizing Softball Player Analyzing Baseball for ESPN," Breitbart, October 8, 2015, http://www.breitbart.com/sports/2015/10/08/radio-host-suspended-for-criticizing-softball-player-analyzing-baseball-for-espn/ (accessed December 16, 2015).

49. "Social Media Guidelines for AP Employees," May 2013, Associated Press, http://www.ap.org/Images/Social-Media-Guidelines_tcm28-9832.pdf (accessed December 16, 2015).

50. Katie Pisa and Tim Hume, "Boko Haram Overtakes ISIS as World's Deadliest Terror Group, Report Says," CNN, November 17, 2015, http://www.cnn.com/2015/11/17/world/global-terror-report/ (accessed December 16, 2015).

51. Larry Atkins, "Hashtag Activism Is a Good Thing Despite Its Conservative Critics," *Huffington Post*, July 29, 2014, http://www.huffingtonpost.com/larry-atkins/hashtag-activism-is-a-goo_b_5368173.html.

52. Catherine Taibi, "Fox News Panel Slams #BringBackOurGirls Hashtag Activism," *Huffington Post*, May 11, 2014, http://www.huffingtonpost.com/2014/05/11/fox-news-bringbackourgirls-hashtag-activism-brit-hume-george-will_n_5305749.html (accessed December 16, 2015).

53. Rush Limbaugh, "Are We Really This Powerless?" RushLimbaugh.com, May 8, 2014, http://www.rushlimbaugh.com/daily/2014/05/08/are_we_really_this_powerless (accessed February 4, 2016).

54. Jonathan Topaz, "Stewart Launches Limbaugh Hashtag," *Politico*, May 13, 2014, http://www.politico.com/story/2014/05/jon-stewart-rush-limbaugh-hashtag-106619 (accessed February 4, 2016).

55. Joshua Keating, "What You Won't Learn about Somali Pirates from *Captain Phillips*," *Slate*, October 11, 2013, http://www.slate.com/blogs/browbeat/2013/10/11/captain_phillips_true_story_of_somali_pirates_is_complicated.html (accessed February 4, 2016); Anastasia Moloney, "5 Humanitarian Crises We Can No Longer Afford to Ignore," *Huffington Post*, December 16, 2015, http://www.huffingtonpost.com/entry/5-humanitarian-crises-we-can-no-longer-afford-to-ignore_us_5671956be4b0688701dbc53e (accessed February 4, 2016).

56. Edward-Issac Dovere and Carrie Budoff Brown, "Behind the Obamacare Surprise," *Politico*, April 3, 2014, http://www.politico.com/story/2014/04/obamacare-affordable-care-act-enrollment-105275 (accessed December 16, 2015).

57. Petula Dvorak, "#YesAllWomen: Elliott Rodger's Misogynistic Ravings Inspire a Powerful Response on Twitter," *Washington Post*, May 26, 2014, https://www.washingtonpost.com/local/yesallwomen-elliott-rodgers-misogynistic-ravings-inspire-a-powerful-response-on-twitter/2014/05/26/dd755e4e-e4e0-11e3-8f90-73e071f3d637_story.html (accessed February 4, 2016); Nolan Feeney, "The Most Powerful #YesAll Women Tweets," *Time*, May 25, 2014, http://time.com/114043/yesallwomen-hashtag-santa-barbara-shooting/ (accessed February 4, 2016).

58. Mary Elizabeth Williams, "Why Is the Media Ignoring 200 Missing Girls?" *Salon*, April 30, 2014, http://www.salon.com/2014/04/30/why_is_the_media_ignoring_200_missing_girls/ (accessed December 17, 2015).

59. Ben Mathis-Lilley, "Nigeria Says It's Rescued 200 Girls from Boko Haram," *Slate*, April 28, 2015, http://www.slate.com/blogs/the_slatest/2015/04/28/nigeria_missing_girls_boko_haram_rescue_200_reportedly_found_along_with.html (accessed December 17, 2015).

60. Julia Greenberg, "Stop With the Millennial Niche News Sites Already," *Wired*, June 8, 2015, http://www.wired.com/2015/06/stop-millennial-niche-news-sites-already/ (accessed January 24, 2016).

61. Sonia Yamada, "New York Times Research Finds Young News Readers Seek Reliable News Sources," INMA (International News Media Association), April 13, 2015, http://www.inma.org/blogs/value-content/post.cfm/new-york-times-research-finds-young-news-readers-seek-reliable-news-sources (accessed January 24, 2016).

62. Amy Mitchell, Jeffrey Gottfried, and Katerina Eva Matsa, "Millennials and Political News," Pew Research Center, June 1, 2015, http://www.journalism.org/2015/06/01/millennials-political-news/ (accessed December 16, 2015).

63. Claire Cain Miller, "Social Media Deepens Partisan Divides. But Not Always," *New York Times*, November 20, 2014, http://www.nytimes.com/2014/11/21/upshot/social-media-deepens-partisan-divides-but-not-always.html?_r=0 (accessed December 16, 2015); Yosh Halberstam and Brian Knight, "Homophily, Group Size, and the Diffusion of Political Information in Social Networks: Evidence from Twitter," NBER working paper 20681, National Bureau of Economic Research, November 2014, http://www.nber.org/papers/w20681.

64. Ibid.

65. Will Bunch, phone interview, October 25, 2015.

66. John Timpane, e-mail interview, November 30, 2015.

67. Steven Beschloss, e-mail interview, December 4, 2015.

68. Larry Atkins, "Federal Media Shield Law Should Extend to Unpaid Bloggers and Citizen Journalists," *Huffington Post*, August 13, 2013, http://www.huffingtonpost .com/larry-atkins/federal-media-shield-law_b_3744539.html.

69. Amy Gahran, "Proposed Federal Shield Law Could Protect Local Newsgatherers Too," Knight Digital Media Center, September 24, 2013, http://www.knightdigital mediacenter.org/blogs/agahran/2013/09/proposed-federal-shield-law-could-protect-local -newsgatherers-too (accessed November 4, 2015).

70. Holly Lafon, Michaela Meaney, and Zachary Vasile, "US Senators Consider If Bloggers and Freelancers Deserve First Amendment Privileges," Medill DC, August 8, 2013, http://dc.medill.northwestern.edu/blog/2013/08/08/ananth-reporter-0708/#sthash .aGgyq6OW.dpbs (accessed August 10, 2013); Scott Bomboy, "Senators Ponder if Bloggers Deserve First Amendment Protection," *Constitution Daily* (blog), National Constitution Center, August 5, 2013, http://blog.constitutioncenter.org/2013/08/senators -ponder-if-bloggers-deserve-first-amendment-protection/ (accessed August 10, 2013).

71. Bomboy, "Senators Ponder if Bloggers Deserve First Amendment Protection."

72. Tom Haydon, "Judge Rules Union County Blogger Is Protected by the State's Shield Law," *Star-Ledger*, April 12, 2013, http://www.nj.com/union/index.ssf/2013/04/ union_county_blogger_scores_vi.html (accessed August 10, 2013).

73. "Internet Issues—A Reporter's Obligation to a Source—Anonymous Comments Online," Reporters Committee for Freedom of the Press, http://www.rcfp.org/first -amendment-handbook/4-confidential-sources-and-information/internet-issues-reporters -obligation; Lucy Dalglish, "Defining a Journalist," Reporter's Committee for Freedom of the Press, http://www.rcfp.org/browse-media-law-resources/news-media-law/news-media -and-law-spring-2008/defining-journalist (accessed August 10, 2013).

CHAPTER 12: IS THE MAINSTREAM MEDIA LIBERALLY BIASED? DOES THE MEDIA TRY TO BE OBJECTIVE AND BALANCED?

1. Dr. Matthew H. Reavy, "Objectivity and Advocacy in Journalism," *Media Ethics* 25, no. 1 (Fall 2013), http://www.mediaethicsmagazine.com/index.php/browse-back -issues/179-fall-2013-vol-25-no-1/3999003-objectivity-and-advocacy-in-journalism (accessed November 21, 2015); L. Brent Bozell, *Weapons of Mass Distortion: The Coming Meltdown of the Liberal Media* (New York: CrownForum, 2004); Bernard Goldberg, *Bias: A CBS Insider Exposes How the Media Distort the News* (Washington, DC: Regenery, 2002); David Edwards, David Cromwell, and John Pilger, *Guardians of Power: The Myth of the Liberal Media* (London: Pluto Books, 2006); Tien-Tsung Lee, "The Liberal Media Myth Revisited: An Examination of Factors Influencing Perceptions of Media Bias," *Journal of Broadcasting and Electronic Media* 49, no. 1 (2005): 43–64.

2. John Dombrink, "Donald Trump Is a Modern Spiro Agnew," *New Republic*, https://newrepublic.com/article/122482/donald-trump-succeeds-modern-spiro-agnew (accessed March 8, 2016).

3. Pat Buchanan, "The Times' Vendetta against Augusta," Townhall.com, December 9, 2002, http://townhall.com/columnists/patbuchanan/2002/12/09/the_times_vendetta _against_augusta (accessed September 25, 2015).

4. Chris Matthews, "Conservatives Are Right: The Media Is Very Liberal," *Fortune*, November 2, 2015, http://fortune.com/2015/11/02/liberal-media/ (accessed December 5, 2015); Tim Groseclose and Jeffrey Milyo, "A Measure of Media Bias," *Quarterly Journal of Economics* 120, no. 4 (2005): 1191–237, http://qje.oxfordjournals. org/content/120/4/1191.short.

5. Timothy P. Carney, "Liberal News Media Bias Has a Serious Effect," *New York Times*, December 21, 2015, http://www.nytimes.com/roomfordebate/2015/11/11/why-has -trust-in-the-news-media-declined/liberal-news-media-bias-has-a-serious-effect (accessed January 9, 2016).

6. James B. Steele, phone interview, December 11, 2015.

7. "Black and White and Re(a)d All Over: The Conservative Advantage in Syndicated Op-Ed Columns," Media Matters, September 2007, http://cloudfront .mediamatters.org/static/pdf/oped_report.pdf (accessed March 4, 2016).

8. Conor Lynch, "The Wing Nut Myth that Refuses to Die: The One Simple Reason Why There's No 'Liberal Media Conspiracy,'" *Salon*, November 2, 2015, http:// www.salon.com/2015/11/02/the_wing_nut_myth_that_refuses_to_die_why_the_one _simple_reason_why_theres_no_liberal_media_conspiracy/ (accessed December 15, 2015).

9. Rob Kall, e-mail interview, November 29, 2015.

10. Ron Dzwonkowski, "New Venture Debunks Notion of Liberal Media Bias," *Detroit Free Press*, August 12, 2012, available at http://www.sportsmenvote.com/news/ opinion-new-venture-debunks-notion-of-liberal-media-bias/ (accessed September 25, 2015). See also T. R. Clancy, "What Media Bias?" *Dearborn Underground*, August 13, 2012, http://dearbornunderground.blogspot.com/2012/08/what-media-bias.html; and The 4th Estate Project, http://www.4thestate.net/.

11. "The Web: Alarming, Appealing, and a Challenge to Journalistic Values. Financial Woes Now Overshadow All Other Concerns for Journalists," Pew Research Center, March 17, 2008, http://www.stateofthemedia.org/files/2011/01/Journalist-report -2008.pdf (accessed September 25, 2016).

12. Cass R. Sunstein, "Republicans Who Fault the Media Show Their Bias," *Bloomberg View*, November 16, 2015, http://www.bloombergview.com/articles/ 2015-11-16/republicans-who-fault-the-media-show-their-bias; Matthew Gentzkow and Jesse M. Shapiro, "What Drives Media Slant? Evidence from U.S. Daily Newspapers," *Econometrica* 78, no. 1 (January 2010): 35–71, http://www.brown.edu/Research/Shapiro/ pdfs/biasmeas.pdf (accessed December 14, 2015).

13. Mark Bowden, e-mail interview, November 15, 2015.

14. Walter Dean, "Understanding Bias," American Press Institute, https://www

.americanpressinstitute.org/journalism-essentials/bias-objectivity/understanding-bias/ (accessed March 4, 2016).

15. Kyle Whitmire, "Trump for America: Let's Face It, There's No Way This Ends Well," AL.com (Alabama Media Group), November 22, 2015, http://www.al.com/opinion/index.ssf/2015/11/trump_for_america_lets_face_it.html (accessed December 15, 2015).

16. Brent Cunningham, "Re-thinking Objectivity," *Columbia Journalism Review*, July/August 2003, http://www.cjr.org/feature/rethinking_objectivity.php?page=all; "The Washington Post Standards and Ethics," ASNE (American Society of News Editors), http://asne.org/content.asp?contentid=335 (accessed September 22, 2015).

17. Matt Taibbi, "Hey, MSM: All Journalism Is Advocacy Journalism," *Rolling Stone*, June 27, 2013, http://www.rollingstone.com/politics/news/hey-msm-all-journalism-is-advocacy-journalism-20130627 (accessed September 22, 2015).

18. Roy Peter Clark, "AP Dumps 'Illegal Immigrant' but Not Neutrality," Poynter, April 4, 2013, http://www.poynter.org/2013/ap-style-dumps-illegal-immigrant-but-not-neutrality/209180/ (accessed September 22, 2015).

19. "SPJ Code of Ethics," Society of Professional Journalists, September 6, 2014, http://www.spj.org/ethicscode.asp.

20. Gary Kamiya, "Iraq: Why the Media Failed," *Salon*, April 10, 2007, http://www.salon.com/2007/04/10/media_failure/ (accessed September 22, 2015).

21. Colin Campbell, "The Republican Party Suddenly Canceled Its NBC Debate Amid CNBC Furor," *Business Insider*, October 30, 2015, http://www.businessinsider.com/rnc-cancels-nbc-debate-reince-priebus-cnbc.

22. Maya Rhodan, "Ted Cruz Goes After the Media in Republican Debate," *Time*, October 28, 2015, http://time.com/4091905/republican-debate-ted-cruz-media-cnbc/; Samantha-Jo Roth, "Ted Cruz Wants Only Conservatives to Moderate Future Debates," *Huffington Post*, October 31, 2015, http://www.huffingtonpost.com/entry/ted-cruz-debate-moderators_us_563531abe4b00aa54a4e7661 (accessed December 15, 2015).

23. "This Line Got the Most Favorable Reaction Ever from a Luntz Focus Group," *Fox News Insider* (blog), October 29, 2015, http://insider.foxnews.com/2015/10/29/frank-luntz-focus-group-reacts-ted-cruzs-criticism-cnbc-gop-debate-moderators.

24. Sara Jerde, "Ann Coulter Defends CNBC Debate Moderators from 'Ridiculous' Attacks," *Talking Points Memo*, October 29, 2015, http://talkingpointsmemo.com/livewire/ann-coulter-donald-trump-cnbc-debate (accessed November 14, 2015).

25. Dylan Byers, "The John King-Newt Gingrich Debate," *Politico*, January 20, 2012, http://www.politico.com/blogs/media/2012/01/the-john-king-newt-gingrich-debate-111596.

26. Josh Voorhees, "Donald Trump's Debate Boycott Won't Change the Race. That's Why He's Doing It," *Slate*, January 27, 2016, http://www.slate.com/blogs/the_slatest/2016/01/27/donald_trump_s_fox_news_debate_boycott_will_help_him.html (accessed February 22, 2016).

27. Michael Smerconish, "Is Media Too Tough on Ben Carson?" *Smerconish*, CNN, November 7, 2015, http://transcripts.cnn.com/TRANSCRIPTS/1511/07/smer.01.html (accessed December 8, 2015).

28. Eric Bradner, "Ben Carson Thanks 'Biased Media' for $3.5 Million in One Week," CNN, November 7, 2015, http://www.cnn.com/2015/11/07/politics/ben-carson -fundraising-3-5-million-media/ (accessed December 8, 2015).

29. Scott Glover and Maeve Reston, "A Tale of Two Carsons," CNN, November 7, 2015, http://www.cnn.com/2015/11/05/politics/ben-carson-2016-childhood-violence/ (accessed December 8, 2015).

30. Nick Gass, "Ben Carson's 15 Most Controversial Quotes," *Politico*, October 9, 2015, http://www.politico.com/story/2015/10/ben-carson-controversial-quotes-214614 (accessed December 8, 2015).

31. "Carson Rips Media for Lying; Rubio Hits Double Standard," *MediaBuzz*, transcript, Fox News, November 15, 2015, http://www.foxnews.com/transcript/ 2015/11/15/carson-rips-media-for-lying-rubio-hits-double-standard/; Lynn Sweet, "Sweet: Carson off Base in Media Complaints; Buck Up and Deal with It," *Chicago Sun Times*, November 15, 2015, http://chicago.suntimes.com/lynn-sweet-politics/7/71/1103274/ sweet-carson-base-media-complaints-buck-deal (accessed December 9, 2015); Howard Kurtz, "Carson Rips Media for Lying; Rubio Hits Double Standard," transcript, *MediaBuzz*, Fox News, November 15, 2015, http://www.foxnews.com/transcript/ 2015/11/15/carson-rips-media-for-lying-rubio-hits-double-standard/.

32. Bryan Monroe, "The Truth about What Candy Crowley Said," CNN, October 20, 2012, http://www.cnn.com/2012/10/18/politics/fact-check-crowley-critics-debate/ (accessed December 9, 2015).

33. John Cassidy, "Did the Media Get the Democratic Debate Wrong," *New Yorker*, October 15, 2015, http://www.newyorker.com/news/john-cassidy/did-the-media-get-the -democratic-debate-wrong (accessed December 9, 2015).

34. Paul Farhi, "How Biased Are the Media Really?" *Washington Post*, April 27, 2012, https://www.washingtonpost.com/lifestyle/style/how-biased-is-the-media -really/2012/04/27/gIQA9jYLmT_story.html (accessed December 9, 2015).

35. Ibid. David D'Alessio teaches at the University of Connecticut at Stamford and is the author of the book *Media Bias in Presidential Election Coverage, 1948–2008: Evaluations via Formal Measurement* (Lanham, MD: Lexington Books, 2012).

36. Ibid. Eric Alterman is the author of the bestselling *What Liberal Media? The Truth about Bias and the News* (New York: Basic Books, 2003).

37. Ibid.

38. Gloria Goodale, "Social Media Age Shocker, on Politics, Newspapers Get More Respect," *Christian Science Monitor*, February 24, 2014, http://www.csmonitor.com/ USA/Elections/Vox-News/2012/0224/Social-media-age-shocker-On-politics-newspapers -get-more-respect (accessed January 15, 2016).

39. Roger Yu, "'Oregonian' Cuts Home Delivery to 3 Days," *USA Today*, June 21, 2013, http://www.usatoday.com/story/money/business/2013/06/20/oregonian-home -delivery-cutback/2442765/ (accessed January 15, 2016).

40. Lymari Morales, "U.S. Distrust in Media Hits New High," Gallup, September 21, 2012, http://www.gallup.com/poll/157589/distrust-media-hits-new-high.aspx (accessed January 15, 2016).

41. Julie Moos, "PEW: 75 Percent of Americans Say Journalists Can't Get Their Facts Straight," Poynter, September 23, 2011, http://www.poynter.org/2011/pew-75-of -americans-say-press-cant-get-their-facts-straight/147038/ (accessed January 16, 2016).

42. Robert Reinhold, "Washington Post Gives Up Pulitzer, Calling Article on Addict, 8, Fiction," *New York Times*, April 16, 1981, http://www.nytimes.com/1981/ 04/16/nyregion/washington-post-gives-up-pulitzer-calling-article-on-addict-8-fiction .html?pagewanted=all (accessed January 16, 2016).

43. Dan Barry, David Barstow, Jonathan D. Glater, Adam Liptak, and Jacques Steinberg, "CORRECTING THE RECORD; Times Reporter Who Resigned Leaves Long Trail of Deception," *New York Times*, May 11, 2003, http://www.nytimes.com/2003/ 05/11/us/correcting-the-record-times-reporter-who-resigned-leaves-long-trail-of -deception.html?pagewanted=all (accessed January 16, 2016).

44. Doug Stanglin, "No Law License for Ex-Writer, Fabricator Stephen Glass," *USA Today*, January 28, 2014, http://www.usatoday.com/story/news/nation/2014/01/27/ stephen-glass-new-republic-fabricator-law-license-denied/4940813/ (accessed January 16, 2016).

45. Neely Tucker, "Whatever Happened To . . . The Foreign Correspondent Who Made Up Stories?" *Washington Post*, July 22, 2011, https://www.washingtonpost.com/ lifestyle/magazine/whatever-happened-to—the-foreign-correspondent-who-made-up -stories/2011/05/11/gIQAmOvgTI_story.html (accessed January 16, 2016).

46. "Boston Columnist Resigns Amid New Plagiarism Charges," CNN, August 19, 1998, http://www.cnn.com/US/9808/19/barnicle/index.html (accessed January 16, 2016).

47. Emily Steel and Ravi Somaiya, "Brian Williams Suspended by NBC News for 6 Months Without Pay," *New York Times*, February 11, 2015, http://www.nytimes .com/2015/02/11/business/media/brian-williams-suspended-by-nbc-news-for-six-months .html?_r=0 (accessed January 16, 2016).

48. Roger Yu, "Study: Americans' Support of First Amendment Grows," *USA Today*, July 3, 2015, http://www.usatoday.com/story/news/2015/07/03/newseum-institute -first-amendment-center-2015-first-amendment-study/29623405/ (accessed September 28, 2015).

49. Ibid.

50. John Hawkins, "Seven Deceptive Mainstream Media Techniques," Townhall. com, July 27, 2010, http://townhall.com/columnists/johnhawkins/2010/07/27/seven _deceptive_mainstream_media_techniques/page/full (accessed September 28, 2015).

51. Dylan Byers, "Chuck Todd Takes Aim at Partisan Media," *Politico*, September 25, 2014, http://www.politico.com/blogs/media/2014/09/chuck-todd-takes-aim-at -partisan-media-196120 (accessed September 28, 2015).

52. Sally Lehrman, "Unconscious Stereotypes Slow Newsroom Diversity," Society of Professional Journalists, http://www.spj.org/rrr.asp?ref=8&t=diversity.

53. Mark Coddington, "CNN," *Encyclo*, August 28, 2014, http://www.niemanlab .org/encyclo/cnn/ (accessed September 28, 2015).

54. Bill Carter, "The F.B.I. Criticizes the News Media after Several Mistaken Reports of an Arrest," *New York Times*, April 17, 2013, http://www.nytimes

.com/2013/04/18/business/media/fbi-criticizes-false-reports-of-a-bombing-arrest.html (accessed September 29, 2015).

55. Bill Carter, "CNN's Ratings Surge Covering the Mystery of the Missing Airliner," *New York Times*, March 17, 2014, http://www.nytimes.com/2014/03/18/business/media/cnns-ratings-surge-with-coverage-of-the-mystery-of-the-missing-airliner.html (accessed September 29, 2015).

56. Ibid.

57. Bill Cromwell, "Readers: CNN's Still Tops in Credibility," *Media Life*, March 2, 2015, http://www.medialifemagazine.com/readers-cnns-still-tops-in-credibility/ (accessed September 29, 2015).

58. David Carr, "Gains for NPR Are Clouded," *New York Times*, March 14, 2011, http://www.nytimes.com/2011/03/14/business/media/14carr.html?_r=0 (accessed September 29, 2015).

59. Amy Mitchell, "Which News Organization Is the Most Trusted? The Answer Is Complicated," Pew Research Center, October 30, 2014, http://www.pewresearch.org/fact-tank/2014/10/30/which-news-organization-is-the-most-trusted-the-answer-is-complicated/ (accessed September 29, 2015).

60. Mark Bowden, e-mail interview, November 15, 2015.

61. Bill Reed, e-mail interview, December 7, 2015.

62. Bowden, e-mail interview.

63. James B. Steele, phone interview, December 11, 2015.

64. Bowden, e-mail interview.

65. Catherine R. Squires, "Young Black People See the News Media's Double Standard," *New York Times*, December 21, 2015, http://www.nytimes.com/roomfordebate/2015/11/11/why-has-trust-in-the-news-media-declined/young-black-people-see-the-news-medias-double-standard (accessed January 15, 2016).

66. T. Becket Adams, "MSNBC's Hayes: Media Biased, but Not Partisan," *Washington Examiner*, November 13, 2015, http://www.washingtonexaminer.com/msnbcs-hayes-media-biased-but-not-partisan/article/2576266 (accessed March 9, 2016).

67. Matt Taibbi, "America Is Too Dumb for TV News," *Rolling Stone*, November 25, 2015, http://www.rollingstone.com/politics/news/america-is-too-dumb-for-tv-news-20151125 (accessed March 9, 2016).

68. Jay Rosen, "On the Deep Grammar of the White House Correspondents Association Dinner," *PressThink*, April 25, 2015, http://pressthink.org/2015/04/on-the-deep-grammar-of-the-white-house-correspondents-association-dinner/ (accessed January 15, 2016).

69. David Roberts, "The Real Reason the Media Is Rising Up against Donald Trump," *Vox*, December 1, 2015, http://www.vox.com/2015/12/1/9828086/donald-trump-media (accessed January 15, 2016).

CHAPTER 13: WHAT'S NEWS? WHAT ARE THE FACTORS USED BY THE MEDIA IN DECIDING WHAT TO REPORT? HOW IS BIAS DISPLAYED IN THE SELECTION PROCESS?

1. Robert C. Kennedy, "On This Day: November 13, 1880," *New York Times*, November 13, 2001, https://www.nytimes.com/learning/general/onthisday/harp/1113.html (accessed January 22, 2016).

2. "Missing Pregnant Woman Found Dead," *USA Today*, August 21, 2005, http://usatoday30.usatoday.com/news/nation/2005-08-20-missing-woman_x.htm (accessed January 22, 2016).

3. Neil Clark, "Terrorism in Africa: A Bigger Threat than in Europe, but Much Less Coverage," RT, January 15, 2015, https://www.rt.com/op-edge/222983-terrorism-africa-threat-nigeria/.

4. Thomas Friedman, "Friedman: So, What Is 'News'?" *Houston Chronicle*, July 27, 2014, http://www.chron.com/news/article/Friedman-So-what-is-news-5650355.php (accessed November 2, 2016).

5. Silpa Kovvali, "'Master of None' Tackles the Empathy Gap: How Nuanced Minority Stories Can Shrink the Emotional Gulf between White Americans and 'Others.'" *Salon*, November 21, 2015, http://www.salon.com/2015/11/21/master_of_none_tackles_the_empathy_gap_how_nuanced_minority_stories_can_shrink_the_emotional_gulf_between_white_americans_and_others/ (accessed December 12, 2015).

6. John Timpane, e-mail interview, November 30, 2015.

7. Arianna Huffington, "Just Say Noruba," *Huffington Post*, May 25, 2011, http://www.huffingtonpost.com/arianna-huffington/just-say-noruba_b_2928.html (accessed December 12, 2015).

8. Tom Foreman, "Diagnosing 'Missing White Woman Syndrome,'" CNN, March 14, 2006, http://www.cnn.com/CNN/Programs/anderson.cooper.360/blog/2006/03/diagnosing-missing-white-woman.html (accessed December 12, 2015).

9. Jonathan Kuperberg, "Tips for Newsroom Tweeting: A Q&A with Los Angeles Times Social Media Editor Stacey Leasca," Official Twitter Blog, June 3, 2014, https://blog.twitter.com/2014/tips-for-newsroom-tweeting-a-qa-with-los-angeles-times-social-media-editor-stacey-leasca (accessed December 15, 2015).

10. Alison Schwartz, "Robin Thicke & Miley Cyrus Twerk It Out at VMA's," *People*, July 1, 2014, http://www.people.com/people/package/article/0,,20302940_20728423,00.html (accessed December 15, 2015).

11. Jeff Rossen and Josh Davis, "What's 'Sizzurp'? A Dangerous Way for Kids to Get High," *Today*, January 23, 2014, http://www.today.com/news/whats-sizzurp-dangerous-way-kids-get-high-2D11976739 (accessed December 15, 2015).

12. Anahad O'Connor, "Consequences of the 'Cinnamon Challenge,'" *New York Times*, April 22, 2013, http://well.blogs.nytimes.com/2013/04/22/consequences-of-the-cinnamon-challenge/ (accessed December 15, 2015).

13. Benjamin Fearnow, "Deadly 'Choking Game' Spreads among Teens on Social Media," CBS St. Louis, August 5, 2014, http://stlouis.cbslocal.com/2014/08/05/deadly -choking-game-spreads-among-teens-on-social-media/ (accessed December 15, 2015).

14. Alan Schwarz, "Risky Rise of the Good Grade Pill," *New York Times*, June 9, 2012, http://www.nytimes.com/2012/06/10/education/seeking-academic-edge-teenagers -abuse-stimulants.html (accessed December 15, 2015).

15. Justin Ellis, "My Team, My Publisher: The New World of Competition between Leagues and Media in Sports," Nieman Lab, April 11, 2013, http://www.niemanlab .org/2013/04/my-team-my-publisher-the-new-world-of-competition-between-leagues -and-media-in-sports/ (accessed December 17, 2015); Jordan Heck, "Joe Buck Responds to Royals Fans Who Don't Want Him at ALCS," *Sporting News*, October 17, 2015, http:// www.sportingnews.com/mlb-news/4658477-mlb-playoffs-2015-alcs-joe-buck-royals -blue-jays-announcer-tv-fox-harold-reynolds (accessed December 17, 2015).

16. Tom Waseleski, "Inside the Opinion Pages," *Pittsburgh Post-Gazette*, March 25, 2014, http://www.post-gazette.com/opinion/2014/03/04/Post-Gazette-opinion-FAQ/ stories/201403040169 (accessed November 1, 2015).

17. "Sen. Bernie Sanders (I-VT) to Brian Stelter on CNN's Reliable Sources: '. . . you have ABC, CBS, and NBC Not Devoting One Minute to the Most Significant Trade Agreement in the History of the USA,'" CNN, May 24, 2015, http://cnnpressroom .blogs.cnn.com/2015/05/24/sen-bernie-sanders-i-vt-to-brian-stelter-on-cnns-reliable -sources-you-have-abc-cbs-and-nbc-not-devoting-one-minute-to-the-most-significant -trade-agreement-in-the-history-of-the-usa/ (accessed November 1, 2015).

18. David Schultz, "Donald Trump and Corporate Media Bias in America," *MinnPost*, December 15, 2015, https://www.minnpost.com/community-voices/2015/12/ donald-trump-and-corporate-media-bias-america (accessed December 1, 2015).

19. Fred Mitchell, "Carlton's Number Finally Up," *Chicago Tribune*, June 26, 1986, http://articles.chicagotribune.com/1986-06-26/sports/8602150759_1_phillies-steve -carlton-national-league-record (accessed November 1, 2015); Bob Verdi, "Carlton, Phils' Silent Star, Lets His Pitching Speak for Itself," *Chicago Tribune*, October 21, 1980, http:// archives.chicagotribune.com/1980/10/21/page/47/article/carlton-phils-silent-star-lets-his -pitching-speak-for-itself (accessed November 1, 2015); Larry Stone, "Let Beast Mode Be: Why I've Changed My Mind about Marshawn Lynch's Silence," *Seattle Times*, January 30, 2015, http://www.seattletimes.com/sports/seahawks/let-beast-mode-be-why -ive-changed-my-mind-about-marshawn-lynchs-silence/ (accessed November 1, 2015).

CHAPTER 14: THE PROCESS OF REPORTING AND HOW IT CAN AFFECT BIAS

1. John Rains, "Across the Chasm," *Highlights & Hindsights* (newsletter), *Fayette-ville Observer*, February 2002, available at Poynter, August 19, 2002, http://www .poynter.org/2002/across-the-chasm/1921/ (accessed October 17, 2015).

2. Mark Bowden, e-mail interview, November 15, 2015.

3. Bill Reed, e-mail interview, December 7, 2015.

4. Will Bunch, phone interview, December 2, 2015.

5. Ibid.

6. Bowden, e-mail interview.

7. Reed, e-mail interview.

8. James B. Steele, phone interview, December 11, 2015.

9. John Timpane, e-mail interview, November 30, 2015.

10. Bunch, phone interview.

11. Maya Rhoden, "Jeb Bush Says 'Stuff Happens' Remarks after Oregon Shooting Taken Out of Context," *Time*, October 2, 2015, http://time.com/4060114/oregon-shooting -jeb-bush-stuff-happens/ (accessed February 17, 2016).

12. Jack and Suzy Welch, "It's True: Corporations Are People," *Wall Street Journal*, July 15, 2012, http://www.wsj.com/articles/SB100014240527023037407045775248233O 6803692 (accessed February 17, 2016).

13. Philip Elliott, "SPIN METER: Obama's 'You Didn't Build That' Echoes," Associated Press, Yahoo News, July 25, 2012, http://news.yahoo.com/spin-meter-obamas -didnt-build-echoes-190033849.html?_esi=1 (accessed February 17, 2016).

14. Sheryl Gay Stolberg, Shaila Dewan, Brian Stelter, "With Apology, Fired Official Is Offered a New Job," *New York Times*, July 21, 2010, http://www.nytimes.com/2010/ 07/22/us/politics/22sherrod.html (accessed February 17, 2016).

15. Judy Faber, "CBS Fires Don Imus over Racial Slur," CBS News, April 12, 2007, http://www.cbsnews.com/news/cbs-fires-don-imus-over-racial-slur/ (accessed October 17, 2016).

16. Nicholas Carlson, "What Was Post Thinking Running Obama Monkey Cartoon," *Business Insider*, February 18, 2009, http://www.businessinsider.com/what-was-post -thinking-running-obama-monkey-cartoon-2009-2 (accessed February 17, 2016).

17. Irving DeJohn and Helen Kennedy, "Jeremy Lin Headline Slur Was 'Honest Mis-take,' Fired ESPN Editor Anthony Federico Claims," *New York Daily News*, February 20, 2012, http://www.nydailynews.com/entertainment/tv-movies/jeremy-lin-slur-honest-mistake -fired-espn-editor-anthony-federico-claims-article-1.1025566 (accessed February 17, 2016).

18. Jay Sharbutt, "Jimmy 'The Greek' Is Fired by CBS," *Los Angeles Times*, January 17, 1988, http://articles.latimes.com/1988-01-17/sports/sp-36803_1_jimmy -snyder (accessed February 17, 2016).

19. "Rand Paul On 'Maddow' Defends Criticism of Civil Rights Acts, Says He Would Have Worked to Change Bill," *Huffington Post*, May 20, 2010, http://www .huffingtonpost.com/2010/05/20/rand-paul-tells-maddow-th_n_582872.html (accessed January 12, 2016).

20. Michael Zennie, "'Game On': Sarah Palin Will Be Host on 'Today' the Same Time as Katie Couric Takes Anchor Chair for 'Good Morning America,'" *Daily Mail*, April 2, 2012, http://www.dailymail.co.uk/news/article-2123652/Sarah-Palin-host-Today -time-Katie-Couric-takes-anchor-chair-Good-Morning-America.html (accessed January 12, 2016).

21. Colby Itkowitz, "A Brief History of the 'Gotcha Question' in Politics," *Washington Post*, February 24, 2015, https://www.washingtonpost.com/blogs/in-the-loop/wp/2015/02/24/a-brief-history-of-the-gotcha-question/ (accessed January 16, 2016); Frank Bruni, "Pressed by a Reporter, Bush Falls Short in World Affairs Quiz," *New York Times*, November 5, 1999, http://www.nytimes.com/1999/11/05/us/pressed-by-a-reporter-bush-falls-short-in-world-affairs-quiz.html (accessed January 16, 2016).

22. Dan Balz and Robert Costa, "Gov. Scott Walker: 'I Don't Know' Whether Obama Is a Christian," *Washington Post*, February 21, 2015, https://www.washingtonpost.com/politics/walker-says-he-is-unaware-whether-obama-is-a-christian/2015/02/21/6fde0bd0-ba17-11e4-bc30-a4e75503948a_story.html (accessed January 16, 2016).

23. Caitlin Cruz, "Trump Accuses Conservative Host of 'Gotcha Questions' that Fiorina Breezes Through," *Talking Points Memo*, September 4, 2015, http://talkingpointsmemo.com/livewire/donald-trump-hugh-hewitt-interview (accessed November 4, 2015); Hugh Hewitt, "Donald Trump on the Day He Took the Pledge," Hugh Hewitt Program, September 3, 2015, http://www.hughhewitt.com/donald-trump-on-the-day-he-took-the-pledge/ (accessed November 4, 2015).

24. "War on Women," MSNBC, http://www.msnbc.com/topics/war-women (accessed March 5, 2016).

25. Tania Ralli, "Who's a Looter? In Storm's Aftermath, Pictures Kick Up a Different Kind of Tempest," *New York Times*, September 5, 2005, http://www.nytimes.com/2005/09/05/business/whos-a-looter-in-storms-aftermath-pictures-kick-up-a-different-kind-of-tempest.html?_r=0&module=ArrowsNav&contentCollection=Business%20Day&action=keypress&region=FixedLeft&pgtype=article (accessed October 4, 2015); Aaron Kinney, "'Looting' or 'Finding'?" *Salon*, September 1, 2005, http://www.salon.com/2005/09/02/photo_controversy/ (accessed October 4, 2015).

26. Ralli, "Who's a Looter?"

27. Matt Stopera, "Actual News Headlines vs. Fox News Headlines," *BuzzFeed*, June 24, 2011, http://www.buzzfeed.com/mjs538/actual-news-headlines-vs-fox-news-headlines#.uyRJxDMo9 (accessed October 4, 2015).

28. Edward Schumacher-Matos, "We Write the Headlines; You Decide the Bias," NPR, September 27, 2012, http://www.npr.org/sections/ombudsman/2012/09/27/161827094/we-write-the-headlines-you-decide-the-bias (accessed October 4, 2015).

29. *New York Daily News* (@NYDailyNews), Twitter, January 15, 2016, https://twitter.com/NYDailyNews/status/687887932603129856 (accessed February 22, 2016). David Wright, "New York Daily News Cover to Cruz: 'Drop Dead, Ted,'" CNN, January 15, 2016, http://www.cnn.com/2016/01/15/politics/new-york-daily-news-cruz-cover/ (accessed February 22, 2016).

30. Don Wycliff, "Outrage about the Fallujah Photograph," *Chicago Tribune*, April 8, 2004, http://articles.chicagotribune.com/2004-04-08/news/0404080206_1_fallujah-picture-propaganda (accessed October 1, 2015); Daniel J. Vargas and Andrew Guy Jr., "Graphic Iraq War Photos Generate Controversy," *Houston Chronicle*, April 2, 2004, http://www.chron.com/life/article/Graphic-Iraq-war-photos-generate-controversy-1956446.php (accessed October 1, 2015).

31. Larry Atkins, "*Time* Magazine Got It Right in Publishing Graphic Cover Photo," *Huffington Post*, August 1, 2010, http://www.huffingtonpost.com/larry-atkins/itimei -magazine-got-it-ri_b_666727.html; Daniel Martin Varisco, "Covering Afghanistan," Tabsir, July 31, 2010, http://tabsir.net/?p=1208 (accessed October 1, 2015).

32. Alicia C. Shepard, "Gruesome Haiti Photo: A Need for Context," NPR, January 25, 2010, http://www.npr.org/sections/ombudsman/2010/01/gruesome_haiti_photo_a _need_fo_1.html (accessed October 1, 2015).

33. Richard Stengel, "The Plight of Afghan Women: A Disturbing Picture," *Time*, July 29, 2010, http://content.time.com/time/magazine/article/0,9171,2007415,00.html (accessed March 12, 2015).

34. Eric Boehlert, "Fox News' Tasteless Exploitation of ISIS Video," Media Matters, February 5, 2015, http://mediamatters.org/blog/2015/02/05/fox-news-tasteless -exploitation-of-isis-video/202427 (accessed December 12, 2015).

35. David Bianculli and Gail Shister, "How TV Covered the Dwyer Suicide," *Philadelphia Inquirer*, January 23, 1987, http://articles.philly.com/1987-01-23/news/ 26187226_1_dwyer-newscast-gun (accessed December 12, 2015); Eleanor Randolph, "Witnesses to Death Journalists Question Their Role," *Washington Post*, January 23, 1987, https://www.washingtonpost.com/archive/politics/1987/01/23/witnesses-to-death -journalists-question-their-role/0542e227-334b-4db0-8289-bc3cca6168e5/.

36. "The View from Inside the Military," *Nieman Reports*, June 15, 2003, http:// niemanreports.org/articles/the-view-from-inside-the-military/ (accessed March 4, 2016); "Embedding Reporters on the Front Line," *Nieman Reports*, June 15, 2003, http://nieman reports.org/articles/embedding-reporters-on-the-frontline/ (accessed March 4, 2016).

37. Jonathan Stray, "How Do You Tell When the Media Is Biased? It Depends on How You See Yourself," Nieman Lab, June 27, 2012, http://www.niemanlab.org/2012/06/ how-do-you-tell-when-the-news-is-biased/ (accessed March 5, 2016).

38. Associated Press, "Altered Images Prompt Photographer's Firing," NBC News, August 7, 2006, http://www.nbcnews.com/id/13165165/ns/world_news-mideast_n _africa/t/altered-images-prompt-photographers-firing/ (accessed October 22, 2015.)

39. Howard Kurtz, "Time's 'Sinister' Simpson," *Washington Post*, June 22, 1994, https://www.washingtonpost.com/archive/lifestyle/1994/06/22/times-sinister -simpson/6659311e-0bc0-4215-96f5-40271e38525a/ (accessed October 26, 2015).

40. Ken Light, "Fonda, Kerry, and Photo Fakery," *Washington Post*, February 28, 2004, https://www.washingtonpost.com/archive/opinions/2004/02/28/fonda-kerry-and -photo-fakery/15bdc6ed-c568-49fc-bddd-ac534c426865/ (accessed October 26, 2015).

41. Larry Atkins, "Seventeen Magazine Promises Real Photos of Real Girls," *Philadelphia Magazine*, July 20, 2012, http://www.phillymag.com/news/2012/07/20/ seventeen-magazine-photoshop-models/.

42. Greg Botelho, "Seventeen Magazine Vows Not to Alter Images, to 'Celebrate Every Kind of Beauty,'" CNN, July 6, 2012, http://www.cnn.com/2012/07/05/us/ seventeen-photoshopping/ (accessed October 26, 2015).

Here is the note from Ann Shocket, editor-in-chief of *Seventeen Magazine*: http://i2.cdn .turner.com/cnn/2012/images/07/05/ann.august.editors.letter.pdf (accessed March 8, 2016).

43. "10 News Photos That Took Retouching Too Far," *AdWeek*, May 21, 2009, http://www.adweek.com/fishbowlny/10-news-photos-that-took-photoshop-too/241284 (accessed October 10, 2015). See also: Sherry Ricchiardi, "Distorted Picture," *American Journalism Review*, August/September 2007, http://ajrarchive.org/Article.asp?id=4383.

44. Jeffrey Goldberg, "About that McCain Photo," *The Atlantic*, September 14, 2008, http://www.theatlantic.com/international/archive/2008/09/about-that-mccain-photo/8825/ (accessed October 10, 2015); Jeffrey Goldberg, "Jill Greenberg Dropped by Photo Agency," *The Atlantic*, September 16, 2008, http://www.theatlantic.com/international/archive/2008/09/jill-greenberg-dropped-by-photo-agency/8830/ (accessed October 10, 2015).

45. Tara Parker-Pope, "Losing Weight by Photoshop," *New York Times*, December 17, 2009, http://well.blogs.nytimes.com/2009/12/17/losing-weight-by-photoshop/ (accessed October 10, 2015); Jennifer Michalski, "The 15 Worst Celebrity Magazine Photoshop Fails," *Business Insider*, October 9, 2013, http://www.businessinsider.com/worst-celebrity-photoshop-fails-2013-10?op=1 (accessed October 10, 2015); "Most Blatant Uses of Photoshop in Magazine Ads," YourCover, http://www.yourcover.com/Articles/Most-Blatant-Uses-of-Photoshop-in-Magazines-Ads (accessed October 10, 2015); "Worst Celebrity Photoshop Disasters Ever," *US Weekly*, June 24, 2013, http://www.usmagazine.com/celebrity-body/pictures/worst-celebrity-photoshop-disasters-ever-2013226/31283 (accessed October 10, 2015).

46. Parker-Pope, "Losing Weight by Photoshop."

47. Abigail Pesta, "The War on 'Teen Vogue': Young Readers Escalate Campaign for More 'Real Girls," *Daily Beast*, July 18, 2012, http://www.thedailybeast.com/articles/2012/07/18/the-war-on-teen-vogue-young-readers-fight-for-real-girls.html (accessed October 10, 2015); Amy Odell, "Are Teenagers Better at Solving the Thin Model Problem than 'Vogue' Editors?" *BuzzFeed*, May 3, 2012, http://www.buzzfeed.com/amyodell/are-teenagers-better-at-solving-the-thin-model-pro#.yqlDK3OPb (accessed October 10, 2015); Olivia Lidbury, "Vogue Editors Unite to Launch Model Health Initiative," *Telegraph*, May 3, 2012, http://fashion.telegraph.co.uk/news-features/TMG9242759/Vogue-editors-unite-to-launch-model-health-initiative.html (accessed October 10, 2015); Associated Press, "Young Activists Say Teen Vogue Was Shockingly Rude to Them after Photoshop Protest," Fox411, July 12, 2012, http://www.foxnews.com/entertainment/2012/07/12/young-activists-say-teen-vogue-was-shockingly-rude-to-them-after-photoshop.html (accessed October 10, 2015).

48. "Debate Heats Up Over Photoshopped Fashion Models," CBS News, February 17, 2015, http://www.cbsnews.com/news/cindy-crawford-photo-sparks-debate-over-photoshopped-fashion-models/ (accessed October 10, 2015).

49. Mark Leibovich, "Chevy Chase as the Klutz in Chief, and a President Who Was in on the Joke," *New York Times*, December 29, 2006, http://www.nytimes.com/2006/12/29/washington/29chevy.html?_r=0 (accessed November 11, 2015).

50. "Top 10 Bushisms: A Fond Look Back at Some of George W. Bush's Less-than-Articulate Moments in Office," *Time*, http://content.time.com/time/specials/packages/article/0,28804,1870938_1870943_1870944,00.html (accessed November 11, 2015).

51. Dan Lamothe, "Obama's 'Latte Salute' Controversy Spins into Second Day," *Washington Post*, September 24, 2014, https://www.washingtonpost.com/news/checkpoint/wp/2014/09/24/obamas-latte-salute-controversy-spins-into-second-day/ (accessed November 11, 2015).

52. Howard Kurtz, "Why Jorge Ramos Crossed the Line in Confronting Donald Trump," Fox News, August 27, 2015, http://www.foxnews.com/politics/2015/08/27/why-jorge-ramos-crossed-line-in-confronting-donald-trump.html (accessed March 15, 2016).

53. Paul Farhi, "Al Sharpton Plays Several Sides in Trayvon Martin Story," *Washington Post*, July 19, 2013, https://www.washingtonpost.com/lifestyle/style/2013/07/19/03edafe2-efd5-11e2-9008-61e94a7ea20d_story.html (accessed March 15, 2016); Kyle Feldscher, "Rev. Al Sharpton Calls for Activism Despite Criticism: 'If You Don't Fight, You Are Guaranteed to Lose,'" MLive, February 27, 2015, http://www.mlive.com/lansing-news/index.ssf/2015/02/rev_al_sharpton_calls_on_conti.html (accessed March 15, 2016).

54. Lloyd Grove, "Stephanopoulos Caught in Clinton Cash Trap," *Daily Beast*, May 14, 2015, http://www.thedailybeast.com/articles/2015/05/14/george-stephanopoulos-gave-75-000-to-the-clintons-and-didn-t-declare-it.html (accessed May 18, 2015).

55. Larry Atkins, "Stephanopoulos Incident Feeds False Republican Myth that the Media is Liberally Biased," *Huffington Post*, May 20, 2015, http://www.huffingtonpost.com/larry-atkins/stephanopoulos-incident-f_b_7346496.html.

56. David Montgomery, "MSNBC's Keith Olbermann Suspended For Contributing To 3 Democratic Candidates," *Washington Post*, November 6, 2010, http://www.washingtonpost.com/wp-dyn/content/article/2010/11/05/AR2010110504496.html (accessed November 5, 2015).

57. Kathryn S. Wenner, "Conflicts of Interest," *American Journalism Review*, May 2003, http://ajrarchive.org/Article.asp?id=3004 (accessed November 5, 2015).

58. Bill Dedman, "TV Reporter Who Supported Candidate Is Out," NBC News, July 11, 2007, http://www.nbcnews.com/id/19415989/ns/politics/t/tv-reporter-who-supported-candidate-out/ (accessed November 5, 2015).

59. Scott Kraus, "Columnist: Call Suspended Me for Riding in Gay Pride Parade," *Morning Call*, June 24, 2006, http://articles.mcall.com/2006-06-24/news/3662328_1_gay-pride-parade-grand-marshals-ethics-policy (accessed November 5, 2015).

60. Howard Kurtz, "Administration Paid Commentator: Education Dept. Used Williams to Promote 'No Child' Law," *Washington Post*, January 8, 2005, http://www.washingtonpost.com/wp-dyn/articles/A56330-2005Jan7.html (accessed November 5, 2015).

61. Associated Press, "Columnist Dropped by Syndicate Over Education Dept. Payments," NBC News, January 10, 2005, http://www.nbcnews.com/id/6798618/ns/us_news-education/t/columnist-dropped-syndicateover-education-dept-payments/#.VunFsOZH6ew (accessed November 5, 2015).

62. Reed, e-mail interview,.

63. Christopher Harper, e-mail interview, December 13, 2015.

64. Ibid.

65. Ibid.; Christopher Harper, "Media Won't Let Facts Stand in the Way of a Good Story," *Washington Times*, April 8, 2015, http://www.washingtontimes.com/news/2015/apr/8/christopher-harper-media-wont-let-facts-stand-in-t/?page=all (accessed December 13, 2015).

66. Bunch, phone interview.

67. Bowden, e-mail interview.

68. Timpane, e-mail interview.

69. Steele, phone interview.

70. "Chris Hayes: From 'Up' in the Morning to 'All In' at Night," NPR, WBUR, March 26, 2013, http://www.wbur.org/npr/175376175/chris-hayes-from-up-in-the-morning-to-all-in-at-night (accessed November 14, 2015).

71. "SPJ Code of Ethics," Society of Professional Journalists, September 6, 2014, http://www.spj.org/ethicscode.asp (accessed November 4, 2015).

72. Alex S. Jones, "An Argument Why Journalists Should Not Abandon Objectivity," *Nieman Reports*, September 15, 2009, http://niemanreports.org/articles/an-argument-why-journalists-should-not-abandon-objectivity/ (accessed November 4, 2015); Alex S. Jones, *Losing the News: The Future of the News that Feeds Democracy* (New York: Oxford University Press, 2009).

73. Tessa Jolls, phone interview, October 19, 2015.

74. James Taranto, "Bully for Whom? Serge Kovaleski and the Trump Paradox," *Wall Street Journal,* November 27, 2015, http://www.wsj.com/articles/bully-for-whom-1448647860 (accessed December 4, 2015).

75. "SPJ Code of Ethics."

76. Ibid.

77. Michael Getler, "More Self-Inflicted Wounds," *PBS Ombudsman* (blog), PBS, September 2, 2015, http://www.pbs.org/ombudsman/blogs/ombudsman/2015/09/02/more-self-inflicted-wounds/ (accessed December 4, 2015).

78. Catalina Albeanu, "Crowdfunding Platforms for Journalists: We All Know Kickstarter, but What Are Some of the Specialized Platforms Out There That Could Help Journalists Fund Their Projects?" Journalism.co.uk, November 21, 2014, https://www.journalism.co.uk/news/crowdfunding-platforms-for-reporters-photographers-video-journalists/s2/a563228/ (accessed February 22, 2015); Bill Mitchell, "Hoyt's Donation to NYT Story Raises Question: Can Journalists Be Both Contributors and Critics?" Poynter, July 23, 2009, http://www.poynter.org/2009/hoyts-donation-to-nyt-story-raises-question-can-journalists-be-both-contributors-and-critics/97403/ (accessed February 22, 2015); Bill Mitchell, "NYT Public Editor, Spot.Us Director: Garbage Patch Story Shows Creative Way to Fund Journalism," Poynter, November 11, 2009, http://www.poynter.org/2009/nyt-public-editor-spot-us-director-garbage-patch-story-shows-creative-way-to-fund-journalism/99352/ (accessed February 22, 2015).

79. T. Rees Shapiro, "Lawyers for U-Va. Dean: Jackie Lied to Rolling Stone, 'Invented' Story," *Washington Post*, January 8, 2016, https://www.washingtonpost.com/news/grade-point/wp/2016/01/08/lawyers-for-u-va-dean-jackie-lied-to-rolling-stone-about-gang-rape-invented-story (accessed January 22, 2016).

80. Neil Levy, "Bias, Balance and the Problems of Media Objectivity?" *On Line Opinion*, June 24, 2004, http://www.onlineopinion.com.au/view.asp?article=2312 (accessed February 22, 2015).

81. Walter V. Robinson and Francie Latour, "Bid Cited to Boost Bush in Guard," *Boston Globe*, September 9, 2004, http://archive.boston.com/news/politics/president/ bush/articles/2004/09/09/bid_cited_to_boost_bush_in_guard/?page=full.

82. Associated Press, "CBS News Admits Bush Documents Can't Be Verified," NBC News, September 21, 2004, http://www.nbcnews.com/id/6055248/ns/politics/t/ cbs-news-admits-bush-documents-cant-be-verified/; "CBS Ousts Four Over Bush Guard Story," CNN, January 11, 2005, http://www.cnn.com/2005/SHOWBIZ/TV/01/10/ cbs.guard/; Howard Kurtz, "Rather Concedes Papers Are Suspect," *Washington Post*, September 16, 2004, http://www.washingtonpost.com/wp-dyn/articles/A24633-2004 Sep15.html; Paul Rosenberg, "George W. Bush's Military Lies: The Real Story about the Undeniable Service Gaps He Got Away With," *Salon*, October 17, 2015, http://www. salon.com/2015/10/17/george_w_bushs_military_lies_the_real_story_about_the _undeniable_service_gaps_he_got_away_with/.

83. Larry Atkins, "Rathergate Misses the Point," *Philadelphia Metro*, September 2004.

84. Dan Gillmor, "Helping the Almost-Journalists Do Journalism," Center for Citizen Media, July 23, 2008, http://citmedia.org/blog/2008/07/23/helping-the-almost -journalists-do-journalism/ (accessed February 22, 2015).

85. Shawn Burns, "'Advocacy' Is Not a Dirty Word in Journalism," *MediaShift*, October 16, 2014, http://mediashift.org/2014/10/advocacy-is-not-a-dirty-word-in -journalism/ (accessed February 22, 2015).

CHAPTER 15: THE POLARIZING EFFECT OF ADVOCACY JOURNALISM ON POLITICS AND SOCIETY

1. Carroll Doherty, "7 Things to Know about Polarization in America," Pew Research Center, June 12, 2014, http://www.pewresearch.org/fact-tank/2014/06/12/7 -things-to-know-about-polarization-in-america/ (accessed September 26, 2015).

2. "Full Video and Transcript: NPR's Interview with President Obama," NPR, August 10, 2015, http://www.npr.org/sections/itsallpolitics/2015/08/10/431244020/full -video-and-transcript-nprs-interview-with-president-obama (accessed September 26, 2015).

3. Major Garrett, "Top GOP Priority: Make Obama a One-Term President," *National Journal*, October 23, 2010, https://www.nationaljournal.com/member/magazine/ top-gop-priority-make-obama-a-one-term-president-20101023 (accessed September 26, 2015); Dan Farber, "Sen. Mitch McConnell Has Some Explaining to Do," CBS News, November 14, 2010, http://www.cbsnews.com/news/sen-mitch-mcconnell-has-some -explaining-to-do/ (accessed September 26, 2015).

4. Carl Hulse, "In Lawmaker's Outburst, a Rare Breach of Protocol," *New York Times*, September 9, 2009, http://www.nytimes.com/2009/09/10/us/politics/10wilson.html (accessed September 26, 2015); Steve Benen, "Yet Another Obamacare Repeal Vote?" MSNBC, September 30, 2015, http://www.msnbc.com/rachel-maddow-show/yet-another -obamacare-repeal-vote (accessed October 26, 2015).

5. "Fox News Has Most Trusted Coverage, or Not, Quinnipiac University National Poll Finds; Tina Fey, Dennis Miller Top Choices to Replace Stewart," Quinnipiac University Poll, March 9, 2015, http://www.quinnipiac.edu/news-and-events/quinnipiac -university-poll/national/release-detail?ReleaseID=2173 (accessed September 26, 2015).

6. Rob Kall, e-mail interview, November 29, 2015.

7. Thomas Carsey and Geoffrey Layman, "Our Politics Is Polarized on More Issues than Ever Before," *Washington Post*, January 17, 2014, https://www.washingtonpost .com/news/monkey-cage/wp/2014/01/17/our-politics-is-polarized-on-more-issues -than-ever-before/.

8. Will Bunch, phone interview, October 25, 2015.

9. John Timpane, e-mail interview, November 30, 2015.

10. Mark Bowden, e-mail interview, November 15, 2015.

11. Nick Gass, "The 11 Best Quotes from the First Democratic Debate," *Politico*, October 13, 2015, http://www.politico.com/story/2015/10/democratic-presidential -debate-quotes-214765 (accessed November 2, 2015); Ryan Teague Beckwith, "Read Joe Biden's Speech about Not Running for President," *Time*, October 21, 2015, http://time .com/4081594/joe-biden-president-campaign-transcript-full-remarks/ (accessed November 2, 2015).

12. Michael Allen, "Rep. Louie Gohmert: Obama Administration Is 'Enemy Within,'" *Opposing Views*, April 15, 2015, http://www.opposingviews.com/i/politics/ foreign-policy/rep-louie-gohmert-obama-administration-enemy-within-video (accessed November 2, 2015); Aric Mitchell, "President Obama Is 'Enemy Within,' Congressman Says: Right or Wrong," *Inquisitr*, April 15, 2015, http://www.inquisitr.com/2013101/ president-obama-is-enemy-within-congressman-says-right-or-wrong/ (accessed November 2, 2015).

13. Thomas Sowell, "Apparently, Obama-Love Is Blind," *National Review*, October 22, 2008, http://www.nationalreview.com/article/226048/believers-barack-thomas-sowell (accessed November 2, 2015).

14. Thomas Sowell, "Idols of Crowds," Townhall.com, September 16, 2008, http:// townhall.com/columnists/thomassowell/2008/09/16/idols_of_crowds/page/full (accessed November 2, 2015).

15. Hank Stephenson, "State Representative Stands by Her Comparison of Obama to Hitler," *Arizona Capitol Times*, October 7, 2013, http://azcapitoltimes.com/ news/2013/10/07/state-representative-stands-by-her-comparison-of-obama-to-hitler/ (accessed November 2, 2015).

16. Dave Lindorff, "Bush and Hitler and the Strategy of Fear," *CounterPunch*, February 1, 2003, http://www.counterpunch.org/2003/02/01/bush-and-hitler-and-the -strategy-of-fear/ (accessed November 2, 2015).

17. Callum Borchers, "'The New Furor': Philadelphia Daily News Front Page Goes There on Donald Trump," *Washington Post*, December 8, 2015, https://www
.washingtonpost.com/news/the-fix/wp/2015/12/08/the-philadelphia-daily-news-front
-page-goes-there-on-donald-trump/ (accessed December 10, 2015).

18. Toby Harnden, "Bush Like Hitler, Says First Muslim in Congress," *Telegraph*, July 14, 2007, http://www.telegraph.co.uk/news/worldnews/1557447/Bush-like-Hitler
-says-first-Muslim-in-Congress.html (accessed November 2, 2015); The Learning Network, "Feb. 27, 1933: Germany's Reichstag Building Set on Fire," *New York Times*, February 27, 2012, http://learning.blogs.nytimes.com/2012/02/27/feb-27-1933-germanys
-reichstag-building-set-on-fire/?_r=0 (accessed November 2, 2015).

19. Melissa Clyne, "Ben Stein: Iran Deal Makes Chamberlain's Pact with Nazis Seem Trivial," Newsmax, July 14, 2015, http://www.newsmax.com/Headline/Ben
-Stein-Iran-deal-Neville-Chamberlain/2015/07/14/id/656912/ (accessed November 2, 2015); "Conservative Media: Iran is Munich," *Huffington Post*, November 26, 2013, http://www.huffingtonpost.com/2013/11/26/iran-nuclear-deal-munich-conservative
-media_n_4343584.html (accessed November 2, 2015); Noah Smith, "Obama Should Play Nixon and Go to Iran," *Bloomberg View*, September 9, 2014, http://www
.bloombergview.com/articles/2014-09-09/obama-should-play-nixon-and-go-to-iran (accessed November 2, 2015).

20. Jonathan Turley, "Is Clerk Kim Davis a Hero or Villain? Why Her Defiance Is More George Wallace than MLK," *Washington Post*, September 3, 2015, https://www
.washingtonpost.com/posteverything/wp/2015/09/03/is-clerk-kim-davis-a-hero-or-villain/ (accessed December 3, 2015).

21. Jesse Lee Peterson, "Kim Davis: Modern Day Rosa Parks," *WorldNetDaily*, September 13, 2015, http://www.wnd.com/2015/09/kim-davis-modern-day-rosa-parks/ (accessed December 3, 2015).

22. Larry Elder, "Bush Led, Bin Laden Dead—Where's the Credit?" RealClear Politics, May 5, 2011, http://www.realclearpolitics.com/articles/2011/05/05/bush_led
_bin_laden_dead_--_wheres_the_credit_109757.html (accessed February 4, 2016).

23. Mark Jurkowitz, "Bin Laden Coverage Still Leads but the Narrative Changes," Pew Research Center, May 14, 2011, http://www.journalism.org/2011/05/14/pej-news
-coverage-index-may-915-2011/ (accessed February 4, 2016).

24. Jonathan S. Tobin, "Back to Full-Time Racial Incitement," *Commentary*, July 15, 2013, https://www.commentarymagazine.com/culture-civilization/popular-culture/
back-to-full-time-racial-incitement-george-zimmerman-msnbc/ (accessed February 4, 2016); Ben Adler, "Conservative Media Smears Trayvon Martin: Right Wing Commentators Are Seizing on Irrelevant Details of Martin's Life to Justify His Death," *The Nation*, March 27, 2012, http://www.thenation.com/article/conservative-media
-smears-trayvon-martin/ (accessed February 4, 2016).

25. Alex Seitz-Wald, "Fox News Adopts George Zimmerman: Outside His Legal Team, Few Have Done More to Help Trayvon Martin's Shooter than Sean Hannity. Here's Why," *Salon*, July 1, 2013, http://www.salon.com/2013/07/01/right_wing_media_adopts
_george_zimmerman/ (accessed February 5, 2016).

26. Mark Hemingway, "Media Malpractice," *Weekly Standard*, April 23, 2012, http://www.weeklystandard.com/media-malpractice/article/636993 (accessed February 5, 2016).

27. Eric Deggans, "Four Lessons from the Media's Conflicted Coverage of Race," NPR, December 6, 2014, http://www.npr.org/sections/codeswitch/2014/12/06/368713550/four-lessons-from-the-medias-conflicted-coverage-of-race (accessed February 5, 2016).

28. Brett LoGiurato, "Joe Scarborough: Sean Hannity Has Been Using the Trayvon Martin Case to 'Gin Up His Ratings,'" *Business Insider*, July 22, 2013, http://www.businessinsider.com/joe-scarborough-sean-hannity-obama-trayvon-martin-race-2013-7 (accessed February 5, 2016).

29. Doug Spero, "How TV News Failed Trayvon Martin, George Zimmerman, and American People," *Christian Science Monitor*, July 22, 2013, http://www.csmonitor.com/Commentary/Opinion/2013/0722/How-TV-news-failed-Trayvon-Martin-George-Zimmerman-and-American-people (accessed February 5, 2016).

30. Marc Caputo, "Poll: Republicans Like George Zimmerman More than President Obama. Independents Not Far Behind," *Miami Herald*, June 14, 2013, http://miamiherald.typepad.com/nakedpolitics/2013/07/poll-republicans-like-george-zimmerman-more-than-president-obama-independents-not-far-behind.html (accessed February 5, 2016).

31. Alexis Sobel Fitts, "Michael Brown Shooting and the Crimes Journalists Choose as Newsworthy: Explaining Why Black Suspects Are Covered at Greater Proportion than They Commit Crimes," *Columbia Journalism Review*, August 28, 2014, http://www.cjr.org/minority_reports/michael_brown_ferguson_media.php (accessed February 5, 2016).

32. "Joe: Rams Protest the Last Straw for Me," *Morning Joe* video, 17:12, MSNBC, December 1, 2014, http://www.msnbc.com/morning-joe/watch/joe--rams-protest-the-last-straw-for-me-365495875637 (accessed February 5, 2016); Al Weaver, "Scarborough Rails Against the Left, Media: Michael Brown 'Is Your Hero? Really?'" *Daily Caller*, http://dailycaller.com/2014/12/01/scarborough-rails-against-the-left-media-michael-brown-is-your-hero-really-video/ (accessed February 5, 2016).

33. Glenn Kessler, "The Biggest Pinocchios of 2015," *Washington Post*, December 14, 2015, https://www.washingtonpost.com/news/fact-checker/wp/2015/12/14/the-biggest-pinocchios-of-2015/ (accessed February 5, 2016); Michelle Ye Hee Lee, "'Hands Up, Don't Shoot' Did Not Happen in Ferguson," *Washington Post*, March 19, 2015, https://www.washingtonpost.com/news/fact-checker/wp/2015/03/19/hands-up-dont-shoot-did-not-happen-in-ferguson/ (accessed February 5, 2016).

34. Timpane, e-mail interview.

35. Darin Watkins, "Study Links U.S. Polarization to TV News Deregulation," WSU News, September 24, 2015, https://news.wsu.edu/2015/09/24/study-links-u-s-polarization-to-tv-news-deregulation/ (accessed February 6, 2016).

36. Deanna Zandt, "Can't We All Just Get Along? Polarization of Politics, the Internet, and You," *Forbes*, August 22, 2012, http://www.forbes.com/sites/deannazandt/2012/08/22/cant-we-all-just-get-along-polarization-of-politics-the-internet-and-you/#47ef1f993d70 (accessed February 6, 2016).

37. Michael Kranish, "The Role of Partisan Media," *Boston Globe*, October 6, 2013, https://www.bostonglobe.com/business/2013/10/05/broken-city-the-role-partisan-media/FctYo09Bx0qHd15IhAuHdL/story.html (accessed February 6, 2016).

38. John Diaz, "The Great American Echo Chamber," *San Francisco Chronicle*, October 31, 2014, http://www.sfgate.com/opinion/diaz/article/The-great-American-echo -chamber-5862035.php (accessed February 2, 2016).

39. "The Press and Polarization," *New York Times Editorial Board*, April 17, 2008, http://theboard.blogs.nytimes.com/2008/04/17/the-press-and-polarization/ (accessed February 2, 2016); Jonathan McDonald Ladd, "The Role of Media Distrust in Partisan Voting," *Political Behavior* 32 (May 19, 2010), http://faculty.georgetown.edu/jml89/ LaddMediaVoting.pdf (accessed February 2, 2016).

40. Nicholas DiFonzo, "The Echo-Chamber Effect," *New York Times*, April 22, 2011, http://www.nytimes.com/roomfordebate/2011/04/21/barack-obama-and-the-psychology-of -the-birther-myth/the-echo-chamber-effect?module=ArrowsNav&contentCollection =undefined&action=keypress&region=FixedLeft&pgtype=blogs (accessed February 2, 2016).

41. David Mikkelson, "Who Is Barack Obama?" Snopes, July 7, 2009, http://www .snopes.com/politics/obama/muslim.asp (accessed March 4, 2016).

42. Dan Amira, "Who Do Members of Congress Follow on Twitter?" *New York Magazine*, September 3, 2013, http://nymag.com/daily/intelligencer/2013/08/who-do -members-of-congress-follow-on-twitter.html (accessed February 2, 2016); Caitlin Dewey, "How Twitter Makes the Political Echo Chamber Worse," *Washington Post*, September 3, 2013, https://www.washingtonpost.com/news/the-fix/wp/2013/09/03/how -twitter-makes-the-political-echo-chamber-worse/ (accessed February 2, 2016).

43. Joshua Bleiberg and Darrell M. West, "Political Polarization on Facebook," Brookings Institution, May 13, 2015, http://www.brookings.edu/blogs/techtank/posts/ 2015/05/13-facebook-political-polarization (accessed February 2, 2016).

44. "The Echo Chamber Revisited," transcript, *On The Media*, NPR, June 17, 2011, http://www.onthemedia.org/story/143347-echo-chamber-revisited/transcript/ (accessed February 2, 2016).

45. Michael Barone, "Barone: Life in a Cocoon Dulls Political Responses," *Washington Examiner*, May 22, 2012, http://www.washingtonexaminer.com/barone-life -in-a-cocoon-dulls-political-responses/article/1307586 (accessed February 4, 2016).

46. James Carville, "Opinion: Disturbing Polarization in Media Worsens Political Partisanship," *The Hill*, October 15, 2013, http://thehill.com/opinion/columnists/james -carville/328731-polarization-in-media-worsens-partisanship (accessed February 4, 2016).

47. "Anderson Cooper 360 Degrees," CNN Transcripts, October 29, 2015, http:// transcripts.cnn.com/TRANSCRIPTS/1510/29/acd.01.html (accessed February 4, 2016).

48. Matthew Levendusky, "Are Fox and MSNBC Polarizing America?" *Washington Post*, February 3, 2014, https://www.washingtonpost.com/news/monkey-cage/wp/2014/ 02/03/are-fox-and-msnbc-polarizing-america/ (accessed February 4, 2016).

49. Steven Beschloss, e-mail interview, December 4, 2015.

50. Ibid.

51. "Bills that Become Laws: No Budget, No Pay," No Labels, http://www.nolabels. org/bills-passed/ (accessed March 2, 2016).

52. AllSides, allsides.com.

CHAPTER 16: THE POPULARITY OF ADVOCACY JOURNALISM AND ITS INFLUENCE

1. Peter Johnson, "More Reporters Embrace an Advocacy Role," *USA Today*, March 5, 2007, http://usatoday30.usatoday.com/life/television/news/2007-03-05-social -journalism_N.htm (accessed September 22, 2015).

2. Greg Garrison, "'All Lives Matter' March Draws Thousands to Birmingham," AL.com (Alabama Media Group), August 29, 2015, http://www.al.com/living/index .ssf/2015/08/all_lives_matter_march_draws_m.html (accessed September 22, 2015).

3. Amy Gardner, Krissah Thompson, and Philip Rucker, "Beck, Palin Tell Thousands to 'Restore America,'" *Washington Post*, August 29, 2010, http://www .washingtonpost.com/wp-dyn/content/article/2010/08/28/AR2010082801106.html (accessed September 22, 2015).

4. Sarah Ferris, "Ebola Disappears from Media Spotlight after Midterms," *The Hill*, November 19, 2014, http://thehill.com/business-a-lobbying/224721-ebola -disappears-from-media-spotlight-after-midterms (accessed September 22, 2015).

5. Dominic Patten, "Fox News Tops Cable Primetime Viewership for First Time in 2015, Bill O'Reilly up Over 2014," *Deadline Hollywood*, March 10, 2015, http://deadline .com/2015/03/fox-news-cable-victory-bill-oreilly-1201389905/ (accessed September 22, 2015).

6. Al Weaver, "Fox News Reigns as Ratings King for 13th Straight Year, CNN Posts All-Time Lows," *Daily Caller*, December 30, 2014, http://dailycaller.com/ 2014/12/30/fox-news-reigns-as-ratings-king-for-13th-straight-year-cnn-posts-all-time -lows/ (accessed September 23, 2015).

7. Mike Allen, "How Fox News Has Stayed on Top," *Politico*, February 1, 2012, http://www.politico.com/story/2012/02/how-fox-news-stayed-on-top-072253 (accessed September 23, 2015).

8. David Zurawik, "New Level of Fox News Dominance Demands Analysis, Not Dismissal," *Baltimore Sun*, November 18, 2014, http://www.baltimoresun.com/ entertainment/tv/z-on-tv-blog/bal-fox-news-ratings-dominance-demands-analysis -20141117-story.html (accessed September 23, 2015).

9. Joanne Ostrow, "In Television and Radio Talk Wars, Why Do Conservatives Drown Out All the Others?" *Denver Post*, February 10, 2012, http://www.denverpost .com/ci_19931372 (accessed September 25, 2015).

10. Nicole Hemmer, "Can Jeb Bush Break Conservative Media," *U.S. News & World Report*, March 24, 2015, http://www.usnews.com/opinion/blogs/nicole -hemmer/2015/03/24/ted-cruz-jeb-bush-and-talk-radios-2016-influence (accessed September 25, 2015).

11. Associated Press, "GOP Chief Apologizes for Limbaugh Remarks," NBC News, March 3, 2009, http://www.nbcnews.com/id/29478402/ns/politics-more_politics/t/gop -chief-apologizes-limbaugh-remarks/#.VtmQeeZH6ew (accessed September 25, 2015).

12. Toby Harnden, "Radio 'King' Angers Daschle," *Telegraph*, November 26, 2002,

http://www.telegraph.co.uk/news/worldnews/northamerica/usa/1414369/Radio-king
-angers-Daschle.html (accessed September 25, 2015).

13. "Top 15 Most Popular Political Website, May 2016," eBizMBA, http://www
.ebizmba.com/articles/political-websites.

CHAPTER 17: WHAT'S GOOD ABOUT
ADVOCACY JOURNALISM?

1. Jim Romenesko, "Study: Young People Consider News to Be Garbage and
Lies," *JimRomenesko.com* (blog), September 10, 2012, http://jimromenesko.com/
2012/09/10/young-people-regard-news-as-garbage-and-lies/#more-24319 (accessed
November 11, 2015); Paula Poindexter, *Millennials, News, and Social Media: Is News
Engagement a Thing of the Past?* (New York: Peter Lang, 2012).

2. Mark Whittington, "NBC Should Drop the Boring Evening News Format and
Hire Craig Ferguson as Anchor," *Examiner*, February 8, 2015, http://www.examiner.com/
article/nbc-should-drop-the-boring-evening-news-format-and-hire-craig-ferguson-as
-anchor (accessed November 11, 2015).

3. Jessica Toonkel, "Tegna CEO Looks to Rejuvenate Local TV," Reuters,
November 25, 2015, http://www.reuters.com/article/us-tegna-ceo-idUSKBN0TE
27W20151125 (accessed December 11, 2015).

4. Roberto Acosta, "MSNBC's Rachel Maddow Tells Flint 'America Is with You
Now' in Water Crisis," MLive, January 28, 2016, http://www.mlive.com/news/flint/index
.ssf/2016/01/msnbcs_rachel_maddow_tells_fli.html (accessed March 4, 2016).

5. Oliver Darcy, "Sean Hannity Travels to Texas Border for Exclusive Tour with
Rick Perry: 'I'm Learning Things Here Today that I Never Knew Of,'" TheBlaze, July 11,
2014, http://www.theblaze.com/stories/2014/07/11/sean-hannity-travels-to-texas-border
-for-exclusive-tour-with-rick-perry-im-learning-things-here-today-that-i-never-knew-of/
(accessed March 4, 2016).

6. John Timpane, e-mail interview, November 30, 2015.

7. Dean Starkman, "The Great Story: In the Run-Up to the Great Recession,
Accountability Journalism Saw the Story that Access Journalism Missed," *Columbia
Journalism Review*, January/February 2014, http://www.cjr.org/feature/the_great_story
.php (accessed March 4, 2016); Dean Starkman, *The Watchdog that Didn't Bark:
The Financial Crisis and the Disappearance of Investigative Journalism* (New York:
Columbia University Press, 2014).

8. Rob Kall, e-mail interview, November 29, 2015.

9. Mark Bowden, e-mail interview, November 15, 2015.

10. Will Bunch, e-mail interview, December 2, 2015.

11. George Rodrigue, "Reporting on Problems with Solutions in Mind," *Cleveland
Plain Dealer*, September 19, 2015, http://www.cleveland.com/metro/index.ssf/2015/09/
reporting_on_problems_with_sol.html (accessed November 11, 2015).

12. "Dean Kirkman Advocacy Journalism Remarks," transcript, American University School of Communication, March 1, 2011, http://www.american.edu/soc/journalism/deans-advocacy-journalism-remarks.cfm (accessed November 11, 2015).

CHAPTER 18: WHAT'S BAD ABOUT ADVOCACY JOURNALISM?

1. Amy Mitchell, Jeffrey Gottfried, Jocelyn Kiley, and Katerina Eva Matsa, "Section 1: Media Sources: Distinct Favorites Emerge on the Left and Right," Pew Research Center, October 21, 2014, http://www.journalism.org/2014/10/21/section-1 -media-sources-distinct-favorites-emerge-on-the-left-and-right/#in-news-sources-we -trust-or-distrust (accessed February 22, 2016).

2. Julie Alderman, "Right-Wing Media Take Obama Out of Context Claiming He Said Paris Terror Attacks Were Merely a 'Setback,'" Media Matters, November 18, 2015, http://mediamatters.org/research/2015/11/18/right-wing-media-take-obama-out-of -context-clai/206936 (accessed February 22, 2016).

3. Ibid.

4. Erik Wemple, "Andrea Mitchell's Wawa Comment is Ill-Informed," *Washington Post*, June 19, 2012, https://www.washingtonpost.com/blogs/erik-wemple/post/andrea -mitchells-wawa-comment-is-ill-informed/2012/06/19/gJQAivbNoV_blog.html (accessed February 22, 2016).

5. Andrew Husband, "Fox News Contributors Suspended For 'Pussy,' 'Shit' Comments Aimed at Obama," *Mediaite*, December 7, 2015, http://www.mediaite.com/tv/ fox-news-contributors-suspended-for-pussy-shit-comments-aimed-at-obama/ (accessed February 22, 2016).

6. Jack Mirkinson, "Martin Bashir Resigns from MSNBC Following Sarah Palin Comments," *Huffington Post*, December 4, 2013, http://www.huffingtonpost.com/ 2013/12/04/martin-bashir-resigns-msnbc_n_4385884.html (accessed February 22, 2016).

7. Paul Farhi, "Ed Schultz Suspended from MSNBC after Calling Laura Ingraham a 'Right Wing Slut,'" *Washington Post*, May 26, 2011, https://www.washingtonpost.com/ lifestyle/style/ed-schultz-suspended-from-msnbc-after-calling-laura-ingraham-a-right -wing-slut/2011/05/26/AGOcV2BH_story.html (accessed February 22, 2016).

8. Nico Lang, "It's Time to Stop Making Every Scandal into a 'Gate,'" *Daily Dot*, October 15, 2014, http://www.dailydot.com/opinion/stop-overusing-gate-suffix-jennifer -lawrence/ (accessed March 10, 2016).

9. "When High-Minded Politicos Buckley and Vidal Took the Low Road," *PBS NewsHour*, PBS, July 31, 2015, http://www.pbs.org/newshour/bb/high-minded-politicos -buckley-vidal-took-low-road/ (accessed February 22, 2016).

10. Michael Smerconish, "The Pulse: The Divide Gets Wider and Wider," *Philadelphia Inquirer*, January 13, 2013, http://articles.philly.com/2013-01-13/news/ 36314465_1_primaries-districts-polarization (accessed September 6, 2015); Michael Smerconish, "Polarization in 4 Steps," *Huffington Post*, March 16, 2013, http://www

.huffingtonpost.com/michael-smerconish/polarization-in-4-steps_b_2470717.html (accessed September 6, 2015).

11. Amy Mitchell, Jeffrey Gottfried, Jocelyn Kiley, Katerina Eva Matsa, "Political Polarization and Media Habits," Pew Research Center, October 21, 2014, http://www.journalism.org/2014/10/21/political-polarization-media-habits/ (accessed September 6, 2015).

12. Lydia Saad, "TV Is Americans' Main Source of News," Gallup, July 8, 2013, http://www.gallup.com/poll/163412/americans-main-source-news.aspx (accessed September 6, 2015).

13. Mark Jurkowitz, Paul Hitlin, Amy Mitchell, Laura Santhanam, Steve Adams, Monica Anderson, and Nancy Vogt, "The Changing TV News Landscape," Pew Research Center's Project for Excellence in Journalism, 2013, http://www.stateofthemedia.org/2013/special-reports-landing-page/the-changing-tv-news-landscape/.

14. Margaret Sullivan, "When Reporters Get Personal," *New York Times*, January 5, 2013, http://www.nytimes.com/2013/01/06/public-editor/when-reporters-get-personal.html?_r=0 (accessed September 12, 2015); Daniel Marans, "Tom Brokaw Invokes Holocaust, Japanese Internment in Powerful Indictment of Trump: Demonizing Muslims Would Repeat Past Mistakes, He Argues," *Huffington Post*, December 9, 2015, http://www.huffingtonpost.com/entry/tom-brokaw-condemns-donald-trump_us_56686500e4b009377b2347a8 (accessed December 12, 2015).

15. "Study Finds Fox News Viewers Least Informed of All Viewers," *Huffington Post*, July 23, 2012, http://www.huffingtonpost.com/2012/05/23/fox-news-less-informed-new-study_n_1538914.html (accessed September 12, 2015); "What You Know Depends on What You Watch: Current Events Knowledge Across Popular News Sources," press release, Public Mind Poll, Fairleigh Dickinson University, May 3, 2012, http://publicmind.fdu.edu/2012/confirmed/final.pdf (accessed September 12, 2015).

16. Andrew Beaujon, "Survey: NPR's Listeners Best-Informed, Fox Viewers Worst-Informed," Poynter, May 23, 2012, http://www.poynter.org/2012/survey-nprs-listeners-best-informed-fox-news-viewers-worst-informed/174826/ (accessed September 12, 2015).

17. Will Bunch, phone interview, October 25, 2015.

18. Mark Bowden, e-mail interview, November 15, 2015.

19. Rob Kall, e-mail interview, November 29, 2015.

20. John Timpane, e-mail interview, November 30, 2015.

21. James B. Steele, phone interview, December 11, 2015.

22. "ACORN Chief Says Videos 'Made My Stomach Turn,'" CNN, October 6, 2009, http://www.cnn.com/2009/POLITICS/10/06/acorn.press.club/ (accessed November 11, 2015).

23. Drew Griffin and David Fitzpatrick, "The Real Story Behind Those Planned Parenthood Videos," CNN, October 20, 2015, http://www.cnn.com/2015/10/19/politics/planned-parenthood-videos/ (accessed November 11, 2015).

24. Joe Strupp, "Spokane Probe: Other Editors Say They Forbid Undercover Operations," *Editor & Publisher*, May 10, 2005, http://www.editorandpublisher.com/

news/spokane-probe-other-editors-say-they-forbid-undercover-operations/ (accessed November 11, 2015).

25. Erik Wemple, "WTTG (Fox5) Reporter Emily Miller Advances Gun-Rights Agenda in Maryland," *Washington Post*, February 10, 2015, https://www.washingtonpost .com/blogs/erik-wemple/wp/2015/02/10/wttg-fox-5-reporter-emily-miller-advances-gun -rights-agenda-in-maryland/ (accessed November 11, 2015).

26. Brian Stelter and Bill Carter, "Lou Dobbs Abruptly Quits CNN," *New York Times*, November 11, 2009, http://www.nytimes.com/2009/11/12/business/media/ 12dobbs.html (accessed November 11, 2015).

27. Ibid.

28. Peter Johnson, "More Reporters Embrace an Advocacy Role," *USA Today*, March 6, 2007, http://usatoday30.usatoday.com/life/television/news/2007-03-05-social -journalism_N.htm (accessed November 11, 2015).

29. Juan Castillo, "Opinion: What We Should Really Take Away from Trump -Ramos Dust-Up," NBC News, August 27, 2015, http://www.nbcnews.com/news/ latino/opinion-what-we-should-really-take-away-trump-ramos-dust-n416601 (accessed November 15, 2015).

30. Patricia Mazzei, "Donald Trump v. Jorge Ramos, Redux," *Miami Herald*, August 26, 2015, http://www.miamiherald.com/news/politics-government/election/ article32489868.html#! (accessed November 15, 2015).

31. Jack Martinez, "Donald Trump and Jorge Ramos: Who Was Right?" *Newsweek*, August 26, 2015, http://www.newsweek.com/jorge-ramos-trump-365995 (accessed November 15, 2015).

32. Bankole Thompson, "Thompson: Advocacy Journalism Lacking in 2016 Campaign," *Detroit News*, September 10, 2015, http://www.detroitnews.com/story/ news/politics/elections/2015/09/09/thompson-advocacy-journalism-lacking-campaign/ 71984330/ (accessed November 15, 2015).

33. Dave Weigel, "Megyn Kelly's Minstrel Show," *The Atlantic*, July 14, 2010, http://www.theatlantic.com/daily-dish/archive/2010/07/megyn-kellys-minstrel-show/ 184788/; Max Read, "Why Is Fox News' Megyn Kelly So Obsessed with the New Black Panthers?" *Gawker*, July 15, 2010, http://gawker.com/5587578/why-is-fox-news-megyn -kelly-obsessed-with-the-new-black-panthers; "REPORT: Fox News Has Hyped Phony New Black Panthers Scandal at Least 96 Times: Fox Devoted More than 8 Hours of Airtime to Discussion of New Black Panthers," Media Matters, July 16, 2010, http:// mediamatters.org/research/2010/07/16/report-fox-news-has-hyped-phony-new-black -panth/167811; Jenée Desmond-Harris, "The New Black Panther Party Explained," *Vox*, April 15, 2015, http://www.vox.com/2014/11/16/7217173/10-questions-you-were-afraid -to-ask-about-the-new-black-panther-party.

34. David A. Graham, "The New Black Panther Party Is the New Acorn," *Newsweek*, July 14, 2010, http://www.newsweek.com/new-black-panther-party-new-acorn -74927 (accessed December 4, 2015).

35. Robert J. Samuelson, "Media Bias Explained in Two Studies," *Washington Post*, April 23, 2014, https://www.washingtonpost.com/opinions/robert-samuelson-media-bias

-explained-in-two-studies/2014/04/23/9dccdcf6-cafd-11e3-93eb-6c0037dde2ad_story
.html (accessed September 10, 2015).

36. Andrew Kirell, "Chuck Todd: Fox and MSNBC Primetime 'Hasn't Been Healthy for Politics,'" *Mediaite*, March 19, 2015, http://www.mediaite.com/tv/chuck -todd-fox-and-msnbc-primetime-hasn%E2%80%99t-been-healthy-for-politics/ (accessed September 10, 2015); Tim Graham, "Chuck 'No Point Of View' Todd Says Fox, MSNBC Are 'Not Healthy For Politics,'" *NewsBusters*, March 19, 2015, http://newsbusters.org/ blogs/tim-graham/2015/03/19/chuck-no-point-view-todd-says-fox-msnbc-not-healthy -politics#sthash.VKEa5I43.dpuf (accessed September 10, 2015); *Mike O'Meara Show*, http://mikeomearashow.com (accessed September 10, 2015).

CHAPTER 19: THE FUTURE OF ADVOCACY JOURNALISM AND BALANCED JOURNALISM

1. Mark Bowden, e-mail interview, November 15, 2015.

2. John Timpane, e-mail interview, November 30, 2015.

3. Elena Groholske, "Beverly Kirk Speaks on Advocacy Journalism at CU's Media Appreciation Luncheon," April 5, 2011, http://www.campbellsville.edu/04052011 beverlykirk (accessed September 4, 2015).

4. Michelle Ciulla Lipkin, phone interview, November 11, 2015.

5. John Avlon, "The Top 25 Centrist Columnists and Commentators," *Daily Beast*, April 1, 2010, http://www.thedailybeast.com/articles/2010/04/01/the-top-25-centrist -columnists-and-commentators.html.

6. Will Bunch, phone interview, October 25, 2015.

7. Ibid.

8. Ibid.

9. John Timpane, e-mail interview, November 30, 2015.

10. James B. Steele, phone interview, December 11, 2015.

11. Philip Meyer, "Public Journalism and the Problem of Objectivity," University of North Carolina at Chapel Hill, http://www.unc.edu/~pmeyer/ire95pj.htm (accessed September 4, 2015).

12. Sarah Hinchliff Pearson, "Objective Failure: Why the Debate About Media Objectivity Threatens the Viability of General-Interest News Outlets," May 3, 2010, http://cyberlaw.stanford.edu/blog/2010/05/objective-failure-why-debate-about-media -objectivity-threatens-viability-general (accessed September 4, 2015).

13. Kellie Riordan, "Does Journalism Still Require Impartiality?" *Guardian*, September 4, 2014, http://www.theguardian.com/commentisfree/2014/sep/05/does -journalism-still-require-impartiality (accessed September 4, 2015).

14. Matthew Yglesias, "Bernie Sanders Is (Still) the Future of the Democratic Party," *Vox*, April 20, 2016, http://www.vox.com/2016/4/20/11466376/bernie-sanders -future-democrats (accessed May 6, 2016).

15. Laura Frank, "The Withering Watchdog: What Really Happened to Investigative Reporting in America," *Exposé*, PBS, June 2009, http://www.pbs.org/wnet/expose/2009/06/the-withering-watchdog.html (accessed September 4, 2015).

16. Jonathan Stray, "Objectivity and the Decades-Long Shift from 'Just the Facts' to 'What Does It Mean?'" Nieman Lab, May 22, 2013, http://www.niemanlab.org/2013/05/objectivity-and-the-decades-long-shift-from-just-the-facts-to-what-does-it-mean/ (accessed September 4, 2015).

17. Tim Rowland, "News These Days Is an Evolution," Herald-Mail Media, December 12, 2015, http://www.heraldmailmedia.com/opinion/tim_rowland/news-these-days-is-an-evolution/article_4b9754a2-e83f-5d5e-9e8c-06a89f02cd71.html (accessed September 4, 2015).

18. Lloyd Grove, "How TMZ Claims Its Celebrity Scalps, Like Ray Rice," *Daily Beast*, September 10, 2014, http://www.thedailybeast.com/articles/2014/09/10/claiming-scalps-the-tmz-way-ray-rice-is-just-the-latest.html (accessed March 22, 2016).

19. Ibid.

20. "L.A. Clippers Owner to GF: Don't Bring Black People to My Games . . . Including Magic Johnson," TMZ, April 25, 2014, http://www.tmz.com/2014/04/26/donald-sterling-clippers-owner-black-people-racist-audio-magic-johnson/ (accessed March 22, 2016).

21. Associated Press, "TMZ Video Shows 76ers' Jahlil Okafor in Second Boston Street Fight," Fox Sports, December 2, 2015, http://www.foxsports.com/nba/story/philadelphia-76ers-jahlil-okafor-second-boston-fight-video-120215 (accessed March 22, 2016).

22. David Knowles, "Lil' Wayne Says He's 'Good' via Twitter Despite Reports He Was Being Read His Last Rites at a Los Angeles Hospital after Suffering Multiple Seizures," *New York Daily News*, March 15, 2013, http://www.nydailynews.com/entertainment/music-arts/lil-wayne-critical-condition-hospital-tmz-article-1.1290388 (accessed March 22, 2016).

23. Nancy Dillon, "Janet Jackson Didn't Slap Paris Jackson in the Face After All, Gossip Website Says," *New York Daily News*, August 1, 2012, http://www.nydailynews.com/entertainment/gossip/janet-jackson-didn-slap-paris-jackson-face-gossip-web-site-article-1.1126749 (accessed March 22, 2016).

CHAPTER 20: THE IMPORTANCE OF BEING A SAVVY MEDIA CONSUMER

1. Michael Robb, "Tweens, Teens, and Screens: What Our New Research Uncovers," Common Sense Media, November 2, 2015, https://www.commonsensemedia.org/blog/tweens-teens-and-screens-what-our-new-research-uncovers (accessed December 1, 2015).

2. "Generation M2: Media in the Lives of 8 to 18-Year-Olds," Kaiser Family

Foundation, January 20, 2010, http://kff.org/other/event/generation-m2-media-in-the
-lives-of/ (accessed December 1, 2015).

3. "How Millennials Get News: Inside the Habits of America's First Digital
Generation." Media Insight Project, American Press Institute, 2015, http://www.media
insight.org/PDFs/Typology/MillennialTypologyFinal.pdf (accessed December 1, 2015).

4. Janna Anderson and Lee Rainie, "Millennials Will Benefit and Suffer Due to
Their Hyperconnected Lives," Pew Research Center, February 29, 2012, http://www.
pewinternet.org/2012/02/29/millennials-will-benefit-and-suffer-due-to-their
-hyperconnected-lives/ (accessed December 1, 2015).

5. Eugene Kiely, e-mail interview, December 18, 2015.

6. Mark E. Andersen, "Fake News Is a Plague on Social Media," *Daily Kos*,
September 13, 2015, http://www.dailykos.com/story/2015/9/13/1419950/-Fake-news-is-a
-plague-on-social-media (accessed December 2, 2015).

7. Samantha Murphy Kelly, "8 Social Media Hoaxes You Fell for This Year,"
Mashable, November 5, 2012, http://mashable.com/2012/11/05/social-media
-hoaxes/#xubXfgelVSqs (accessed December 2, 2015).

8. Kevin Fallon, "Fooled By 'The Onion': 9 Most Embarrassing Fails," *Daily
Beast*, November 27, 2012, http://www.thedailybeast.com/articles/2012/09/29/fooled-by
-the-onion-8-most-embarrassing-fails.html (accessed December 2, 2015).

9. Brian M. Rosenthal, "Planned Parenthood Cleared, But 2 Indicted Over Videos,"
Houston Chronicle, February 2, 2016, http://www.chron.com/news/houston-texas/
article/Harris-grand-jury-indicts-pair-behind-Planned-6782865.php (accessed February
22, 2016); Manny Fernandez, "2 Abortion Foes Behind Planned Parenthood Videos are
Indicted," *New York Times*, January 26, 2016, http://www.nytimes.com/2016/01/26/
us/2-abortion-foes-behind-planned-parenthood-videos-are-indicted.html?_r=0 (accessed
February 22, 2016); Drew Griffin and David Fitzpatrick, "The Real Story Behind Those
Planned Parenthood Videos," CNN, October 20, 2015, http://www.cnn.com/2015/10/19/
politics/planned-parenthood-videos/ (accessed February 22, 2016); Jeremy Breningstall,
Elizabeth D. Herman, and Paige St. John, "How Anti-Abortion Activists Used Undercover
Planned Parenthood Videos to Further a Political Cause," *Los Angeles Times*, March 30,
2016, http://graphics.latimes.com/planned-parenthood-videos/; Ted Andersen, "Why
the Undercover Planned Parenthood Videos Aren't Journalism," *Columbia Journalism
Review*, May 12, 2016, http://www.cjr.org/analysis/why_the_man_who_made
_undercover_planned_parenthood_videos_isnt_a_journalist.php.

10. Walter Dean, "Journalism as a Discipline of Verification," American Press
Institute, https://www.americanpressinstitute.org/journalism-essentials/verification
-accuracy/journalism-discipline-verification/ (accessed December 3, 2015).

11. John Christie, "Anonymous Sources: Leaving Journalism's False God Behind,"
Poynter. April 23, 2014, http://www.poynter.org/2014/anonymous-sources-leaving
-journalisms-false-god-behind/249037/ (accessed December 3, 2015).

12. Frank Langfitt, "Covering the Sago Mine Disaster," *Nieman Reports*, June
15, 2006, http://niemanreports.org/articles/covering-the-sago-mine-disaster/ (accessed
December 3, 2015).

13. A. Brad Schwartz, "The Infamous 'War of the Worlds' Radio Broadcast Was a Magnificent Fluke," *Smithsonian*, May 6, 2015, http://www.smithsonianmag.com/history/infamous-war-worlds-radio-broadcast-was-magnificent-fluke-180955180/?no-ist (accessed March 9, 2016).

14. David Morgan, "15 Best April Fools' Day Hoaxes," CBS News, April 1, 2012, http://www.cbsnews.com/media/15-best-april-fools-day-hoaxes/ (accessed March 9, 2016).

15. "Trick or Treat? Needles in Halloween Candy Turns Out to Be Hoax," NBC Philadelphia, November 6, 2015, http://www.nbcphiladelphia.com/news/local/NATL -PHL-Needles-Halloween-Candy-Hoax-341713352.html (accessed March 9, 2016).

16. Morgan, "15 Best April Fools' Day Hoaxes."

17. Michelle Ciulla Lipkin, phone interview, November 11, 2015.

18. Ibid.

19. Kiely, e-mail interview.

20. Kathleen Tyner, e-mail interview, November 6, 2015.

21. Lipkin, phone interview.

22. Leann Davis Alspaugh, "How to Identify Bias," OLE Community, Pearson's Online Learning Exchange, April 11, 2012, http://olecommunity.com/election/how-to -identify-bias/ (accessed December 4, 2015).

23. Tyner, e-mail interview.

24. Kiely, e-mail interview.

25. Dan Giancaterino, e-mail interview, November 9, 2015.

26. Ibid.

27. Brad Wilmouth, "Matthews: Obama Speech Caused 'Thrill Going up My Leg,'" *NewsBusters*, February 13, 2008, http://newsbusters.org/blogs/brad-wilmouth/2008/02/13/matthews-obama-speech-caused-thrill-going-my-leg (accessed February 23, 2016).

28. Bradford Plumer, "Hack in Business: Dick Morris's Tea Party Payday," *New Republic*, December 7, 2010, https://newrepublic.com/article/79059/hack-dick-morris -tea-party (accessed February 3, 2016).

29. Howard Kurtz, "Karl Rove Rejects Reality," CNN, November 28, 2012, http://www.cnn.com/2012/11/09/opinion/kurtz-karl-rove/ (accessed February 3, 2016).

30. Michael Calderone, "Fox's Beck: Obama Is 'a Racist,'" *Politico*, July 28, 2009, http://www.politico.com/blogs/michaelcalderone/0709/Foxs_Beck_Obama_is_a_racist .html (accessed December 15, 2015).

31. "Mark Levin: Barack Obama Is an Anti-Semite, 'How Dare You Lecture We the People?'" RealClearPolitics, December 8, 2015, http://www.realclearpolitics.com/video/2015/12/08/mark_levin_rages_at_president_obama_we_dont_need_your_damn _lectures_something_is_seriously_wrong_with_you.html (accessed December 15, 2015).

32. Keith Olbermann, "Pathological Liar or Idiot-in-Chief?" MSNBC, December 6, 2007, http://www.nbcnews.com/id/22134108/ns/msnbc-countdown_with_keith _olbermann/t/bush-pathological-liar-or-idiot-in-chief/ (accessed December 8, 2015).

33. "North Korea's Tightly Controlled Media," BBC News, December 19, 2011, http://www.bbc.com/news/world-asia-pacific-16255126 (accessed December 8, 2015).

34. Ian Burrell, "Al Jazeera Chief: We Don't Take Orders from Qatar on IS, or

Anything Else," *Independent,* November 5, 2014, http://www.independent.co.uk/news/ media/tv-radio/al-jazeera-chief-we-don-t-take-orders-from-qatar-on-is-or-anything -else-9842178.html (accessed March 1, 2016).

35. Dan Sabbagh, "Al-Jazeera's Political Independence Questioned Amid Qatar Intervention: Al-Jazeera English Journalists Protest After Being Ordered to Re-Edit UN Report to Focus on Qatar Emir's Comments on Syria," *Guardian,* September 30, 2012, http://www.theguardian.com/media/2012/sep/30/al-jazeera-independence-questioned -qatar (accessed March 1, 2016).

36. Margarita Simonyan "Putin Talks NSA, Syria, Iran, Drones, in RT Interview," transcript, RT (Russia Today), June 12, 2013, https://www.rt.com/news/putin-rt-interview -full-577/ (accessed March 1, 2016); Max Fisher, "In Case You Weren't Clear on Russia Today's Relationship to Moscow, Putin Clears It Up," *Washington Post,* June 13, 2013, https://www.washingtonpost.com/news/worldviews/wp/2013/06/13/in-case-you-werent -clear-on-russia-todays-relationship-to-moscow-putin-clears-it-up/ (accessed March 1, 2016).

37. Elizabeth Wahl, "I Was Putin's Pawn: What It Was Like to Work for the Russian Propaganda Machine, and Why I Quit on Live TV," *Politico,* March 21, 2014, http:// www.politico.com/magazine/story/2014/03/liz-wahl-quit-russia-today-putins-pawn -104888_full.html (accessed March 1, 2016).

38. Ibid.

39. Federica Cherubini, "Fact Checking Is on the Rise, but There Are Many Challenges," Poynter, July 2015, http://www.poynter.org/2015/fact-checking-is-on-the -rise-but-there-are-many-challenges/360553/ (accessed November 4, 2015).

40. "Bias," AllSides, http://www.allsides.com/about-bias (accessed March 9, 2016); "Fact-Checking," Duke Reporters' Lab, http://reporterslab.org/fact-checking/.

41. Arthur S. Brisbane, "Should the *Times* Be a Truth Vigilante?" *New York Times,* January 12, 2012, http://publiceditor.blogs.nytimes.com/2012/01/12/should-the-times-be -a-truth-vigilante/ (accessed November 4, 2015).

42. Bill Adair and Angie Drobnic Holan, "The Principles of PolitiFact, PunditFact, and the Truth-O-Meter," PolitiFact, http://www.politifact.com/truth-o-meter/article/2013/ nov/01/principles-politifact-punditfact-and-truth-o-meter/.

43. FactCheck.org, http://www.factcheck.org/

44. Kiely, e-mail interview.

45. Snopes, http://www.snopes.com.

46. Glenn Kessler, "About Fact Checker," *Washington Post,* September 11, 2013, https://www.washingtonpost.com/news/fact-checker/about-the-fact-checker/ (accessed November 4, 2015).

47. Glenn Kessler, e-mail interview, December 18, 2015.

48. Peter Roff, "Who's Checking the Fact Checkers? A New Study Sheds Some Light on What the Facts the Press Most Likes to Check," *U.S. News & World Report,* May 28, 2013, http://www.usnews.com/opinion/blogs/peter-roff/2013/05/28/study-finds -fact-checkers-biased-against-republicans (accessed November 4, 2015).

49. Alex Seitz-Wald, "Study: Republicans Are 'the Less Credible Party': PolitiFact

Rules GOP 'False' More Often than Democrats, with Bachmann One of the Worst, a New Report Reveals," *Salon*, May 28, 2013, http://www.salon.com/2013/05/28/study _republicans_are_the_less_credible_party/ (accessed November 4, 2015).

50. "About Us," Media Matters, http://www.mediamatters.org/about.

51. Craig Silverman, "New Research Details How Journalists Verify Information," Poynter. February 27, 2013, http://www.poynter.org/2013/new-research-details-how -journalists-verify-information/203728/ (accessed November 5, 2015).

52. Ibid.

53. P. B. Brandtzæg, M. Lüders, J. Spangenberg, L. Rath-Wiggins, and A. Folstad, "Emerging Journalistic Verification Practices Concerning Social Media," *Journalism Practice*, March 13, 2015, http://www.academia.edu/11440031/Emerging_Journalistic _Verification_Practices_Concerning_Social_Media (accessed February 22, 2016).

54. Joseph Lichterman, "How Storyful Is Turning Slack into an Extension of Its Newswire," Nieman Lab, November 12, 2015, http://www.niemanlab.org/2015/11/ how-storyful-is-turning-slack-into-an-extension-of-its-newswire/ (accessed February 22, 2016); Storyful, https://storyful.com/.

55. Slack, https://slack.com/.

56. Angela Moon and Melissa Fares, "Two Years after Acquisition, Apple Shuts Social Analytics Platform Topsy," Reuters, December 16, 2015, http://www.reuters.com/ article/us-apple-topsy-idUSKBN0TZ2NV20151216.

57. Peter Kafka, "Social Curation Service Sulia Shuts Down," *Recode*, October 21, 2014, http://www.recode.net/2014/10/21/11632086/ social-curation-service-sulia-shuts-down.

58. Trackur, http://www.trackur.com/.

59. "About TinEye," TinEye, https://www.tineye.com/about.

60. "Frequently Asked Questions," FotoForensics, http://fotoforensics.com/faq.php.

61. Jane Elizabeth, "The American Press Institute's Fact-Checking Project, Explained," American Press Institute, May 6, 2014, https://www.americanpressinstitute .org/fact-checking-project/american-press-institutes-fact-checking-project-explained/ (accessed February 22, 2016).

62. Paul M. J. Suchecky, "The Funders Behind the Fact Checkers," *Inside Philanthropy*, April 9, 2015, http://www.insidephilanthropy.com/home/2015/4/9/the -funders-behind-the-fact-checkers.html# (accessed February 22, 2016).

63. "American Press Institute Announces Major Project to Improve Fact-Checking Journalism," American Press Institute, February 6, 2014, https://www.american pressinstitute.org/news-releases/american-press-institute-announces-major-project -improve-fact-checking-journalism/ (accessed February 22, 2016).

64. Patrick Cockburn, "Embedded Journalism: A Distorted View of War," *Independent*, November 22, 2010, http://www.independent.co.uk/news/media/opinion/ embedded-journalism-a-distorted-view-of-war-2141072.html (accessed March 1, 2016).

65. Mary Walton, "Investigative Shortfall," *American Journalism Review*, September 2010, http://ajrarchive.org/article.asp?id=4904 (accessed November 22, 2015).

66. Tessa Jolls, phone interview, December 14, 2015.

67. Dean Howard Schneider, phone interview, December 2, 2015.

68. Asawin Suebsaeng and Dave Gilson, "Chart: Almost Every Obama Conspiracy Theory Ever: Fake Birth Certificates, Ghostwriters, Teleprompters, a Teenage Trip to Mars, and More of the Most Paranoid and Bizarro Obama Conspiracy Theories Out There," *Mother Jones*, October 2012, http://www.motherjones.com/politics/2012/10/chart-obama-conspiracy-theories (accessed February 5, 2016).

69. Chris McGreal, "9/11 Conspiracy Theories Debunked," *Guardian*, September 5, 2011, http://www.theguardian.com/world/2011/sep/05/9-11-conspiracy-theories-debunked (accessed February 5, 2016).

70. Jolls, phone interview.

71. Lipkin, phone interview.

72. Tyner, e-mail interview.

73. Schneider, phone interview.

74. National Association for Media Literacy Education (NAMLE), http://namle.net/.

75. Lipkin, phone interview.

76. Jolls, phone interview.

77. Samuel Reed III, "No 'Love Train' for Media Literacy in Philadelphia," *Philadelphia Public School Notebook*, August 2, 2011, http://thenotebook.org/articles/2011/08/02/no-love-train-for-media-literacy-in-philadelphia (accessed November 12, 2015).

78. Tyner, e-mail interview.

79. Lipkin, phone interview.

80. Schneider, phone interview.

81. Giancaterino, e-mail interview.

82. Jolls, phone interview.

83. Tyner, e-mail interview.

84. Katie Donnelly, "5 Great Media Literacy Programs and How to Assess Their Impact," *MediaShift*, April 21, 2011, http://mediashift.org/2011/04/5-great-media-literacy-programs-and-how-to-assess-their-impact111/ (accessed November 2, 2015).

85. Ibid.

86. "Schools and Organizations," NAMLE, http://namle.net/grad-student/schools-orgs/ (accessed November 2, 2015).

87. "Media Literacy Education," College of Education, University of Florida, http://education.ufl.edu/english-education/specializations/media-literacy/ (accessed November 2, 2015).

88. "What is News Literacy?" Stony Brook University Center for News Literacy, http://www.centerfornewsliteracy.org/what-is-news-literacy/; "About Us," Stony Brook University Center for News Literacy, http://www.centerfornewsliteracy.org/about-us/ (accessed November 4, 2015).

89. "The Gatekeepers: Guide to Top Program Officers & Foundation Executives," *Inside Philanthropy*, http://insidephilanthropy.squarespace.com/insider-guide-to-program-offic/david-d-hiller-robert-r-mccormick-foundation.html# (accessed November 4, 2015).

90. Schneider, phone interview.

91. Ibid.

92. Rory O'Connor, "Guest Post: Practical Tools for Teaching News Literacy," *New York Times*, October 8, 2014, http://learning.blogs.nytimes.com/author/rory-oconnor/?_r=0 (accessed November 4, 2015).

93. "The CML Five Key Questions of Media Literacy and Five Core Concepts," Center for Media Literacy, 2005, http://www.medialit.org/sites/default/files/14B_CCKQPoster+5essays.pdf (accessed December 11, 2015), © 2002–2015 Center for Media Literacy.

94. Jolls, phone interview.

95. "CML Five Key Questions," © 2002–2015 Center for Media Literacy.

96. Ibid.

97. Ibid.

98. Ibid.

99. Jeff Share, Tessa Jolls, and Elizabeth Thoman, *Five Key Questions that Can Change the World: Lesson Plans for Media Literacy*, Center for Media Literacy, 2007, http://www.medialit.org/sites/default/files/02_5KQ_ClassroomGuide.pdf, © 2002–2015 Center for Media Literacy.

100. "CML Five Key Questions," © 2002–2015 Center for Media Literacy.

101. Jolls, phone interview.

102. Ibid.

103. Ibid.

104. Ibid.

105. United States Media Literacy Week, https://medialiteracyweek.us/; [Canadian] Media Literacy Week, http://www.medialiteracyweek.ca/.

106. Lipkin, phone interview.

107. "What Is Media Education?," Media Literacy Week, http://www.medialiteracyweek.ca/about/what-is-media-education/ (accessed March 1, 2015).

108. Ibid.

109. National Association for Media Literacy Education (NAMLE), https://namle.net/publications/media-literacy-week-november-2nd-6th-2015/.

110. Kiely, e-mail interview.

111. Ibid.

112. Lipkin, phone interview.

113. Tyner, e-mail interview.

114. Giancaterino, e-mail interview.

115. Jolls, phone interview.

116. Schneider, phone interview.

117. "Decision 2012: Media Literacy," Newseum Digital Classroom, http://www1.newseum.org/digital-classroom/modules/decision-2012/media-literacy/default.aspx (accessed November 3, 2015).

118. Lynh Bui, "Schools Demanding News Literacy Lessons to Teach Students How to Find Fact Amid Fiction," *Washington Post*, April 15, 2013, https://www.washingtonpost.com/local/education/schools-demanding-news-literacy-lessons-to-teach-students

-how-to-find-fact-amid-fiction/2013/04/15/e67b9c26-963d-11e2-9e23-09dce87f75a1
_story.html (accessed November 3, 2015).

119. Ibid.

120. Larry Magid, "Online Youth Need Critical Thinking Skills," CNET, August 6, 2009, http://www.cnet.com/news/online-youth-need-critical-thinking-skills/ (accessed November 3, 2015).

121. Schneider, phone interview.

122. Ibid.

123. Ibid.

124. Lipkin, phone interview.

125. Schneider, phone interview.

INDEX